THE COST OF FREE LAND

THE COST of FREE LAND

Jews, Lakota, and an American Inheritance

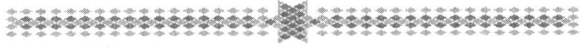

REBECCA CLARREN

VIKING

VIKING
An imprint of Penguin Random House LLC
penguinrandomhouse.com

Grateful acknowledgment is made for permission to reprint the following:
Lines from *How the West Was Really Won* copyright © 1980 by Somerset Press
(a division of Hope Publishing Co., www.hopepublishing.com).
All rights reserved. Used by permission.

Image credits may be found on page 321.

LIBRARY OF CONGRESS CATALOGING-IN-PUBLICATION DATA
Names: Clarren, Rebecca, author.
Title: The Cost of Free Land : Jews, Lakota, and an American Inheritance / Rebecca Clarren.
Other titles: Jews, Lakota, and an American Inheritance
Description: [New York] : Viking, [2023] | Includes bibliographical references and index.
Identifiers: LCCN 2023017505 (print) | LCCN 2023017506 (ebook) |
ISBN 9780593655078 (hardcover) | ISBN 9780525507628 (ebook)
Subjects: LCSH: Jews, Russian—South Dakota—History. | Sinykin family. |
Sinykin, Harry, 1859–1945—Family. | Immigrants—South Dakota—History. |
Indians—Relations with Jews. | Lakota Indians—Land tenure—South Dakota. |
Frontier and pioneer life—South Dakota. | South Dakota—Ethnic relations—History.
Classification: LCC F655 .C63 2023 (print) | LCC F655 (ebook) |
DDC 978.3/004924—dc23/eng/20230612
LC record available at https://lccn.loc.gov/2023017505
LC ebook record available at https://lccn.loc.gov/2023017506

Printed in the United States of America
3rd Printing

Book design and map illustration by Daniel Lagin

For Jude and for Louie

He [Rabbi Tarfon] used to say:
It is not your duty to finish the work,
but neither are you at liberty to neglect it.

—PIRKEI AVOT 2:16

CONTENTS

LAKOTA LANDS AND SURROUNDING AREA

✦✦✦ 1851–PRESENT DAY ✦✦✦

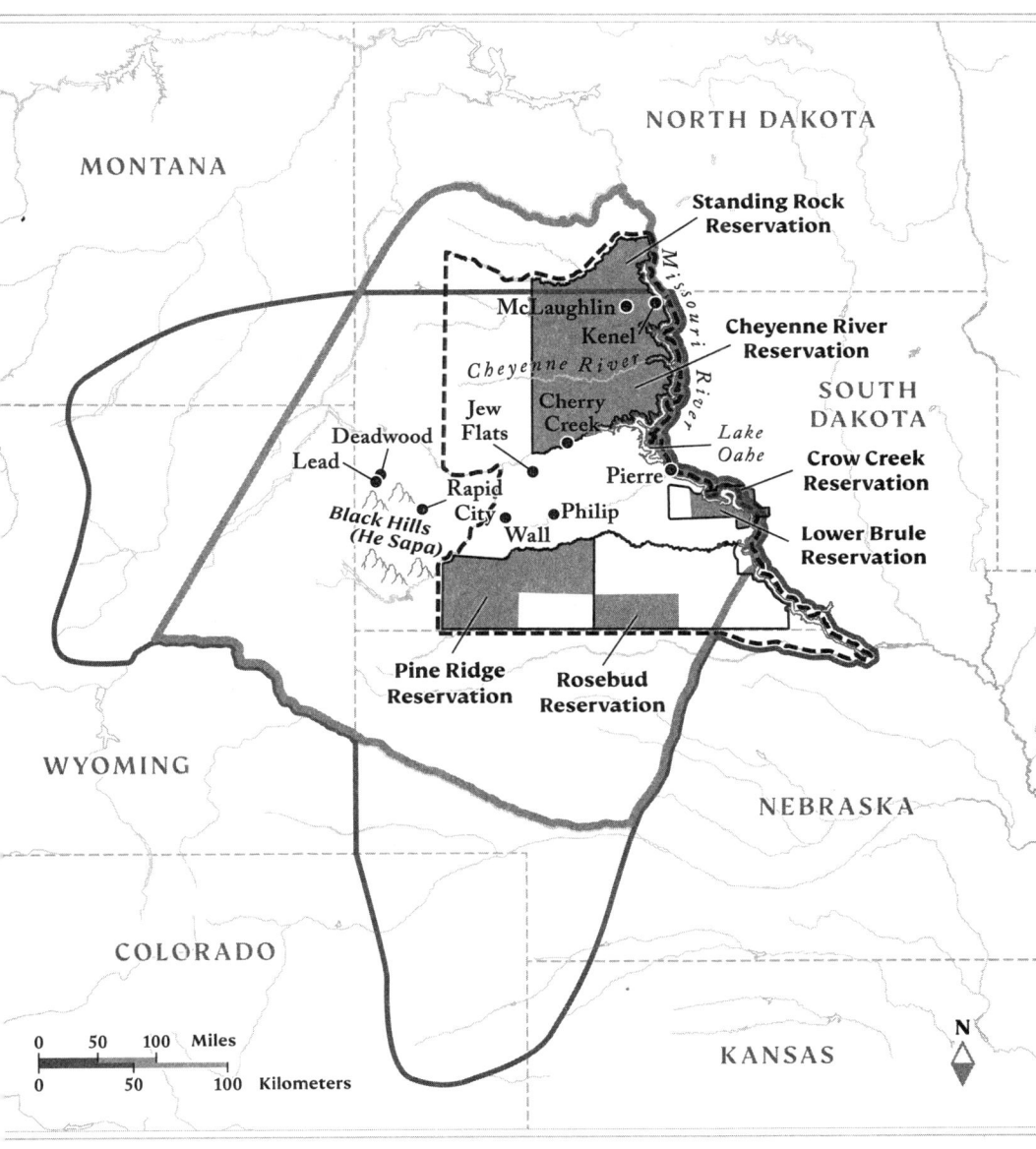

DIMINISHING LAKOTA LAND

☐ 1851 Fort Laramie Treaty

☐ 1868 Treaty, Great Sioux Reservation, including unceded territory and hunting grounds

⌐⌐ 1877 Taking the Black Hills

☐ 1889 Great Sioux Agreement

■ Present day size of six reservations

NOTE ON TERMINOLOGY

For most of the United States' official history, the Oceti Sakowin people have been called Sioux. This was not a name of the Nation's choosing. Their enemies, the Chippewa, referred to them as *naduwessi*, meaning "enemies" or "snakes"; French traders mispronounced the term and abbreviated it to "Sioux." This book is primarily concerned with one of the seven Nations that comprise the Oceti Sakowin, the Lakota, of which there are another seven sub-bands. The Lakota refer to themselves by the name of their dialect, which translates as "council of friends." In an effort not to repeat mistranslations of the past, I have chosen to use that name outside legal or historical references to the Sioux. For the most part, I've followed the advice of Gregory Younging's *Elements of Indigenous Style: A Guide for Writing By and About Indigenous Peoples*.

Many terms used to identify Indigenous people are controversial. Over the course of more than twenty years of reporting on Indigenous communities in the United States, I've met people who call themselves Native, Indian, Indigenous, American Indian, Alaska Native, and Native American; some individuals use these terms interchangeably, depending on who they're with and where they are. The writer David Treuer, who is of Ojibwe and Jewish descent, offers sensible advice: if you are concerned about what to call someone, simply ask them their preference. The terms used in this book are a reflection, whenever possible, of the quoted person's choice.

THE COST OF FREE LAND

PROLOGUE

※※※※

Twenty-two years ago, while on a reporting trip to the Pine Ridge Reservation in South Dakota, I found myself sitting shotgun in a truck with a man who would later become president of the Oglala Sioux Tribe. He was smoking weed. When he offered me some, I declined, hoping to indicate a level of professionalism that, as a reporter visiting an Indigenous community for the first time, I certainly couldn't claim.

We had driven off a dirt road and were parked at the top of a rise. Before us were green rolling hills and the flat plains beyond. It was gray outside. I later described the day this way: "thick clouds the color of ash hang low in the sky, and the damp and cold air sinks into my bones like a long depression." A herd of buffalo, with their dark brown backs, dotted the landscape.

Officially, I was there to write an article about how a group of Lakota were defying federal drug laws to grow industrial-grade hemp. More than an effort to build a foothold in a niche market, this was a way for them to wield their sovereignty. Treaties signed with the federal government more than a century earlier established the Lakota as an independent and equal Nation that was allowed certain authority within its borders. According to the hemp grower, this meant he and his family could create their own rules about what to grow on their land, even if those rules conflicted with United States law.

It is likely that I was wearing jeans and a plain gray T-shirt; back then, this was more or less my uniform for reporting trips, as I believed that, by wearing clothes with limited personality, I could signal to sources that my identity didn't matter. In my bag beside me were a camera, a DAT recorder, and my slim reporter's notebook with the binding at the top. I had one great question prepared, which I had learned from a *This American Life* comic book about how to be a reporter. My boss had told me to write down every single thing that I saw and heard and smelled, but, nonetheless, I failed to record whether the man beside me in the truck smoked a pipe or rolled a joint, or if he seemed very high, or how I felt about any of it.

Sitting there in the small cab, the dank cloud of smoke lacing the air between us, I was uncomfortable with the quiet. I had yet to learn how to follow a source's lead; I had yet to learn so many things. In my nervousness, I decided to share something about myself.

I told him that my family used to own land in South Dakota. That we'd had a ranch somewhere known as Jew Flats. I told him I had an uncle who everyone called Bronco Lou. I remember thinking this might make him see we had something in common, that this might endear me to him.

He was polite, or maybe just stoned, and nodded. His smile was thin in a way I couldn't read. It would take me years to realize what my words would immediately mean to any Lakota citizen.

The 9/11 attacks had taken place the week before I visited Pine Ridge. One evening while I was there, over a paper plate of food that the hemp growers had shared with me at a family gathering, I said something banal about the horror of the recent events in New York. Sitting beside me, a former American Indian Movement (AIM) activist stared at me, her mouth a flat line, and said, "Now you know what it feels like to be attacked and invaded. It's about time for Americans to understand how that feels." The day before, an Oglala elder had told me, "When I saw those people running through the streets with terror, I was reminded of my ancestors running in fear at Wounded Knee." Even then, I failed to connect certain dots, certain historic realities between her, the Lakota, and myself.

All these years later, what stays with me from that reporting trip— what seems now to be the clear central narrative—appeared at the time to be only tangential to the article I was there to write.

✧ ✧ ✧ ✧ ✧

IN 2001, I KNEW ONLY THE MAJOR PLOT POINTS OF MY FAMILY'S HISTORY in South Dakota. I knew that my great-great-grandparents had six children, three girls and three boys, and that they came to America as part of a wave of Jews who fled Russia and its antisemitism at the turn of the twentieth century. I knew that they, like many other immigrants at the time, received free land from the federal government: a cool 160 acres that was theirs to keep if they could turn the wild prairie into farmland. I knew their life was hard and strange. The stories that relatives had told me, well worn from years of retelling, underscored an unfailing tenacity, a specific toughness, as if it were a part of our DNA.

One such story went like this: It was cold, because it was winter in South Dakota. My great-great-grandmother Faige Etke Sinykin sent her two youngest daughters, who were as young as ten and twelve years old, outside, armed with an axe or log to crack the ice-choked eddy of the creek behind the house. Once they succeeded, Faige Etke went to the creek, stripped, and dunked herself in the freezing water. This was her mikvah, a Jewish ritual bath that religious women take at the end of their menstrual cycle. That my great-aunt and several cousins referred to this story as *cute*, as in, *Do you want to hear a cute story?*, tells you something about the women in my family.

Another selection from our greatest hits: when one of the six Sinykin children was old enough to pass for an adult, they would write "21" on a small piece of paper and stick it inside their shoe. Then, they would walk into the Land Office and ask to file a homestead claim on their very own 160-acre parcel. The land clerk would look them in the eye and ask if they were of age, and they would swear, without lying, *Yes, sir, I'm over 21.*

That my family handed down these particular stories—selected from the slush pile of history, leaving other, more problematic plotlines behind— is instructive. Because, of course, both the stories we choose to tell and our decision not to tell others create the myth we pass to future generations.

I grew up looking at mysterious, never-explained photographs of my relatives posing with Indigenous people in South Dakota. In one, my cousin

Vivian is at a roadside stand, the Badlands behind her. She is wearing a breastplate, its beads made of bone, over her Peter Pan–collared blouse and pleated skirt. She and the man beside her are wearing matching eagle-feather war bonnets. In another sepia-toned photo, my great-great-uncle Jack, his gun holstered over his jacket, shakes hands with a man whose skin is a few shades darker than mine. The man wears full regalia and holds a beaded bag and pipe. This man was always identified—inaccurately, it would turn out—as Chief Red Cloud. That we were related to someone who knew a famous chief was a source of pride, but not of curiosity. There was no handed-down story about the Lakota and our relatives. We never talked about our family's neighbors on the nearby reservations.

I have spent almost my entire adult life reporting on the American West, attempting to write articles that expand our fixed ideas about the region, highlight inequities, and tell the stories of people and places often overlooked. When writing, for example, about the environmental and public-health effects of oil and gas development or the dangerous working conditions endured by farm workers, I have tried to deepen my reporting with

Louie Sinykin posing with Indigenous men near Sylvan Lake, South Dakota, early 1930s.

historical context. Yet, when it has come to my own ancestors' history on the South Dakota prairie, I maintained a blind spot. Only after years of reporting in Indigenous communities did it dawn on me that my family, that I myself, had benefited from the centuries of federal mistreatment of Indigenous people in the United States.

It would take many other reporting trips to other reservations in the years after I first went to Pine Ridge for me to deepen my suspicion that my family's singular focus on specific moments—*she dunked herself in the freezing water*—disconnected us from those who didn't share our genetics. Our stories of the prairie clearly imparted the values of toughness and religious commitment, but they failed to convey nuance and complexity. I would begin to suspect that, in fact, our history and that of the Lakota intertwined like a double helix—invisible, and yet shaping everything.

IN 2017, I FOUND MYSELF PACKING FOR ANOTHER REPORTING TRIP. MY TWO kids, ages two and five at the time, sat on the edge of the bed and watched me pack: into the roller bag went a favorite red shirt, pink scarf, my digital recorder, extra batteries, and two reporter's notebooks.

"Don't go, Mama," the littlest one said. "Why do you have to go?"

I explained about being a reporter, about how interviewing people in the place where they live and work helps to tell a better story. But I looked into their serious brown eyes and thought: good question.

The sludgy discomfort I was feeling in the face of an upcoming reporting trip wasn't exactly new. By then, I'd been reporting for nineteen years, packing one roller bag or another to go on assignment for various national magazines, but this feeling had never gone away. Despite being a card-carrying extrovert, I almost always have a tentative feeling before setting out to talk to strangers. Will my questions be the right ones? Will I know enough to hear what isn't said?

The next morning, before the kids were awake, I caught a flight to San Francisco and then a cab to Noe Valley to meet Abby Abinanti, chief justice of the Yurok Tribal Court and a former judge for the California State Superior Court. I had been hired by an investigative-journalism nonprofit to write about Abinanti's unique and compassionate approach, how her implementation of traditional Yurok religion and culture in her courtroom was becoming a model for state and federal judges nationwide. Her court is far more likely to ask defendants to devise ways to "make things right" than to send them to jail, which Abinanti considers a last resort. Nearly seventy years old then, she was well known in legal circles as a fierce trailblazer, someone who *doesn't take any crap.*

We met in a café, and the silence between us was deafening. Abinanti was shy. I felt so awkward that, when I went to the restroom, I stared at myself in the mirror and said, aloud, "Shit." But once in the car, rescued from the need to make eye contact, with 333 miles to cover before we'd reach the Yurok Reservation in northern California, we fell into comfortable conversation. She told me to call her Abby, but, like many people, I would come to call her Judge. I put my notebook in my lap and let my digital recorder run.

As I peppered her with questions, and she patiently answered, John Denver, Willie Nelson, and Hank Williams sang to us from her radio; at times, Judge hummed along. Outside, the dry California grasses flipped their long necks in the wind. We passed tawny hills and slips of river that were more sand than water. The September sky was a pale blue, a perfect day for a drive.

I pushed away the question I longed to ask, the one that had much more to do with me than with her. Instead, I asked her an obvious one about what it was like to be the first Native female attorney in the state.

Judge Abby grunted, and a sharp laugh fell from her mouth. "The first thing a judge ever said to me is, 'You can't be a lawyer, you're an Indian.' Other lawyers spit on me. I'd rather be shoved than spit on. It was a rugged start."

I shook my head, but not exactly in disbelief. Such racism, I had come to understand, was endemic to the experience of most Indigenous people in the United States. Still, I wondered aloud how she kept going.

She turned her head to stare at me; her eyes narrowed. *Are you dumb?* she seemed to be asking me silently. *Are you wasting my time?* Then she turned back to watch the winding highway. "I don't know," she said, shrugging. "I guess it's just what I do." It was quiet between us for what felt like ten miles. I sighed internally. By then, I was used to being the uninformed white lady in the room. I knew how much I didn't understand.

She turned off the radio and put on an old CD of Yurok brush songs and dances. It sounded to me like a thumping heartbeat and the sound of walking through dry, thigh-high grass. Judge explained that, when she gets worried, she thinks of the traditional Yurok dances and they calm her. I began to notice how central worry is to her job description as fierce auntie and revered judge.

Eventually, toward the end of our long drive north from San Francisco—when we were almost to the place where the Klamath River, which the Yurok consider the lifeline of their people, meets the ocean—I built myself up to be bigger than the question I wanted to ask. Staring out the window at the shade cast by redwoods, I told her about my dawning suspicions. I had, at last, begun to wonder about the role my homesteader ancestors might have played, directly or indirectly, in the story of their Lakota neighbors. How exactly had my family gotten their free land and at what cost?

She was squinting, listening hard, as if trying to solve a puzzle. Then she told me that I had to seek out the truth, even though it likely wouldn't be easy.

"Every story is a strand inside that truth, and you have to go out and collect as many stories as you can. It's kind of like interviewing eyewitnesses for a murder trial. If you interview ten people, you get ten different stories, and they were all there, they all saw it happen. But taken together, you find a summary, which adds up to an objective truth. Then you decide what to do about it."

What to do about the truth isn't a question that journalists are trained to ask. Our job is to disrupt, to expose. To personally take part in any kind of solution isn't typically part of the job. But this question was impossible to ignore. I lobbed the word *reparation*.

"Reparation is a bank word. With reparations, everything has a price. I think the bigger concept is healing. Reparations can be part of that or not. People talk about truth and reconciliation. I'm not a big fan of reconciliation. I'm a fan of healing."

Then, she told me another thing that would change my life. She told me to study the culture and traditions of my own people to learn how to respond to a harm. She told me that, if I was lucky, eventually some Lakota might trust me enough to share their own cultural concepts of contrition, for how to make something right after you've done a wrong. "Every culture has experience with being wrong, with finding a way forward," said Judge. "We're all humans, and we all make mistakes."

I grew quiet in the car, thinking. The light died outside, and we drove over a mountain pass and through a herd of elk, their brown necks craning toward the thin strip of grass beside the highway. Again, I wondered about those old photographs of my family members and Lakota. Again, I wondered just what had happened one hundred years ago on that South Dakota prairie.

Over the coming months and years, I would pack that roller bag again and again, traveling to the western prairie and beyond in search of answers about both the past and the future. In response to Judge Abby's guidance, I would undergo several years of hevruta, a traditional Jewish form of paired study. Every other week, my rabbi and I would meet to read ancient Jewish texts that proscribe how to atone and reconcile after a harm has been committed, even and especially one that a person didn't cause directly but did benefit from. We would find, in every layer of Jewish writing—from the pre-Israelites, who dealt with sin by killing heifers, to the famous Spanish rabbi Maimonides, all the way to the rabbis of today, who are writing about America's amoral history of slavery and land theft—that, before you can fix anything, you must tell the truth, not just to God, but out loud to the entire community.

This book is my effort to take this first step, to dig into the past and reveal the cost of that "free" land on the prairie, and then the next step, the grappling about what to do with such truth, even when the truth— what I thought I knew, what I've learned—remains as slippery as an eel in a basket.

What follows here isn't a complete history of either the Lakota or immigrant Jews but a narrative of the connective tissue between these groups. The ways their entangled histories pull and push against each other refute the idea that pieces of the past exist in isolation. At its most basic form, this is an American story. It belongs to us all.

1

❊❊❊❊

BEYOND THE PALE

To understand how a Jewish community ended up settling on Lakota land, we must begin in Odesa in the spring of 1881, when my great-great-grandfather Harry Sinykin was around nineteen years old. It was unseasonably hot. In fields outside the city, crops were wilting. An economic downturn had left thousands of factory workers unemployed. People were hungry. A dry wind blew incessantly, raising dust and dirt that fell from the sky like ash.

Months earlier, terrorists had assassinated the Russian tsar, Alexander II. Rumors boiled in the streets and the countryside, blaming Jews. Though unfounded, the accusations flourished: Jews had long been reviled as different, as Christ-killers. In early May, as out-of-work men spilled from taverns, they formed a mob and stormed the streets, looking for Jews. Some later reported hearing the chants from blocks away: "The Jews drink our blood!"

Harry Sinykin, drawing on the survival instincts that would serve him well on the South Dakota prairie two decades later, dove under his bed as soon as he heard the angry rioters. If he was armed at all, it was, at best, with a kitchen knife, as it was illegal for Jews to own guns. Others would later recall having only rocks and slabs of wood with which to defend themselves.

Harry heard men yelling. He heard the windows shattering. He heard the door crash to the ground. The mob smashed every mirror in the house, they broke all the furniture, and then Harry felt the heavy wooden bed frame crash onto his face. His nose broke. Blood was everywhere. The peasants or the soldiers, whoever they were, found him. They beat him. They broke every one of his ribs, set fire to the house, and left him for dead.

The looting of Jewish shops and homes and the attacks on Jewish people continued in Odesa for six days. (Such violence toward Jews was so common, so systemic in Eastern Europe that it had a name, *pogrom*, which comes from a Russian word that means both "to destroy" and "to conquer.") Somehow, Harry survived and escaped the burning house. For the rest of his life, he would suffer from the effects of the beating and smoke inhalation. Even so, he was lucky to be alive.

This is an immigrant story. Like all immigrant stories of survival—of leaving the known world to flee to a new place—it begins with fear and relies on luck. My family's stories about Harry have always followed a classic script: we highlight his pluck and how he overcame adversity on the road to opportunity. We fail to acknowledge the reverberations of our family's good fortune, or the fact that it came at the expense of others.

ON A COLD SEPTEMBER DAY IN 2018, MY GREAT-AUNT ETTA, HARRY'S granddaughter, sits across the table from me in her sitting room. Stacks of black-and-white photographs fan out between us. She tells me that Harry had twinkling brown eyes, and that he always kept his Prince Edward goatee perfectly trimmed.

"I remember, I was a little girl, and my grandpa, Harry, pointed to a scar on his nose and said, 'You see this here? This was from the pogrom in Russia.'"

Then eighty-five, Etta is our family matriarch and expert on all things Sinykin. I have flown to Minnesota to learn how Harry and the rest of my ancestors managed to escape Russia and came to live on the South Dakota prairie, in a place that locals still call Jew Flats, on land that some say was stolen from the Lakota. I want to know what my ancestors thought about their Lakota neighbors. Had they ever considered the implications of their "free" American land? Answers will not come quickly. Etta's short white hair is neatly curled. Her pink lipstick perfect. She wears a blue cotton zippered sweatshirt and matching pants. She might look like a fragile, adorable old lady, but she is the one in charge.

Etta has lived in this two-story modern colonial, in a neighborhood of Minneapolis sometimes referred to as St. Jewish Park, for fifty-four years. It doubles as home and family museum. The chinoiserie wallpaper, which she chose before her daughter's bat mitzvah in 1975, is covered with family photographs. A large silver samovar, brought over from Russia in the 1930s by relatives, is displayed like a sculpture in the corner of the dining room. The closet in her kitchen, where others might store coats or food, is filled with cardboard boxes of photographs and yellowing letters. On the nearby mantel is a clear plastic box containing my great-grandmother's riding gloves, a doll, and a purse, all of them adorned with gorgeous beadwork. Etta refers to the style simply as "Indian."

Somewhere, Etta is sure of it, are the original homesteading documents, signed by President Woodrow Wilson himself. But there is no Dewey decimal system for this collection, and there is no directing this interview.

I point to a photograph of my great-grandfather and his cousin standing beside a white horse and a pony; they're wearing bandanas, cowboy hats, chaps, and boots that lace to the knee.

"What was it like for them on the prairie?" I ask.

She answers by telling me a story about her father's education at a heder, a Jewish school in Russia.

Again, I try to steer the conversation back to South Dakota. It doesn't work.

Etta tells me, firmly but not without kindness, "I have to tell this story from the beginning. Let me go back. Let me tell you the names of my grandparents' parents."

I take a deep breath, surrendering. Etta takes a sip of Coca-Cola and smiles. It will take forty-three minutes before she gets to a story about South Dakota. Eventually, I will come to see the wisdom in her line of thinking: to fully understand a story, you must go back, back to the historical forces dictating its creation.

TO BE A JEW IS TO LIVE LIFE WAITING FOR THE OTHER SHOE TO DROP. CEN-turies of not knowing what danger lurks in the near future has left a legacy of anxiety, of unease with the unknown. Although I live a seemingly safe and privileged life in a liberal, accepting city, I have inherited it, too. I lay awake at night thinking of my Jewish kids and those who would hurt them. I gravitate toward newspaper accounts that meet my fears: stories of mass shootings in synagogues, of Jewish cemeteries desecrated by red swastikas spray-painted across the Hebrew names, of the fires set to Jewish-owned stores and organizations. Once, as a child, when leaving synagogue, my mother told me to tuck my Star of David necklace under my blouse. She never had to tell me again.

From a historical perspective, this paranoia is practical, even adaptive.

As early as the second century, and for hundreds of years to follow, Jews were routinely burned at the stake for practicing their religion. In the fourteenth century, Jews throughout Europe were accused of causing the bubonic plague, the devastating epidemic of its time, and in some places, such as Provence and Catalonia, more Jews died from the subsequent mas-sacres than from the disease. The following century, all Jewish children in Portugal were forcibly taken from their parents and baptized under threat of death. For more than two millennia, there has been an unending pat-tern of forced conversions, massacres, and expulsions. Jews didn't wander, they fled.

By the 1300s, many Jews exiled from countries throughout western Europe had escaped to Poland, where King Casimir the Great welcomed them, betting that an influx of literate people, many of whom had financial know-how, would enrich small towns throughout his country. For several hundred years, Jews experienced relative peace there. They kept their own language, Yiddish, a mixture of medieval German and Hebrew with Slavic elements. They prayed and studied. Some were doctors and moneylenders, artisans and merchants; many lived in poverty. But when Russia annexed a chunk of Poland in 1772, Jews became ruled by long-standing antisemites who feared them for both their religious differences and the competition they posed to Russian businessmen. Empress Catherine the Great required Jews to live within a narrow slice of land that stretched from the Baltic Sea to the Black Sea and today includes parts of Poland and Ukraine, plus all of Lithuania, Belarus, and Moldova. They didn't call it a reservation, they called it the Pale of Settlement.

Here, Jews were generally not allowed to own land. They were restricted to certain jobs. They resided primarily in shtetls, the Yiddish word for small towns, where most Jews lived in extreme poverty. Beginning in 1827, as part of a state-sanctioned effort of assimilation, the Russian government encouraged its army to take Jewish boys as young as twelve to be raised by members of the military, or in military facilities, until they turned eighteen, at which point they were required to serve twenty-five-year stints. There are stories of boys much younger than twelve being taken. According to family lore—that I have no way of verifying—the brother of my great-great-grandmother was stolen away at the age of six; he was converted and became a high bishop in the Russian Orthodox Church. In 1856, the new tsar abolished the practice of drafting Jewish children and shortened all military service to six-year terms, with soldiers selected by lottery. Even so, family stories convey there was still much to fear as Jewish soldiers were regularly put at the front lines and coerced to convert to Christianity.

When Tsar Alexander II was assassinated in March 1881, life for Russian Jews went from hard to hideous. A handful of newspapers printed fictitious rumors that Jews, bent on revolution and clambering for more rights, had orchestrated the assassination. Though the reports were quickly reversed, the allegations were like tinder in a socioeconomic powder keg.

For centuries, Russians had considered Jews both social pariahs and economic rivals. When Harry was a young man, Russian newspapers published reams of articles not only accusing Jews of using Christian blood in religious ceremonies but blaming them for causing widespread economic devastation.

"They beat us with the ruble, sucking the juice from the inhabitants among whom they live," wrote one article about Jews just weeks prior to the Odesa pogrom.

Modernization of industry and agriculture over the previous decades had left many Russian peasants without work, a situation exacerbated by the severe drought, which caused crop failure and widespread famine. Whether the peasants would be allowed to retain the land rights granted to them by Alexander II wasn't clear, and tensions were high. Land—who has it and who doesn't—propels this narrative from the beginning.

When rumors proliferated that the new tsar, Alexander III, wanted the Russian masses to avenge the murder of his father by attacking Jews and looting Jewish businesses, the powder keg exploded.

Throughout the following year, there were pogroms in 259 Jewish communities throughout Russia. The looting and outright damage of Jewish homes and businesses totaled millions of rubles, possibly far more. No good data exists to determine the number of people injured, murdered, or raped in these attacks. In all, the pogroms were estimated to have harmed more than one hundred thousand Jewish families, of which twenty thousand became homeless.

IT WAS DURING ONE OF THESE POGROMS THAT RUSSIANS ATTACKED MY great-great-grandfather Harry. He was so injured and traumatized that he left Odesa, never to return, traveling more than six hundred miles north to his mother's house in Kapulye, a shtetl near Minsk. Today this is in Belarus. Then, it was just another village in the Pale. His father didn't go with him; Harry's parents had divorced when he was young, because his father wasn't religious enough, and no one seems to know anything about what happened to him during or after the pogrom.

At some point in the following year, after Harry's bruises had faded, he visited a nearby village where, according to relatives who were born there, the women were so handy and religious they could "do three things at once: nurse a baby, make the babies, and pray." Stopping by the town's water well, Harry met a tall young woman with deep-set, sky-blue eyes. Enter Faige Etke, my aunt Etta Fay's grandmother, for whom she is named.

"He tells his mother, 'I met this beautiful younger woman. Can you help me get to know her?'" Etta tells me, laughing, glad to tell a happy part of the story. We are sitting at her card table looking at the steady gaze of

Faige Etke Sinykin, circa 1883; her hair
had been ritually cut after her wedding.

six generations of Sinykins frozen in family photographs crowding out the
books on the nearby shelves. "So, she checks her out and, PS, they eventually get married."

This PS, this abridged version, is unexpected in a family that loves a
good story, lives for a tangent, and doesn't throw anything away, be they
details, tax returns, or nightgowns. It tells me that little is known about
the beginning of this marriage, a union that, while fruitful in some ways,
would be a disaster in others.

They made a life for themselves, Harry and Faige Etke, or as much of
a life as was possible in Kapulye in 1883. Jews at the time were not allowed
to work with fancy metals like gold and silver, but tin and copper were
deemed common enough for Jewish hands. Harry, having trained as a tin-
smith in Odesa, opened a successful business with his wife. He and his
twelve employees made utensils, pans, and graters, samovars, even the domed
copper tops of the local cathedrals and synagogues. Faige Etke got pregnant with twins; they both died, one right away, one at age three. She got

The five oldest Sinykin children, taken in
Russia, circa 1896. From left to right, back row:
Jack, Fanny, Ted. Front row: Ruth, Rose.

pregnant again, and this time the baby survived. In time, they had six
children.

They were relatively wealthy: they always had four or five first-rate horses,
and they lived in a rented, two-level home with a basement, a porch, and
separate bedrooms for the parents and children. Their son would later describe the house as "one of the nicest in all of Kapulye."

This isn't necessarily high praise. In Jewish archives, letters, and oral
histories, Kapulye, a town of around five thousand people set amid forested
hills, is described as a "backwater." There were no hospitals, no sewers, no
running water, and no coal. Light was derived from the sun, a candle, or
a kerosene lamp. Most of the wooden houses had straw roofs or shingles
blanketed with moss. Faige Etke's brother kept his cows inside his house
during the cold days of winter. Most Jews were artisans, like Harry, or store-

keepers, while most of the Christians worked in the thousands of acres of fields owned by a Russian aristocrat, who my family called the poritzer.

The biggest event, aside from the upheaval of the pogroms, was the advent, in the late 1890s, of a town outhouse with different entrances for men and women. S. Y. Abramovitsh, one of the greatest Yiddish authors, based his fictionalized town of Kabtsansk (translated as "Paupersville") on Kapulye, where he grew up in the mid-nineteenth century. In his Kabtsansk, Jews are miserable, naïve, idle, and helpless in the face of intractable poverty.

There were two parallel roads that led into town: one led to the Jewish side, past the cemetery and toward the highest part of the hills, the other to the side streets behind the hills, where the Christians and a small population of Muslims lived. While Jews held a slight majority, and while one relative recalled that "most people were so poor they had little reason to be jealous of each other and mostly got along well," the cohabitation was uneasy. The threat of a pogrom was always there.

Actual danger persisted, too. The tsar's soldiers would regularly come through town and, not having any barracks, stay for days at a time with shtetl families. As a matter of course, they would rape the women. A cousin, born and raised in a nearby shtetl, remembered of her family, "they were always scared."

The risk to Jewish boys of conscription into the Russian army was a central obsession. To avoid the draft, one of Harry's younger brothers drank lye; he would avoid the army but die from lung disease in his sixties. Another relative poured hot oil in his ear. Another, also desperate to avoid the draft, either took identification papers off the body of a Dutch non-Jew killed in a pogrom or bought a dead man's papers. Either way, he changed his last name and, free of his Jewish status, avoided conscription.

That threat was compounded in May 1882, when Alexander III, following a year of pogroms, passed a series of laws ostensibly to "improve the relations between the Jews and the native population in the Pale of Settlement." In truth, these "May Laws," as they're commonly called, were just the latest policy designed to repress Jews economically. Described by historians as "legislative pogroms," they restricted where Jews could live within the Pale, and forbade Jews from working on Sundays and from owning land and mortgages. In response, hundreds of thousands of Russian Jews fled to America in search of a better life. Included among this initial throng was Harry's younger brother Sam, who arrived by steamship into New York City in 1891.

For his first six months in America, Sam stayed with a cousin, and seemingly every other Jew from Eastern Europe, in the overcrowded and chaotic Lower East Side. Most immigrants worked seventy hours a week alongside children in sweatshops where no one had ever heard of a weekend. The tenements were rife with tuberculosis. The neighborhood was "the eyesore of New York and perhaps the filthiest place on the western continent," *The New York Times* wrote on July 30, 1893. "Cleanliness is an unknown quantity to these people." Here in the Promised Land, antisemitism was alive and well.

If Sam had opened a newspaper or magazine, he might have seen the ads for resorts reading: NO DOGS. NO JEWS. NO CONSUMPTIVES. Seeing cities flooded by these Yiddish speakers, Ivy League schools, posh hotels, and country clubs banned Jews. Real estate agents drafted both informal and coded neighborhood agreements to block Jews from buying homes. While none of this affected Sam directly—he, like most Jews from the Pale, was far too poor for such things—this growing wave of antisemitism greatly worried the more established, self-styled German Jews who'd been living in East Coast cities like New York, Philadelphia, and Baltimore for decades.

As early as the 1830s, and throughout the mid-nineteenth century, antisemitic persecution and economic hardships in central Europe had prompted thousands of Jews from Germanic countries to emigrate. In America, they blended in the best way they knew how: by speaking English or German rather than Yiddish, prospering in business, and going to synagogue on Sundays. But these new Eastern European arrivals, including Sam, threatened their safety and ambition. Something, they decided, must be done.

The answer cooked up by a group of Jewish philanthropists, who unfortunately called it "a solution to the Jewish problem," was to send these embarrassing immigrants away from East Coast cities to the American

West. For several decades already, Congress had been clearing the prairie of Indigenous peoples and buffalo to make way for white settlers, who, by farming the land, could assist the national effort of colonization. The Homestead Act of 1862 had made 10 percent of the nation's land, nearly 300 million acres, available in 160-acre plots to anyone willing to make a go of it, even those who had yet to become citizens, even Jews.

The idea of a Jewish farmer had deep roots. Thousands of years earlier, Jews in Israel and Babylon tilled the earth. The Jewish calendar reflects this heritage with rituals and holidays tied to an agrarian cycle of planting and harvest.

As early as the 1880s, in the face of Russian pogroms, American and European Jewish machers (translated as both "successful businessmen" but also, generally, "those who get things done") realized that the Homestead Act could be a ticket to Jewish freedom and began raising money to send Russian Jews to create utopian, secular farm colonies in the United States. This movement, dubbed Am Olam, meaning "eternal people," preached that, by embracing the plow, Jews could attain "full manhood and citizenship." Am Olam chapters spread throughout the Pale, financing and creating more than twenty-six settlements in America. The constitution of one based in South Dakota proclaimed it was there to "help the Jewish people in its emancipation from slavery . . . the colony shall demonstrate to the enemies of our people the world over that Jews are capable of farming."

These Jews were not, in fact, capable of farming. By the time Sam arrived in America, in 1891, almost all of the Am Olam colonies had failed, largely due to a lack of farming experience. But the East Coast businessmen, determined to get something done, doubled down on the plow. Though their efforts would come too late to help Sam, they would pave the way for tens of thousands of Jewish farmers. This was plugged as survival; they were, said one program booster, saving Jews from "a worse hell than was ever invented by the imagination of the most vindictive Jew-hater of Europe."

Beginning in 1901, the Jewish Agricultural Society's Industrial Removal Office helped fresh arrivals from the Pale acquire free (or cheap) federal land, train tickets, loans for farming equipment, and a modicum of farming skill. Over the next two decades, the organization sent approximately seventy-five thousand Jewish immigrants out of crowded East Coast cities into less-populated places. Those places included the Catskills, but also (in what is most relevant to this book) nearly two thousand western communities, most of which were built on land that had until recently been reserved for Native Nations. The Galveston Movement, funded by a German-born macher and New Yorker, brought another eight thousand Jews from Eastern Europe directly into non–East Coast ports, settling them in states such as Nebraska, Texas, Colorado, Oklahoma, North Dakota, California, and Iowa. By the time such aid was on offer, however, Sam Sinykin, the first of my family to arrive in America, no longer needed the help.

SAM HAD SPENT HIS FIRST SIX MONTHS IN AMERICA WORKING IN A SHOE factory, taking English classes at night, and hating New York City's noise and crowds. He'd heard that a number of Jews from Kapulye had already established themselves at the end of the rail line in Sioux City, Iowa. A few were heads of department stores and meatpacking plants and able to help their landsmen find work. When Sam could afford a train ticket, he did what most immigrants do: go where they know someone. When he arrived in Sioux City in 1892, there were so many people from his former shtetl already living there that there was a synagogue named after it: the Anshe Kapulie. The Sioux City Jews were so uniformly from that general region of the Pale, speaking with the same Litvak accent, that a local history would remember that there were only two Jewish immigrants from Poland. They must have stuck out like soft pickles.

(A brief public service announcement: Two thirds of all American Jews living today are Ashkenazi, meaning their ancestors lived in Central and Eastern Europe. They get the most airtime, but the American Jewish community is diverse, full of descendants from people whose customs and languages were forged in Spain, northern Africa, and the Middle East.)

Sam's letters from Sioux City back to Harry in Kapulye, describing America as a place where a man could get ahead, were like a gateway drug to an obsession with the New World. The work wasn't glamorous. Like most Jewish immigrants in the West, Sam became a peddler, something akin to a traveling salesman. With a horse and a cart, or a backpack stuffed with a hundred pounds of dry goods, he traveled between farms throughout Iowa and into South Dakota selling everything from pans to dried beans. Every week, he put the little bit of money he had earned into a bank in Dell Rapids, South Dakota, a small town north of Sioux City. After a year, the banker and the mayor approached him; they had noticed his work ethic. The town needed a dry-goods store, and they offered him financial assistance to open one. By 1894, according to my aunt Etta, Sam wrote to Harry to come to America and help him. Faige Etke, pregnant with their fourth child and the primary caretaker of her aging parents, told her husband to go ahead and look over this "Promise Land."

Such independent thinking gives weight to my aunt Etta's stories about Faige Etke, how she was "a ball of fire" and someone who could "do anything." Educated by her brothers, she had a quick mind for math and took care of the business's books. Trained by her own mother as a midwife, Faige Etke delivered many Kapulye babies, and the women of the shtetl regularly came to her for advice about marriage and childbirth. When Harry left, and even before he did, she handled the finances, and still managed

The two oldest Sinykin children, Fanny and Ted, by the "hinterish," or back house, in Kapulye around 1900, in a photograph likely sent to Harry in America.

to do all the baking and keep a kosher, religious home. "Undaunted and strong, she met every crisis," Etta wrote.

That Faige Etke was tough is undisputable. Remember the ice baths on the South Dakota prairie in the middle of winter. The balls she was juggling make my modern feminist challenges look easy. But it wasn't so uncommon for Jewish women of the time to hold jobs while their husbands were off studying and praying at shul. And often in those years, husbands left Russia first and sent for their family later. Still, I wonder, was there another reason Faige Etke wasn't opposed to putting thousands of miles and an ocean between herself and her husband?

There are stories that we tell in my family that are told only in low tones, chin down, lower lip pulled to the side. No one is supposed to know these stories, and yet, somehow, everyone does. "I think Harry may have sustained some brain damage, not to mention emotional trauma, from the beating in that pogrom that could've affected his behavior," says my mom, leaning on a family trait of creating empathy through medical diagnoses. "He really suffered. He really might have been challenging."

HARRY ARRIVED IN AMERICA IN 1895; BY AUGUST 1897, AT THE AGE OF thirty-six (or thirty-eight, depending on the document), he became a citizen of the United States, renouncing forever his allegiance to the tsar of Russia. By then, his brother's store had become, according to Sioux Falls's *Argus Leader*, "a large mercantile establishment" with "an immense stock," a one-hundred-foot-long storeroom, and two entrances.

By 1903, Harry's two oldest children, Ted and Fanny, and his brother, Sol (the one who drank lye to avoid the draft), had joined him. At some point, family lore has it, Harry invented a new tool for use in a Sioux City meatpacking plant. The money he made on the patent allowed him to travel back and forth to Kapulye at least twice. Each time, Faige Etke got pregnant. Meanwhile, the situation for Russian Jews was getting worse. There were more pogroms. There was less food.

"Kids in Europe were afraid of two things: basements and attics. That's where they killed [Jewish] kids," Jack, the third Sinykin child, told my cousin Cathi in a taped interview in 1983. With Harry and the two oldest children in America, Jack became Faige Etke's favorite, the one she relied on, if she relied on anyone. So, when Russian revolutionaries began to lure young boys to the forest outside town to roast kielbasa by a fire and talk philosophy, Faige Etke made Jack promise he'd never "run with that gang."

Like so many preteens, he blew off his promise. With scores of other boys (thousands throughout the nation), he listened eagerly as the men explained how they would overthrow the government. "They told us not to stay by our mother's apron, to be a man, to take a stand," Jack told Cathi.

Faige Etke, connected as she was to everyone and everything in town, quickly learned what Jack had gotten up to, and she was terrified. Soldiers patrolled Kapulye's dirt roads. If caught with the socialists, Jack would be forced into the tsar's army or sent "straight to Siberia," he later recalled. Faige Etke—remembering her younger brother, who was conscripted into the army at the age of six, remembering all the young Jewish boys who marched in front of revolutions and wars and never lived to have bar mitzvahs—immediately went to work finding permits and tickets to send Jack to the United States. She squeezed the business for the cash to send her boy away from harm. Within sixteen months, Jack had a cheap ticket on a German boat to America. At his departure, Faige Etke blessed her son and sent him off alone. He was twelve years old.

AROUND THE TIME THAT JACK WAS TRAVELING TO AMERICA, LIKELY 1905, my family story first collides directly with the story of the Lakota. It was at this juncture that newspaper ads and posters, plastered in train stations and on the walls of buildings, proclaimed, as one such broadside did: YOU NEED A FARM! HERE IS ONE YOU CAN GET BY SIMPLY OCCUPYING IT. In bold type, it announced that thirty million acres, or two million farms, of "fertile prairie" in western South Dakota were becoming free for the taking. Even non-citizen immigrants, those who'd simply declared their intention of becoming Americans, were eligible.

Harry must have seen or heard about these ads, but I doubt that he knew much about the land itself. Other Jewish homesteaders described the

Dakota prairie as a place "untouched by human toil since the beginning of time." This, of course, wasn't true. Indigenous peoples had been living in the Dakotas, hunting buffalo, gardening, collecting wild plants, and setting up tipis on this "fertile prairie" for millennia. Federal treaties between the United States and the Great Sioux Nation signed when Harry was a child, in 1851 and 1868, had reserved this land as permanently belonging to the Oceti Sakowin. But important details, such as how this land had been acquired or why it was free, weren't mentioned in the ads.

When Harry wrote to Faige Etke to tell her about the opportunity to homestead and to ask her what she thought about her husband becoming a farmer, she responded, according to a letter my aunt Etta once saw: *You have poor health. It would be very healthy for you to live in the country. You should do it.*

It's unclear whether Faige Etke knew the extent of Harry's poor health, or what kind of father she was sending Jack to live with. Despite the family narrative that, in America, Harry worked with his brothers in the dry-goods shop, was getting land, and getting ahead, the digging I've done has revealed a darker story—a story that has everything to do, once again, with that pogrom in Odesa.

When Jack arrived in South Dakota, his father was more than unwell. Harry was unhinged. The first night, and again the second and the third, Jack woke to see his father standing at the darkened window of his sod house in Dell Rapids, holding a loaded gun, and shouting at imaginary Cossacks in the street. "God dammit," Harry yelled and fired. "Son of a bitch."

"His nerves were shot," Jack told Cathi. "He was unhappy. This wasn't the life for Harry Sinykin." Dell Rapids was a small slip of a town with dirt streets and wooden boards for sidewalks. Unlike in Kapulye, Harry had no connections here, no respect. The legacy of the pogrom attack dogged him: he had a double hernia, he constantly coughed from his asthma. His physical pain was like an extra limb. Maybe this explains why Harry doesn't appear in city directories as a co-owner of the Sinykin Store and why he was relegated to life as a peddler. His brothers worked together in their shop, but Harry was on his own, just another Hebe with a broken accent and a broken nose. For Jack, he told Cathi, that first year in America was awful.

The news of Harry's decline and the reality of life in America for her children reached Faige Etke. Bringing everyone back to Russia wasn't a good bet. A new wave of deadly pogroms had swept across the Pale in 1905; Russians are estimated to have killed more than eight hundred Jews and injured thousands more in Odesa alone. The slogan of the Black Hundreds, a nationalist group, was "Beat the Yids and Save Russia!" Mobs led by priests chanting "Kill the Jews" stormed synagogues on the Sabbath, when religious Jews spend the day devoted to prayer and family. Rabbis told their congregants to chant prayers while Russian men beat them and trashed their holy temples.

Faige Etke decided it was time. She packed up her piano, her silver candlesticks, her best linens, her dining room table, her writing desk, and her violin. Everything else, she sold. She said good-bye to her father, knowing she would never see him again. Nor would she run her own business. With all her remaining worldly goods, she and her three youngest children—Louie, who was four, Ruth, ten, and Rose, twelve—left Kapulye on a horse and buggy, like, Etta tells me, something out of *Fiddler on the Roof.*

They caught a train from Minsk. For days, they traveled across Europe on hard wooden benches. Upon arrival in the Port of Antwerp, they joined crowds of other emigrants to wait in long lines for predeparture medical inspections. Rose was found to have an eye infection, and they were not allowed to board their ship. For months, Faige Etke and her three children waited in limbo. Undaunted as she apparently was, Faige Etke made the best of things. Rose told Etta how they traveled to London and saw Big Ben.

Finally, on November 1, 1906, they boarded the SS *Manitou*, a 475-foot-long black steamship with a white band around the funnel and four masts. A sister vessel of the *Titanic*, the ship offered the Sinykin children a glimpse of unknown luxury.

"They did not ride steerage," Etta says, sitting at her kitchen table late at night, surrounded by stacks of photo albums and letters. Over the next few years, she will tell me this no less than six times. Several cousins repeat this fact. Unlike many immigrant Jews—including Jack, who slept in the hold where wooden bunks were crowded so closely together it was as

if the passengers were livestock—"they had their own room," Etta remembers. "Rose told me they ate in a beautiful dining room with very nice white
tablecloths. She was very taken with the white tablecloths."

There seems to be a longing to underscore that we were special. Unlike
so many Jews, we didn't arrive in America penniless. This story is basically
true, but it requires some critical revision. It wasn't entirely the success of
the Kapulye business or Harry's peddling that paid for their voyage. It appears from family letters that Harry took out a $900 mortgage on his new
free homestead on the South Dakota prairie—the first of many such loans—
and it was that money that helped pay for Faige Etke and her three youngest children to escape Russia. Even before her arrival, Faige Etke's life was
entwined with Lakota land.

WHEN THE *MANITOU* LANDED IN BOSTON AFTER ELEVEN DAYS AT SEA, FAIGE
Etke and her children joined the masses of fresh Jewish arrivals. Between
1881, the year of the pogrom in which Harry's face was smashed, and 1924,
an estimated 2.5 million Eastern European Jews, almost all of them from
the Pale, came to America. Upon landing, they immediately had more status than they'd had in Europe, where, for centuries, the major class line
was the division of Jew from non-Jew. Here, what mattered most was skin
color. The Sinykins weren't fully white—they were still on the Ku Klux
Klan's short list—but they weren't as vilified or vulnerable as Blacks or Native Americans. That class distinction would propel them forward in more
ways than they could imagine. They were the lucky ones.

Only a few decades later, the Germans would efficiently complete the
project that Russians had attempted in fits and starts for generations. In 1941,
the Nazis came to Kapulye. They created a ghetto, sectioning off a slice of
town with a wooden fence trimmed with barbed wire, and imprisoned approximately two thousand Jews inside. "Not a single day would pass without murder victims, without the pouring of blood and the terrible screams
of pain," wrote one survivor. The following year, storm troopers returned
without warning and selected twelve hundred people, seemingly at random, to be locked in a synagogue. Over the next three days, in "a wild

orgy," everyone, except eleven young people who managed to escape, was shot. Several months later, a special branch of the German military came to the shtetl armed with cannons and automatic guns. The plan was to "liquidate" the remaining Jewish population. They were met by a surprise resistance, perhaps the same people who once fed Jack a sausage in the woods. A hailstorm of bullets flew at the Nazis from cellars, attics, and ditches, killing at least forty-eight Germans.

But the Nazis were good at this. They brought in barrels of benzene and poured the volatile liquid over houses and roads. When they set it on fire, almost the entire ghetto was destroyed, more than five hundred homes. Some reports say that the remaining Jews who weren't burned alive were marched at gunpoint to a riverbank near the edge of town, told to dig a pit, to strip, and then, in lines of maybe ten at a time, they were shot. Their bodies fell into the freshly dug holes. The Nazis had killed 2,965 Jews of Kapulye and the surrounding shtetls. In another shtetl miles away, Nazi gunmen efficiently murdered Harry's cousins, who had stayed in Europe too long. They were the unlucky ones.

Thanks in part to their new free land on the South Dakota prairie, Faige Etke and her children avoided this fate. In the early days of 1907, they boarded a westbound train in New York City, leaving behind her sister and her nieces and nephews, and headed toward the American Plains.

Faige Etke may have been uneasy, worried that, in this new land, her children would lose their religion and their culture. As they sat on the train, watching New York slip away outside the window, the English clanged around her. She didn't understand a word. A piece of paper pinned to her coat was her only tether to this new place. It stated that she must get off in Sioux City and that a Harry Sinykin would meet her there. But who was this man? She hadn't lived with him regularly for more than a decade. How would her three oldest children have grown and changed in this new country? She believed she was headed to land that was, by all accounts, "uninhabited." She believed the homesteads would be something like dachas, the cozy countryside vacation homes of wealthy Russians. She had no idea what she was getting herself into.

2

***

THE HOLOCAUST AT HOME

L et me make clear something that Faige Etke may not have understood: In the aftermath of the Civil War, the United States was bent on seeding the northern Plains with white people who would support, just by being there, a transcontinental railroad linking the new state of California, and its raft of natural resources, to the rest of the country. Standing in the way of this vision were millions of buffalo and tens of thousands of Native Americans. Inconveniently, earlier in the century, the United States had determined that the Great Plains were useless for both agriculture and industry, so Congress had made legal agreements with sovereign Nations like the Lakota reserving Indigenous rights to the land. So, promises made became promises broken.

IN THE WINTER OF 1880, JUST ONE YEAR BEFORE HARRY HID UNDER THE bed during that pogrom in Odesa, Joseph White Bull went hunting for buffalo. He was only around thirty-one years old, but it would be one of his last hunts. White Bull's world, like Harry's, was churning, agitated by distant forces.

The snow that day was wasma (Lakota for very deep). The winter had been harsh, even by South Dakota standards; White Bull and his five fellow hunters had run out of tobacco and nearly all their food. The Plains were mostly void of trees and offered little shelter. The hunters needed to find the herd, or for the herd to find them.

White Bull was broad shouldered, taller than six feet, his dark black hair a curtain at his back. His left arm bore the scars of three bullet wounds incurred in battles with the United States Army. On that winter day, due to the legacy of those broken promises, he was required to carry a permit issued by a white man that allowed him to travel. His gun was likely borrowed, as he was no longer allowed to own one.

White Bull is often noted for being the nephew of Sitting Bull, one of the most famous men of his time and widely lauded today as one of the greatest chiefs from that era. But White Bull himself, known for bravery and charisma, was no slouch. As an old man, he would describe his younger self as a "he-man" (he was married, Lakota-style, around eighteen times). Respected and beloved by his people, his list of titles reflects the dynamic era in which he lived: accomplished warrior—he was in more than twenty-six battles with both the United States and other Native Nations; chief of the Mnicoujou Lakota; Tribal judge; sergeant at arms; church leader; and Tribal Chairman of the Cheyenne River Reservation.

What mattered in this particular moment was that he was one of the "outstanding buffalo hunters of his day," according to an article that ran fifty-six years later in the *Rapid City Journal*. The story credits that statement to White Bull himself. Though he wasn't known for humility, he was nothing if not honest; his famous uncle and his father had taught him that lying was a sign of weakness, and as foreign to the Lakota as smallpox.

On four different occasions, by his own account, White Bull shot his arrow so straight and strong that it pierced a buffalo's tough hide and came out the other side. This was impossibly hard—even bullets couldn't pass through a bison—making him something like the Michael Jordan of buffalo hunting.

On that snowy day in 1880, White Bull heard the buffalo from a distance, their hooves like the sound of thunder. The thousands of animals massed together appeared like a single moving body. It was possible in those days to travel for forty miles without losing sight of a herd.

As the buffalo smelled humans and began to stampede, gasping for

Joseph White Bull (Pte San Hunka) as a
young warrior.

breath, White Bull and his fellow hunters charged. White Bull reached the
herd first and shot eleven tatanka, Lakota for buffalo. "By the time we had
skinned and dressed our meat it was already dark, about 9 p.m.," he said
years later. The next day, they again went hunting, and again he was the
first to reach the herd. That time, he killed seven of the thousand-pound
animals. "The meat made a heavy load for my pony."

Within a few years, the American bison would be decimated. Within
twenty-five years, the trail White Bull most likely took to travel from his
home to these hunting grounds would become a road joining thousands of
claim shacks and ranches, including land that would belong to my great-
grandparents. This was entirely by design of the United States government.

I FIRST MEET JOSEPH WHITE BULL'S GRANDSON, DOUG WHITE BULL, IN JUNE
2019. At seventy-five years old, he tells me, he's the oldest living descendant

of the man he calls "Grandpa Joe." I've come to visit him at his house on the Standing Rock Reservation, led here by an old photo from the Sinykin archives. In the picture, Harry's son Jack is shaking hands with an older man in Lakota regalia. On an earlier visit to the Dakotas, Lakota historians had determined that the older man was Joseph White Bull (rather than Red Cloud, as my family had always believed), and so I find myself looking for answers in Doug's low-slung, thin-walled house that he shares with his grandson, who was then thirteen.

Doug is short and a little stooped; he walks with a shuffle and a walking stick decorated with turquoise stone. We sit and chat at his small wooden kitchen table. Behind him hangs a large traditional Lakota star quilt in green, yellow, and white, the colors of his beloved Green Bay Packers. On the wall above him are a collage of framed photographs of his family, of Kamala Harris, who he's hoping will become president, and a painting of Jesus. Nearby hang braided timpsila, prairie turnip, a food he's been digging and eating his entire life.

This visit will be the first of many. I will come to know that Doug is partial to long talking, light teasing, historical facts, Ernest Hemingway, and felt fedoras. A celebrated teacher and coach for forty years, now retired, he is famous in Lakota communities. "Oh, Doug White Bull, sure I know him," strangers say, their words bent by the weight of respect, their eyes taking me in, at last.

Doug's eyesight isn't great, and neither is his hearing. Like most Lakota his age, Doug has diabetes. Both of his wives died of kidney failure associated with the disease. Diabetes is so widespread here that Prairie Knights, the beautiful casino on Standing Rock, stocks each hotel bathroom with needle dispensers. Within the first year of the pandemic, the coronavirus, posing higher risk to those with such prevailing health issues, would kill Indigenous people in the Dakotas at an estimated rate nearly double that of white people in those states. Two elders who had shared parts of their stories with me, but who both had more to tell, would die of heart attacks.

According to Doug, such dismal health statistics are directly connected to the federal effort to decimate the bison. "When we had the buffalo and we lived the way we wanted to, we were a healthy people," says Doug. "There wasn't one single obese Native American."

Papers published in leading economic journals agree. When the Lakota's diet consisted of bison, other wild game, wild fruits, and the vegetables they grew, they were among the healthiest people in North America. Not only did they have living standards equal to or better than their European contemporaries, but people who were dependent on buffalo were the tallest in the world, according to *American Economic Review*.

In the 1700s, when the first white men came to the Plains, there were anywhere from thirty to sixty million buffalo in North America. Even today, the land where my family homesteaded retains evidence of this abundance: the top lands of the ranch are pocketed by wallows showing where buffalo once rolled and drank from shallow pools, their depressions most evident under a crust of snow at dusk.

"The [buffalo] would come in the morning, and they'd be passing by all day. This is what the old people say," says Doug, explaining that the buffalo weren't afraid of the Lakota and would come walking right into and past their camps. "Then nightfall came, and I think they must have rested, and then [the buffalo] would be going by all the next day. Days and days they'd pass."

By the early 1800s, due in large part to their prowess at hunting buffalo, the Lakota were experiencing the most prosperity they'd ever known. They had learned to ride and breed horses, which were originally introduced to the region by Spaniards in New Mexico. This was a real upgrade from their former dependence on dogs to carry their supplies and belongings between camps. Powerful warriors and adept horsemen, the Lakota, with a population estimated at around thirty thousand, controlled a territory that stretched from the western lip of Lake Superior to the Bighorn Mountains in Wyoming. Living in tipis made from cottonwood poles and the skins of buffalo, they would periodically relocate to established campsites in order to provide fresh grass for their ponies. Once there, some would plant large gardens near rivers and lakes; Mnicoujou, the Lakota band of which White Bull would be chief, translates as "Planters by the Water."

Buffalo meat was divided evenly among a tiyospaye, a group of families related by blood or through marriage that could include anywhere from a handful of families to more than twenty. These tiyospayes traveled and camped together year-round within a specific territory. Every part of the buffalo would be dispatched for critical use. The sinew would become strings for bows. The skins would become moccasins, robes, and tipis; the horns, tools. The bones would be cracked and boiled to release the oil, good for cooking and for curing leather. Pemmican, a mixture of berries, meat, and fat kept in a bag made of a buffalo stomach, could last for up to three years, a defense against the months sapped by blizzards and drought.

The handful of American explorers and soldiers who visited the Plains in the early nineteenth century were blind to the prairie's bounty. Major Stephen Harriman Long, an explorer for the U.S. Army, reported that the Great Plains were "entirely unfit for civilization" and a "Great Desert" that was completely unsuitable for agriculture. In 1834, relying on this intelligence, the Andrew Jackson administration officially designated the entire prairie west of the Missouri River, some fifteen hundred miles wide, as "Permanent Indian Frontier." This declaration should have been written in pencil; it wouldn't last long.

In 1842, the first pioneer train, eighteen covered wagons traveling together, rolled across Lakota territory headed to Oregon. Within the decade, gold would be discovered in California's American River, and more than ninety thousand settlers a year would be stampeding across the Permanent Indian Frontier, lured by the promise of easy riches. "Covered wagons were stringing out like wild geese, pushing westward with an insane desire for gold," wrote Josephine Waggoner, a Húŋkpapȟa Lakota historian who collected oral histories from scores of elders in the early 1900s.

In their wake, these pioneers left a trail of literal shit, rotting animals, broken furniture, unmarked graves, and wagon ruts—deep scars in the grassland. The settlers took good wood and left disease. The buffalo fled the stench and ecological destruction, and the Lakota's centuries-old hunting routes and camping spots were suddenly obsolete. Tiyospayes were forced to forge farther to the west and the north to follow the bison on which their lives depended.

These settlers, who were breaking American law by trespassing on Lakota land, were hailed by President James Polk as shining instruments of Manifest Destiny, the notion, coined by newspaperman John L. O'Sullivan in 1845, that none other than God himself wanted white people, who were dedicated to "the great experiment of liberty," to "overspread and to possess the whole of the continent." This idea of a God-given right to control western land became the foundation of every law affecting Indigenous people living in the United States.

In what was probably 1849, amid this massive disruption to the Lakota way of life, Joseph White Bull—Doug's Grandpa Joe of hunting fame—was born into a powerful family in the He Sapa, what American maps call the Black Hills of South Dakota. White Bull's father and grandfather had been chiefs of the Mnicoujou Lakota, and his mother was a sister of Sitting Bull.

"The men of that family were courageous, intelligent, generous, and fecund," wrote Stanley Vestal in *Warpath*, a 1934 biography of Joseph White Bull. "They planned to make [White Bull] a great warrior and a chief, and spared no pains to bring him up to walk in the tracks of his grandfather."

I spent days reading the heavy cursive notes biographer Vestal took in 1932, when, for several weeks, he sat on the dirt or cardboard floor in White Bull's one-room log cabin interviewing the old man, the conversation translated from and to Lakota by younger relatives. Both White Bull's words and the eagle feathers and war bonnet he kept in his home are evidence that he was raised with the sort of high expectations not unfamiliar to any high achiever. Both his uncle and his father told him he must make his name great. The day he became a chief himself, in 1881, his father instructed him to protect and help the old and orphaned, to safeguard the land, and to be wise and patient.

"God sees you," White Bull remembered his father telling him. "Don't forget these words. Love your people. Be a good friend to good men. Don't leave the Indian road. Think every day."

White Bull, today, remains widely admired. He followed his father's instruction. And yet, for all his accomplishments, the path his family planned for him would be trampled beyond recognition.

❖ ❖ ❖ ❖ ❖

THE FIRST THREE DECADES OF WHITE BULL'S LIFE WERE MARKED BY A
series of treaties between the Lakota and the United States. Each new legal
agreement was less favorable to his Nation and claimed even more land for
America. The official map of Lakota Territory would be drawn and redrawn
five times in little more than fifty years. These negotiations would be crippled by miscommunication, some of it unintentional, but much of it stra-
tegic and sly. At times, the United States government would resort to
bloody military operations and massacres.

For American politicians—in a tradition that continues today—
doublespeak was diplomatic recreation. Laws were made with all possibility
of amendment. As N. Scott Momaday, a Kiowa scholar and writer once
put it, "the whites thought nothing of breaking the word." To the Lakota
and other Plains Nations, words were considered sacred. To speak honor-
ably and truthfully was as fundamental as drinking and eating. Important
conversations began with the sharing of a pipe, so that the smoke between
people rose to the sky, forming a ladder upon which their voices reached
the Creator. So, for the Lakota, negotiations for this series of treaties were
doomed from the start. As Judge Abby Abinanti explains, "It's easy to lie
to people who don't have lies as a part of their culture, because they have
no defense against it."

On a September morning in 1851, when Joseph White Bull was two
years old, the United States gathered ten thousand people of various Plains
Nations—including not only all seven Lakota bands but also their enemies
the Crow and Ree—together along the banks of Nebraska's Horse Creek.
The Americans were intent on making a treaty to secure a lasting peace
and enable the unmolested creation of a transcontinental railroad. Colonel
David D. Mitchell, a regional superintendent of Indian Affairs told the assembled Nations that the "Great Father," President Millard Fillmore, wanted
them to stop warring among themselves. Also, he continued, each Nation
must create boundaries of their lands, so that, if and when white people
were harmed on their journeys across the Plains, it would be clear which
Nation was to blame. If they agreed to these terms, the feds would provide

$50,000 worth of provisions each year for fifty years, to be divvied up proportionally among the Nations. Mitchell explained that, in the future, when the buffalo were gone, the Great Father would provide farming equipment, cattle, and pigs.

Mitchell took care to speak slowly, but his meaning wasn't entirely conveyed. The Lakota language has no words for "progress," "private property," or "extinction." Translators listening to Mitchell were challenged to convey these ideas. Consider the scene: thousands of people were gathered outside, surrounded by wind and buzzing insects, trying to hear one guy speak without any amplification. "One can imagine this cacophony of nine languages being spoken at the same time," writes Raymond J. DeMallie, a treaty scholar and anthropologist. In the following days, Mathó sap'ic'iye, an Ihanktonwan chief commonly known as Painted Bear, would put it plainly: "This is the third time I have met the whites. We don't understand their manners, nor their words."

Not only were key concepts lost in translation, but the Indigenous Nations and the United States were working with totally divergent worldviews that went beyond differing concepts of honesty. While it was obvious to Mitchell that the buffalo would soon be extinct, to the Plains Nations, who had no firsthand experience with extinction, the animals were an inalienable gift from the Creator that would last forever if the people properly cared for the natural world. Also, while it was possible to make a short-term alliance between enemy Nations—such a thing had happened before—the long-term truce Mitchell wanted would require a transformation of Lakota culture. Not only would a lasting peace eradicate war, but it called for an end to capturing enemy horses, a practice that brought honor and achievement to young men, many of whom would give their prize away to a less fortunate community member. The Lakota view animals and rivers as their relatives and live *with* the land; they couldn't own what they considered a sacred gift. They couldn't sell their family. Mitchell's maps meant nothing to them.

After nine days of deliberation and confusion, a treaty was "signed" (twenty-one chiefs touched a pen while a white man used it to sign an *X*) and approximately sixty million acres was reserved as "the territory of the

Sioux or Dahcotah Nation." Lakota women, who had powerful status within
their Nation, weren't invited to sign the treaty, the first of many colonial
steps to diminish matrilineal power. A jubilant Mitchell wrote to Congress
that he had secured a lasting peace. The Lakota walked away with a completely different narrative. The year we made "peace with the Crows," they
called it in their annual Winter Count, a painted buffalo hide inscribed with
one statement and picture to describe each year. The only reference to the
United States was a picture depicting piles of blankets and beads.

The peace guaranteed by the treaty was brief. Within three years, a
settler's lame and skinny cow wandered away from the Oregon Trail and
into a Lakota camp. A young Mnicoujou warrior killed the lost cow, a culturally appropriate act for the Lakota, who didn't believe cows or buffalo
could be owned. The Mormon settler who owned the skinny cow saw things
differently. He enlisted twenty-nine cavalry from a nearby fort, and together they rode into the Lakota camp circle demanding they be offered
compensation. Chief Frightening Bear offered several horses, but the settler
refused, wanting money. How much time Frightening Bear was given to
negotiate is lost to history, but, before too long, the soldiers opened fire
and killed the chief. The Lakota responded by killing twenty-eight of the
twenty-nine Army men.

The next two decades would be marked by scores of violent interactions
between Lakota and white soldiers and settlers. Hundreds, if not thousands, were killed on both sides (soldiers tended to overstate their losses,
and Native Americans carried their dead away from massacres and battle-
fields, making it difficult for the white people who reported such things to
arrive at any reasonable accounting). That said, the Lakota were clearly the
superior fighters, a fact grudgingly acknowledged by military officers in a
number of reports to Congress. White Bull came of age during this time,
fighting from horseback, armed with a rifle. "My father was a chief and
because of this I showed no fear. It was because of him that I wanted to be
in the thick of the fight," White Bull wrote years later about one of his early
battles. "It was a hard thing to do but I accomplished it. They were all
shooting at me but they didn't hit me."

A gold strike in Montana lured thousands more settlers across Lakota hunting grounds, again devastating miles of grasslands and diminishing the buffalo population even further. From the U.S. Army's perspective, this was all for the good. "Kill every buffalo you can. Every buffalo dead is an Indian gone," an Army colonel told his troops in 1867. Soldiers were encouraged to kill bison for food, sport, or simply for target practice. Their efforts at extinction were aided by a leap in tanning technology, discovered in Germany, that enabled buffalo hides to become fine leather used for robes and hats. Swarms of white hunters killed an estimated two million bison per year for several years running. There are photographs of buffalo skulls piled higher than a two-story house. The smell of the decomposing bodies wafted for fifty miles. Coyote and wolf hunters turned dead bison into poison traps. By lacing carcasses with strychnine, they created indiscriminate death zones that killed scavengers and silenced birdsong across the prairie.

It was a desperate time. "The whole country was unsafe . . . the [white] soldiers were hated more than anything," recalled Waggoner, the Húŋkpapȟa

Pile of buffalo skulls, circa 1892.

historian. With the demise of buffalo, Lakota were "living on bark, dead horses and cattle," reported one Indian Affairs Agent in 1866.

The movie *Dances with Wolves*, about a Civil War soldier who befriends a Lakota tiyospaye, takes place on the Plains during the late 1860s, during this period of decimation. I remember the movie as a little cheesy and one-dimensional, but for Doug White Bull, it has profound meaning.

"They came upon a scene where all these buffalo were laying out in the prairie, and the white buffalo hunters shot them, skinned them, and took their hides," he tells me one day. "That's all they took, the hides. These buffalo laying all over. They just stopped, and that scene, boy." Doug starts to cry, unable to speak for a while.

Many months later, I ask Doug what it is about that movie, about that history, that affected him so much. He starts by telling me things that don't immediately seem connected to the film: how more than half of Standing Rock Lakota are unemployed, and how their teenagers attempt suicide at devastatingly high rates.

"That loss of the buffalo is a part of that. If the white man would've sat down with our people, the knowledgeable ones, and asked them about our culture and language and talked about, 'How did you live on this continent for so long in all this weather?' They would've learned something. If we still had the buffalo, I think the world would be better off right now."

Amid the buffalo slaughter, something happened that no newspapers, politicians, or generals had predicted: the Lakota beat the U.S. Army. The fierce Indigenous warriors drove the military away. In a remarkable moment in American history, the U.S. Army lost and let the victors set the terms for peace.

The resulting Fort Laramie Treaty of 1868, signed by Joseph White Bull and more than 150 other Oceti Sakowin Head Men, pledged to keep white people from living north of the Platte River, preserving an area where the Lakota and other Native Nations could continue to hunt the diminished but still-roaming herds of buffalo. Critically for what was to soon unfold, it required any future agreement over land takings to be ratified by three fourths of Oceti Sakowin males. But, once again, what was said and what was understood wasn't the same. The treaty created the Great Sioux Reservation, and cut Oceti Sakowin landholdings by 32.9 million acres, more than half of what had been preserved by the 1851 treaty. But this wasn't exactly done on the up and up: the treaty reserved an additional 32 million acres for the Oceti Sakowin to use to hunt buffalo, but only for as long as the buffalo existed in numbers that "justified" the chase. Such vague language was a setup for misinterpretation. Many scholars believe that the Head Men may not have realized that their territory had in fact been shrunk.

And once again, America's words would have little meaning. Within months, people at the highest levels of the government conspired to undercut the treaty. No wonder the Lakota word for white person is *wasicu*, or fat-taker. To be a wasicu is to behave as if you have no relatives, no one to account to, and to be selfish and independent. That could also describe a capitalist who pulls themself up by their bootstraps.

By 1871, longing for more freedom to pursue Manifest Destiny and expand the country's western range, Congress declared it was done making treaties with Indigenous Nations. By then, hundreds of Nations had signed nearly four hundred treaties with the United States resulting in the transfer of more than 1.3 billion acres, or more than 68 percent of the eventual Lower 48 away from Native American control. Rutgers professor Jameson Sweet, who is Lakota and Dakota, has found that, at the core of every single treaty negotiated by wasicus was "some kind of fraud . . . some kind of coercion, they're taking advantage of some extreme poverty or something like that so they can purchase the land at rock bottom prices."

WHEN SOME OF MY RELATIVES SET SAIL FOR AMERICA, THEY HAD HEARD that the streets here were paved with gold. They never considered where that gold might have come from or what this new country might have done to make that gold its own.

In the aftermath of the Civil War, the United States was in the worst debt of its young life, owing more than $2.7 billion—more than forty times what it had owed only five years earlier. Rumor persisted that gold could be found deep in the Black Hills of the Dakota Territory. Such treasure could pay the national debt and enable America to rebuild the razed South, pay out pensions to Union veterans, and expand its westward railroad. But the Black Hills were, by federal treaty, the Lakota's property, and the Black Hills were not for sale.

"The Great Spirit gave us this land and we are at home here," Sitting Bull told a Catholic missionary who had been tasked, in 1868, with convincing the Lakota to sign a revised treaty that ceded the Hills. "I will not have my people robbed. We can live if we can keep our Black Hills. We do not want to eat from the hand of the Grandfather [the United States]. We can feed ourselves." But the wasicus would not take no for an answer.

In the summer of 1874, Lieutenant Colonel George Armstrong Custer, a golden-haired Civil War hero, was charged by Congress to lead a scientific expedition into the Hills. He declared it would be "one of peace." To demonstrate this "peace," he traveled with a column of one thousand soldiers, three Gatling guns, the latest make of automatic rifle, and two hundred rounds of ammunition per man. Included in the ranks were a geologist, "practical miners," a photographer, and "a pack" of embedded reporters. In truth, the mission was simple: find gold. It was an open secret. A private in the U.S. Army who kept a diary during the expedition wrote, "Does the treachery and blood-shedding by the redskins justify the Government of the United States in staining its honor? by the violation of the existing treaty? or by a monstrous fib about a peaceful expedition? I say, 'No!'"

Custer's expedition spent weeks getting lost, its horses and gear stranded in deep, unforgiving canyons. Bumbling around, "the expedition spent about as much time picnicking as standing watch," wrote historian Edward Lazarus. But after nearly a month, while taking a dip in a creek, one of their party saw something shiny in the water: approximately forty pinhead-size flecks. With a shout of joy, he cried, "Boys, I've got it!" The men threw up their hats, ran in circles, and jumped up and down, some of them crying, some of them laughing, wrote historian Waggoner, who interviewed one of the two Lakota guides who accompanied the expedition. (The participation of these Indigenous men was imperative to Custer's success; for the rest of their lives, they were spurned by many in their community for what was deemed a great betrayal.)

Custer exaggerated the size of the lode, and the newspapermen followed suit, relaying a trumped-up version of events. GOLD IN THE GRASS ROOTS AND IN EVERY PANFUL OF EARTH BELOW read the front-page headline in *The Bismarck Tribune* on September 2, 1874, continuing with the subhead, ANYBODY CAN FIND IT—NO FORMER EXPERIENCE REQUIRED. Within a year, thousands of amateur gold miners would be camped, illegally, in the hills.

Again, Congress sent commissioners to the Lakota. Again, they offered to buy the Black Hills. Again, the Lakota refused. "One does not sell the land the people walk on," said Crazy Horse, the famous Oglala Lakota warrior. When offered $6 million for the land, Oglala Chief Red Cloud countered that such a price was "just a little spit out of my mouth," because the He Sapa were "worth seven generations."

The commissioners returned to DC empty-handed, but instead of accepting defeat, Congress simply changed the rules. The 1868 Fort Laramie Treaty had promised regular payments of cash and food. Now, the government decided that, until the Lakota ceded the Black Hills, it would cease those promised deliveries, an action sure to cause starvation given the decimated buffalo herds. Still, the Lakota were unmoved.

President Ulysses S. Grant had pledged, during his 1872 reelection campaign, to keep peace with Indigenous people in the American West. In secret, he wanted the gold of the Black Hills at all costs. By November 1875, he and a small group of military advisers made plans for how the Lakota should, as the president put it, "be whipped." The following summer, the Army launched an undeclared war on the Lakota. They would soon have reason to regret it.

"I could whip all the Indians on the continent with the Seventh Cavalry," Custer had once bragged. In June 1876, he and seven hundred men, operating under bad intelligence that vastly underestimated their opponents' numbers, attempted to surround more than two thousand Lakota, Cheyenne, and Arapaho camping along the Little Bighorn River in southeastern Montana. Custer's soldiers never made it across the water. George Standing Bear, an Oglala Lakota warrior who was there, told his son, "When we rode into these soldiers I really felt sorry for them, they looked so frightened . . . They seemed so panic-stricken that they shot up in the air." Joseph White Bull recalled that Custer was so scared that, in his fear, he threw a gun that had run out of shells.

According to firsthand accounts from Native warriors, the battle was basically over in less than a half hour. For hours afterward, Indigenous women and boys walked among the wounded soldiers, killing them with their clubs and stripping the bodies. "The boys got some good clothes," said Standing Bear. Custer was found with bullet wounds in his head and chest. That night, White Bull recalled, the gathered tiyospayes celebrated with a big dance, unaware of what was coming.

(The National Park Service and most American historians refer to this fight as the Battle of the Little Bighorn, but the Lakota call it the Battle of Greasy Grass for how the grass looked emerging from the nearby river.)

The question of who killed Custer greatly interests many historians, practically all of them men. One entire book posits that White Bull himself killed Custer. I admit, this matters little to me. The point is that Custer died. The point is that the Lakota, Cheyenne, and Arapaho had landed the bloodiest blow to U.S. forces in the history of the Indian Wars. "Custer's Last Stand" became a national tragedy of epic proportion; the deluge of public grief was considered by some even greater than that experienced in the wake of Abraham Lincoln's assassination. Calls for revenge echoed throughout the land, with towns and cities of all sizes pledging to send volunteers to dispatch what reporters, aka "ink-bottle generals," called the "merciless" Sioux. Much of what would follow, for both the White Bulls and the Sinykins, stemmed from this national mourning and embarrassment.

FOUR MONTHS AFTER CUSTER'S DEFEAT, IN THE FALL OF 1876, U.S. ARMY colonel Nelson A. Miles and an estimated two-thousand Mnicoujou Lakota met near the Yellowstone River in what is today eastern Montana. What was said is subject to debate; what the two sides understood were two vastly different things. The Mnicoujou thought peace with the white man had been won. The official Army reports described this new understanding as "surrender."

As part of the agreement, several Head Men, including White Bull's uncle White Hollow Horn, agreed to travel with Miles by steamboat to a nearby Agency of the federal Indian Office. But within days, word reached White Bull that soldiers had seized the Lakota's weapons and ponies and were treating them as prisoners.

Hearing the news, White Bull remembered that his famous uncle, Sitting Bull, had recently told him not to fight in war, that peace was required for the safety of their people. And yet, White Bull could not allow the army to hold his relatives prisoner. Years later, he would tell his biographer Vestal that he spoke to the warriors with whom he was camped and said, "We must go into the Agency. From this day on, the Grandfather will take over the nation that used to be ours; he will take our guns, and knives, and horses—everything. That is the price he demands for peace—*everything!*"

When he and the other fifty warriors reached the Agency at Fort Bennett, five thousand soldiers—one fifth of America's entire military—were already there. A captain with a line of armed soldiers behind him announced via interpreter that the warriors must give up their guns.

"I have a family to support," White Bull said, refusing. "They will starve unless I hunt for them, and I cannot hunt without my gun."

"We are taking all the guns and the names of the Indians here," said the captain. "Some day, when the wars are over and the Sioux have cooled off, these guns will be given back or will be paid for, or shotguns will be issued to the Indians for hunting."

White Bull handed over his gun. In Vestal's account, he did so because he believed the captain was telling the truth. I find this hard to believe. It seems more likely that White Bull was making a difficult choice in a no-win situation. As Vestal also writes, "he was afraid that, if he had a weapon, he might lose his temper later and use [it to] kill someone. Then the white troops would punish his relatives and things would be worse than before."

Things would, in fact, be worse than before. Over the next six months, soldiers, wielding the threat of starvation and violence, took more than seven thousand Lakota horses, as well as rifles and ammunition, though many Lakota hid their guns. Congress's plan was to sell the horses, use the proceeds to buy cows, and coerce the Lakota into becoming ranchers. But of the more than two thousand horses taken from the Standing Rock and Cheyenne River reservations, only 429 went to auction. The discrepancy was the result of a combination of disease, bureaucratic incompetence, corruption, and outright theft. The animals "had been disposed of along the route by the herders in exchange for all sorts of favors, including a ten dollar bill, a quart of whiskey, rental on a livery team, and 18 tons of hay," later reported the *St. Paul Pioneer Press*. At the federal Agency on what would become the Pine Ridge Reservation, the U.S. Army received $4,169.84 (nearly $100,000 today) from the sales of the horses; it never used the money to buy cattle or to repay the Lakota.

Under threat of imprisonment, White Bull wasn't able to leave the reservation for four years, and after that could do so only with a permit. Without ponies or guns, and with soldiers and settlers still killing thousands of buffalo a day, Lakota couldn't easily hunt wild game. Meanwhile, the rations promised by the earlier treaty had been weaponized: until the Lakota sold the Black Hills, there would be no food.

"Here and there we could see men and women laboriously dragging wood home or carrying small quantities on their backs," an elder later told Waggoner. "Every tent seemed to be silent except where children were crying for food. Silence, because there was no enjoyment in talking, no enjoyment in singing, only a wailing song at times came with the wind, a song of grief and regret."

Amid such starvation, Congress sent federal representatives back to the Dakota Territory, certain that the hungry Lakota would sell the Black Hills in exchange for food. When the vast majority of Head Men refused, the commissioners switched tactics.

According to the testimony of Lakota men who were in the room where it happened, the commissioners sent to parlay served liquor. Outside the warehouse where they met was a cannon pointed at them, and "squads of armed soldiers were at the door." In exchange for rations to feed the starving, some of the Head Men agreed to lease the minerals in the "land above the pines." At no point did they agree to sell. In the end, only 10 percent of those eligible to sign touched the pen, far from the 75 percent required by the earlier treaty.

"Those who signed the Treaty did so because they were afraid, and if they had not been afraid they would not have signed," a Lakota chief who was there later recalled.

Again, the American government's official version of events wasn't anywhere close to the Lakota version. The commissioners returned to Washington, DC, and declared that they had a bill of sale for the Black Hills as well as the approximately thirty-two million additional acres that had been set aside as hunting territory in the 1868 Fort Laramie Treaty.

"And that," White Bull told his biographer, "was the end." Except it wasn't, not quite.

IN THE YEARS THAT FOLLOWED THE TAKING OF THE BLACK HILLS, THE United States, intent on clearing space for railroads and white immigrants like my ancestors, doubled and tripled down on its failure to keep its word, taking even more Lakota land. I'm going to leap ahead for a moment, through fourteen years of Lakota hardship, poverty, grief, and resistance, because the devastating consequences of the Battle of the Little Bighorn wouldn't be fully felt until 1890, on the banks of Wounded Knee Creek.

That year, news came to the Standing Rock Reservation of a new religion, one that was being embraced by Indigenous people on dozens of reservations throughout the West. Several years earlier, a Paiute man in Nevada named Wovoka had experienced a vision from God. The version of this vision that reached the Lakota, carried by letter, telegram, and word of mouth, was that, if they were peaceful, honest, and prayed, a messiah—sometimes called Christ or Jesus—would push the whites back across the ocean, and all the Indigenous people and all the buffalo that had ever lived would be home again, eternally happy. By dancing in a circle until the participants fell into a trance, the Lakota would hasten this coming era. This Ghost Dance, which had roots in Paiute religion but was influenced by the Christian churches now blanketing Lakota Country, offered a bridge, a way to maintain tradition in a changing world.

In 1884, the Department of the Interior, acting without permission from

Congress, had outlawed Native religious practices; those caught practicing ceremonies such as the Sun Dance, a sacred tradition, could have their rations withheld and be thrown in jail. Within a year of the Ghost Dance's arrival in the Dakotas, one third of all Lakota—around six thousand men, women, and children—embraced it, often adapting elements of the Sun Dance, such as placing a cottonwood tree in the midst of the dancing circle. Lakota dancers, many wearing white ceremonial shirts that they believed made them impervious to bullets, danced until they fell into a trance, in which they saw the coming paradise. Joseph White Bull himself participated three times, but after having a vision of violence, he never danced again. It may have saved his life.

For the first year of the Ghost Dance's presence on reservations, there's limited evidence that white settlers or federal officials were worried about the practice. But in November 1890, with two South Dakota congressional seats up for grabs, and the Republican agenda hanging in the balance, Republican president Benjamin Harrison decided to use the Ghost Dance for political gain.

"Sending in the army would be popular with settlers," historian Louis S. Warren wrote in *God's Red Son: The Ghost Dance Religion and the Making of Modern America*, "because large numbers of soldiers meant profits for local merchants and military contractors."

Under the president's direction, one third of the U.S. Army was sent to South Dakota. It was the largest campaign since the Civil War. As in Odesa less than a decade earlier, the newspapers printed inflammatory rumors. Suddenly, white settlers were reading that impassioned dancing would lead to violent revolt, that there were as many as fifteen thousand armed Lakota, that attack was imminent, that Ghost Dancers had already murdered settlers and soldiers. Some articles inaccurately stated that the dancing Lakota became cannibals, thirsty for white men's blood and inspired to bash in children's brains. Homesteaders closed their schools. Mass meetings were held.

Harrison's gamble worked: both South Dakota seats went Republican.

Within weeks, upwards of fifteen hundred soldiers swarmed Lakota Country, arresting and jailing Ghost Dancers. Up at the Standing Rock

Agency, the federal agent in charge ordered the Indian police to arrest Sitting Bull for fomenting dancing. What happened next changed history.

As Sitting Bull's wife watched her husband forcibly taken from their home, she began to sing a death song. Her mournful tune made the Indian policemen, who may have been drinking, even more nervous. As members of Sitting Bull's tiyospaye began fighting to rescue him, the scene turned to chaos, and one of the policemen shot Sitting Bull. He would die within days from his wounds.

(The fact that these policemen were themselves Lakota complicates this story, introducing in bold the dynamics of colonization: that, for some, the only way to survive is to adopt the attitudes of the oppressor. As Paulo Freire writes in *Pedagogy of the Oppressed*, "almost always, during the initial stage of the struggle, the oppressed, instead of striving for liberation, tend themselves to become oppressors, or 'sub-oppressors.'")

In the hours after Sitting Bull was murdered, hundreds of his people fled his camp in fear, including Doug White Bull's maternal grandfather and great-grandmother, and headed south seeking the protection of Mnicoujou Chief Spotted Elk. A few days later, after walking in the winter cold for approximately seventy-five miles, these starved, footsore, and ragged men, women, and children reached Spotted Elk, a respected Head Man and Ghost Dancer whom the American soldiers called Big Foot. Spotted Elk's cousin urged him to surrender to the U.S. military, but early morning the following day, he led both Sitting Bull's followers and his own into the hills and headed toward a stronghold to the south, where he'd heard other believers would be dancing and praying and waiting for the Messiah.

More than a century later, on a warm June day, I peer over the edge of a razor-like road cut into the green hills of the Cheyenne River Reservation. Deep gullies dotted with pine and sage drop away from the road. "This is the route they could take without detection," says Donovin Sprague, the great-great-grandnephew of Spotted Elk, a Lakota historian and author, and my guide for the day. As his ancestors traveled farther south, they likely crossed land that would, within fifteen years, be owned by my great-grandparents.

Later that week, my cousin Aviva and I, tourists to this tragedy, visit

Bigfoot Pass in Badlands National Park. While another visitor practices guitar in a shaded picnic area, we stare at a sign that reads JOURNEY TO WOUNDED KNEE. It notes that here the Lakota lowered their wagons over the mesa's ledge and down a cliff. Sprague explained that they used ropes of braided sinew. The sign fails to explain how they managed this, particularly in the snow, particularly as Spotted Elk had pneumonia and, unable to walk, had to be carried by cart.

There in the Badlands, the Ghost Dancers found neither their brethren nor the Messiah. "We were afraid and did not want to be alone," Paul High Back, who had been a young man at the time, recalled in a 1940 radio recording. They headed east, toward what they thought was the protection of Red Cloud on what is today the Pine Ridge Reservation. Instead, a cordon of soldiers intercepted the 340 Lakota on the road and escorted them to the banks of Wounded Knee Creek. Spotted Elk raised a white flag of surrender. The Lakota made camp and tried to sleep. All night, they heard horses moving, iron clanking, "a thousand things scared us," one Lakota man later recalled. "We wondered what the whites would do."

The following account of what happened next is based on interviews with both soldiers and Lakota who were there that day, conducted between the 1940s and 1970s, and now housed at the University of South Dakota. To the best of my knowledge, no one has written about the events at Wounded Knee Creek based on these transcripts.

The next morning, the Lakota woke to find that an army of nearly five hundred men had moved four Hotchkiss guns, the semiautomatic weapons of their time, to the hillside above them, their rotating barrels pointed at the tipis and tents below. The soldiers told the Lakota to surrender their weapons. What happened next is unclear. Most Indigenous witnesses recalled that an old man who was deaf and dumb accidentally fired his gun as he was handing it over. Soldiers, watching from the hill, reported that an old man threw dirt in the air, a sign to his comrades to fight back. Others reported that an old woman hit a lieutenant on the head with her "tomahawk." Regardless of the reason, the soldiers on the hill unleashed a hail of shells, chunks of lead the width of an old silver dollar, on the mostly unarmed men, women, and children below.

U.S. soldiers and the guns they used at the Wounded Knee Massacre, taken at the Pine Ridge Agency, January 1891.

The several hundred soldiers on the hill were none other than the surviving members of the Seventh Cavalry, the unit the Lakota had defeated at the Battle of the Little Bighorn. As the Lakota ran through flaming sheets of gunfire, some heard the soldiers yelling "Remember Custer!"

"Shoot 'em down, shoot 'em down. Let us get through with it," Robert Norman, a recent immigrant from Norway and new recruit who was two days shy of his twenty-first birthday, recalled the soldiers up and down the line saying. Pete Lemley, another soldier, recalled an Irishman, a gunner who "went to shooting every Indian he could see. And the last bunch he shot at was a old buck going up the draw with a covered wagon and he had it full of squaws and Indians . . . he hit that wagon and killed them, blowed the wagon all to the devil and there was just one little Indian baby, that's all there was alive."

Many survivors were hit in the feet and legs. They hid under dead bodies, waiting until dark to escape for fear of the soldiers who, High Back recalled, spent the afternoon "searching among the draws and brush for Indians still alive and shooting them down." One woman was shot and killed while running, her baby boy on her back. The wails of the child pierced the air as he crawled onto his dead mother and tried to breastfeed. Doug's grandfather, age five or six, ran with his mother to hide near the creek and managed to survive.

The cavalry killed an estimated three hundred Lakota, most of them Mnicoujou and Húŋkpapȟa; most of them women and children. Spotted Elk's body was riddled with bullets. The soldiers "piled them up just like cordwood," said Norman, and threw the bodies in a fifty-foot-long trench. A photographer snapped a picture of the soldiers wearing fur caps and wool coats, posing above the narrow trench filled with corpses. Google "Wounded Knee dead, Nazis" and you can find this image posted alongside a more recent picture, striking in its similarity, of Nazis standing above an open pit filled with dead Jews.

The press called the massacre a critical military victory. L. Frank Baum, the author of *The Wizard of Oz*, who was the editor of South Dakota's *Aberdeen Saturday Pioneer* at the time, wrote in an editorial six days after the slaughter at Wounded Knee, "Our only safety depends upon the total extirmination [*sic*] of the Indians. Having wronged them for centuries we had better, in order to protect our civilization, follow it up by one more wrong and wipe these untamed and untamable creatures from the face of the earth."

For their actions that day, ultimately twenty soldiers were given the Medal of Honor, the U.S. Army's highest military decoration, an award "bestowed only to the bravest of the brave," according to the U.S. Army's website. For context, consider this: of the more than sixty-four thousand South Dakotans who fought in World War II, only two received the Medal of Honor. A bill currently in Congress that would rescind these medals has received, as of this writing, only twenty-eight cosponsors. History textbooks published as recently as 2017 (and used by students in South Dakota) refer to the events at Wounded Knee as a battle, rather than a massacre.

HARRY'S BROTHER SAM ARRIVED IN AMERICA WITHIN MONTHS OF THE Wounded Knee Massacre. By that time, white settlers and the diseases they introduced had slaughtered millions of Native Americans. The national Indigenous population had been decimated to around 15 percent of their population prior to the arrival of Christopher Columbus. The buffalo had been eradicated: of the estimated thirty to sixty million that roamed across North America prior to the arrival of European settlers, there were approximately five hundred left, many of them in zoos. The federal government had seized more than one hundred million acres of land from Plains Nations. Nearly all Lakota were living on reservations, where the price of leaving without a permit could be imprisonment, starvation, or death.

These calculated strategies to deal with the "Indian Problem" would inspire none other than Adolf Hitler. In a 1928 speech, he applauded the way Americans had "gunned down the millions of Redskins to a few hundred thousand, and now keep the modest remnant under observation in a cage." Hitler "often praised to his inner circle the efficiency of America's extermination—by starvation and uneven combat—of the red savages who could not be tamed by captivity," wrote John Toland in *Adolf Hitler: The Definitive Biography*.

Hitler's studies of American Indian reservations influenced his creation of concentration camps. America's westward expansion, justified by Manifest Destiny, served as Hitler's template for what he called *Lebensraum*, "living space," his justification for invading the countries east of Germany and murdering millions of Slavs living there. In 1942, the head of the Nazi legal department, Hans Frank, called the Jews of Ukraine (the site of Harry's torture during the pogrom) "Indians."

One January day in 2019, the day after International Holocaust Remembrance Day, Doug White Bull and I speak over the phone.

"Last night, I was watching something on television about the Holocaust and these old people who were survivors, and I thought of you right away," he says. "Your people and our people went through the same thing. But our people had a holocaust that lasted for four hundred years. Americans condemn Hitler, which you should, he should be condemned, but at the same time, they should condemn themselves."

I remember his voice coming through the speaker on my cell phone as I drove home in the rain, the dark outside crowding in. I remember a slight turn inside myself, a moment when I began to look at things in an entirely new way. I thought when I set out to write this book that I was writing about America, but, with Doug's help, I'd see a dizzying pattern emerge that crisscrossed both the globe and our shared history.

As a preteen, I was obsessed with Anne Frank. I read every book about the Holocaust I could get my hands on, prompting many weird daydreams of myself as patient and tough, hiding in attics, and longing for oranges. But I never knew, until Doug told me, how America had inspired the Nazis. The more I looked, the more I would rethink everything I thought I knew about resilience and freedom, about America and my place in it.

3

JEWFACE ON THE FRONTIER

I n true American fashion, the horror of the Indian Wars, of massacres and land theft, quickly became family entertainment. On a hot summer day in Sioux City, sometime in the first decade of the twentieth century, the sweet smell of cow manure from nearby stockyards mingled in the air with the dust rising from thousands of boots shifting nervously from the packed tiers of the local fairgrounds. Those in the stands, squeezed shoulder to shoulder, held their breath, as dozens of half-naked Lakota, Cheyenne, Pawnee, and Arapaho actors rode bareback into the arena, chests painted, their war bonnets flying. With war whoops, they circled a pioneer cabin. The cries of the white family inside pierced the hazy air. As one of the warriors lit a torch and held it aloft, threatening to burn the settlers inside, a taut line of tension stretched through the crowd, the white family crying for mercy, the warriors hollering against the horses' hooves, the music swelling until the moment stood to break.

On cue, entering the fairgrounds on his beautiful steed, was the famed buffalo- and Indian-killer himself, William Cody, aka Buffalo Bill, creator of this spectacle, the *Wild West* show. Within minutes, Cody dispatched the buckskin riders, stifling their war cries. The crowds, totaling an estimated thirty thousand people, nearly the size of Sioux City's entire population, cheered and clapped. (Though I don't have any ticket stubs to prove it, it's likely some of the Sinykins were in attendance.) Many waved the show's program high in the air. Its copy pronounced that the bullet used by settlers, soldiers, guides, and scouts in the American West was "the pioneer of civilization . . . without the rifle ball we of America would not be today in possession of a free and united country."

The *Wild West* show was the biggest extravaganza going, something like today's Super Bowl. For thirty years, it toured America and Europe reenacting theatrical scenes of recent conflict between Native Americans and settlers on the prairie. To the millions of people who attended, Cody's depiction of the West was fact (Cody himself had served as a scout, tracking and killing Native Americans for the U.S. Army). Over the course of the several-hours-long program, the show depicted "Custer's Last Stand," and then used Custer's death to justify the massacre at Wounded Knee, which was also portrayed in a popular later act. Many Seventh Cavalry soldiers were hired to act in the show. Cody and the audience hailed them as heroes.

Other "true to nature and life" depictions included Indians attacking

Poster from the *Buffalo Bill's Wild West and Congress of Rough Riders of the World* show catalog, undated.

settlers in wagons crossing the Plains, buffalo hunts using scores of the last surviving buffalo, battles between cowboys and Indians (the cowboys always won), and Native American "war dances." The Sioux City reporters lauded the show as "realistic and faithful in historical facts" and "a correct representation of life on the plains."

This was mythmaking at its height.

The glorification of homesteaders who defended their lands from Indigenous people not only justified American land-taking but telegraphed to the audience that it was the bravery of settlers, settlers soon to include the Sinykins, that made this country extraordinary. Missing from the show was any indication of land theft or attempted genocide. Instead, it told a story of American exceptionalism written in bold type and void of any complicating details. It was only one of many such misrepresentations about their adopted country that my family may have swallowed whole.

Faige Etke arrived in Sioux City by the spring of 1907. She and her youngest children, Rose, Ruth, and Louie, would spend less than one year there while Harry traveled back and forth to the homestead, four hundred miles away, where he drilled a well to ready it for their arrival. Yet, their brief time in this frontier city was their crash course in American myth, bias, and code.

Faige Etke had escaped pogroms, she'd reconnected with her husband and her children, and she, like most recent immigrants, was eager to shed the image of herself as a victim and embrace her new country. I can only imagine that she and the rest of my relatives were wielding grit and hard work as passkeys for belonging. And yet, she remained a stranger in a strange land. From what I can tell, one way that my family and other recent immigrant Jews managed this central anxiety was to distance themselves from Native Americans. Whiteness in America is graded on a curve. Adopting the stereotypical and racist ideas about Lakota and other Indigenous peoples could only help Jews appear a little more white, a little more American.

THE SINYKIN KIDS COULD WALK TO THE LOCAL DEPARTMENT STORE AND, for eight cents, buy the sheet music to the latest hit, "Yonkle, the Cow-Boy

Sheet music for "I'm a Yiddish Cowboy
('Tough Guy Levi')."

Jew," who "Went out west one day; Just to shoot wild Indians, That's what
the neighbors say." "I'm a Yiddish Cowboy," another popular song of the
day, describes "tough guy" Levi, a Turkish Tobacco–smoking Broncho
Buster who "don't care for Tomahawks or Cheyenne Indians, oi, oi," and
isn't afraid to "marry a squaw or start a war, for I'm a fighting guy."

When these songs were performed by vaudeville acts, the comedians
wore putty noses shaped into large hooks and portrayed bumbling immigrant Jews, their Yiddish accents so thick the butchered words became a
Yinglish. One such act, Jordan & Harvey, "the Yiddish Parody Kings,"
came to Sioux City's Orpheum Theatre, six blocks from the Sinykins' place,
in April 1908. It was, in the words of one showbill, "a laugh a second for
twenty minutes."

This was Jewface. Like most of vaudeville at the time, it trafficked in
stereotype: the bumbling, clueless immigrant, the money-grubbing ped-

dler, the emasculated and weak Jewish man dressed up as a ridiculous and, therefore, hilarious Western cowboy.

Jewface was so antisemitic that, in 1909, the Central Conference of American Rabbis formally condemned these shows as among the most significant sources of prejudice against Jews and set out to investigate how to prohibit what was called "the stage Jew." Complicating their argument and fears was that, though originally staged by gentiles, Jewface productions by the early 1900s were acted, produced, and, in the main, attended by Jews themselves. The fact that it was offensive didn't stop it from being funny and useful.

"To laugh at the Jews on stage and think 'that Jew is flunking the attempt to be a real American' was a way for people like your great-grandfather to distance themselves from the performers," says Jody Rosen, a *New York Times* cultural critic who, in 2006, curated the album *Jewface*, a collection of sixteen hits from the turn of the twentieth century. "By laughing, he's saying, I'm not *that* clueless, and feels, as a result, more American."

Jewish vaudeville actors didn't only depict peddlers but also portrayed Jews married to "Indian princesses" and donned red face paint and Native regalia to play the Indigenous people themselves. (The offensive trope of a Pocahontas-like daughter of a Native American chief defending her white lover had long predated Jewface and had been used to justify colonization and the settlers' right to Indigenous land.)

By perpetuating stereotypes of Native Americans, Jewish actors and comedians could shake off their own suspect status and appear whiter. When Jews dressed up in redface and pretended to be Indigenous, they made good on the promise of the melting pot and even asserted a "spiritual connection to the American landscape," writes historian Philip J. Deloria in *Indians in Unexpected Places*.

This trend continued for decades. In the 1930 movie *Whoopee!*, a New York Jew moves out west for his health and, after being captured by Indians, is invited to join the tribe. The Jewish character, while dressed in Indigenous garb, opts for a Yiddish accent while saying, "Me Big Chief Izzy Horowitz," as he tries to rip off a rich white man over the sale of a blanket and a doll (the joke being that a Jew would've haggled more deftly over land prices). As Michael Rogin wrote in *Blackface, White Noise*, redface wasn't a "disguise but rather calls attention to the Jew under the costume."

In the era of Buffalo Bill, these redface shows were billed as realism, and it would have been almost impossible for my ancestors' life experiences to disprove such billing as the racist stereotype it was. Though Indigenous people had lived for millennia on the banks of Sioux City's Floyd River, by the time my family arrived, the Indigenous population was almost nonexistent.

Joseph White Bull himself came through town for a few days, missing Faige Etke's arrival by a matter of months. He was on his way to Wyoming, where he would help the U.S. Army forge a peace with the Utes. While in town, he stayed in a hotel, went to the movies, and, in his green shirt and red tie, sat for a photograph.

For a few days after learning about White Bull's time in Sioux City, I wondered whether this could have been the moment when Jack Sinykin and Doug's grandfather posed together for a photograph. The lead, one of dozens I followed to find the origin of this picture, ran cold. Additional interviews dissuaded me from the idea that a teenaged Jack would've had any interaction with the famous White Bull. Even Jewish immigrants had more status than Native Americans—the groups rarely mixed.

"Native people were a subclass; they would've been considered barely human, if that," says Reverend Dr. Marilyn van Duffelen, who runs the St. Paul's Indian Mission in Sioux City.

Throughout the time the Sinykins lived in Sioux City, the local press disparaged Indigenous people. In a back-of-the-envelope sort of investigation, I searched archival issues of *The Sioux City Journal* between 1902 and 1908, finding that Native Americans in its pages were described as either lazy ("He makes the squaw do the drudge work" and "Nowhere does the Indian do a great deal") or stupid ("Their outlook as a race is not bright"). If not dumb and unambitious, they were depicted as "blood thirsty," as people to fear.

Reflecting the prevailing racism of the day, the newspaper's coverage of Indigenous people was biased and unbalanced. When a "pioneer" killed an "Indian," the paper described the crime as self-defense and manslaughter. When three Lakota men, being held in jail while awaiting trial, were lynched by a crowd of angry whites, the paper described the crowd in two different places as both "quiet" and "orderly." There was no mention of any consequence for "their work of vengeance." (The journalist Isabel Wilkerson in her 2020 book *Caste*, uses the word *pogrom* to describe this form of vigilante justice.)

The newspaper coverage of White Bull's 1906 visit dripped with condescension, describing the celebrated chief as "a very vain person," who, while preparing to have his picture taken, "primped like a girl," and whose "features are typical of the thoroughbred American red man, the class which is rapidly disappearing."

Sioux City wasn't an isolated bastion of racist thought but a reflection of the nation. In 1907, *World Today* magazine ran an article titled "Shaping the Future of the Red Man," which determined that the "shortcomings" of the Indian were "insuperable deterrents to the success of our new policy of standing [him] upon his feet and teaching him to walk alone." The next year, *Harper's* stated that "the Indian" was deterred by a "strong streak of childishness." Open nearly any news story at the time about Indigenous people, and it will read along the same lines.

I used to believe that if I were alive when there was an Underground Railroad, I'd have hidden people in the cellar. I used to believe that if I were alive during Wounded Knee, I'd have protested in the streets. But the more I understand about the fear and unrelenting racist messaging woven into white society, the harder it is to convince myself I'd be a braver or more compassionate version of my ancestors, especially when considering the real threat their Jewishness posed to them as they lived in Sioux City with their thick accents and thin pocketbooks.

"SUSPICION, JEALOUSY, AND HATRED" WERE THE WORDS USED IN 1912 BY A local Jewish historian to describe how Iowans viewed their Jewish neighbors. Though there were more than seventy-five Jewish-owned businesses in Sioux City in 1905, many of those that tried to set up shop outside Jewish

Harry's brother Sam Sinykin (center, hand on jacket) in one of his stores.

neighborhoods failed because, according to a 1934 history of one Sioux City suburb, "our people will not patronize a Jew. . . . For forty-four years it seems that our people have declared and enforced an open season on Jews." When my family lived in Sioux City, the local paper ran a cartoon depicting a hook-nosed man meant to represent Yiddish merchants, merchants like the Sinykins.

By 1907, when Faige Etke and her three youngest children had arrived, Sam Sinykin and his brothers were doing all right. They'd gone bankrupt in Dell Rapids but had opened a new shop in a Jewish neighborhood in Sioux City, hiring their newly arrived relatives to work as peddlers, hawking their goods to farmers in the surrounding area. My aunt Etta's dad, Jake Kozberg, and her uncle Jack, both fresh off the boat, would sleep in farmers' barns and travel throughout Iowa and the Dakotas until they'd sold out. Their rabbit-fur capes, dyed in a variety of colors, were a big hit among the farmers' wives. Until it rained.

On a return trip, a farmer met the two boys with a loaded shotgun.

His wife had worn the fur to church and the blue dye had stained her best dress. He pointed the shotgun at the two immigrants, demanding they pay him back for both the fur and the dress.

"My father is saying to Jack, 'Let's give him the money and let's get out of here,'" Etta told me over the phone one day during the pandemic. She's been lonely with so many of us who love her staying away to try to keep her safe, but she finds herself laughing while relating this story. "Jack is trying to soft talk him and say, 'I'm so sorry,' and my father kept saying, 'Don't talk anymore, Jack, he's going to shoot us, give him the money.' They told this story one year at Passover. I remember it so well, by the time they were done telling us how they finally gave him the money, they were falling off their chairs laughing so hard. Tears were in their eyes. That was one of the cutest and funniest stories they told."

Even after Etta tells me this story several subsequent times, I still don't get it. Was it funny that they were almost shot, or was it funny that they were selling faulty goods? Maybe you had to be there. Maybe it was funny to think of the powerful men that Etta knew as ever being powerless. It was, at that moment, staring down the barrel of the gun, that Etta's dad, my great-grandfather, decided he was done with peddling. He wanted to work for himself. All these decades later, it seems to me to say something about the chutzpah it took to survive.

Jack and Jake lived with Faige Etke, Harry, and the rest of their children in East Bottoms, the poorest neighborhood in Sioux City. The soundtrack to their new existence was the blast and honk of trains from the nearby railyard, the foreign accents of immigrants from all over Europe, and the heavy rains turning the streets to mud. The smell of coal dust, sawdust, cattle manure, and cooking grain from the nearby mills filled the air. Industrial exhaust hung over the neighborhood like a soiled rag. Jobs were easy to come by, but Jews were often robbed, and the cops were not inspired to help.

Despite the circumstances, Harry's condition had improved. He was no longer watching the window at midnight, loaded gun at the ready. He had found work designing a major expansion of one of the city's biggest meatpacking plants. Under his direction, it would include such modern conveniences as a water-purifying plant, a cold-storage building, and a 250-ton ice machine.

Harry, working at last as an artisan, his entire family finally together in America, was less depressed, yet he remained something of a cipher. For weeks that stacked to become months, Faige Etke wondered why his brother Sam's family was living with them, crowding their small rooms. Some combination of good breeding and a language barrier prevented her from speaking directly to her in-laws. It took six months before she understood that this house was not, in fact, Harry's, but his brother's. That it was she, not they, who was indebted. It took even longer for her to realize that what he promised to be building for them up on their homestead wasn't the sort of house she'd had in mind.

Faige Etke might have taken strength from the fact that Jews have long been insecure about their housing. In many ways, it's the clear central narrative of both Jewish myth and history. The Torah, the Hebrew Bible, opens in Genesis with the story of God kicking Adam and Eve out of the garden of Eden, a place where they were safe and fed. This is not a prologue but a foreshadowing of repeated exile. When Cain kills his brother, he is punished by God with ceaseless wandering. Abraham, at God's prompting, leaves his country to establish a new homeland hundreds of miles away. The central drama of the Torah, a narrative we retell every year during the spring holiday of Passover, is the Israelites' escape from slavery followed by forty years of wandering in the desert. While Moses sees the Promised Land and is assured that his people will reach that longed-for place, they never get there. As readers, we never do, either.

The Torah ends with Moses dying as he looks toward Israel. Each fall, after reading this final scene, Jews have a big party called Simchat Torah, where we dance in a huge circle to unroll the scrolls of the Torah and then, promptly, rewind and begin again at Genesis, with the exile from Paradise.

Most of contemporary Jewish ritual has been divorced from land. We carry our culture in portable technology like food, prayer, and books. We keep telling the story of exile, in part because it has resonated for thousands of years: since at least the fifth century, during which many ancient Jewish texts were written, Jews have routinely been expelled from their homes. This happened in Alexandria and Constantinople. It happened several hundred years later in England, then France, Spain, and Portugal. From there, some Jews fled to Brazil, others to Italy and Germany—within a hundred years, the Jews in each of those places were again banished. By the sixteenth century, many Jews were living an uneasy existence in Poland, parts of which would become Russia's Pale of Settlement. Which brings us, in whiplash fashion, to the Sinykins' journey from Kapulye to Sioux City.

"Exile proves to be the rule, not the exception," writes Arnold M. Eisen, a leading scholar of American Judaism. "Home remains an affair of the imagination, located in the future perfect tense."

All of this explains why, on the day Faige Etke boarded the train in Sioux City and rode north toward her South Dakota homestead, the land where they were headed was, in her imagination, a paradise. This was likely at some point in late 1907 or early 1908. With her was an assortment of her children, cousins, and landsmen from the Pale. In light of everything that was to come, I cannot stress enough the significance of this moment. Those who wander cannot farm or ranch. The Sinykins believed that having land was the hedge against exile, and the hedge is the central concept, the lace that keeps the shoe from dropping. They believed that they had, at last, arrived. Yet, packed with all their belongings was new baggage, an assortment of fears and prejudices that had been stuffed into their heads and that would shield them from certain realities about the cost of this free land.

4

❖❖❖❖❖

"KILL THE INDIAN . . . SAVE THE MAN"

Around the same time that the Sinykins were settling onto their home-stead, Joseph White Bull's niece Sarah Buffalo was moving across the prairie in the opposite direction. In 1909, in a horse-drawn wagon driven by a stranger, Buffalo was traveling away from her family, away from the only home she'd ever known, away from the prairie dogs and the grass sea, away from the cottonwoods that blazed like fire. This was collecting season, and she and the other children in the wagon were the collection.

"I was taken to school at Rapid City when I was eight years old," Buffalo said in a 1971 interview. Pay attention to that wording: *I was taken.* This wasn't her choice, or her parents' choice. They most likely wouldn't see each other for at least nine months.

Upon arrival at the Rapid City Indian School, a place created and run by the United States government, Buffalo was scoured with soap, her hair cut, and her clothes taken and replaced by a uniform of wool and ging-ham. Boys and girls were separated. Because no one expected her to excel at learning, to become a doctor or a politician, more than half the day was spent, not reading or writing, but on an "industrial" education: how to iron, cook, and fold laundry, that is, how to have a job that didn't rely on land. Between classes, the children practiced military drills and marched in straight lines. Buffalo wasn't allowed to speak Lakota, the only language she knew.

If they "hear us talk Indian, they pull our ear or hit us across the head with something. And tell us to talk American," recalled Silas Condon, a Lakota child from the same part of the Cheyenne River Reservation. When he was taken to Rapid City Indian School, he was five years old.

This age isn't theoretical for me. As I write this, my youngest child is six. He needs my help to wash his hair. He, like most children his age, can't tell time or tie his shoes. If there is an empty lap, he will crawl into it. I have never been away from him for more than five nights in a row. To imagine him being taken from me is to imagine the apocalypse.

In 1891, decades before Buffalo and Condon were first sent to Rapid City, Congress passed legislation requiring that all Indigenous children attend boarding schools, called Indian Industrial Schools. Parents who refused to hand over their kids were often jailed or not given the biweekly food rations promised by treaties between their Nation and the United States. With the buffalo practically extinct, going without rations could mean starvation. The year my family settled on the prairie, more than 24,000 Indigenous children throughout the United States, including 4,216 Lakota, were collected and taken to federal boarding schools run by former army generals or missionaries. By intention, the majority were located too far away from the reservations to enable regular parental visits. Compulsory attendance didn't end until the 1970s. By then, Congress had funded at least 408 Indian Boarding Schools nationwide; more than one hundred thousand Indigenous children were taken away.

(This strategy of forced assimilation has a long history: in Spain, during the seventh century, many Jews opted to convert rather than be forced to leave the country. But out of fear that these recent converts would secretly teach their children Jewish traditions, the Spanish government forcibly removed Jewish children from their parents and gave them to Christians to be raised and educated.)

The time Doug White Bull spent at boarding school, a place he calls a concentration camp, was the worst time of his life. Such schools were rife with disease. Teachers and administrators sexually assaulted and otherwise physically abused children. When Sarah Buffalo was at Rapid City Indian School, students who spoke their native language or tried to run away faced punishments that were used at the time by the military—children were caged in guardhouses and forced to chop wood all day long while wearing a ball and chain. Despite periodic official guidelines banning the use of corporal punishment, violent discipline remained a regular practice at some Indian Boarding Schools into the mid-1980s. A recent federal report found that tens of thousands of children died at these places, buried in unmarked graves, the coffins built by students learning carpentry.

Congress sold the idea of these Indian Schools to the public using the language of altruism and "social uplift." Using the wildly popular theory of unilinear evolution (which postulated that, like individual humans and many other organisms, societies develop through predetermined stages of infancy, adolescence, and adulthood), politicians and bureaucrats boasted that they could use education, religion, and agriculture to hasten the evolution of Indigenous people from "savage" to "civilized." This theory would later be used to justify Nazism, as it placed Aryans at the pinnacle of human progress.

The stated goal of federal Indian Boarding Schools, according to their architect, Brigadier General Richard Henry Pratt, was "that all the Indian there is in the race should be dead. Kill the Indian in him and save the man." Teddy Roosevelt, prior to becoming president, wrote about such schools, "We are trying to turn the Indian from a child into a man." But for all the talk of progress and peace, this campaign of assimilation, what today we call cultural genocide, was designed to tighten the national wallet.

By the early 1880s, Congress had determined that keeping soldiers in the field fighting Lakota and other Northern Plains Nations was too expensive, costing, on average, more than $2 million a year (approximately $500 million today). By weaponizing not only education but religion and agriculture to obliterate traditional Native culture, America aimed to reshape Indigenous life, replacing movement with stasis, resistance with submission.

First Communion class, Standing Rock Agency Boarding School, Fort Yates, North Dakota, 1911.

⋆ ⋆ ⋆ ⋆ ⋆

EDITORS TELL REPORTERS TO FOLLOW THE MONEY. IN THIS CASE, LAND IS money. *Follow the land,* I tell myself and watch as power topples and swells across the prairie. I follow the land and watch how what America had promised to the Lakota came to belong to my family.

It's no coincidence that Congress's desire to populate the western states coincided with millions of immigrants from eastern Europe flooding the Eastern Seaboard. The press and politicos blamed those immigrants, as Sam Sinykin quickly learned, for overcrowded cities and strained infrastructure. Suddenly, western senators had allies among eastern legislators in the cause of white settlement on Indigenous lands, and both had the critical backing of the most powerful corporations of the time: the railroads.

The railroads had discovered that the real money was not in long-distance commerce between California and New York, but in local travel. Little communities that needed rail access to receive dry goods and ship their cattle to market represented a fortune waiting to be made. To seed the prairie with settlers, the railroads published maps and pamphlets advertising cheap government lands near rail lines. These corporations were interested in a particular stock of settler, one that leaned Aryan. To that end, in 1882 alone the Northern Pacific Railway distributed 632,590 circulars throughout America and Europe advertising free land on the American Plains. The circulars weren't written in Yiddish or Italian, but in English, Swedish, Dutch, Danish, and Norwegian. But standing in the way of new rail lines was the Great Sioux Reservation, which covered almost all of western South Dakota.

By this point, Lakota prosperity had already been severely diminished. Over the previous three decades, Congress, ignoring the promises it had made in both the 1851 and 1868 treaties, had allowed settlers to pass through Lakota land and had encouraged these settlers, as well as U.S. soldiers, to slaughter the buffalo to near extinction. With nothing close to the signatures of three quarters of the Lakota men required by the 1868 treaty, the United States had robbed the Lakota of the gold-rich Black Hills using the threat of cannons and withheld rations.

You already know this, you read it in chapter 2, but the chronology of federal land grabs can be confusing, as it goes from bad to worse, and then worse again. By 1888, Lakota were restricted from traveling beyond the Dakotas and were living on less than twenty-one million acres, a loss of more than 65 percent of their land in less than forty years. Wielding the banner of Manifest Destiny, Congress set out to take even more.

"The white man has laid his rapacious eye upon it, and the white man is going to have it," said one congressman on the House floor in 1889. To clear the way for railroads and settlers, the United States sent General George Crook to the Dakotas to gather the necessary signatures for what it called the Great Sioux Agreement, which aimed to grab more than half of the Lakota's remaining land. To return without the signatures was not an option.

Though not recorded in any official federal record, Joseph White Bull later told his biographer that "Three Stars," aka Crook, offered him $200 cash, the equivalent of more than $5,000 today to sign the agreement. White Bull refused and refused again in the days to come. Crook hosted a big meal, giving cash or horses to Head Men and one dollar each to the "common people." The vast majority remained unmoved. This couldn't have been a surprise—sixty-four Lakota chiefs, Sitting Bull among them, had already traveled to Washington via train to voice their objections to proposed legislation.

(There is a bigger story to tell here about Lakota activism, about the ways men like Sitting Bull, Red Cloud, and White Bull, stripped of their guns and their horses in the aftermath of the Battle of the Little Bighorn, used the tools they had—diplomacy, patience, and, they believed, the law—to bend the arc of justice their way. But my job here is primarily to recount what was done on behalf of immigrants, of my ancestors.)

When bribery didn't work, Crook leaned on fear, threatening in public meetings that if Lakota didn't sign, Congress would take their land by conquest and move them far away. With their guns and horses confiscated, many Lakota despaired at the idea of war. Still, there were many, includ-

One of the many Lakota diplomatic efforts to promote their rights, including leaders such as Joseph White Bull (front row, second from right with rifle at his knee), Pierre, South Dakota, 1908.

ing Sitting Bull, who continued to protest the agreement—in response, Crook barred them from the meeting. In the end, with some fraudulent math, Crook secured the needed signatures, and, within short order, Congress passed the Great Sioux Agreement of 1889. It would dramatically reshape the Great Plains.

The agreement was a Lakota-specific version of a piece of federal legislation passed two years earlier called the General Allotment Act (you may know it as the Dawes Act, so named for its author). The key to unlocking the civilized soul of the Indian, said Henry Dawes, was to change his relationship to land. The idea was "to take Indians out one by one from under the tribe, place him in a position to become an independent American citizen, and then before the tribe is aware of it, its existence as a tribe is gone," wrote Dawes in a wholesale reversal of the nation-to-nation relationship that had been established less than twenty years earlier with the signing of hundreds of treaties. Under his law, Indigenous individuals received the equivalent of a homestead, with acreage determined by age, gender, and position. Give him a farm, the thinking went, and he will spring into the shape of an independent capitalist, transforming the reservation into the Jeffersonian ideal of a society of farmers. I'm using "him" here intentionally: though in traditional Lakota society, growing crops was primarily the domain of women, under the Allotment Act, Indigenous women received half as much land as men, if they received any at all. Married women were entirely excluded.

Sitting Bull worried that such assimilation would erode female authority and pleaded with a white anthropologist affiliated with the Interior Department to "take pity on my women . . . The young men can be like the white men, can till the soil, supply the food and clothing. They will take the work out of the hands of women. And the women . . . will be stripped of all which gave them power."

The real winner of the Great Sioux Agreement was arguably the Chicago, Milwaukee, and St. Paul Railroad. The guts of the law make evident the influence of corporate power: it granted the railroad a six-mile-wide, eighty-mile-long strip of land, called a right-away, across the northern edge of the Cheyenne River Reservation, a place for cowboys to push their cattle to train depots. In the agreement, the verbiage clarifying the rights of the railroads runs nearly ten times longer than that detailing water rights, a not-insignificant thing when farming in a dry place.

Supporters from coast to coast praised these allotment laws as the "Indian's Emancipation Proclamation," and newspapers hailed such policy for "bettering" the Indian. This legislation would, in fact, do the opposite. Under both the Allotment Act and the Great Sioux Agreement, all Native lands, which now were completely allotted to individuals, would be held in trust by the federal government for twenty-five years, a time period deemed sufficient for Indigenous people to "evolve" from savages into citizens. Rather than experience some sort of emancipation, the Indigenous farmers would remain under the dominion of the Indian Office. Members of the Lakota Nation were shunted onto five much smaller reservations, and the Great Sioux Agreement sliced 11 million acres away from the Lakota. This is the moment when my family becomes inextricably tied up with the Lakota, because among those acres were the 5,840 that would become my family's ranch. Soon, as intended by the Allotment Act, the government would take even more land.

After the reservations were divvied up into individual farms, the left-over acreage was deemed "surplus to Indian use," and sold cheaply to the railroads or settlers. Legal scholars today describe this as "a huge form of affirmative action for white people." For Indigenous people, it certainly would be nothing like the freedom the newspapers had promised.

ONE REASON WHY THE UNITED STATES WANTED TO CREATE SMALLER RESERVATIONS was the hope that in confined spaces it could more easily control every aspect of Lakota life, something it had been trying and largely failing to do for two decades. To learn how exactly they attempted to do this is to reconsider everything you've been taught about America's separation of church and state.

By 1869, President Ulysses S. Grant had appointed Christian missionaries to serve as Indian Agents, official federal representatives on the reservations. These men were, in theory, moral and beyond corruption, and

Grant charged them to "civilize" Indigenous people by turning them into Christians. (Jews, not in the business of missionary work and having suffered forced conversions themselves for centuries, were deemed by President Grant to be ineligible for the job.) In what he called a "peace policy," Grant divvied up seventy-three Indian Agencies among thirteen Christian denominations, as if, wrote the famed Dakota writer Vine Deloria Jr., "they were choosing sides for touch football." Initially, the Episcopal Church received exclusive rights to the Dakota franchise and, with it, 26,929 Lakota souls. Soon enough, the Methodists, Catholics, and Congregationalists would set up shop, as well.

Charles Hall, a missionary in North Dakota in the late nineteenth century, liked to say that his aim was the same as Custer's, but, instead of using a gun, "my weapon is the Word of God."

The Christian Indian Agents made it illegal to practice the Sun Dance, or any other traditional Lakota ceremony. The loss of such religious practice, particularly one conducted after family members died, made some Lakota say they felt istelya, diminished to the level of a nonhuman. For Lakota women, whose cultural importance had been elevated by legends of female deities and female-specific ceremony, Christian patriarchy, with its focus on a male god and the insistence that women change their family names to their husbands', "virtually eclipsed the autonomy of Native women," wrote Beatrice Medicine, a Sihasapa and Mnicoujou Lakota scholar.

For Lakota who were caught practicing their religion, the punishment was jail time or forced labor. It was the loss of such religious practice that historians link to the rise of the Ghost Dance. Also punishable by as much as thirty days in the guardhouse were having a relationship outside of marriage or drinking alcohol, two activities in which I am certain members of my own family engaged. Of course, they were never arrested for such things, living as they did off the reservation, where the rules were different.

The progress that the Indian Affairs Office was making in its civilization efforts was tracked by Indian Agents with actuarial precision. Beginning in the late nineteenth century until at least 1935, the Indian Office tracked the exact number of Lakota who had been baptized and attended church services. Also recorded were the number of missionaries, how many

Indigenous people had married whites, the number of Indigenous people wearing "modern attire," how many spoke or wrote English, and how many farmed and raised cattle. Conversion to Christianity was, for the Indian Office, the gold star of assimilation, and by 1916 the Cheyenne River Reservation's Indian Agent proudly reported to his boss that almost every adult and child had been baptized.

For the Lakota, as it had been for Jews in medieval Spain and ancient Rome, conversion wasn't capitulation but continuity. As Joseph White Bull said in 1935, "the Indian religion and the Christian religion are equally good since they prayed alike to one god." Almost a century later, Doug would tell me almost the exact same thing. He and many of his family attend Catholic services in a church with traditional Lakota star quilts hanging from the rafters and a pulpit made from a wide stump of cottonwood. But Doug has also performed ancient Lakota ceremonies that were maintained in secret for generations. (Included among those ceremonies practiced in secret was the Ghost Dance, which Lakota and other Indigenous people continued to perform into the twentieth century, especially in concert with protests over land takings.)

With conversion, the Christian churches received more than souls. America gave them land. By 1910, the Indian Office had allotted nearly three thousand acres to twenty-seven churches on the Cheyenne River Reservation. As of today, churches own at least twenty-five thousand acres on reservations nationwide. South Dakota reservations appear to remain the most impacted: churches own nearly nine thousand acres of Indigenous land in the state. In 1990, the Catholic Church still owned approximately ten thousand acres on reservations nationwide, including the mineral rights on some of that land. In more recent years, the Catholic Church and the United Church of Christ have worked to return land to South Dakota Native Nations. That said, it's also been common in recent decades for churches throughout the state to lease their reservation lands to private entities, sharing none of those monies with Indigenous communities, according to Cleve Her Many Horses, a former Bureau of Indian Affairs superintendent who now runs the Tribal Land Enterprise for the Rosebud Sioux Tribe. To this day, the Episcopal Church makes money on land it was given on South

Dakota's Rosebud Reservation, leasing it for hay, cattle grazing, and to a cell phone tower company.

"It has been said of missionaries that when they arrived they had only the Book and we had the land; now we have the Book and they have the land," wrote Vine Deloria Jr. "Kindly old missionaries were really land agents who helped rape the tribe of its land base."

FOR MANY YEARS, THE INDIAN AGENCY, NEVER KNOWN FOR EFFICIENCY, made no big rush to divvy up reservations into individually fenced farmland where Lakota could no longer live by collective effort. During this time, vast swaths of the reservations remained as they had been: roadless oceans of grass, neck-high, unfenced, and rolling in green. Those living on the Cheyenne River and Standing Rock reservations continued to live in family groupings along rivers, the highways of the time, with ready access to water and shade. Most had made good effort to adapt, to trade their skill and know-how with buffalo for that lesser beast, the cow. This adoption of ranching allowed Lakota to step toward both innovation and the survival of their culture: those with larger herds could afford to butcher cows and share them at ceremonies. By running herds with horses, these Lakota cowboys maintained the horsemanship of their ancestors. If it wasn't a transition they had wanted, it was one at which they were excelling.

From the less than six hundred cows and four bulls the government supplied in 1877, as part of an earlier land negotiation, by 1901, Lakota ranchers on Standing Rock had grown the herd to twelve thousand head. On the Cheyenne River, Lakota ranchers were producing one million pounds of beef annually, more than half the meat needed to feed their reservation's residents. Nearly every family had at least a few head of cattle and horses and a farm of anywhere from one to five acres.

One would think that this success would elate American politicians, all of whom continued to raise their glasses to allotment and celebrate it as a tool of civilization. What happened instead once again exposes the vast difference between what America promised and how it acted. I know I sound like a broken record, but frankly the record is broken.

By 1900, thirteen years after the passage of the Allotment Act, the Indian Office had divided and allocated most reservations nationwide into individual parcels. If Henry Dawes's theories of social Darwinism had been correct, Indigenous people, with their embrace of the plow, should've been leaping into capitalism with money in their pockets. Instead, they were more impoverished than they'd been prior to allotment. This was spun as good news.

"When we make an Indian tribe rich, we delay its civilization," said Connecticut senator Orville Platt, arguing that the government should stop paying such "high prices" to the Lakota and other Nations for their land. "The easiest Indians in the country to civilize are the blanket Indians and they have no money, no funds, no land, no annuities."

Instead of seeing allotment as the problem, the latest crop of politicians, led by President Theodore Roosevelt, determined that it was Native Americans themselves that needed time to adjust. The new best way for Lakota to learn to run the land would be by watching experts. White experts. Out-of-state experts.

In 1901, the Indian Office leased nearly 3.5 million acres, nearly half the Cheyenne River Reservation and three quarters of Standing Rock, to cattlemen from Texas and New Mexico. No matter that many Lakota families lived and ranched amid these lands. No matter that "a fair price" to lease grasslands elsewhere in South Dakota in the early 1900s was twenty-five cents an acre; the Indian Office, without the consent of any Indigenous authority, offered Lakota land to white cattlemen for four cents an acre. Following the land, at this point, leads in a straight line to Joseph White Bull, alone and freezing in a jail cell, being held on trumped-up charges.

THE LAKOTA TRIBAL COUNCIL, A GROUP OF ELECTED HEAD MEN THAT INcluded Joseph White Bull, had asked the Indian Agent of Cheyenne River to write to his superiors to inform them that the Lakota were against the proposed lease of so much of their land to white cattlemen from Texas and New Mexico. When the Agent refused, White Bull, by then a chief for more than twenty years, and another elder rode ninety miles to Pierre to send a letter themselves. When they arrived home, the Agent, who had learned of their letter, had them arrested and thrown in jail. The chief of police cut White Bull's long hair. White Bull was held without trial for three months.

This was in 1901, when White Bull was fifty-two. Only months earlier, he'd narrowly survived a rough case of smallpox; the scars from the pox made potholes in his skin. The cell where the police kept him at the back of the station had no chair, no bed. This was meant as punishment, but Steve Vance, the Cheyenne River Sioux Tribe's historic preservation officer, speculates that White Bull, a man of the old ways, would've preferred the floor, to be close to the earth, where he could pray and think.

White Bull hadn't broken any American law; if he'd been a citizen, his arrest would have been illegal. But White Bull, like all Indigenous people in the United States at the time, wasn't a citizen but a national. As such, he was denied the right to vote and other inalienable rights. (This dual system of rights provided further inspiration for Adolf Hitler. When Nazi legal scholars drafted laws to make Jews second-class citizens, they would justify their thinking with America's treatment of Indigenous people and Blacks.)

While he was imprisoned, the police made White Bull dig ditches, clean yards, and grade roads. He was never paid for this work. While covering the lease agreement over the following year, the newspapers failed to interview a single Lakota, instead reporting the Agent's line that "the Indians themselves want the leases made." Another quoted the Agent as saying "there is no resistance to any of the orders intended to further their civilization." In early February 1902, President Roosevelt heard from a delegation of Standing Rock Lakota asking him to fence six miles on either side of the Grand River to protect Indigenous lands from white ranchers. Noting that this would make the land worthless to the cattlemen, President Roosevelt dismissed their request and promptly endorsed the lease deal.

With White Bull's signature no longer required for the lease agreement, the Indian Agent released him, at last telling him why he'd been arrested, saying, "first, for leaving the reservation, and second, for kicking against what Commissioner Jones decided to have done." As the Agent opened the jail, White Bull stood up straight and told it straight.

"You are a Government Agent, sent here to help the Indians, but instead of doing that you are cheating them. You are doing things the Indians do not like. I cannot be friends with a man like that," White Bull said, as he relayed to his biographer Stanley Vestal years later. White Bull recalled telling the Agent, "this reservation belongs to the Indians and I will use all my power to make the best of it."

Within short order, what White Bull predicted came to pass. The southwestern ranchers brought more than eighty thousand cattle onto the grasslands. The cows overgrazed, stripping the land of ancient minerals. Ranching outfits allowed their cows to graze off their leased lands, destroying fences and Lakota-owned hay. The corporate cattle were so destructive that a later Indian Agent on the Cheyenne River Reservation asked his bosses to stop the leasing program. The Agent from Standing Rock wrote to his superiors in DC that the Lakota "feel that the 'Great Father' in Washington is asleep and has forgotten them and certainly it would appear that they were not wholly incorrect in this assumption." And yet, the opinions and well-being of the Lakota, if they ever had mattered to Congress before, were soon to be inconsequential.

In 1903, a Kiowa man argued that the treaty his Nation had signed with the United States made the U.S. government's recent land takings illegal. The case, *Lone Wolf v. Hitchcock*, went all the way to the Supreme Court. The justices determined that Congress was entitled to pass laws that violated its former treaty promises. This case looms with import, wobbling like a house built without a foundation, a monument to what is fact and what can be edited.

After *Lone Wolf*, America's earlier treaty promise, that the consent and signature of three fourths of all Lakota men were required prior to any new land takings, became obsolete. Once again, the wasicus went back on their word. And this time, it was enshrined in a SCOTUS decision.

Between 1905 and 1910, the population of western South Dakota more than doubled from the previous five years. These settlers, which included my ancestors, were quickly realizing that their measly government-sponsored lot of 160 acres wasn't big enough to survive on. The only way to persist—let alone compete—with the large southwest cattle companies was to have more land. But with what money? And what land?

Like heroes with capes, elected officials drafted legislation to open what they called additional "excess" reservation land to their homesteading constituents. The Lakota used every tool of resistance possible. They stalled. Tribal Councilmen wrote letters of protest. They traveled to DC to explain that this was unjust. At the very least, they said, Congress should keep the promise it had made only a few years earlier that it would allot reservations to individual Lakota before releasing the leftover land to settlers. Congress ignored their requests. And after *Lone Wolf*, the Lakota had little recourse.

By 1904, all five Lakota reservations had been allotted. The government deemed 9.3 million acres of land set aside by the Great Sioux Agreement to be surplus to the Lakota's needs and opened it up for white settlement. Over the following decade, the United States passed a series of new laws that resulted in the transfer of an additional 8 million acres of Lakota land to settlers. In 1908, the year the Sinykins planted their first crops, Congress determined that an additional 2.9 million acres on the Cheyenne River and Standing Rock reservations were surplus to the needs of the Lakota and opened the land to non-Indigenous people. Local settlers and businesses hailed the news. This, like earlier land takings, was done without Lakota consent. The terms were terrible. Though one senator estimated that the land was worth as much as ten dollars an acre, Congress set the price at $1.25. The Interior Department also allowed settlers to defer payment for more than fourteen years. Congress continued to extend such deferred payments, and to this day many of these homesteads were never paid for.

Many Lakota didn't learn that their land had been given away until white settlers arrived in their wagons. There's an apocryphal story of a Lakota family seeing some tired travelers and offering them dinner. At the end of the meal, the hosts asked, *Where are you headed?* The white people answered, *We're home, this is our land now.*

Much of the best farmland, the flatlands with the high grasses, was given to homesteaders. Driving across the land where Doug White Bull grew up, an allotment his parents inherited, I feel the tug and plummet of a roller coaster. The tawny grass rises steeply to rocky buttes, then drops, then rises again.

"You should take a movie here. You can show your kids you going up and down hills," Doug tells me one day as we off-road with a friend out to the old site. I laugh and tell him they wouldn't believe it. "They'd see the sky," chuckles Doug as the van points almost directly up toward the clouds.

This wasn't a place to prosper with a plow, especially without the chance to string multiple units together. While congressional action had enabled settlers to do just that, to consolidate lands, something my family would find critical to their success, Indian Agents intentionally spaced apart individuals from the same family. Fearful that collective farming would perpetuate traditional Lakota culture and government based on family groupings, and fearful that it would douse the assimilation mission, the Indian Agency assigned Joseph White Bull his acreage more than thirty miles away from his kin.

A 1909 map of the Cheyenne River and Standing Rock reservations stretches across a sepia-colored paper. The rivers and creeks drawn across the land look, to me, like a wide, interconnected root system. Railroad tracks crisscross the land like black stitches. But it's the color that gets your attention. The land that remains under Lakota ownership is yellow, much of it dramatically covered by a pale red the color of dried blood; that color indicates the land that had been taken away. By then, approximately 98 percent of the land set aside for the Lakota by the 1851 treaty was owned by white settlers and the railroads. Between 1868 and 1939, the Homestead Act gave nearly 1.5 million families title to 246 million acres in the United States, an area almost the size of Texas and California combined.

"This land is your land, this land is my land . . . this land was made for you and me." When Jennifer Lopez sang that famous song during Joe Biden's presidential inauguration in 2021, Native Twitter erupted.

I KEEP RETURNING TO THE QUESTION OF WHAT MY ANCESTORS KNEW about what was happening on the reservation on the other side of the Wakpá

Wašté, what American maps call the Cheyenne River. That distance was collapsed, as the river, then undammed, was "easily forded at any point along the stream," according to a local history. Were the Sinykins aware of such persecution being done in this land of the free? Maybe. Probably.

Newspapers published throughout western South Dakota between 1908 and 1910, the exact period during which my family was first settling on the prairie, reported that Cheyenne River and Standing Rock Lakota didn't want their reservations opened, and that they had signed treaties protecting these lands as their property. Despite this awareness, settlers urged public officials to open the reservation to them, justifying themselves in a way that inverted all that old language of social uplift and do-gooding.

"The opening of the Sioux Indian lands is developing them from that of the homes of indolent dependents of the government to the farm residences of thrifty Americans," ran a 1908 article about the opening of the Rosebud Reservation to white settlement. "The Indians who have been

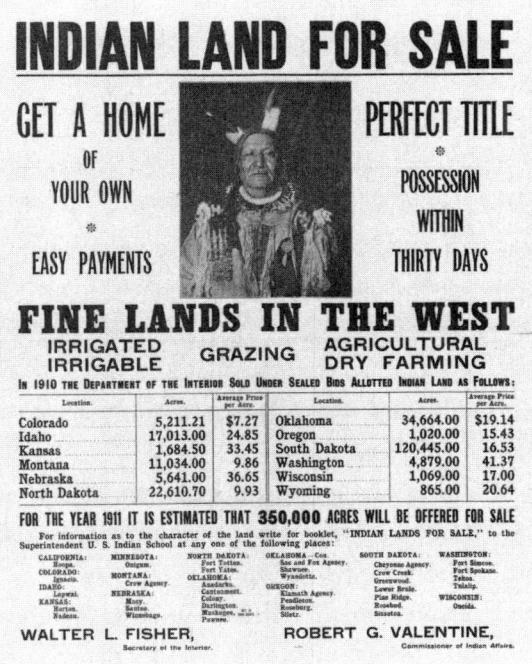

U.S. Department of the Interior broadside, 1911.

content to live lazily on the fertile soil and draw their liberal allowances will soon see more of their lands converted to useful purposes."

The Indian Agent at Cheyenne River, after hearing incessant requests from non-Indigenous ranchers to sell off the reservation, wrote to his boss in 1912 that "white men . . . in the vicinity of this reservation care very little about the Indian, except for what they can make of him."

As far as I can tell, my family never bought any of these lands, and they weren't among those making incessant requests, but that doesn't mean they were ignorant of what was happening. My inability to definitively answer this question frustrates the journalist in me, the one who likes to know. Here I have access to such a trove of family stories and documents, thanks in large part to Etta and to her parents before her, and yet mysteries remain.

Judge Abby, knowing more about the world than I do, is less uncertain. "Everyone knew what was happening to Indians," she tells me. But, in her way, she is quick to offer my ancestors empathy for seemingly not doing anything about it. Because of both the bigoted messages they'd learned in America as well as the brutality they had experienced, which we now call trauma, Judge tells me, they couldn't consider how the free land and other opportunities they received from the government harmed Native Americans.

"What do you expect of people who survived genocidal attacks but to survive, for god's sake. When someone is fleeing for their life, if you're on a dead run, you're not stopping to have a restorative-justice conversation or question why you're being helped."

It's now the job, she gently reminds me, of my generation, those of us who have grown up free of such upheaval, to do the work of considering the harms of this entangled history. At Judge Abby's urging, I set out to study my own culture for guidance.

Although I've had a bat mitzvah and belong to a synagogue, although I say prayers most Friday nights, lighting Shabbat candles and blessing my children, I'd never studied Jewish text in a serious way before. Fortunately, I didn't have to do it alone. My rabbi, Benjamin Barnett—who describes himself as part mystic, part skeptic, who I would describe as a mensch— agreed to meet with me regularly, to study together in an ancient practice called hevruta, or studying in pairs. Together, we read places in the Torah and the Talmud, ancient Jewish texts, that describe how to make amends. We looked at and discussed the sermons of other rabbis throughout the country who are looking to these old stories and laws for direction in their efforts for social justice.

What would immediately become clear is that Jews have spent centuries considering how to atone for their sins or the mistakes we make that estrange us from God and from one another. (The word for sin in Hebrew, *chet*, comes from an archery term that simply means to have missed the mark.) The concept of repair in the face of harm, of creating a more just world, is so central to our culture that there are daily prayers dedicated to it. Our most sacred time of the year, the weeks leading up to the Jewish New Year, revolves around a practice called *t'shuvah*, which means "repentance" or, more literally, "return." Rabbi Benjamin likes to say it's "about returning to the inherent goodness of your nature." During this time of year, the Torah instructs us to seek forgiveness directly from anyone we have harmed or who has been negatively affected by our actions.

"To confront the ways we've missed the mark is the beginning of that repair and healing. Doing this work isn't a sign we're doing something wrong. We're human. We're going to make mistakes. T'shuvah is part of the rhythm of life," Rabbi Benjamin tells me one winter day in 2019. He is wearing a knit yarmulke, a T-shirt, and jeans. We drink coffee while rain slides down the window beside us. "Almost two thousand years ago, Jews would atone through animal sacrifice, but today I think the offering and the sacrifice is both economic and it's truth-telling, and the truth-telling, that's the harder part."

Over the course of the next three years, I'd come to understand just what he meant.

5

LITTLE SHTETL
ON THE PRAIRIE

My blue shadow stretches long across the rolling South Dakota prairie. I am here as a tourist to my personal history, to assess and haul its bulk into the future. To stand in the middle of this land is to feel myself go small, to feel like a speck in the middle of a grass ocean. The wide sky swallows me whole. It is not unlike the feeling of investigating the past.

More than one hundred years ago, the Sinykins, their cousins, and friends—around thirty Jewish families—homesteaded here on what was then recently Lakota land. On this frigid day in mid-February 2019, the light is low in the sky, and it settles on the snow crust and wheatgrass. Locals still refer to this place as Jew Flats. Not far from here is where Faige Etke used to strip naked and dunk herself in the frozen creek for her mikvah. Even though I'm wearing two down coats, long underwear, and two pairs of socks, my body aches. I clearly missed something critical in the genetic lottery: a predisposition to withstand the cold is not part of my inheritance.

The northern boundary of Jew Flats is approximately thirteen miles from the southeastern corner of the Cheyenne River Reservation. Despite proximity, my ancestors and the other immigrants with whom they shared the prairie didn't consider the Lakota their neighbors. An invisible wall separated the reservation from the land owned by settlers, the rules different for each side.

For my family's "Mini-Kin Sinykin Reunion" in 1977, my aunt Etta wrote a history that included old pictures, a family tree, and songs about us written to the tune of "Tea for Two" and "Cabaret." In it, Etta described our ancestors as "representative of the times they lived in . . . They had to subsist and 'make it' on their own."

This official storyline of scrappy independence is a trope in every Horatio Alger story, in every tale about pioneers from *Little House on the Prairie* to Willa Cather's back catalog. That narrative has given me confidence, even if it is likely undeserved: on some level, I believe that because of what my ancestors survived, I, too, can endure anything.

On this cold February day at the outset of my research for this book, I walk the land in search of the leavings of my ancestors' lives. Here, the crusted snow dips in the depression of an old cellar, impossibly small. Here is the faint outline of buffalo wallows, where bison once rolled in mud. Here is the butte, its rocky slabs like horse's teeth, where my cousins, while growing up here in the 1950s, found arrowheads.

The Jews of Jew Flats didn't all arrive at once, and it's unclear, despite the official documents I've collected, exactly when Faige Etke and her children first joined Harry on the prairie, though, by 1908, they'd sowed their first crop. If I squint, I can see them walking onto the land for the first time. Up they go, climbing the steep hills beside horse-drawn wagons laden with their remaining ties to the Pale. Inside the bundles would've been their candlesticks and white linens. With them was furniture that seems a questionable choice for ranch life: a wooden writing desk and a piano. If the Jews of Jew Flats spoke to one another, it wasn't in English but Yiddish. Every one of them was not only from Russia but from the same region, if not the same shtetl. Many of them were related, a fact that wouldn't stop some from marrying. There are the cows and sheep lumbering beside the wagons. There are the crates filled with chickens; watch them squawk at the air.

Articles that ran like ad copy in the Sioux City newspapers had promised that this land was an "Earthly Paradise for the Farmer and the Livestock Man . . . in truth you will soon have a home that is a real 'Home Sweet Home' . . . the farmer who desires a home for himself and family can do no better than to locate in this part of this splendid state . . . where the climate is perfect, where crops are sure, and where the poorest man if industrious can soon own a home of his own."

They had finally escaped exile; they believed they were no longer wandering. I hope they felt a thrill, a sense of pride. For the first time in generations, they were standing on their own land. I hope it was months rather than minutes before that feeling dropped like a stone down a well.

HERE IS WHAT I KNOW: HARRY, ON EARLIER VISITS TO THE HOMESTEAD, had stayed in a cave. Faige Etke insisted that Harry build her a little house on the prairie before she left Sioux City. Their youngest child, Louie, told *The National Jewish Post and Opinion* many decades later, shuddering at the memory, that their first house on the claim wasn't made of stone or wood but of dirt, its walls the cut bank of a hill, with roots and grass jutting from the roof. Harry could argue, I guess, that a dirt house was still a house, better than a cave, but for Faige Etke, who had lived in *one of the nicest houses in Kapulye*, this welcome must've set a certain tone.

The good news about soddies, these houses built from dirt and grass, is that they stayed relatively warm when temperatures dropped to negative forty, as happens regularly in the Dakotas. The bad news: they were dirty. When it rained, it rained through a hole in the roof made for the stove pipe, and the floor liquefied to mud. They also tended to be dark and to smell, I can only imagine, like bong water.

A hole in the ground under a board on the floor served as both a "refrigerator" and a place to hide from the not-infrequent tornados. A cave in the back (perhaps the same cave where Harry once slept) housed their animals. The well they'd paid to have drilled was full of sour, hard water. Dried buffalo dung, known by the more attractive name "buffalo chips," served as fuel for the woodstove, as there were very few trees nearby. Wind thrashed the prairie in all seasons. The sun, rarely cased in clouds, rarely thinned by trees, beat down on the Sinykins. When Faige Etke's oldest grandchild was as young as five, he'd clear the path to the outhouse every morning of rattlesnakes.

"It was a place like the End of the World," Faige Etke's middle daughter, Rose, once wrote to my grandmother Pauline. "The land went for miles and no one around. Twenty-five miles from a railroad station, seven miles from a post office, three and a half miles from any neighbors. The walking was very hard—over hills and draws. It was a lonely life, especially for the young."

Within a span of approximately forty-four square miles, the Jews of Jew Flats had forty-five noncontiguous homesteads, islands of Jews in the midst of non-Jewish homesteaders, many of them also immigrants, many of them Germans, German-speaking Russians, and Norwegians, the result of the railroads' efforts to colonize the Plains. The language barrier between this Aryan type of immigrant and the Jewish one made for more isolation.

That first winter, like other winters to come, was so cold that at night they could lie in bed, dressed in layers of clothing, and watch their breath freeze on their blankets. When a blizzard clobbered the prairie, my great-grandmother Ruth, age twelve the year they arrived, got lost in a lashing white storm. She once told my mother that she survived by keeping close to the cows and drafting off their warmth. Summer brought other threats: prairie fires, swarms of grasshoppers, and winds so hot they blistered their faces. At night, the only sound outside was the piercing howl of the coyote.

"It was one bitchy place to have to live," Herbie Marsh, my ninety-year-old cousin tells me on a mild day in Los Angeles, where he has lived for nearly seven decades. His face is deeply wrinkled, like a topographical map. It is early 2020, weeks before the pandemic will shut everything down and months before he will die; this lunch would be our last visit. When a young man notices Herbie's "Korean War Vet" hat and approaches our table to thank him for his service, Herbie grimaces and waves him off. Never one to suffer fools, Herbie tells everything straight.

"It was the border of the Sioux reservation, just the most desolate area in the world. Oh, it was just a miserable time in history for the family."

Herbie looks like his mother, Rose, both of them narrow through the face with alert, dark eyes. But where Herbie was once an excellent dancer and athlete (though he did once run ninety-five yards with a football in the wrong direction, earning the nickname "Wrong Way Marsh" from the local paper), Rose was, in the parlance of the day, a hunchback and kept inside to help her mother in the kitchen while Ruth, her younger sister, rode horses for miles. In one telling, Rose got her hump as a baby in Russia when she was dropped somehow. In another telling—more reliable, frankly—she, like her oldest sister, Fanny, and other members of the family, had scoliosis. It was left untreated, and her case was far more severe than her sister's. According to Etta, when Rose was bullied at school, Faige Etke told her daughter, "Because your back is crooked, you're going to have a hard life. You must learn to be strong and feisty."

Such harsh words from Faige Etke. I see her from this distance standing in the dull light of the sod, her face pinched by a stack of trouble, a woman grasping to stay in control amid this vast sea of grass. Her hobbies were chatting and loving God. Both passions were constrained by prairie life.

Besides her children, there weren't many people for her to sit with, sharing a pot of tea and talking into the day. Her sister lived in New York, her parents were dead, the other Jew Flats homesteaders were a long walk away. Yes, she had her mikvah, and she said her daily prayers, but the worry she had carried with her from the Pale, that, in America, her children would be less Jewish, less traditional, was, in some ways, becoming realized.

One of the handed-down stories I heard from several cousins makes this tension clear: Faige Etke's daughter Ruth, my great-grandmother, is riding bareback across the prairie, and she is certain that she is dying. Blood seeps through her clothes onto the horse's back. Her stomach hurts. She thinks something must have burst inside her. She rushes the horse home, and on arrival, she runs inside to Faige Etke. "I think I'm dying," she tells her mother, "I can't stop bleeding between my legs." At which point, Faige Etke slaps Ruth across both cheeks and says, "Mazel tov. You're a woman now. May you have many children."

Faige Etke had almost certainly been slapped in this way. Her mother, too. For hundreds of years, Jewish and non-Jewish women throughout Eastern Europe, Greece, and Turkey slapped their daughters on first acknowledgment of their periods, possibly in anticipation of the shame associated with fertility. Jews adopted the tradition as a form of superstition, akin to telling an actor to break a leg. But for my family, this ritual ended on the prairie. Ruth, I'm more than a little relieved to report, didn't slap her daughters. America would change the Sinykin children: they would each choose to practice only some of the traditions passed down to them.

Despite the pain this may have caused, despite the unfamiliarity of her new life, according to family lore, Faige Etke never complained. Her son Jack later told Etta that "the average woman couldn't go through what she did. . . . She always made the best of things as they came." And the best chance she had, the best chance her children had, was to find a way to make the land make money.

·Jack and Louie both would remember Faige Etke's insistence that they grow up to become multimillionaires, and that the key to their wealth would be in the South Dakota prairie. After researching Jewish history, I now believe that this pressure to be financially successful wasn't only about ambition. It was about security. For thousands of years, as long as Jews were important to a country's economy, either as artisans, merchants, or money-lenders, they were allowed to stay. Many times, countries intent on ridding themselves of their Jewish populations would make special provisions for those who were wealthy. Faige Etke was looking to protect her children in this new, foreign place. But converting land into dollar bills was hardly a sure bet.

THE SINYKINS' 160 ACRES WERE FREE, BUT ONLY IF THEY COULD, UNDER the rules of the Homestead Act, "improve" upon them by building a house and planting at least ten acres within three years. If they failed to "prove up," the borrowed land would be returned to the feds.

By the spring following their arrival, the Sinykins had planted five acres of corn and wheat. Faige Etke had her own vegetable garden, of which, multiple sources report, she was very proud. Over the following years, the family quadrupled their yield and expanded the family landhold-ings as the four oldest children, at the insistence of Faige Etke, filed their own homestead claims.

Almost immediately, they learned what Joseph White Bull and his family had known for generations: farming the Plains anywhere but near the riverbanks was nearly impossible. The heavy clay soil, known as gumbo, couldn't be changed, only endured, making travel in mud season very difficult. Settlers liked to say, "If you stick to this country when it's dry, it will stick to you when it is wet."

The temperature could swing fifty degrees in one day. The rivers to the north and the south were, at that moment, undammed and undiverted. Hail the size of baseballs fell from the sky. Prairie fires whipped through the fields. Stem rust, a plant disease, was common in wheat varieties of the time, causing up to 70 percent crop failure.

Within a year or two, having seen the dismal financial returns on corn and oats, the Jews of Jew Flats went in for cattle. In a sepia-toned picture postcard unearthed from a box in Etta's study, a Sinykin cousin and Jew Flats homesteader sits astride a white horse in the midst of cows in the nearby town of Philip. The back of the picture reads, in my great-grandmother's cursive, "Sale Day." Another photograph shows children feeding the cows, their mother and grandmother looking on; "Sinykin cows," reads the note on the back. But the switch from farmer to rancher wasn't a sure thing.

Jew Flats, sod structure in background. Pictured right to left: Faige Etke Sinykin, her daughter Fanny, grandson Benny, son Louie, granddaughter Cecelia, and daughter Rose, circa 1911.

"One hundred and sixty acres was enough to starve," says Rich Smith, a local rancher, age 100, on a cold morning in 2019, as the light streams through his kitchen window, a cup of coffee steaming from a mug. The house where he grew up and still lives is just to the north of Jew Flats. He explains that, on the grass-sparse prairie, the quarter square mile of land the feds provided as a homestead wasn't sufficient to raise enough cattle to make a living, wasn't enough to keep a family fed.

It must have been stressful. Harry had never farmed before, and I think that his head injury from the pogrom made him unpredictable. While he, like so many immigrants, was doing his best to take advantage of new opportunities, he remained bent by the terror he'd endured in the Pale.

"For many immigrants, if you move here with trauma, you're going to do what it takes to get by," writes Cathy Park Hong, referencing her own family, in *Minor Feelings: An Asian American Reckoning.* "You cheat. You beat your wife. You gamble. You're a survivor and, like most survivors, you are a god-awful parent."

And yet nothing—none of the stories Etta told me about Harry and his "keen sense of adventure"—prepared me for what I learned from sticking my nose into the past. I was sitting on the floor of my parents' basement in Seattle, sifting through documents my grandmother had kept in a safe-deposit box. In a tea-colored letter written in the 1930s, one of Harry's sons-in-law describes events from the early days on the prairie. I had to reread it several times, my eyes widening.

"What H.S. did to his wife and how she fainted and we worked over her for five hours trying to bring her back to life. His son Ted Sinykin was there and other boys and Ted wanted us all to tie him up with a rope and declare him insane."

The exact details of what Harry did to Faige Etke to make her pass out for five hours are missing. But the fights, mentioned in future worried letters between Ruth and Rose, continued. Jack credited their father's bad temper to the stress and pressure he was under. Harry did love Faige Etke, Jack insisted, and she knew, for the most part, Jack once told Etta, "how to handle him." Etta herself has a hard time believing that such violence was routine as, throughout her own childhood, she only ever heard Harry speak of his late wife with love and respect.

In none of the family stories is Faige Etke described as a victim. This was the woman who was "undaunted and strong, [who] met every crisis," as Etta wrote in her family history. For all the hardships Faige Etke endured on the prairie, the narrative line is one of strength, not weakness. This is the challenge of trafficking in story. Even if I had letters or journals in which Faige Etke described her experience, they would provide only a selection of thoughts. There will always be a disconnect between what happened and what we talk about, especially when what happened is cast in shame.

LIKE THE TWO ROADS THAT RAN INTO KAPULYE, THERE'S ANOTHER VERsion of life on Jew Flats that runs in parallel to the narrative of struggle and hardship. The alternate storyline handed down about this little shtetl on the prairie is that this land was the makings of a wonderful life. In this version, there wasn't just dust or gumbo for what felt like fourteen months at a hitch, but wildflowers, thick across the prairie in blues and whites and yellows. There were thickets of wild cherries, plums, and grapes that grew along the creeks, free for the taking.

"With all the hardships that were faced in the day to day living of farming and raising cattle, they did have an appreciation for their land," reads the history Etta wrote for the Mini-Kin Sinykin Reunion. "They were no longer fearful of soldiers and pogroms and could sleep peacefully through the night."

In multiple conversations, my aunt Etta stresses this point: they loved the land. "I can remember my mother and Rose talking about it, they always called it 'the good earth.'"

They always had enough to eat. Faige Etke was, according to the family story, "a wonderful cook and seemed to be able to make a good meal out of very little." They had time for leisure—there were baseball games in the nearby towns, they had bicycles, and they went to parties in claim shacks, where they moved the furniture onto the prairie and danced all night long. I have pictures of them at picnics, men holding violins, a woman with a banjo, others with fishing poles.

In family lore, every Sinykin child became not only a good horseman but an "expert rider." Harry had a matched pair of bay horses named Molly and Dolly. It was said that Ruth was "the best bareback gal" in the county. I have pictures of her on horseback, dressed in a hat and a duster.

This skill may have produced ill-gotten gains—or not. "Your mom's family is just a bunch of horse thieves," my great-aunt Fanny's son-in-law would say about the Sinykins, a big smile on his face. No one ever got caught; I can find no record to validate such a claim. And, in fact, another family member told me that his dad, Faige Etke's grandson, was in a posse to catch such thieves. Certainly, horse thieving was common on the Plains at the time: between 1905 and 1920, South Dakota newspapers wrote about it at least seven hundred times. One newspaper from a neighboring county reported, in 1910, "horse stealing seems to be an epidemic that is spreading rapidly."

In one way or another, by the winter of 1910, the Sinykins and their Jewish neighbors had amassed horses and cattle. The four oldest Sinykin kids had all filed on their own homestead. Though Rose may have felt lonely, the prairie had become crowded.

Enticed by the ads in the newspapers and the railroad broadsides, homesteaders built claim shacks on almost every parcel across the prairie. Between 1900 and 1915, more than one hundred thousand settlers, many of them immigrants, moved to western South Dakota. The light of kerosene lamps flickered through windows; cracks in the tar paper glimmered "almost as thick as the stars," recalled one neighbor.

By this time, the Sinykins had built the shacks required to prove to the government that they were in it for the long run and deserving of that free land. In the sparsely wooded Plains, most settlers opted to build using cheap, thin plywood hauled from faraway towns and lined with tar paper. Built in a matter of days, these "houses" were no more impressive than a packing box.

These humble American beginnings stayed with my aunt Fanny,

Harry's oldest daughter, her entire life. She told her children in a taped conversation that, the first time she went on an airplane, amazed by the clouds and sky outside the window, her first thought was, "Never did I ever dream that I'll be in a plane like that when I was livin' in South Dakotee in a shack ten by twelve."

And yet, they must have been proud of these one-room homes, a serious promotion from a sod house and a cave. In an undated photograph, on which the photographer wrote "Company on the Claim," my great-grandfather, an uncle, and four other men pose in front of a claim shack. Two of them have guns. One holds a rolled newspaper and a pipe. My great-grandfather, his eyes exactly like my brother's, like my nephew's, looks stunned.

"Even though it was hard, they loved it," says my aunt Etta, her voice warming to the memory. "Their lives were so much narrower in Russia, and I think they were so happy to be free to be able to go and come and do."

By the time my family was on Jew Flats, more than seventy Jewish

Men on Jew Flats posing in front of a claim shack. My great-grandfather Jake Kozberg second from right. My great-great-uncle Ted Sinykin third from the left.

farm communities, composed of anywhere from a few dozen to twenty-five hundred people, had been established in the United States, many in the West. By 1912, there were an estimated twenty-five thousand Jewish farmers in forty-six states. In the Dakotas, an estimated one thousand Jews were homesteaders like the Sinykins. (Keep in mind, they represented a sliver of Dakota settlers, estimated at less than 0.5 percent.) The Jewish machers on the East Coast who had worked to get Eastern European Jews out west, called Jewish farms "the visual and tangible sign of religious liberty and political emancipation," according to the Jewish Agricultural and Industrial Aid Society's annual report from 1908.

To ensure greater success, JAIAS offered grants and low-interest loans to Jewish farmers; in 1910 alone, it provided nearly $210,000 to 353 farmers. The society created the first agricultural schools in the country to provide a deep and quick immersion for immigrants headed to work the plow. Later, the organization financed scholarships for Jewish youth to attend non-Jewish agricultural schools in their home states and even offered fire insurance. Its publication, *The Jewish Farmer*, was the first Yiddish-language newspaper in the world dedicated to farming, and by 1912 it had more than five thousand subscribers. Its pages were crammed with helpful tips, such as how to keep eggs fresh and the best time to plant alfalfa.

I can find no evidence that my family subscribed, or that they got in on any of these loans or grants. What I can find is that the American system of commerce was supporting them well enough—within the first decade of homesteading, the Jews of Jew Flats took out more than $24,000 in mortgages on the value of their land (what today would be around $606,000). They used the money to buy equipment and expand their landholdings, but also to leave and start other businesses in other parts of the state (under the Homestead Act, settlers had to live on their land for only six months in a row per year).

Homesteading was more than a financial boost, it was the platform shoes of social class. These settlers of former Lakota lands were praised by reporters as "all that was good, all that was real in America," writes historian Paula M. Nelson. Carrie Ingalls, whose older sister Laura's books romanticized their homesteading childhood on the eastern side of the state, worked for newspapers throughout western South Dakota when my family was newly arrived. Carrie's own homestead wasn't far from Jew Flats; she used to commute by mule to the *Pedro Bugle*, the local newspaper.

Editors such as Ingalls, desperate to keep settlers on the Plains as they expanded their readership and ad-buying consumer base, used their column inches to rally and inspire. "The cowards and those afraid to try stay east; while the ambitious, the hustlers, the real continent builders, come out to God's own good, free country," read one newspaper in western South Dakota at the time. Pioneers who stuck it out through the drought and hard times were described in local papers as "heroes and heroines" and "strong and steadfast."

Both the narrative of difficulty and the narrative of glory can be true, but I find that I am increasingly caught on the meaning that falls in the gap between these two versions of events. What I didn't realize when I visited the prairie that cold February day in 2019 was that the pride I take in my ancestors' endurance had obstructed me from seeing a fuller story, one that acknowledges the systemic benefits that the federal government extended to us because we weren't Indigenous but white, at least white enough. Not only were harms imposed upon those living on reservations, freedoms were extended outside the reservations, creating inequity in two directions. To look only at one piece of this history is to ignore the depths of this unfairness.

UNLIKE THEIR LAKOTA NEIGHBORS, WHO'D BEEN PERSECUTED FOR EM-bracing the Ghost Dance and who were still at risk of being jailed for practicing their ceremonies and religion, the Jews of Jew Flats were free to worship how they liked. They had their mikvah. They had their own rabbi, Hyman Kozberg, Harry's cousin, who was educated in the Pale's Slutsk Yeshiva (apparently a very big deal) and trained as a shochet, a Jewish butcher able to kosher meat. He taught the children Hebrew and led services using a Torah they'd brought with them from Sioux City. Despite her worry, "in the midst of the prairie, [Faige Etke] maintained her rigid piety and a kosher home," again, from Etta's 1977 family history.

Unlike their Lakota neighbors, whose children were regularly taken from their communities for nine months at a stretch to be assimilated at federal schools, the Sinykins were free to educate their children however they wanted. They hired their non-Jewish neighbors, the Calloway siblings, to teach their children and some of the adults in twin claim shacks a few miles away. Unlike the segregated Indian Boarding Schools, here Jews and non-Jews, boys and girls were all taught together.

Unlike the Lakota, whom the Indian Agents tried to keep from farming or ranching in family groups with the intention of breaking apart traditional communal culture, the Sinykins and their cousins and friends survived by collective effort, unbothered by government interference.

Unlike the Lakota, whose marriages and divorces were regulated by the Indian Agent, the Jews of Jew Flats could marry and breakup with whomever they wanted. Unlike the Lakota, who were denied citizenship, which prevented them from voting and accessing a slew of rights, immigrant citizens (at least the men) could vote even when they couldn't speak or read English.

Unlike most Lakota, who couldn't get a bank account or handle their own money, let alone leave the reservation to pursue jobs elsewhere, the

Children of homesteaders at a school near Jew Flats. Sinykins pictured: Rose, second from left; Ruth, third from left; and Louie, end of the right-side row in overalls, 1908.

Jews of Jew Flats could and did leverage the worth of their land for a mortgage or bank loan.

Again, I return to the question of what my ancestors understood about this inequity. Later, my uncle Jack will pose with Joseph White Bull, and other family members will take snapshots at roadsides with people in traditional Dakota and Lakota dress. Later, there will be rumors of bootlegging on the reservations and of distant cousins who helped Lakota to bury their dead. But at this point, in the early days of their homesteads, it seems they knew their Lakota neighbors only enough to fear them.

My aunt Rose told her children and her grandchildren how scared she was when Lakota would walk past the house, as they did when taking their children to boarding school or traveling to see relatives on distant reservations. When Rose saw them coming, she'd kill a chicken or harvest things from the garden to give to the Lakota. This wasn't generosity, but a hedge. Her granddaughter Marcia told me, "What she was doing was to give the Indians something so that they wouldn't just take everything. She believed they would've just taken everything. This was her way of protecting their livelihood."

One homesteader who had been a child on the prairie wrote about the Mnicoujou across the river, "the Indians never gave my folks any trouble, but the women were scared of them." Another settler in the county had a visiting cousin who put her child to sleep on a chair beside the bed. In the night, the baby fell and rolled under the cot. The mother woke up and "became hysterical, screaming that the Indians had stolen her baby."

When a Jewish woman in North Dakota was in labor, two Indigenous men, hearing her screams, came to the house. Within ten minutes, two Native women joined them and helped her deliver her child. But this immigrant woman didn't feel a bond of friendship and gratitude. Her grandchild recalled, "After that, my grandmother insisted on moving off the farm."

This fear wasn't based on lived experience—I can find zero accounts of any Lakota attacks on settlers during this time. In reality, Lakota had the most to fear. One government official wrote in 1912 that the feeling of settlers near the Cheyenne River Reservation was "that the Indian is fair game for anyone who can hit the mark."

It is easy to judge the dead but to do so in this case is to fail to recognize the systemic forces behind their ignorance and bigotry. The settlers' fear of Indigenous people maintained a segregated prairie, and that was "evidence of a successful federal Indian policy," explains historian Mikal Eckstrom, whose ancestry is German, Norwegian, and Nimiipuu, and who is one of a handful of historians who have studied the relationship between Jews and Native Americans. By keeping these spaces separate, the Office of Indian Affairs believed it could more easily control Indigenous people and, says Eckstrom, "keep settlers safe."

For as long as I can remember, I have leaned toward storytellers. My own children ask me all the time for *a real story, something that really happened, that's funny.* Rarely, in any of these stories, the ones I was told and the ones I tell now, does the narrator cast themself as the bad guy. It's only recently that I find myself listening to these stories with an ear toward what is left unsaid. Listening in this way, the spine of each narrative cracks to reveal a far more potent meaning.

My ancestors left Europe as victims of oppression; they arrived in America to find more of the same and were only too aware that things could get worse. One rabbi in North Dakota during this era, like many rabbis throughout the country at the time, was "anxious to go along with the congregation in the matter of Americanization," as his son put it, and thus went by the title not of *rabbi* but of *reverend.*

"Everything he did, how well he worked with horses, or even how he sharpened an axe, was intended to demonstrate that Jews really *were* capable of hard physical labor, as much as any non-Jew!" reads the 1942 novel *Jewish Cowboy,* about a Russian Jew ranching in North Dakota. Throughout the country, Jewish farmers felt compelled to disprove the stereotypes that Jews "disdained honest toil."

My own family must have felt some of this same pressure. Non-Jewish classmates on the prairie called my uncle Louie, then in elementary school, "Lou the Jew"; he hated that nickname. A descendent of German homesteaders who grew up Lutheran not far from Jew Flats told me that, while there wasn't a total lack of interaction between his family and Catholics and Jews, his grandparents expected him to speak only German. His family wasn't going to get close to their Jewish neighbors.

All of which explains something about these dingy, handed-down tales about dangerous Indians. For Faige Etke and others from the Pale, anyone who wasn't Jewish was someone to fear, explains David S. Koffman, another one of the historians considering the intersection of Jews and Native Americans. By conflating Lakota with Cossacks or other would-be attackers, both Jewish and non-Jewish settlers could rewrite their old narratives, could be not victims but heroes, facing their fears and emerging triumphant. To cast Lakota as dangerous elevated Jews and other immigrants to the "good guys in the historical drama," says Koffman.

History moves in a circle. What I doubt my ancestors realized is that the federal policies that separated the Lakota from the settlers on the prairie were not so different from the policies of the Russian tsars that had placed Jews in the Pale. Both were spurred by the perceived threat to a dominant culture. Russian laws that stripped Jews of their rights and pogroms like the one in which Harry was clobbered on the head, eventually led my family to the prairie, onto Lakota land.

Few of us who descend from settlers still live on the prairie, but that doesn't mean that our fear, or the systemic racism that fosters fear, has disappeared. It has followed us to our gentrifying urban neighborhoods.

"This is our inheritance, for those of us who imagine ourselves pioneers," writes essayist Eula Biss, connecting *Little House on the Prairie* to life in modern-day Chicago in her essay "No Man's Land." "We don't seem to have retained the frugality of the original pioneers, or their resourcefulness, but we have inherited a ring of wolves around a door covered only by a quilt. And we have inherited padlocks on our pantries. That we carry with us a residue of the pioneer experience is my best explanation for the fact that my white neighbors seem to feel besieged in this neighborhood. Because that feeling cannot be explained by anything else that I know to be true about our lives here."

It's not only fear that has followed me home to my quiet street in Portland, Oregon. Resting on the window frame above my desk is a gray and weathered slab of wood punctured by a rusted and bent nail. I found it one summer while walking Harry and Faige Etke's homestead with my cousin Aviva and the kind woman who now owns the ranch. With her permission, I brought the old slab home. My husband accurately described it as junk, but I believed it to be significant, somehow connecting me to Jew Flats.

Only after several subsequent visits to South Dakota, where I walked the land of my ancestors waiting to feel something profound, did I realize what is likely obvious to you. Having grown up in the Northwest—among evergreen trees draped in shawls of moss and craggy, snow-capped peaks— I'm not moved by the palette of brown hills, by the grass sea of Jew Flats. Just because my ancestors lived there does not give me a claim on belonging. Today, I look at the wooden slab and see only the dead weight of nostalgia.

BY 1911, MOST JEW FLATS HOMESTEADERS HAD ENDURED GUMBO AND blizzard and had proved up, meaning the land was officially theirs to sell or pass to their progeny. But they remained vulnerable to a life still beyond their control, to years best summed up as a catalog of catastrophe.

There was no rainfall from the autumn of 1910 until the following October; climate data indicates it was among the driest periods of the century in Pennington County, home to most of Jew Flats. It was so hot, you could crack an egg in a frying pan and watch it cook under the sun. Wells went dry. The rivers and creeks became nothing more than "potholes of dirty water." The threat of prairie fire was constant. There were no hoses or fire engines then, so the best defense was a furrow around the house and wet rags on the roof. A fire in Montana that summer was so big that the South Dakota sun became an orange ball in the haze, the air harsh in the lungs. The best crops that year were prairie dogs, rattlesnakes, and Russian thistle. For two years running, Faige Etke and Harry lost their entire crop. Corn planted in spring never grew through the sod. One farmer in the county remembered that it was "so dry you couldn't see a spear of grass."

And so, an exodus. People left almost as fast as they had come. More than half of all homesteaders in my family's county gave up, drifting away to win the West somewhere else. One settler left with a sign on the back of his wagon that read: FORTY MILES FROM WATER, FORTY MILES FROM WOOD, I'M QUITTING THIS DAM COUNTRY AND I'M QUITTING IT FOR GOOD. The Jew Flats families that left split for western cities, which, far more than rural places, would become home to Jewish immigrants. One Jew Flats homesteader had so little money left that he had no choice but to walk the hundreds of miles back to Sioux City. He traveled for days through dust and heat, seeing nothing but wild horses and abandoned prairie shacks.

But those immigrant Jews who went bust left with something important. "The act of demonstrating their capabilities in the open spaces of the West would help [Jewish homesteaders] find a self-respect they might not have found otherwise," writes historian Debra Shein. Time on the prairie allowed immigrant Jews, desperate to shed their old skins, the opportunity to metabolize a new identity, allowed them to bridge the conflict between their Jewish and American selves.

At least fourteen Jew Flats settlers returned to Sioux City; within a year, they all had new jobs listed in the city directory, steps toward their eventual success as butchers and merchants. One distant cousin and former homesteader would sell horses to Buffalo Bill and have his own Western road show, for which he'd call himself "Teton Bill."

Those who failed at the homesteading experiment were key to the success of the settlers who stayed. Homesteaders who remained on the prairie, who managed to outlast the drought, harvested their former neighbors' abandoned hay and crops. By paying their departed neighbors' back taxes, the remaining settlers received title to new land, doubling and tripling the expanse where their cows could graze. It appears that none of the land abandoned by homesteaders throughout this time period was made available to the Lakota or the other Native Nations from whom it had been taken.

My family felt more American because they owned a swath of American soil. How does it change our sense of ourselves to learn that our land had been taken from the Lakota at gunpoint or threat of starvation? What does it mean to survive oppression only to perpetuate and benefit from the oppression of others?

✦ ✦ ✦ ✦ ✦

BY 1915, FAIGE ETKE AND ALL FOUR OF HER AND HARRY'S OLDEST CHILDREN had proved up on their homesteads, expanding the Sinykin landholdings to 720 acres, enough land to survive on, enough land for leverage. The drought ended. They were now having their best years yet. Their yields had doubled and doubled again. Several of their sons and cousins took out mortgages on their land and left to open saloons and a liquor-distribution company in other parts of the state, bringing in money that wasn't contingent on weather.

Faige Etke and Harry drilled a second well and were so proud they took its photograph. Harry had received his own cattle brand, which was an *H* being hoisted onto the top curve of an *S*, as if the letters were acrobats. They had a chicken house, two barns, and more than eighty fenced-in acres. They'd built a new, four-room frame house, furnished from the Sears catalog and wallpapered. This was living large on the prairie.

Their fortunes and landholdings would soon grow even greater through what can only be described as the marriage plot in this family history. All three Sinykin daughters would wed fellow Jew Flats settlers (or, in the case of my aunt Fanny, divorce one and marry another). These marriages begat children, a fur coat company, major shares in a glove business, various liquor businesses, and a cosmetics company that fronted for something less than legal. Most critically for the purposes of this book, the marriages would greatly expand the Sinykin landholdings, eventually growing the ranch to more than five thousand acres. When each daughter married a Yiddish-speaking Russian immigrant like herself, her wedding served as a plot point on an arc of assimilation.

Faige Etke arranged for her daughter Rose to marry their Jew Flats neighbor Issie Moskowitz. Called by his grandson Steve a "bull of a man," and by his son Herb "a real son of a gun," Issie started and ended each day with a shot of schnapps. Family lore has it that he once killed four wild dogs with his bare hands when attacked in the woods near Minsk. For all his toughness, he got cold feet one week before the wedding and left Jew Flats for Colorado to work in a mine. In direct rebuttal to the weak-minded

Jewface stereotypes, two Sinykin brothers and a future brother-in-law strapped on their six-shooters and followed him there. The wedding proceeded as planned in the summer of 1915.

Three weeks later, Ruth Sinykin, Faige Etke's fifth child and my great-grandmother, wed Jake Kozberg, her first cousin once removed ("basically a second cousin," Etta always reminds me). A naturalized citizen of two years, a saloon owner in the Black Hills, and a part-time rancher whose land on Jew Flats had "fine herds of cattle and horses," according to the *Lead Daily Call* in 1914, Jake Kozberg was a catch. He and Ruth married in St. Paul, Minnesota—not in a synagogue, of which there were three to choose from, but in a hall "beautifully decorated in pink and white," according to a faded newspaper account that someone clipped, pasted to cardboard, and passed down until it languished in a box in my parents' basement. "The bride's gown was of ivory satin, made on princess lines and trimmed with plain lace and pearls . . . while a full court train hung from the shoulders of the pretty bride. Her veil was of Grecian effect, and she wore a band of pearls around her head." Note the Grecian effect. Note the princess lines. After the ceremony, the three hundred guests in attendance enjoyed dinner and dancing. This wasn't a shtetl wedding. This was making it.

Jake and Ruth would spend a month of their honeymoon on Jew Flats readying their soil for the winter wheat crop. From there, they took a left turn, literally: they headed approximately eighty miles west, into the heart of the Black Hills. They kept their ranch, but they made their home in Lead. What they created there fortified their prosperity. It would come, once again, at a cost to the Lakota.

6

IN DI SHVARTSE BERG*

When my great-grandparents, Jake and Ruth Kozberg, née Sinykin, arrived in Lead, deep in the Black Hills, in 1915, they tucked their Yiddish accents under their English words and set out to make a mint from what was then known as the richest hundred square miles on Earth. In the center of town was a giant hole—the Homestake Mine, the most productive gold mine in the Western Hemisphere. In 1915 alone, the mine produced more than 311,020 ounces of gold, the equivalent today of more than half a billion dollars, creating the best-paying jobs in the state. Square-roofed houses rose into the recently logged hills like keys on a typewriter. The clank of hammers, the grind of new Model T engines, and the clatter of horse hooves filled the air. Between the mine, the mills to process the gold, the sawmills to build the timbers to hold up the mine, and the trains connecting everything, the hills were alive with the sound of money. For immigrants like the Kozbergs, it was an American anthem they were learning to sing.

Lead and its nearby sister city, Deadwood, wore their newfound wealth like a nouveau riche dripping in designer bling. Look too closely, and you could notice signs of stress: the streets of Lead buckled, the possibility of a mine cave-in was imminent, and to anyone who read the papers, there

---

* Yiddish for the Black Hills.

was a different threat—assertions from the Lakota, now living on reservations to the east, that this land was illegally occupied. But for the average
recent arrival, such news was easy to ignore.

Downtown Lead, all four square blocks of it, was lined with modern
hotels that had steam heat and electric lights, a major upgrade from the
Sinykins' claim shack's woodstoves and kerosene lamps. There were cafés
where diners could listen to Victrola records. Hat shops and merchants
stocked the latest styles at bargain-basement prices. Unlike the dirt roads
of Jew Flats and Sioux City's East Bottom, the streets in Lead were paved
with vitrified bricks, their sidewalks made of imported Colorado sand-
stone. The newly built opera house had 1,016 seats of mahogany upholstered
in green velvet from which people could catch a play or a movie for a nickel.
There was an indoor pool, a bowling alley, and a free library for miners and
their families. Every half hour, from dawn to dusk, Ruth and Jake could
catch an electric trolley and be in Deadwood, a bastion of gambling and
dance halls, in fifteen minutes.

The newly married Kozbergs settled into an apartment above Jake's
saloon and bottle shop, the Lobby Liquor House. Here, men could step
up to a dark wooden bar, pay five cents for a glass of wine, drink a Gold
Nugget Lager from the tap, and spit in a white bucket on the floor. In the
narrow room, devoid of tables and chairs, pipe smoke wafted up to the tin
ceilings. Across the street was the train depot, where, twice a day, the Chicago and North Western trunk-line train arrived with everything from
California oranges to sixty-foot-long Douglas fir timbers to packages from
the Sears catalog. Also people, thirsty people, from as far away as Omaha,
Minneapolis, and Chicago. In a photo from 1913, the linoleum floor of the
saloon is tracked with wet boots, and snow covers the leaded-glass windows. Jake, all of five foot six in good shoes, presides behind the bar wearing a suit and tie, his watch tucked into the pocket, his wavy hair combed
back. He looks rich. It wasn't an act.

My great-grandfather wasn't a big romantic. Unlike another suitor
who called Ruth *tsuker pushkele*, which translates as the weird-but-charming
"sweet piggy bank," Jake wasn't big with endearments. He complained in

Jake Kozberg, in a dark suit, behind his bar in Lead, South Dakota. Wall calendar shows January 1913.

a letter to Faige Etke that "I'm a boy that doesn't like to write about this stuff," meaning his love for Ruth. But, he wrote, he cared about Ruth more "than I care about myself." What he lacked in the romance department he compensated for with an incredible work ethic that, in my family, as I've mentioned, is a love language all to itself.

Here's proof: When he first moved to the Hills, Jake worked not as a merchant or a scholar but as a gold miner deep in the bowels of the Homestake mine. As a newbie, he almost certainly was a mucker. Every day, for around ten hours, he would lift ten-pound rocks off the mine floor and load them onto carts, someone else would take the carts to train cars, which would haul the rocks to the mill where they would be crushed to release their gold. The average mucker hauled thirty-two hundred pounds per shift. Jake's personal protective equipment consisted of a felt hat, cotton gloves, and jeans. He didn't last long down there.

The mine, he told Etta, "was no place for a good Jewish boy. You have to use your head." Etta adored her father. One of her earliest memories is of him holding her and singing to her when she was sick. This story about him getting out of the mining business is another favorite, a tell about the value our family placed on hard work: "He has a very big Norwegian friend, and the two of them decide they don't like going down in the ground. They like to see the sunlight. What can they do to earn money? Well, what do the miners want to spend their money on? They want to spend it on women and wine. My father said, this was his words, 'I was not about to open a brothel. We decided to open a saloon on the main street.' And from that day on, he made a good living."

(Arguably, this is a story about quitting. But it's also a story about seeing opportunity and trading one kind of hard work for another.)

This period of my great-grandparents' life was the halcyon days of their marriage. They had escaped Russia, they had survived drought and prairie fire, blizzards, and rattlesnakes. They had made it out of Jew Flats and had their own apartment and their own friends—tons of them, Jews and non-Jews alike.

According to Jake's letters and tax returns, by the time he brought Ruth home to Lead, his saloon was making today's equivalent of $17,000 a month. The following year, the local paper would refer to him as "one of

Newlyweds Jake and Ruth Kozberg in Lead, South Dakota, 1915.

the prominent businessmen of Lead." Jake's ability to ride his economic achievement to heightened social status was almost unimaginable for a Jew living anywhere but the American West.

A PIECE OF HISTORY THAT HAS, TO A LARGE DEGREE, BEEN LEFT ON THE cutting-room floor is that the Black Hills, renowned for being a bastion of gamblers and rough, gold-hungry drunks, was settled, in part, by hundreds of Jews.

"There was mining, and the Jews were mining the miners," says Ann Haber Stanton, a former reporter who refers to herself as "the one-woman Jewish historical society of western South Dakota."

Despite their rough reputation, mining towns in the early twentieth-century American West were welcoming, and accessible to Jews. This rare lack of antisemitism was partly related to a recent history of exiling Native Americans to reservations. Because Lead and Deadwood—like Trinidad, Colorado, or Prescott, Arizona—were built on land recently taken from Indigenous Nations, they had more of a blank political and social slate than the long-established communities in the East. Jews in what historians call "frontier cities," these upstart communities in the West, were just one ethnic group of many in these burgeoning towns.

The Black Hills were home to more foreign-born immigrants than almost any other place in the state. The European newcomers were proud of their heritage; the streets were regularly filled with parades and bands playing ethnic music to celebrate one foreign holiday or another. The day of Jake's naturalization hearing at the Deadwood Courthouse, there were men with him from Italy, Austria, Sweden, Ireland, and England. Though I've found no accounts of Jews marching in the streets with their Torah, the conspicuous displays of multiple cultures created what local historians call a "cosmopolitan" place where Jews, with their own customs, were accepted, or at least relatively more accepted.

(There was an exception to the rule, unfortunately. The large number of Chinese immigrants who populated the Hills, many owning restaurants and laundries, were also proud of their culture and hosted Chinese New

Year festivals, wearing pink silk shirts, giving out free candy and whiskey, and blasting firecrackers. Yet, while these immigrants contributed significantly to the local economy, they were routinely abused and "despised"—crowds of boys threw rocks and snowballs at "the Chinamen," according to reports in the local paper.)

Not only were most Jews whiter, and therefor more acceptable, than their Chinese peers, they had another advantage over most other immigrants in the region: they were educated. Most Jewish boys in the Pale attended heders to prepare for their bar mitzvahs. "I once asked my dad, 'How did you get so smart?'" Etta tells me. This is another instructive story, this one about the value of education. "He only had like a sixth-grade education, but he told me, 'At these schools, we didn't just learn Hebrew, we learned math and geography and all about what was going on in the world. We read the newspapers. Our minds were opened.'" Such literacy enabled Jewish men to open businesses.

Ruth and Jake could walk around the corner from their apartment to buy furniture from Joe Seelig, also a former Jew Flats homesteader. They could buy groceries, jewelry, dry goods, hardware, clothing, shoes, stationery, and, of course, liquor from Jews. Ruth's uncle started a mineral-water company. One brother worked for a time in real estate, developing land deals for mining companies. Jewish men created the first telephone system in the Hills, owned mines, and built opulent hotels. At one point during the early decades of settlement, an estimated one third of all the buildings in Deadwood were owned or rented by Jews. Until the 1950s, the tops of the buildings were emblazoned with the type of names usually associated with the Lower East Side: Goldberg, Levinson, Jacobs, Schwarzwald.

Jews in the Black Hills and other Western mining towns leveraged this economic success for political power. Jewish merchants in the Black Hills became mayors and city councilmen, served as judges and on the boards of directors of banks. Sol Star, the hardware store owner on HBO's *Deadwood*, was a real person who became a South Dakota state senator.

Sure, these Jews worked hard and were gritty and tough, but they were also often bent on assimilating, casting themselves as less Jewish and more white. (The 1915 census lists Jake as Norwegian. I have no idea if this was by mistake or design.)

White people of all origins had lived in the Black Hills for only a generation, maybe two, giving them no inherited claim to social currency and capital. Jews could ride a status elevator that relied on a culture of racism toward Blacks, Chinese immigrants, and, notably, the Lakota, who were considered "lesser people. I hate to say it that way," a board member of the Black Hills Mining Museum tells me. The Homestake Mine has no record of ever hiring an Indigenous person.

This book, like all books, reflects the time in which it is written—it speaks as much to the present as to the past. For my ancestors, shaped as they were by capitalism, trauma, and ambition, the Black Hills was a land of opportunity. But there is a blank space around the edges of this telling, a void of curiosity or concern for the fact that their wealth was made possible by the recent taking of this land from Lakota and other Indigenous peoples. Their apathy wasn't murder. It wasn't theft. But it allowed such harms to persist. It took me a long time to look at this chapter of their lives and see past the surprising parts to notice what had been there all along, what would remain after they were gone, what would come to me as mine to hold.

The Torah teaches that, even if we as individuals haven't committed such harms directly, we are responsible for them, as sin has a communal effect and must be dealt with collectively. In Deuteronomy, there's a teaching that, if a murdered person is found in the road and no one knows who the murderer is, the crime must be absolved by those who live nearby (in ancient days, this involved a bloody ritual involving a river and a heifer). To determine which community should incur the economic damage of sacrificing animals for this ritual, the leaders of the closest towns would measure their distance from the victim, and those living closest to the corpse would assume responsibility. But if nothing was done, the land would become polluted, endangering everyone.

"Sin is not a private affair, sin is social, and its effects are felt by the entire community," writes Rabbi Toba Spitzer about this Torah portion.

She urges us all to ask ourselves, "What measuring stick links me to the foundational sins of this nation? How am I connected?"

Measuring my own distance from the theft of Indigenous land requires a more detailed history lesson than the sort I was taught in school.

FOR MANY THOUSANDS OF YEARS, AS FAR BACK AS COLLECTIVE MEMORY extends, Lakota have come to the Black Hills, which they call the He Sapa, a mountainous and forested marvel that towers above the plains like a heart-shaped island. Here, in the shadow of the peaks, beside the rivers and pines, they could escape both drought and blizzard. But this place was more than refuge. When Joseph White Bull was a child and a young man, his tiyospaye regularly visited the He Sapa, not only to hunt but to conduct sacred ceremonies such as the Sun Dance. Lakota have likened the He Sapa to a cathedral, the sacred home of their religion and culture. The Oglala Lakota Holy Man, Black Elk, a contemporary of White Bull's, described its highest point, which rises more than seven thousand feet above sea level, as the center of the world.

For the Lakota, the stars are "the holy breath of the Great Spirit," and the location of certain constellations at certain times of the year are read as instructions for where and when to do specific ceremonies. Many of these are mapped above the He Sapa, creating a calendar of ceremony and place, where the Spirit World is entwined with the land.

"Each spring, a small group composed of especially devoted members from several Lakota bands journeyed through the Black Hills, synchronizing their movements to the motions of the sun along the ecliptic," writes Ronald Goodman, a former instructor at Sinte Gleska University on the Rosebud Reservation, in his book *Lakota Star Knowledge*. "As the sun moved into a particular Lakota constellation, they traveled to the site correlated with that constellation and held ceremonies there. Finally, they arrived at Devil's Tower at midsummer for the Sun Dance where they were joined by many western Lakota bands."

The He Sapa was "an altar where they worshipped their God," wrote the Oglala Lakota author James La Pointe in his book *Legends of the La-*

kota. "It is only natural, therefore, that through close association with the sacred place, and because of their spiritual devotion to the Hills, many legends have emerged, woven out of both fact and fiction." Many of these include the Lakota origin story of humankind.

Long ago, according to an ancient Lakota story, humans lived deep underground in a Spirit Lodge. The only way to travel to the surface of the Earth was through a hole in a cave out of which cold air always blew. One day, Iktomi, a spider and trickster spirit, aided by either a wolf or a double-faced woman, lured some Lakota to the Earth's surface. When they stepped through the hole, they became buffalo. Many seasons later, after the world was better suited for human life, the Creator instructed the Lakota who'd remained under the world to come through the hole. They did and remained human. This origin story has almost as many variations as there are storytellers, but in each version the cave is specific. It is Washun Niya, also known as Wind Cave, in Wind Cave National Park, in the southern part of the Black Hills.

As the people emerged, the first thing they saw was a buffalo hoof-print. The Creator told them to follow the buffalo, and that the animals would provide everything necessary to survive. In some versions of this story, the buffalo emerged from the hole not as humans but as a string of ants that expanded to their current size by breathing the outside air. In other versions, the buffalo don't appear at all. In all versions, this story is meant to be told aloud in Lakota, not written in English by a Jew.

Doug White Bull and others have told me repeatedly that the Lakota culture lives in its language, that every time a fluent speaker dies, part of the culture dies with them. It took my fifth trip to Standing Rock before I really understood what that meant, to understand why this legend, for example, must be recounted in Lakota for it to be truly understood, for it to teach and convey meaning as intended.

For starters, the Lakota language is verb-heavy, unlike English, which is laden with nouns. This linguistic difference means that stories told in Lakota leap to their feet. When an elder recounts this tale out loud, often with chanting and gestures and at specific times of the year, they bead their words with action, each word or phrase illustrating plot, relationship, and responsibility between characters, depicting how the Lakota are interconnected with the world around them. There are scores of traditional stories about the He Sapa. These stories loop the past to the present. This happens not only by the telling but again within the structure of the language itself.

There is no present tense in Lakota. There's future tense and then a tense for everything that has happened up to the current moment. One elder explained to me that, in this way, history isn't stuck in the past, it's still happening right now. The United States sending Custer into the Black Hills to look for gold, thousands of gold-hungry men descending on the Hills with their pickaxes and pans, other immigrants laying thousands of miles of roads and rail tracks, felling acres of old growth, muddying rivers, when any of that history is recounted in Lakota, it has the immediacy of contemporary tragedy. Academics argue about whether worldview is shaped by language or if it's the other way around. Either way, how the Lakota see the Black Hills is completely different from how Ruth and Jake saw them.

Yiddish, the language my great-grandparents and most other Ashkenazi Jews spoke, is a language of displacement, of landless people in diaspora. The writer Michael Wex postulates that Yiddish is laden with elaborate idioms of complaint to discourage speakers from getting comfortable, to remind them that they remain in exile. Yiddish refers to land in terms of its utility. (Israel is the exception. Despite the Jews' expulsion from their homeland almost two thousand years earlier, by the time my family was living in South Dakota, land from Israel remained so revered that traveling salesmen throughout America sold jars of Israeli soil so that people could be buried beside earth from the Holy Land.)

Yiddish speakers in the Black Hills might have appreciated the beauty around them, they might even have, as my great-grandparents did, called it "God's Country." But western settlers like Jake and Ruth saw the Hills not as sacred but as a place marked with dollar signs. They may not have understood that mining and paving the He Sapa was analogous to razing the Wailing Wall and building a shopping mall on the rubble. They may not have understood that, for the Lakota, to walk away from the He Sapa, to give up the Black Hills, was impossible.

* * * * *

WITHIN SHORT ORDER OF CONGRESS DECLARING, IN 1877, THAT AMERICA owned the Black Hills, Lakota leaders were protesting to anyone who would listen, and even to those who wouldn't, that they'd never sold their land. This was not a sale, they reiterated, only a lease, and only for the land above the trees. But by this point, they knew this was more than misunderstanding. By this point, the Lakota had been living with broken and edited treaties for a generation.

"Do not let the white men fool you," Joseph White Bull's father told him when he was selected to be a Mnicoujou chief in 1881, five years after the United States took the Hills. "Guard the [He Sapa] and also this Reservation."

Within the following two decades, White Bull and other Lakota throughout the region held as many as one hundred councils to discuss how to combat the government's taking of the He Sapa. In one such meeting in July 1904, more than a thousand tents were pitched at Cherry Creek, White Bull's home on the Cheyenne River Reservation. Delegates from the entire Lakota Nation strategized both retaking their lands and surviving the reservations. Six years later, a convention of the Oceti Sakowin and Arapahos, with representatives from reservations in four different states, organized a committee to investigate all relevant records. Within months, they enlisted an attorney, a young man who had been born on Cheyenne River and raised in Lakota Country. The eager Ralph Hoyt Case (he is almost always described as "eager" in history books) promised to deliver them American justice. The Lakota argued that, because the Agreement of 1877 authorizing the taking of the Black Hills wasn't signed by three fourths of male adults, because it was never translated into Lakota, and because those signed were forced to do so under "extreme fear," the agreement was illegal.

Over the next decade, the main talking point from American politicians and Indian Office bureaucrats was that there was no need for such justice. The Lakota had been conquered, they said. The Hills were the spoils of war. By then, by some accounts, the Department of the Interior had deeded more than 75 percent of the Black Hills to homesteaders. By then, my uncles and great-grandfather were living in Lead, making a living off the land, or off the men making a living off the land.

The Indian Office declared that the Lakota couldn't pursue a claim of wrongdoing without Congress passing a law allowing such action. Thus ensued another long fight that the Lakota ultimately won. It took until 1923 for the young and eager Ralph Case, now less young, to finally file a claim in federal court alleging that the United States owed the Great Sioux Nation restitution for the taking of the Black Hills.

That summer, when Case returned to South Dakota after filing the claim, the crowd of Lakota that met him was jubilant, believing that, after forty-six years of delays, justice, in the form of financial compensation, was soon coming. "Case would be the Moses of the Sioux," the superintendent of Pine Ridge told the crowd as he introduced him, this according to historian Edward Lazarus in his book *Black Hills/White Justice*. "Like Moses leading the Jews out of Egypt, Case would lead the Sioux out of the bondage of their poverty and despair and into the promised land of American prosperity."

That Moses himself never made it to the Promised Land was not lost on Case, who paused, considering this, before addressing the crowd. His hesitancy was prescient: the legal fight over the Black Hills would outlive every person celebrating that day.

Two years later, in 1925, the United States hired sculptor Gutzon Borglum to carve the sacred mountains of the Black Hills with the faces of four U.S. presidents. Borglum had previously worked on a monument to Confederate soldiers in Stone Mountain, Georgia, a homeplace for the Ku Klux Klan. Borglum's belief in Nordic superiority and his insider status with the Klan did not seem to prevent him from making friends with two of Ruth's brothers, my uncles Louie and Jack, both of whom visited him several times while he was sculpting Mount Rushmore; there are pictures of them both hanging from ropes during construction and posing with Borglum's son, Lincoln. To carve the monument, Borglum blasted the mountains of the He Sapa, defacing the sacred Lakota ground. Today, the Mount Rushmore National Monument is referred to as "The Shrine of Democracy," but not by most Lakota. They are more likely to call Mount

Louie Sinykin (left) and Jack Sinykin (right) posing
with Lincoln Borglum at Mount Rushmore, likely
between 1939 and 1940.

Rushmore "The Shrine to Hypocrisy," as the four presidents honored by
Borglum each oversaw the theft of Indigenous lands and crafted policies
to cripple Indigenous families and cultures.

The legal case over the Black Hills wound its way through the court
system for decades, the delays and setbacks legion—government attorneys
once took six years to answer a simple motion, something that is typically
accomplished in less than a month. After more than a century of Indigenous activism and a moving cast of attorneys and judges, the case was finally
heard by the U.S. Supreme Court in 1980. The verdict stunned the nation.

"A more ripe and rank case of dishonorable dealings will never, in all
probability, be found in our history," read Justice Harry Blackmun's majority opinion. The Court ruled that the United States had violated the
Fifth Amendment, and that Grant had broken his treaty obligation to prevent trespass into the Hills. For the first time since the passage of *Lone*

Wolf, the legal case that gave Congress the power to take Indigenous land regardless of earlier treaty promises, the Supreme Court ruled that America must pay for such land takings. In an 8–1 decision, the court found that the United States owed the Lakota approximately $106 million for the taking of the Black Hills. But by then, the Lakota didn't want the money. They wanted the land.

This was probably always the goal, writes historian Jeffrey Ostler, author of *The Lakotas and the Black Hills.* Earlier in the century, the Lakota felt that making the return of the land the centerpiece of their activism wouldn't be pragmatic, but by the time of the Supreme Court ruling in 1980, recovering the Black Hills seemed more plausible, as, by then, Indigenous legal organizations had been winning court cases restoring land and water rights for at least a decade.

Just weeks after the Supreme Court ruling, the Oglala Sioux Tribe filed suit in district court for the return of the Black Hills plus $11 billion in damages. For the first time, the lead attorney on the case was a Lakota, one who'd grown up on Pine Ridge. He declared upon filing, "We hereby reject any award money . . . and do not abandon our claim to the lands taken by the Act of 1877." Doug remembers the handmade signs all over Lakota Country that read THE BLACK HILLS ARE NOT FOR SALE.

"We are like the Jews," Patrick Janis, an Oglala Lakota, told *Rolling Stone* in 1987. "The Jews always had it in their minds to come back to Israel, and for 2,000 years it was impossible, but they did it. The same with us. Someday we're going to do it. We're going to get back the Black Hills if the people really want it in their hearts."

The legal fight over the return of the Black Hills is still occurring today. It is considered the longest ongoing legal case in America's history. Due to interest that has accrued on the original settlement amount, there is now more than $1 billion sitting untouched in a federal bank account.

"How, in a world where everything revolves around money, can the poorest people in America refuse to accept millions of dollars?" wrote Tim Giago, the Oglala Lakota founder and editor of the *Lakota Times,* the country's first independently owned Indigenous newspaper, in 2022. "Because they consider the land that was stolen from them to be sacred and as they say, 'One does not sell their Mother.'"

In the meantime, the Black Hills continue to make America rich. It's tricky to say exactly how rich, but consider the following: the Homestake Mine, which closed in 2002, was the longest continuously operating gold mine in the country's history. The gold pulled from that mine alone (not to mention the other gold, silver, and lead mines in the Hills) was worth an estimated $1 billion. The U.S. Forest Service owns 1.2 million acres of the Black Hills. It has been logging pine there since 1899, and the agency boasts that it is among its most productive forests. Tourists have been coming to the Hills for generations to visit Mount Rushmore, hike in the National and State forests, swim in the alpine lakes, and camp. In recent years, tourism in the Hills has generated more than $3 billion annually.

The Black Hills remain a flashpoint over Indigenous sovereignty, and while politicians have championed the cause over the years, they have been few and far between. Notably, in 1985, Senator Bill Bradley introduced legislation that would have returned all federal lands in the Hills to the Lakota, but it died in committee. At campaign stops in 2008, Barack Obama told Lakota that, if elected, he would try to return the Black Hills; Lakota turned out in droves for him, but President Obama let them down. As of this writing, there is not a single congressional ally working to help the Lakota reclaim their land.

In 2020, President Donald Trump held a rally at Mount Rushmore to celebrate Independence Day. He was met by a blockade of hundreds of Dakota and Lakota activists wearing eagle feathers, coupsticks, and sage, chanting, "Land back!" Trump supporters, in what has got to count among the most clueless of political strategies, yelled at the protesters to "go back to where you come from."

THE WEEK FOLLOWING TRUMP'S VISIT TO THE BLACK HILLS, I'M THERE, too, on a mash-up of reporting trip and vacation. As my husband and kids let me drag them around to the many tourist traps on offer, I begin to see a through line. I begin to understand how *go back to where you come from* can flourish in a place dedicated to a specific kind of erasure.

On a hot, dusty July day, my family and I sit on the curb of Deadwood's Main Street, crowded with other tourists, to watch one of the three daily live shootouts that, according to the town's website, "bring history alive." The kids get "deputized" by an actor playing a sheriff and wear their plastic star badges while we watch what constitutes historical entertainment: three men pretend to get drunk in a bar, and two of them threaten to shoot each other over a gambling disagreement.

Designated a National Historic Landmark in 1961, Deadwood is a tourist trap with history as the honeypot. Visitors are welcomed with the sign: DEADWOOD, WHERE THE WEST STILL LIVES. The visitor information booth is a covered wagon. You can pan for gold, eat at a historic ranch, and ride in horse-drawn carriages. You can hike the Seventh Cavalry Trail. By city ordinance, no signage can be plastic. The buildings that line Main Street—mostly saloons, hotels, and merchants selling T-shirts, jewelry, and tchotchkes—have historic brick facades.

At the Mt. Moriah Cemetery high on a hill above the town, pines sway in the wind as a load of tourists, most of them gray haired, several with canes or walkers, step haltingly off a painted former school bus.

"Wild Bill is just up the hill, and he's dying to meet you," shouts the guide through a bullhorn. While most beeline to the graves of Buffalo Bill and Calamity Jane, they blithely pass a historical marker enlightening visitors about the Jewish past here in the Black Hills. Nearby, it explains, is Hebrew Hill, or Mt. Zion, the Jewish section of the cemetery where eighty-nine Jewish pioneers are buried, many of their graves etched with Hebrew letters. Erected in 2005 by the Jewish American Society for Historic Preservation, the sign, like two others downtown, lauds the importance of Jewish businessmen, how they helped "stabilize" the community.

"Jews were not cowardly interlopers, after the frontier had been settled, but were part of the frontier American experience from the beginning," wrote Jerry Klinger, president of the JASHP, explaining what he hoped visitors reading these signs would learn.

Such lauding of early Jewish settlers is "agenda driven," says Jonathan

L. Friedmann, president of the Western States Jewish History Association, who has examined how Jewish historical organizations often use these signs more as a hedge against antisemitism than as an attempt to tell the full story. But Jews aren't the only ones with an agenda here in the Black Hills.

Amid all this celebration of the tough spirit of these early pioneers, there is almost no explanation that these pioneers arrived in the Hills illegally, breaking federal treaty and law. It is possible, even easy, to visit the Black Hills and leave without ever learning that these towns are built on stolen land.

"There are no depictions of Lakota or Sioux in town. They're not talked about," says Hannah Marshall, a former archivist with Deadwood History, a local nonprofit. "It's as if no one existed here before 1876, when Custer found gold."

At one museum, an exhibit describing the disappearance of buffalo is written in the passive voice. "The region's distinctive large animals were driven to near extinction or displaced, even as all of the tribal societies were moved and confined" reads the sign beside a large cut-out picture of a buffalo. It offers no explanation for how exactly the animal was eradicated. A nearby room displays a variety of Indigenous clothing, moccasins, and arrowheads behind glass. The people to whom these artifacts once belonged were not survivors of genocide, according to the sign, but people who "always had to adapt and have done so with grace and beauty."

Even at sites run by the National Park Service, descriptions of Lakota history are minimal. At Mount Rushmore, when I have trouble finding any reference to Native Nations, a ranger tells me of exactly one place with mention of the Treaty of 1868, which, she then inaccurately explains, "gave the Black Hills to the Lakota."

At the Little Bighorn Battlefield National Monument, located west of the Hills in Montana, past the huge American flag waving under the low-hanging clouds, past the monument atop the mass grave, is a sculpture constructed in the early 2000s to honor those Native Americans who died in the battle with Custer. Designed by a non-Indigenous sculptor who incorporated elements inspired by the Mayans and Aztecs, the memorial quotes Lakota warriors describing a hard battle and says that the Seventh

Cavalry "came on us like a thunderbolt." This runs counter to every story I've heard or read about the battle from a Native American, all of whom have described it as a rout that was over in less than half an hour.

"It's good to have a memorial but it's not realistic to what happened there," says Dana Dupris, who is Mnicoujou and Itazipacola Lakota and was, at the time of our interview, Cheyenne River's cultural preservation specialist. Dupris attended advisory meetings with the Park Service in which he and others made comments and suggestions to make the memorial more accurate. Many of their suggestions, he says, were not incorporated.

While Lakota history in the Hills has been largely erased, George Armstrong Custer, the golden-haired man who led the illegal mission into the Hills, is widely celebrated. There are Custer counties in South Dakota, Montana, Idaho, Nebraska, Oklahoma, and Colorado. While driving to, and in, the Black Hills, we pass Custer National Forest, Custer State Park, and through the town of Custer, where a place advertises gun sales and Trump T-shirts in an efficient drive-through. Later that day, we met up with Doug White Bull, his daughter Juliana, and granddaughter for a picnic at the edge of the Hills in a place many Lakota call Racist City. As we talk over our burritos, I ask Juliana what it's like to be here.

"We were driving in these neighborhoods, and all these people are working on their lawns. And if I walked on their property, they'd probably call the cops. But this is our land. Do they even realize it?" Juliana shook her head. "I try not to think about it too much."

If not for certain historic events, one of those houses might've been mine.

MY GRANDMOTHER PAULINE WAS BORN IN 1916 AND BROUGHT HOME TO her parents' apartment over the saloon in Lead. Her parents, Ruth and Jake, pushed her baby carriage down Main Street and spoiled her from the start, dressing her in the nicest clothes. But within a year, the young family would leave the Hills, never to live there again. Jake didn't want to leave. He felt they had no choice, which is different from actually having no choice. The reason that sent them packing tightens the knot around the entangled history of the White Bulls and my ancestors: Prohibition.

In 1917, the sound of broken glass echoed through downtown Lead; gallons of hooch, enough to get a man drunk for weeks, sloshed into the road. It was the smell of good times gone bad.

DESTROYED BOOZE read the all-caps headline from the *Lead Daily Call* on July 26, 1917. Old-time sots named the Norwegian Kid and Linky Lee watched as the chief of police and state attorney stood on the platform of the North Western Railway's freight station and made batting practice out of three barrels' worth of brandy bottles, a five-gallon keg of sherry wine, and a half-barrel of the oddly nonspecific "alcohol." The mournful spectators "wept bitter tears." This $900 worth of booze was partly owned by Jake and intended for sale in his Lobby Saloon.

Just weeks earlier, South Dakota had become one of the first states west of the Mississippi to make both the sale and consumption of alcohol illegal. Jake wasn't the only one affected: two of Ruth's brothers were in the liquor business in the region. Overnight, with the passage of South Dakota's bone-dry law, their time in the Black Hills, built on bar money, turned into a bad bet.

Why South Dakota leapt to embrace Prohibition before any other state in the West hasn't been well researched, but based on the history of Dakota politics, I suspect it was driven by fear of both Native Americans and immigrants. For decades, nothing seemed to scare bureaucrats and politicians more than the idea of an "Indian" with a stiff drink. One of the first laws passed by the newly created Dakota Territory in 1862 was a ban on selling alcohol to Native Americans. This was a national obsession: in 1909 alone, Congress appropriated $40,000 (the equivalent of an estimated $1.3 million today) to suppress the traffic of liquor to Indigenous people. The Indian Office was so centrally obsessed with limiting intoxicants on reservations that, throughout the early 1900s, nearly half of the annual survey questions asked of Indian Agents concerned how easily Lakota could access alcohol.

Despite such grand effort, the Lakota had little trouble finding hooch. Bootleggers on and off the reservation made a steady business. On the

Cheyenne River Reservation during this time, the most common offense prosecuted in Tribal Court was the unlawful introduction of liquor. Though never arrested by Tribal police, it's possible my ancestors were among the suppliers: one story, impossible to verify, is that one of my distant cousins living on Jew Flats helped the Lakota learn to make their own whiskey.

Amid the great influx of settlers descending on homesteads throughout the Dakotas, the drive to prohibit liquor expanded beyond the reservation to the entire state. The Anti-Saloon League, a national Prohibition organization, established a chapter in South Dakota as early as 1896 and began having success drafting and passing "anti-saloon measures." Most of the saloon owners in the Dakotas, like most of those who worked in the alcohol business nationwide, were foreign born or the children of immigrants, according to census data. Many of the foreigners were Jews or Catholics. The Anti-Saloon League, founded and filled almost entirely by white Protestants, believed that taking jobs away from these recent immigrants would spur them to leave. In the case of my family, it certainly worked.

Throughout the summer of 1917, as Prohibition took hold, Jake turned his saloon into a soft-drink emporium—no real surprise, it flopped. His ranch on Jew Flats was in solid shape, being run by relatives and neighbors, but the real money wasn't ever going to be in ranching. It was always going to be in what the land could create as leverage. In August, Jake took out a $1,000 mortgage on his Jew Flats ranch with a bank in Lead, the equivalent of nearly $30,000 today. The money would be seed for a new business, one that would allow the Kozbergs to soar, to find a specific form of American success, at least temporarily. With Sinykin relatives already making money selling and distributing liquor out of St. Paul, where such a thing was still legal, all signs pointed east. Ruth's brother Ted had scouted a new saloon for Jake, one in the heart of the city. The place, Ted wrote, was "good for $10,000 a year" (more like $270,000 today).

Within days of drawing the mortgage, Jake, Ruth, and my grandmother boarded the North Western Railway for St. Paul. For the rest of her life, Ruth would come to the Hills on vacation, swimming in its lakes and walking amid the cool pines. She would bring her children to stay in hunting lodges, not for hunting, but to fill their lungs with good, clean air.

She would teach her daughters to horseback ride and swim and to balance such outdoor pursuits with music lessons and a love of theater.

The sort of musicals and Broadway shows that my family would come to adore were a horse of a different color from the pageantry being staged on reservations throughout the Dakotas when the Kozbergs left.

7

※※※※

THE ARROW FOR THE PLOW

In 1916, in what had to have been a first (and should have been a last) in the history of American governance, the Interior Department decided to stage a mini-play. Throughout the following eighteen or so months, hundreds of Indigenous people on reservations throughout the West would play themselves, and they would read from a script written by the U.S. secretary of the interior. On one cold December day, 101 Lakota gathered on the eastern edge of the Cheyenne River Reservation in front of a crowd and released arrows into the white sky. Through frost smoke and air so cold it burned, the morning light lit the fletchings so that they seemed to blaze as the arrows arced and then, as intended, hit nothing but the cold ground.

"You have shot your last arrow," read the official from the Indian Office who was acting as narrator, and hoisted his prop, a large American flag, into the air. "You are no longer to live the life of an Indian. You are from this day forward to live the life of the white man." He then asked each Indigenous man to put their hand on a steel plow as the narrator told them "this act means that you have chosen to live the life of the white man—and the white man lives by work."

The interior secretary, a job not typically associated with playwriting, wasn't striving for nuance. For the final scene, the civil servant handed Lakota women a purse for saving money and a small American flag, in that

Last Arrow ceremony, Standing Rock Reservation, McLaughlin, South Dakota.

order, because capitalism, in this telling, holds hands with democracy. Then each Lakota, pledging hereafter to use only a "white name," was granted citizenship. At last, the script announced, they were free and equal to their white brothers. Now, they could vote and manage their own land and money. Most important to the large crowd of settlers in the audience cheering and clapping while a cowboy band struck up a tune, this was an opportunity. These newly made citizens were free to sell their land.

The Interior Department staged these Last Arrow ceremonies in an effort to lure Native Americans away from their traditions, culture, and collectively held lands with the bedazzling charms of private property, citizenship, and voting rights. Such assimilation rituals were unique to Indigenous people living in the United States—at no point did any of the Sinykins need to change their name or braid their last challah to become citizens.

By this point, America was at war in Europe and, fat with national fervor, vibrated with the question of what made someone American. President Woodrow Wilson (whose signature is on many of my family's land deeds) had grown tired of the idea that Indigenous people needed time to "evolve" into farmers. Abuzz with the civilizing effects of private property, he and Congress worked in tandem to dissolve Indigenous lands and Nations as quickly as possible. Such a goal seemed to be within reach.

At that point, the Lakota were living on five reservations in the Dakotas, on around 1.3 million acres, just 2 percent of the land they'd reserved by federal treaty in 1851. What's more, this land was no longer legally under their control: under the Allotment Act, back in 1887, Congress had placed all Indigenous land in trust, meaning the United States owned the title to the land, administering it for "beneficial use." This meant that federal bureaucrats, not Tribal Councils or individual Native Americans, had the final say over how reservation land and the minerals under that land were used. Further legislation passed in 1906, called the Burke Act, had given the secretary of the interior himself the power to take parcels of land out of trust status and convert them into private property for those Indigenous people deemed "competent" by local superintendents. During the era to follow, the one that birthed the Last Arrow ceremonies, Congress and an assortment of presidents would strive to speed the pace of this transition, aiming to make good on what President Teddy Roosevelt had stated in 1901 as the function of the Allotment Act: "a mighty pulverizing engine to break up the tribal mass."

This new era of federal policy, built on the shoulders of outright genocide and cultural genocide, would be delivered not by soldiers or lawmakers but, in the main, by bureaucrats armed with the tools of policy, taxation, and flagrant mismanagement. The old assimilationist phrases, grimy from overhandling, began to fall apart. During the teens and twenties, America would reveal once again that the welfare of Indigenous people wasn't as important as the taking of their land.

DOUG'S DAD, JACOB WHITE BULL, NEVER STARRED IN A LAST ARROW CEREMONY. For the duration of their run, he was a volunteer in the U.S. Army shooting at German soldiers from the trenches of France.

"All he said about war is that it was hell," says Doug one day, showing me a photo of his dad in a group of a dozen uniformed young men, all new recruits from Standing Rock. Jacob, with his big ears and full lips, looks

Doughboys from Standing Rock, including Jacob White Bull, front row, second from right.

like his son, but unlike Doug, whose eyes tend to flicker with humor, Jacob is unsmiling, his hands coiled in his lap.

When he returned home after eighteen months at the front, Jacob had no injuries or scars, at least none anyone could see. But for the rest of his life, he never wanted to talk about what happened. He hardly wanted to talk about anything at all—Doug figures his dad might have said all of one hundred words to him during his entire life. When Doug was young, Jacob would get his pension check and drink it down. This bothered Doug for a long time, until he got old enough to understand.

"How stressful that war must have been," says Doug shaking his head and staring at the file folder of family pictures in his lap. "To be at the front, always scared you're going to die."

When I first started reporting in Native American communities, I was surprised by how many veterans I met. Why would people who had been so mistreated by America want to defend it? My own relatives had swallowed lye and poured hot oil in their ears to avoid military service under tsarist Russia. I hadn't realized the important and respected place warriors held in so many Indigenous cultures. By becoming a soldier, I was told, young men could experience the closest approximation on offer of their ancestors' way of life (though, of course, people join the military for countless reasons). More than twelve thousand Native Americans served in World War I. For their sacrifice, they would be rewarded not with yellow ribbons or ticker-tape parades, not with money for college or a new house—they would lose their land.

During the war, as part of this effort to convert land held in trust to taxable private property, President Wilson's commissioner of Indian Affairs assigned bureaucrats (again, they were almost always men) to identify Indigenous people who were ready for the "responsibility" of owning a deed. These Competency Commissions would enter reservation homes and look for what they considered to be indicators of a civilized mind: if the floor was clean, or if men had cut their hair short. Anyone who could read or was good at their job and making a decent living was deemed ready for private property and would receive what was called a land patent. Soldiers and war heroes like Jacob White Bull were especially likely to be seen as suitably assimilated. The reward for land ownership was citizenship and, sometimes, a role in a Last Arrow ceremony.

Whether or not an individual wanted this honor, it wasn't always up to them—the superintendent (the new title given to the Indian Agents) or the competency commissioners could decide on a person's behalf. This involuntary, unceremonious transfer of land was called a "forced fee patent." Many people learned that they held a deed only when a county tax bill arrived in the mail. If people complained to the reservation superintendent, they were told all decisions came out of Washington, DC. By the time a letter could be written and processed, the tax bills were piling up, and the amount owed was typically far more than the per capita income of the Lakota on Cheyenne River. Most people had no choice but to sell their land or risk losing it to foreclosure.

While many Indigenous soldiers were in Europe fighting for America, the Interior Department put their land in forced fee patent. Unaware of this new status, some veterans returned home to find a stack of unpaid taxes. In some cases, the county government had put their land in foreclosure and sold it off to the highest bidder. In some cases, these veterans were obliged to "dispose of their property." In both circumstances, the land was "very frequently sold for a very inadequate consideration," according to the *Congressional Record*.

Within a year of Jacob White Bull's return from the European front, the superintendent converted his land to private property without his permission. Soon tax bills began to pile up against the door. An independent spirit who had run away to attend an Indian Boarding School because he wanted a better education than was offered on the reservation, Jacob, Doug tells me, had been doggedly supporting his family with ranching and both working as a typesetter and playing fiddle with Lawrence Welk, back in the days before Welk had his famous TV show. Doug remembers his dad as proud, a hard worker, but as my ancestors had found, making a living off 160 acres in a dry climate was almost impossible, especially when competing with the large, southwestern-style cattle ranches trampling wide swaths of the reservations.

"These white guys, they went to my dad and said, 'We'll buy that land from you for forty-five cents an acre,' so that's what my dad did," says Doug, staring out on the rolling hills of his relative Fred DuBray's buffalo ranch on Cheyenne River. "He couldn't pay no taxes on it. As far as our culture, nobody owns land. All the land belongs to the people. So taking land and putting ownership on it was a thing we didn't understand."

Fred explains how his great-grandparents were like a lot of Lakota. They had no experience with private property or taxation, and so when the government forced the land into a fee patent, Fred's ancestors didn't understand that they needed to pay a tax. For failure to pay more than two decades of land taxes, the county seized Fred's family's land and sold it at public auction for one dollar an acre, with the money going not to the DuBrays but to the county to cover the back taxes. One day, Fred approached the white man whose ancestors bought his great-grandparents' land.

"I said to him, 'Just so you know, this land you're farming used to belong to my family. You guys basically stole it.' And he said, 'We didn't steal it, we paid good money for that.' I said, 'One dollar an acre? That's just legalized stealing. I'd like to have it back, and if I get a chance to buy it, I want to buy it, and if I get a chance to steal it, I'm going to steal it.'"

Pointing to the flat lands to the north of his property, Fred says, "all that forced patent fee land was flat land and farmable."

This dynamic occurred nationwide. For example, when the Competency Commission for Oklahoma's Quapaw Nation assessed the land of six hundred Tribal members, more than half asked that their land remain in trust, knowing exactly what was likely to happen if it was forcibly turned into private property. "My children are landless," said one. "I want to make sure I can keep it," said another. But their requests made no difference.

A superintendent from the Cheyenne River Reservation, writing to his boss around the time when DuBray's great-grandfather lost his land, estimated that 95 percent of patented land on the reservation had been sold or mortgaged, the vast majority to settlers or real estate developers, those most slippery of prairie residents. And it is at this point, with this knowledge that forced fee patents led to the diminishment of Indigenous land-holdings, that the Indian Office revealed the racism that had always been at the center of its bureaucratic heart.

THE STATUE OF LIBERTY, WHICH MY AUNT ROSE REMEMBERED SEEING FAR off in the distance as my family arrived from Europe, famously declares on its base: "Give me your tired, your poor, your huddled masses yearning to breathe free." It doesn't say that such freedom is contingent on skin color, but under the next policy directive issued by the Wilson administration in 1917, whiteness would serve as gatekeeper and passkey to American democracy. The next stage of land grabbing would be overtly about race.

"The beginning of the end of the Indian problem," announced Indian Affairs commissioner Cato Sells, a Texan banker with zero previous experience working with Native Nations. The policy would rely not on a person's interest and ability to own land, but instead on their genetics. Any Indigenous person with 51 percent or more white ancestry would be automatically deemed competent and immediately issued a forced fee patent.

"It is almost an axiom that an Indian who has a larger proportion of white blood than Indian partakes more of the characteristics of the former than the later. In thought and action, so far as the business world is concerned, he approximates more closely to the white blood ancestry," wrote Sells, adding that this new plan would be "the ultimate absorption of the Indian race into the body politic of the Nation."

Sells had his minions draw up lists of the eligible, and with an alacrity that should stun anyone now familiar with the Bureau of Indian Affairs, within the year, by the spring of 1918, the agency turned nearly 780,000 acres of Indigenous land into private property. In so doing, said Sells, "thousands of Indians [had] been given their freedom." As a side hustle, he arranged to allow "incompetent Indians" to sell (or for the superintendent to sell for them) any of their unused lands. By 1919, the Interior Department expanded "presumption of competence" to include those who had 50 percent Indigenous ancestry.

The media hailed this policy as "courageous." The progressive and popular magazine *The Outlook* found it better that some individuals "be lost" under this new model than "the whole Indian race should be denied the opportunity for that kind of human development which comes only in the atmosphere of freedom and in its bearing the burdens of responsibility which freedom entails."

In more than ten thousand pages of annual reports written throughout this era by superintendents at Cheyenne River to their bosses in DC, the evidence pops: everyone at Indian Affairs knew exactly what they were doing. They knew that Lakota were selling their lands to white men almost immediately after receiving a forced fee patent. They knew these policies were turning the reservation maps into patchwork quilts.

I picture them, pencils aloft, considering how to spin the news.

One superintendent from a South Dakota reservation wrote that taking their land would force Indigenous people to get jobs. In 1913, the superintendent at Cheyenne River—noting that half of those who received a fee patent didn't make any money—wrote, in his best bureaucrat-speak, that losing land was an educational experience, teaching "independence and self-reliance." In 1920, another Cheyenne River superintendent wrote to his superiors that he had dismissed several Lakota requests for their land to be reverted to trust and that "the final disposition of the remaining tribal lands and the opening of the reservation should not be delayed longer than two years from the present time. . . . If it could be accomplished sooner it should be done."

Former president Teddy Roosevelt, upon witnessing the huge number of land sales that immediately followed the finale of a Last Arrow ceremony in South Dakota, wrote to the commissioner of Indian Affairs that it was best to "let them suffer the hardships which their own fault brings." Historian Philip J. Deloria explains that reporting sold allotments as "squandered [rather] than as swindled" removed any blame from white people.

By the time Wilson left office in 1921, his administration had converted the lands of at least ten thousand Indigenous people into private property. Of these 1.5 million acres, more than one million had been sold to settlers. A decade later, only four hundred Indigenous people had managed to hold on to their land, according to a congressional investigation. Subsequent laws allowed these landowners to reclassify their allotments as Trust Land, and some of them were able to get their tax dollars back. But for the estimated ninety-six hundred others, "the Indian is without recourse," said one congressman. Nearly a century later, neither Congress nor the courts has ever done anything to remedy the fact that, by its own admission, America broke the law.

Nowhere in the country were more forced fee patents issued than in South Dakota. No other Indigenous Nation lost as much land under this system than the Oceti Sakowin. This inequity sharpens when including the world beyond the reservations.

Across the prairie, white ranchers were toiling under the same dry sky as the Lakota, and they, too, often couldn't afford their taxes. The list of delinquent taxpayers in 1921 filled nine columns in the local newspapers and included the names of leading businessmen and a county commissioner. The government was foreclosing on hundreds of farmers. There were rumors reported in the press of men hanging themselves from shame of failure. In response, the federal government again rushed to rescue these white settlers.

The railroads still needed homesteaders on the prairie to make long-distance hauls financially viable, and politicians still wanted to empty American cities of recent immigrants. In what functioned as both insurance policy and incentive, Congress created special banks and special credit just for farmers. In 1917 alone, there was almost $30 million available, much of it going to the Great Plains. These loans were low interest and long term, allowing settlers not only to pay their taxes but to buy new machinery, to modernize, and to expand their lands or buy new animals. Not one of these loans, as far as anyone can tell, went to an Indigenous person.

Such money seems to have been important to my ancestor's ability to keep their land. Rose and her husband, Issie, received $800 from the South Dakota Rural Credit Board in 1922. The following year, they and Rose's youngest brother, Louie, got a $10,000 mortgage from the Federal Land Bank of Omaha. More than a decade later, the same bank would give another Sinykin kid $10,000 on his South Dakota ranch, and by then he was hardly more of a farmer than I am.

After digging through the deeds, I can't find evidence that anyone in my family bought land on any of the allotted Lakota reservations. They did not come to know their Lakota neighbors through such a business transaction. And yet somehow, around this time, Ruth's older brother, my uncle Jack Sinykin, the guy who'd been caught eating sausages in Kapulye, the one with Faige Etke's deep-set blue eyes, befriended Doug's ancestor, Joseph White Bull. At least, that's one theory.

AROUND THE YEAR 1919, JACK AND JOSEPH WHITE BULL TOOK A PICTURE together in a studio that printed the image onto a postcard. These "real-photo postcards," made between 1905 and 1920, tended to depict rural America and are most famous for documenting lynchings. The picture of Jack and Joseph creates more questions than it answers. The two men are shaking hands, but Jack, dressed in a suit and tie, has a pistol strapped to the outside of his jacket. Joseph wears a traditional feathered war bonnet and holds a canunpa, the ceremonial Lakota pipe. According to Lakota archivists and historians, the woven bag used to carry the pipe isn't White Bull's. The men stare at each other, unsmiling.

At the time, Jack was bouncing around between his ranch on Jew Flats, an apartment in the Black Hills, and a flat in the train-line town of Philip,

Jack Sinykin and Joseph White Bull shaking
hands, circa 1919.

selling shoes, real estate, and anything else to make money. Based on census records, it's likely Joseph was spending some of his time in Cherry
Creek on the Cheyenne River Reservation, not far north of Philip. This
wasn't a photo to celebrate a land deal, as Joseph, now in his seventies, had
no land to sell. A staunch traditionalist who often kept his long hair braided,
Joseph would keep his land in trust until the end of his life.

When I started this project, I thought that, by understanding this picture, I could collapse the line between the past and today. I could measure my
proximity to history in the way that Rabbi Spitzer advises. I thought I might
learn that it was Joseph's ancestors who dropped the arrowheads my cousins found on Jew Flats. This longing, more than anything else, reveals my
old ideas about land ownership, about the colonialism that has shaped me.

"It can be tempting to decide that something is important simply

because we have a photograph of it," writes Princeton historian and photography curator Martha A. Sandweiss. "Because we value the evidence
we have at hand, we can be led to imagine that the moment fixed in the
photographic image holds great explanatory power. That is not always
true . . . they depict fleeting moments, but they do not explain how they
came about."

Photographs don't tell stories. Photographs lead us to stories. Despite
extensive research in national, state, and Indigenous archives, I still don't
know why Jack and Joseph took this photo together. But not having solved
this mystery doesn't matter as much to me anymore. The fact that their
lives intersected at all has led me to know Doug White Bull and his relatives, whose insights and stories have changed the way I understand both
American history and my own. Our conversations and the history they've
inspired me to study have been a measuring stick for my own culpability.
When I look at this picture now, I see the world beyond the frame. I see
the forces pushing both men to assimilate and pulling them apart. I see the
thread linking both of their lives to mine.

Today, the distance between Joseph's and Jack's descendants can be
measured in many ways. The story that follows is just one example that says
something about the mutable nature of freedom in America.

Doug White Bull and I spent more than a year and a half trying to get
his ancestors' land records from the Bureau of Indian Affairs. We made
phone calls, sent emails, knocked on the glass door of the brick building
that houses such data. After Doug threatened to have a Tribal judge send
a letter on his behalf, it seemed something might shake loose, but nothing
ever did.

During this same time period, I was able to waltz into nearby county
offices and pull all the deeds and mortgages held by the residents of Jew
Flats. During the pandemic, when I couldn't fly to South Dakota, much
of this work wasn't even done by me but by a whip-smart researcher who
pulled the records on my behalf. Journalists learn that these sorts of records
make fact of anecdote. They are the scaffolding on which a story hangs.

The roadblocks that Doug has faced to access his own records are unsurprising to anyone who has ever tried to get information from the Bureau

of Indian Affairs. There's a popular joke in Native America that BIA stands for "Bossing Indians Around," something it seems like the agency has been doing for time immemorial.

HISTORY, LIKE THIS BOOK, MOVES FORWARD AND BACKWARD IN STEPS large and small until the footprints between eras merge, quashing the idea that the past can be put in a box. For example, the way the Indian Office treated men like Joseph White Bull in the early 1900s both reflected the recent past and foreshadowed the present.

A hundred years ago, employees from the Indian Office deemed that Joseph White Bull, with his long hair and refusal to speak English, was too traditional to own private property or manage his own bank account. Instead, Congress had put reservation superintendents in charge of his assets. Keeping the land in trust meant that at least White Bull wouldn't lose it outright, but it still didn't keep his land or any money he made from it anything close to secure.

These superintendents controlled Lakota bank accounts and the money accumulated from former treaty payments and settlers who were leasing their land. Both the superintendents and their bosses at the Indian Office routinely declined requests from grown men and women who had the audacity to want to spend their own money on groceries, clothing, or additional land. Superintendents reported to their bosses that they were certain that, if given access to their accounts, Lakota would burn their savings on "frivolities or alcohol." In a further eradication of female power, superintendents deposited the lease money earned by married women into their husband's accounts. Though superintendents were required to distribute lease payments every six months, in some cases, Lakota waited for their money for almost two years. On the Pine Ridge Reservation, some people died of starvation while waiting for their funds.

The Indian Office's mismanagement of these individual bank accounts would continue for generations. In the 1990s, Elouise Cobell, a banker herself and citizen of the Blackfeet Nation, sued the federal government to prompt an audit of accounts managed by the Bureau. The case revealed a catalogue of financial abuses, estimating that more than $300 billion of Indigenous money had been stolen, lost, or mismanaged over the previous century.

The delay in payments made America money. During this time, the U.S. Treasury was making interest off the funds it held in trust for Indigenous Nations and their members. No records were kept of exactly how much money was in these trust accounts, so it's not possible to track exactly how much was made. However, it certainly was enough for the Indian Office to pay for everything from its own salaries and housing to the hospitals, schools, and annuities Lakota were owed by the treaty agreements they or their ancestors had signed. Let me underscore this point: the money Lakota were supposed to receive in exchange for their land was not only not theirs to use as they chose, it was being used to fund their continued confinement. One superintendent from a Lakota reservation bragged to a visiting congressional committee in 1925 that, for the past decade, he'd covered all his expenses with "moneys belonging to these Indians. . . . No gratuity appropriation has been used."

Not only did the superintendents effectively control the bank accounts, they controlled the land held in trust. In the early 1900s, prior to the advent of forced fee patents, most Lakota had horses and cattle, and many of them were having great success. But the superintendents had the authority to lease trust lands regardless of the approval or desire of the Indigenous landowner. The money Lakota made from leasing wasn't great—while my ancestors could lease their lands at an average rate of forty-five cents an acre, the reservation rate could go lower than ten cents. (These low rates would persist: in 1935, the superintendent leased Joseph White Bull's 480 acres for $22.40 a year, less than $500 today.)

By 1920, Lakota ranchers, sick of their lands being leased without their consent, protested at public meetings. At one meeting that year, about twenty-five men from Cheyenne River demanded the superintendent stop leasing their land to non-Indigenous farmers, because, as one man said, the benefits were "very small, not enough to bother with." He went on to describe his reservation as "covered with cattle like a whole lot of worms on it. I cannot raise any garden and cannot do anything." The superintendents, who were often friends with the white ranchers living on reservations, renewed the leases anyway.

As a result, within four years, there were practically no cattle owned by Lakota on the Pine Ridge and Rosebud reservations, according to testimony at a congressional hearing. Joseph White Bull, who had once had "many cattle and horses," would eventually, like most Lakota ranchers, sell them to survive.

Due to the double-barreled impact of paternalism and greed, by the late 1920s, Lakota, like Native Americans almost everywhere, were starving. Of the thirty-two thousand Lakota allottees who had been given a patent, 80 percent were now landless, a loss of more than 3.5 million acres of Indigenous land. At a federal hearing in South Dakota, a man from Pine Ridge told the assembled congressional committee, "We have not got any cattle now and no money to buy them with." Another man from there added, "I am eating horses and I only have four or five left and when I eat them up there will be no food and I cannot go anywhere. I eat so much horse meat I hear the horse heh-heh-heh-heh in my sleep." The superintendent on that reservation had butchered around two thousand horses in one year to feed the hungry.

Though the government still provided biweekly rations promised by federal treaty, the amount of coffee, flour, sugar, bacon, and beans was enough to last only a few days. The food itself was often rancid, the bacon yellow. "I do really think some of our deaths are caused by eating this bacon," one man said at the hearing.

During this time, while my family continued to leverage their Jew Flats land to impressive effect, their Lakota neighbors, like the majority of Native Americans, were, in the words of a federal report titled "The Problem of Indian Administration," "poor, even extremely poor . . . the health of the Indians as compared with that of the general population is bad . . . the general death rate and the infant mortality rate are high." In a daring choice for bureaucratic writing, the report concluded, "Several past policies adopted by the government in dealing with the Indians have been of a type which, if long continued, would tend to pauperize any race."

By then, two thirds of Indigenous people in the United States either had no land at all or didn't have enough land to subsist on. Allotment, the federal policy through which reservations were carved up into small pieces for individuals and families, would later be called "one of the most destructive Indian-specific policies ever enacted by Congress." In the course of forty-seven years, from 1887 to 1934, allotment, accessorized by policies like forced fee patents, had led to the total loss of around 90 million acres of Indigenous landholdings nationwide (that's the approximate size of nearly all of America's national parks combined). Let me reiterate this point: by the time the United States had ceased the practice of allotment, Indigenous landholdings had shrunk from 138 million acres to 48 million.

This entire era of Indigenous history in the United States, of allotment and leasing and forced fee patents, is rarely taught in American classrooms. I've heard historians jokingly referring to it as the time when nothing was happening to Native Americans. Even at the time when it was happening, when national headlines were preoccupied with the economic crash and the war in Europe, arguably the biggest news story out of Native America wasn't about land loss or starvation but an act of pageantry starring Joseph White Bull himself.

OVER THE COURSE OF THREE DAYS AT THE END OF JUNE 1926, THE UNITED States military staged a commemoration of what was then called Custer's Last Stand on the fiftieth anniversary of that battle. Invited by the War Department, both Indigenous and white veterans of the fight gathered in south-central Montana to, in the words of the promotional materials printed by the Chicago, Burlington and Quincy Railroad, "smoke the ancient peace pipe and to renew the pact of esteem and friendship which followed closely the tragic events on this spot in the heart of the Indian Country."

For all this talk of peace, the reality of Indigenous and non-Indigenous relations at the time was such that, when a contingent of military officers came to the Dakotas to invite Joseph White Bull and other Lakota elders to participate in the day's activities, many of the elders were afraid for their lives. "'I am afraid that, when the soldiers get us together there, they will get to thinking about their dead comrades and rub us out,'" White Bull remembered some of the invited Lakota as saying. Eventually, the men were convinced it would be safe and would give them great honor. Whether it did or did not depends entirely on whom you ask.

On the day of the reenactment, under a cloudless sky, more than fifty thousand spectators, including thousands of Indigenous people, watched from the hillsides surrounding the former battlefield. Joseph wore his eagle-feathered war bonnet and led 100 mounted Lakota and Cheyenne. Among them were dozens of warriors who, like Joseph himself, were veterans of the battle. On the opposite ridge, a column of more than 250 Seventh Cavalry approached, flags waving.

As the two groups neared, a U.S. general who had ridden with Custer raised a saber. In response, White Bull raised his open palm in a sign of peace. Meeting in the middle, the general "sheathed his sword," and he and White Bull shook hands.

This could not have been further from the bloody rout that had taken place fifty years before, when the Lakota killed Custer within less than a half hour. This was a chance for the government to recast Custer's defeat as an act of martyrdom, "to clear the path for civilization," in the words of a program from the event.

The following day, in a second act, a Lakota warrior literally buried a hatchet, a sign of peace, inside the tomb of the unknown soldier. One of the U.S. military veterans told the crowd that the great change that had come to the Plains since what he called "Custer's Last Battle" was not only a benefit to whites but was "a benefit to our Indian brother. They have learned a better way." As a sort of finale, the final speaker of the day closed the proceedings by saying the Indian "has accepted a life with new rights and new opportunities which the relentless march of civilization demands that he assume, and there is peace in his soul. He and his former foe have indeed Buried the Hatchet."

White Bull later told his biographer that this ceremony honored him and elevated his importance in front of thousands of people, including, he said "great generals, great chiefs." It was, he said, one of the happiest days of his life. But for his descendants, these sorts of reenactments, which continue today, aren't anything to celebrate.

Every June, the Hardin [Montana] Chamber of Commerce hosts a Little Bighorn Days festival complete with parade and a reenactment on the original Little Bighorn battle site. The event draws hundreds of people from across the country. In 2010, the actor who plays Custer every year was invited by the Department of Veterans Affairs to participate in a powwow color guard dressed as the Lieutenant Colonel. The Indigenous protest that followed made it clear that the narrative of acceptance was a lie and that the past was not, in fact, buried. The Húŋkpapȟa Lakota emceeing the powwow told *Indian Country Today* that inviting someone dressed as Custer was no less than a hate crime. "Custer and his men killed the wife and children of my grandfather. [He] should never have been allowed within our circle. . . . Would you take a Hitler impersonator to a synagogue?"

Doug only ever attended one reenactment of the Battle of the Little Bighorn. It was back in the early 1990s and, as he remembers, there were only Lakota people there. What struck him was how scared the white soldiers must have been in the face of his Grandpa Joe and the other fierce warriors. But his mind doesn't settle there—it leaps to how the embarrassing defeat of white soldiers was used to justify all the efforts to weaken Native Americans, and the more we talk, the more he thinks about what was taken from him and his family. It wasn't only land, he tells me, it was the history of the Lakota people that wasn't taught in boarding school. It was the Lakota language his own parents were afraid to teach him out of fear that his teachers would wash his mouth out with soap, like they had done to his older brothers who spoke Lakota. It was the insidious nature of growing up in a country that taught him he shouldn't be proud of his identity.

"When I was in Pierre Indian School, we liked to play cowboys and Indians," he says, remembering how the staff at the boarding school would show him and his classmates Western movies twice a week, movies in which, unlike at the Battle of the Little Bighorn, the Indigenous characters were almost always the ones slaughtered. "When we chose sides, nobody wanted to be Indian, everybody wanted to be John Wayne shooting the Indians with a pocketknife and a six-shooter. We wanted to be on the winning side."

8

✻✻✻✻✻

A SHANDA

On a wretched day in what was probably 1923, my aunt Rose stood under a blazing sun and watched smoke rise like a claw tearing apart the sky. By then, something that had been set in motion on the Cheyenne River and Standing Rock reservations decades before was barreling across Jew Flats, brakes off, gears whining.

The Sinykin cows, of which there are more pictures than the family dog, had likely contracted anthrax, a deadly and highly contagious disease that prevents blood from clotting. Sick animals will bleed out of every orifice. On that awful day, Rose's husband, Issie, shot their cows in the head, dug a pit, and torched them. It was worse than the house burning down. In the words of a neighbor, it was like setting a wallet on fire and watching it burn, if that wallet was alive, if that wallet had lungs.

Anthrax isn't normally a threat in the United States, but in July and August 1923, there was an epidemic of anthrax throughout more than half the counties in South Dakota. Around a thousand cows died. One theory for why this happened exposes how interconnected life was on the prairie, belying the notion that federal Indian policy affected only Indigenous people.

The rod-shaped bacteria *Bacillus anthracis*, which can cause anthrax, lurked deep underground. Over generations, cows can develop herd immunity to such a disease, but the cows brought from Texas to populate the non-Lakota ranches on Cheyenne River and Standing Rock most likely had little immunity, because anthrax rarely grew in the Southwest. During periods of drought, the grasslands, both on and off reservations, withered. Cows, never the smartest of creatures, dug deeper and deeper into the soil, searching for grass. What they unearthed killed them. Once anthrax took hold of cows on the reservation, it could spread across the prairie, carried by insects.

Such details of cause and effect were no doubt lost on the Sinykins. The thing that mattered, as they stood there for hours watching the horror show of flies and smoke, the metallic smell of blood filling the air, was that tragedy had found them again.

Growing up, I loved *Little House on the Prairie*, how, in every episode, the Ingalls family survived one dramatic threat after another. Now, I think it wasn't as Hollywood as it seemed to us in our warm Seattle house.

A short list of things that had happened to Aunt Rose on Jew Flats in the six years after Ruth and Jake left for Minnesota: Lightning struck her house and put her two-year-old daughter in a coma that "lasted several days." Rose's oldest son, still a young child, was running from a tornado toward the safety of the storm cellar when the wind picked him up, carrying him a long ways until he was somehow able to reach the ground, cling to the dirt, and survive. When another tornado tore Rose's sister Fanny's house from its foundation, Fanny and her husband and kids left for Utah. Rose was left on the prairie to care for her parents.

By then, Faige Etke's children were worried about their mother. Strict in her observance of Jewish dietary laws, she ate only meat that was ritually slaughtered, and prairie dogs weren't kosher. The rabbi who once koshered meat on Jew Flats now ran a butcher shop in Omaha. There was no electricity, no running water. Faige Etke regularly suffered from debilitating headaches. Rose wrote to her sister Ruth, now living in St. Paul, that if they didn't remove their mother from the prairie, she would die out there fighting with their father.

But for all their hardships, the Sinykins, unlike their Lakota neighbors, not only held on to their land but expanded it over the following decade, working to buy all the original Jew Flats homesteads and beyond.

Yes, they worked their tuchuses off. Yes, the government gave them loans. But a large part of what kept the ranch afloat came from a more intimate source of funds, money made not off the land but in St. Paul, where most of the Sinykins were now living.

WHILE AUNT ROSE STRUGGLED IN SOUTH DAKOTA, HER SISTER, ETTA'S mother, Ruth, was living an alternate version of the American dream. She and Jake and their children—my grandmother Pauline and her sister, Betty—lived on a lovely street lined with elms in St. Paul. They had a live-in maid, Oriental rugs, and closets of bespoke dresses. Ruth's brother Jack, the one who'd taken that photograph with Joseph White Bull, had also prospered. He lived for several years at the St. Paul Hotel, a grand

My grandmother Pauline riding her pony, a gift from her uncle Jack, circa 1922, St. Paul, Minnesota.

place of ballrooms and crystal chandeliers, where both politicians and gangsters regularly stayed. Jack owned racehorses and bred show dogs. He bought my grandmother, his niece, her very own pony.

Jack and Jake had enough money to buy an entire apartment building a few blocks from their own houses for Harry to manage, a means of getting Faige Etke off the prairie. The city Sinykins traveled together, often for months at a time. They went camping in Yellowstone, bringing live chickens in the back of their Model T to cook for dinner. They visited various sanitoriums throughout the Midwest and Florida, where they got massages and ate breakfast in their bathing suits. They rode ponies in Cuernavaca and smoked cigarettes in Mexico City. They become philanthropists, donating regularly to a host of mostly Jewish organizations that fed the hungry and housed the poor. As early as 1927, Jack started training guide dogs for the blind, likely the first person in the United States to do so. These good deeds are important to my family; they tilt the scales from the shanda, the Yiddish word for *shame*.

On the books, the money funding this big life came not only from a glove factory and real estate (the land in South Dakota had not only been mortgaged to start businesses but had more than doubled in value) but, most critically, from two different wholesale drug-and-cosmetics companies. But being in the drugstore business back then wasn't like owning a CVS.

Wholesale drugstores made their own products to line the shelves. Jack and Jake, in business together, manufactured paint, oil, shampoo, hair tonics, and all manner of fancy cosmetics, all of which required one key ingredient: alcohol. By this point, it was against the law to buy or sell alcohol as a beverage.

In 1919, a little more than two years after Ruth and Jake arrived in St. Paul, Congress passed the Volstead Act, extending state Prohibition laws, like South Dakota's, to the entire nation. Once again, Jake's primary source of income, his liquor store, was illegal. But there was no going back, not to the shtetl, not to the soddie. My family had been sold the American idea of progress, which, they understood, was measured in money and moved in only one direction. To survive and thrive, they traded their liquor stores for drug stores. They became bootleggers.

Here's how it worked, as far as I can tell: my great-grandfather and great-great-uncles took some of the alcohol they were legally permitted to acquire for the manufacture of their perfumes and hair tonics and sold it to Chicago mobsters and others who redistilled it into drinkable hooch. In 1922, Jack and Jake were allegedly part of what the papers described as a "rum ring," one that, in five months of that year alone, had made more than $1 million, the equivalent of more than $16 million today. Jake told a Minnesota newspaper that he'd had no idea anything illegal had gone on, that when he sold his denatured alcohol to a Minneapolis bluing company, he'd operated in good faith, believing that they simply made laundry soap. He and Jack were exonerated, at least that time.

Jack's older brother, Ted, also living in St. Paul and also formerly in the liquor business, began making Swee-Tone, "a high-grade home perfume spray." It was sold in two sizes: a diminutive quart bottle, with "a free mouth spray" included in each package, and glass gallon jugs, the exact size in which he'd once sold whiskey. Enclosed in the packaging were step-by-step instructions for how to avoid removing oil from the perfume so that it couldn't possibly be turned into something fit to drink.

Within three years, this perfume business was snared in part of an enormous case alleging that nearly two hundred individuals, including my uncle, had diverted one million gallons of legal, government-permitted alcohol to be used in the manufacture of drinkable alcohol. This $60 million enterprise was "the largest liquor conspiracy since the enactment of national prohibition." (When the indictment arrived, my uncle was away at a sanitorium in Michigan. He waited out the trial in California, afraid to come home for years for fear of arrest. Ultimately, he was exonerated.)

Another cousin, a former Jew Flats homesteader also now living in Minnesota, who had once been arrested and caught with $1,000 worth of liquor after a high-speed chase with a federal agent, was robbed in 1921, the bandits finding more than $1,300 of booze, diamond rings, and $1,800 in cash among his possessions.

Throughout this time and beyond, Ruth routinely wrote in her diary how late Jake was coming home, about his trips to Minneapolis, where "I know what he's doing. Everyone thinks I'm dumb, but I know everything."

The Sinykins, in 1926, on the steps of the new house of Jack and his wife, Genivieve, on Summit Avenue, "the most beautiful street in St. Paul." From left to right: Fanny, Jack, Faige Etke, Louie, Harry, Rose, Ted, and Ruth.

What she may or may not have known was that, at some point, her husband and brother were no longer simply selling their permitted alcohol to other men. According to family lore, trucks emblazoned with "La Salle," their drugstore's name, hauled alcohol to a farm up in Iowa, where my relatives had two large, underground vats. Rumrunners would come there to fill their trucks and then, presumably, distribute alcohol throughout the region.

DESPITE THE SINYKINS' STEADY SUCCESS SINCE ARRIVING IN THE UNITED States, I now see insecurity as a dominant thread in their story. Would they, Jewish immigrants, be accepted and safe here in America? The Sinykins' time on the ranch had elevated them as pioneers, as white settlers of the Plains, part of a master plan of domination. But with their move to St. Paul, their status was once again vulnerable and would remain so for decades.

One day, my aunt Etta, myself, and my cousins Cathi, Noah, and Aviva drive around St. Paul on a self-guided tour of former Sinykin and Kozberg homes. Etta, wearing big, black glasses and a blue-and-white outfit, is our tour guide, directing her daughter Cathi to "stop here, now stop," as she points to her childhood home. This stucco house lined with mature elms was on a "good street" far away from the neighborhoods of poor immigrant Jews.

Later in the evening, our family will gather around a long table to celebrate Shabbat, the Jewish sabbath. There'll be a big crowd; there often is, because, as Etta likes to quote a favorite phrase of her mother's, "you can always put more water in the soup." Before we eat, Etta will light the candles, the flames shining in her eyes, and, as we sing the blessings over wine and bread, our voices will bend and braid into each other. My family has been singing together in this way for generations, even when this embrace of culture was done with caution.

"It was so important to them to lose their foreign accents. They were looked down on if they were immigrants, but in their homes, they lived Jewish lives," Etta tells me. Though she herself swears she never suffered any real antisemitism throughout her childhood, she also told me this: "When we would go out to restaurants and we talked about something Jewish, we always lowered our voices. We didn't want anybody to hear our conversation."

What might sound a little paranoid now was smart at the time. By 1924, at least twenty-five hundred people in St. Paul were Ku Klux Klan members. Included on the rolls were more than a dozen police officers and elected officials. Jews were excluded from civic organizations, resorts, apartment buildings, and social clubs. Even some insurance companies publicly declared that they wouldn't "accept any risks on Jews." Minneapolis, just across the river, had the distinguished honor of being the nation's capital of antisemitism.

Such antisemitism, flourishing throughout the nation, had been a huge driver of Prohibition. The dominant narrative was that the Volstead Act was passed to protect the wives and children of alcoholic batterers who drunk up their paychecks while their families starved. This was partly true: the Woman's Christian Temperance Union had been working, for these reasons, to legislate alcohol abstinence since 1874. But arguably far more powerful was the Anti-Saloon League, the outfit that had been so effective in South Dakota. The ASL worried that the influx of immigrants from Europe, in particular Jews from Eastern Europe and Catholics from Italy and Ireland, threatened the character of white Protestant America. Their stated reason was the immigrants' devilish work in the liquor business.

Henry Ford, a major financial supporter of the Anti-Saloon League, would later describe how "the Jew is on the side of liquor and always has been." Historian Marni Davis, in her book, *Jews and Booze*, wrote that Ford spent money and time spreading his belief that Jews, with their financial power, "dragged American morality through the mud."

The reason so many Jewish immigrants worked as makers and purveyors of booze was, in fact, a hangover from the oppression that Jews faced in the old country. Back in Europe, where Jews generally couldn't own land and were usually excluded from artisan and craft guilds, selling and making liquor was one of the few stable jobs available. Russian noblemen preferred to put Jews in charge of their taverns, because, according to a Yiddish encyclopedia of Jews in Eastern Europe, their "sobriety and restraint were felt to lead to greater profits." In the nineteenth century, in the region of the Pale where the Sinykins and Kozbergs had lived, Jews had managed as much as two thirds of the distilleries in the area.

It's impossible to say how many Jews became bootleggers in America. It's not like anyone kept track, and arrest records tell only a small slice of the story. On the one hand, most stills nabbed by federal agents in the early 1920s were in the South, a region relatively unpopulated by Jews. However, there were so many Jews bringing Canadian alcohol across Lake Erie that it was nicknamed "the Jewish Lake." The family behind the Seagram's empire named one of their boats the *Mazel Tov*.

Even rabbis got in on the game: the Volstead Act allowed Jewish families to have as much as ten gallons of wine per year for use during religious ceremonies (that works out to about a bottle of wine a week per person, to be drunk, presumably, on Shabbat). Suddenly, rabbis with last names like Houlihan and Maguire claimed to have found "'religion' in the Hebraic persuasion," wrote Daniel Okrent, author of *Last Call: The Rise and Fall of Prohibition*. In 1925, the Bureau of Prohibition, the nation's liquor cops, arrested rabbis for procuring wine for the dead, for invented congregants, and for distributing vermouth, champagne, and crème de menthe, not exactly the fruit of the vine used for Jewish rituals. The bureau determined that rabbis and religious wine sellers were one of the major sources of illegal alcohol. Among my family's papers were receipts from the La Salle Drug Company showing their own rabbi buying more than 650 gallons of wine for sacramental purposes. (Of course, this could have been all above board. Or not.)

Regardless of whether Jews and other immigrants were, in fact, the largest pushers of hooch, Republican politicians used it to ride a wave of nativist anxiety. President Calvin Coolidge was reelected in 1924 on a tide of xenophobia, having told Congress the previous year that "America must be kept American. For this purpose, it is necessary to continue a policy of restricted immigration."

In keeping with this tenor, Congress worked to limit immigration, particularly from southern and eastern Europe, and the antisemitism wasn't subtle. The State Department had provided testimony to Congress that Jews were "subnormal," "twisted," "deteriorated," and "full of perverted ideas." One congressman dismissed Jews as the opposite of lauded immigrant settlers who "hewed the forests . . . conquered the wastes and built America. These are beaten folk." In this line of thinking, it's the Jews' failure to colonize America, to conquer Indigenous people, that made them un-American.

To restrict this inferior stock that was corrupting America, Congress and Coolidge banned or severely limited immigration from everywhere but the Aryan and Nordic parts of the world with the passage of the Immigration Act of 1924. The law effectively ceased Jewish immigration, stranding millions in Europe as the Nazis rose to power.

What is often dropped from this widely told piece of history is that, just a week later, driven by similar motives of white supremacy, Congress passed the Indian Citizenship Act. Four years after women obtained the right to vote, all Indigenous nationals, regardless of whether they'd become owners of private property or acted in a Last Arrow play, became American citizens. And yet, while citizenship was an expansion of individual rights, it stripped power from Indigenous governments and further gutted the Indigenous sovereignty created by treaties.

Once again, we return to Hitler. In 1928, he lauded this series of laws affecting Jewish immigrants and Indigenous citizenship as the world's prime example of völkisch, or nationalist, citizenship legislation. Hitler argued that America's exclusion of the "foreign body" of "strangers to the blood" from the ruling race gave Germany the legal authority to strip Jews of citizenship.

"In the early twentieth century the United States was not just a country with racism. It was *the* leading racist jurisdiction," writes James Whitman in *Hitler's American Model: The United States and the Making of Nazi Race Law.*

Motivated in part by rising antisemitism, a significant number of progressive Jewish Americans joined President Franklin Roosevelt's Interior Department throughout the 1930s to help create the Indian New Deal, a series of policies that, for the first time in the agency's history, weren't specifically intended to suppress and diminish Indigenous people, but instead to nurture sovereignty and self-determination. This era ended the policy of allotment, created Tribal governments, and formed a commission allowing Native Americans to seek redress for previous U.S. actions.

Felix S. Cohen, an Interior lawyer and the brains behind many reforms of the era, would later explain that "the Native American is to America what the Jew was to the Russian Czars and Hitler's Germany. For us the Indian tribe is the miner's canary, and when it flutters and droops we know that the poison gasses of intolerance threaten all other minorities in our land."

Though well intentioned, these reforms were created with limited input from Indigenous people themselves, and thus broadly missed the mark, calcifying colonialist assumptions that money is equal to land, and that the model of American democracy is superior to traditional forms of Indigenous governance and justice.

FOR MY AUNT ROSE, THE EXISTENTIAL ANXIETY WROUGHT BY BOTH HOME-
grown and European antisemitism was likely eclipsed by the endless struggle to make two thousand acres viable in a dry land. Years later, she would
list what they created, each animal and building a stitch on a wound. They
had 125 head of cattle, 45 horses, 150 chickens, 8 sows, 9 milk cows, 25 geese
and ducks, and 300 acres under cultivation with an annual crop of 300
bushels of corn and wheat, plus 9 miles of fence. They had 3 hired men. Their
home had 4 rooms, a second story, and a porch, all of it decorated with rugs
and drapes. They had a granary and a cattle shed. I list them all here because, even though it wasn't the life Rose wanted, it was a life she could
make, a life that, if she had been born Lakota, without access to loans and
mortgages, would've been impossible. When she and her husband, Issie,
struggled to pay their taxes, they were saved from foreclosure not only by
federal farm supports but also by their rich bootlegging relatives.

Rose and Issie Marsh (formerly Moskowitz) with fur coat and tractor on Jew Flats,
1920s.

But Rose, who'd dreamed of becoming a nurse or a secretary, had never liked the ranch. This was Issie's dream, not hers. By the late 1920s, she'd had enough of giving birth on the kitchen table beneath flies and wood-smoke. She'd had enough of tromping through snow to hang wet clothes on the line, clothes that, during winter, never fully dried. She'd had enough of smelling like cows and chickens, the odor seeping into her clothing and the curtains of the house. She'd had enough of dirt roads and a yard with-out grass. She'd had enough of the isolation. For years, she'd been begging Issie to move. For years, she'd written to her brother Jack, begging him to get Issie a job in St. Paul. According to her letters, Jack blew her off, ap-parently wanting the family to keep a foothold on Jew Flats. But everyone has a moment that breaks them, and for Rose, it was this:

Issie had been sick in bed for a month, and the work of both run-ning the ranch and caring for their three children fell to Rose. Every day, she had to hitch the buggy to the horse and drive her kids to school three miles away, dropping off the two eldest and then driving back with the youngest, who was not yet school aged, sitting on her lap. One day, on the way home, when she jumped off the wagon to open a gate, the horse bolted, dragging away the wagon with Rose's little girl alone in the back, screaming.

Rose knew that if the horse got past the outer gate, which was certainly open, he would head straight for home. It was rough terrain, and she was certain the wagon would crash and her daughter wouldn't survive.

"I ran and screamed and cried and God just seemed to hear my cries," wrote Rose years later. "A man was working on the fence and he heard me and I raved he should run to that gate and he saw the horse running and he grabbed his horse and got there just in time."

Rose fell to the ground, weeping and thanking God. When the man brought her the horse and buggy and her crying child, Rose, overcome, couldn't speak.

"After that, I made up my mind. No matter what, I am going to move."

By 1930, Rose and Issie had leased their ranch to the neighbors, and their fourth son, Herbie, was born in a hospital in St. Paul. Jack and Jake hired Issie to work in the factory of a new venture: the Cinderella Cosmetics Company. The job was good money, but it was good like a double shot of whiskey is good: potent, reliable, but often riskier than anticipated.

THE COSMETICS COMPANY WASN'T JUST A FRONT. IT WAS A REAL AND TRUE success, doing a steady business selling "color harmony" makeup for the new Technicolor film industry in Hollywood. Jack rented a nice house in Beverly Hills and made friends with movie stars. Then-famous starlets like Grace Hayes and Claire Windsor modeled the company's perfumes, face powder, and lipsticks. To showcase their products, and their success, Jack and Jake hired a Fox Studios art director to design and build, in St. Paul, an Art Deco marvel of a building that a magazine called "a veritable fairyland of chromium, silver and nickel plating."

By now, they were light-years from that shtetl life. How far is perhaps best portrayed by the following entries from my grandmother's journal from when she was almost fifteen. The year was 1931, in the midst of the Great Depression, when most people could barely afford food.

JUNE 6   I took a music lesson. I decided I would have my own recital in the fall.

JUNE 7   I played tennis with Helen today. I walked over there. I walked 21 blocks.

JUNE 8   I played tennis again. I walked about 10 blocks.

JUNE 10   We got a new car tonight a La Salle. It is green. It was Uncle Jack's old car. Mother was quite angry. I felt very melancholy and then very happy.

JUNE 12   I was in a recital and Betty was also. I played the "Fantasy in A Minor." Everybody liked it. I got a new blue silk dress with embroidery. I wore it.

JUNE 14   I played a game of tennis with Helen M. Went to a show and saw "Ladies' Man" with William Powell & Carole Lombard & Kay Francis.

JUNE 16   I played tennis with Helen M and walked 12 blocks. I wanted to go someplace tonight but I didn't.

JUNE 17   I went to a music lesson.

JUNE 19   Walked 10 blocks. Took a music lesson. I played tennis with Eleanor O. We had a good game. I went downtown and bought a dress myself (a green knit suit). It is real cute and I went to a show with Helen M.

Such wealth built from such risk came at a cost. One night, Ruth's youngest brother, Louie, who was also working for Jack and Jake, was jumped at the cosmetics factory by mobsters. Presumably there was some dispute over money. They pushed Louie down an elevator shaft and the fall broke his back. He spent eight months in hospitals and several more recovering in Ruth's living room.

Ruth was often "taking sick with nerves," according to journals and letters. She developed an ulcer and insomnia, regularly staying up so late it became early. Jack's wife, Genivieve, paced the floors at night. Jake contracted jaundice, the result of alcohol-related liver failure. The bonds of family cracked under the strain.

It seems like everyone was fighting all the time. Jake often slept in a chair instead of in bed with Ruth. My eighteen-year-old grandmother was told by her uncle never to trust anyone. Her mother, Ruth, and a close family friend sat her down and gave her unfortunate advice, telling her not to be a fool, not to be sincere, even with a future husband. "All my ideals of honor, truth and sincerity have fallen," wrote my grandmother in her journal.

And in the midst of all this trouble, the worst happened: in 1931, Faige

Etke, only sixty-seven years old, died. On her deathbed, she whispered to one of her sons, "Never sell the land."

According to the official death certificate, Faige Etke died of coronary sclerosis, but for the rest of her own life, Ruth would tell her daughters that her mother had died of a broken heart, presumably due to the bootlegging and all its attendant stress. My aunt Etta repeats it to me, "she died of a broken heart." Hiding in the line is another lesson, a way to underscore that our actions have impact beyond our own sphere, that we have the power to slay our elders with thoughtlessness.

I was raised to understand that, in Ashkenazi tradition, Jewish death happens twice. The first time is when your body dies. The second is when no one remembers you. As a way to sustain their memory far beyond the grave, we name our children for the dead. Ruth, newly pregnant with her third child, named her daughter, who was born the following spring, Etta Fay, for her mother. But the legacy of Faige Etke unspools far beyond her name.

I grew up understanding, without being told, that what matters is in the doing. Friendship and love are accrued by good deeds. My mom has always brought soup to sick people, tutored the kids in her neighborhood, marched to raise awareness for climate change, and donated money to all manner of good causes. I know most of my cousins do the same sort of thing. I now understand that this is, at least in part, because of Faige Etke.

Her gravestone, the tallest in the cemetery, is inscribed HER DEEDS DO PRAISE HER. Her children described her as an untrained social worker, dedicating her time in St. Paul to helping poor Jewish immigrants. Faige Etke brought them food and paid to send strangers to college and religious schools. She was known to give these new arrivals money for bus tickets so that they could visit out-of-town relatives. She did so many good works that one of the many charitable organizations where she volunteered dedicated a Torah in her name, the highest of honors.

Ruth told her own daughters never to play cards in their free time, that if they were fortunate enough not to have to work outside the home, they should volunteer. And they did: almost every one of Faige Etke's daughters

and granddaughters led at least one if not several major Jewish organizations, many of them dedicated to helping the poor. Despite or because
of Faige Etke's violent marriage, her daughters were all fierce, stubborn
women, each of them a fighter unafraid to stand up for herself and others,
a skill they would continue to need, a skill they would pass along to their
children, a skill that my aunt Etta has very clearly inherited.

IN THE LATE AFTERNOON OF A JUNE DAY IN 2021, ETTA AND I SIT ON
either side of her perfectly made white-and-blue bed. I have tears in my eyes.
She is not, as she told me earlier that day, "softhearted like you and Aviva."
She will not cry. But her face is tight and drawn with displeasure.

Over the previous few days, Etta has let me go spelunking in her closets. Layered within the strata of boxes, desk calendars, alumni magazines,
and medical journals was genealogical gold. The day before, with the con-
tents of a different box at our feet, Etta had told me how glad she was that
I was writing this book, how much she trusted me, how much it meant to
have a journalist, the daughter of her beloved niece, my mom, doing this
project.

Today, on the bed between Etta and I, sprawl dozens of letters handwritten in Yiddish, tax returns from 1911, forty-two receipts for donations
Ruth and Jake made to various Jewish organizations, and a box of more
than thirty of Ruth's diaries.

I pick up the green bound volume from 1937 and thumb through until
I find the entry for March 22. By this point, I've dug through old news clips,
and I know what I'm hoping to find.

On that day, Jack had been on trial in what was the grand finale of our
family shanda. By then, Prohibition had ended. The Eighteenth Amendment was repealed in 1933, and the Volstead Act was declared a complete
failure, having led to more drinking nationwide, not less. But in 1935, according to arrest records, Jack and more than twenty other business owners
in St. Paul had taken some of the tax-free denatured alcohol used in their
cosmetics companies and diverted it to stills, where it was cooked and
turned into "magic" whiskey. It was the biggest illicit liquor case since Pro-

hibition had ended. Jack and the others, some of them friends of the family, had allegedly robbed the government of hundreds of thousands of dollars in taxes.

My relatives disagree about how and why Jack was caught. Etta's version of the story, which is the one I knew growing up, was that Jack's business partner, her father, Jake, had said, *Jack, it's getting too hot. Jack, we got to get out.* But Jack, ignoring the advice, made one more deal and was caught by federal agents who had tapped his phone. The other version, told to me by other Sinykin descendants, is that both Jack and Jake, and maybe Issie, too, were all involved in this scam, but that Rose and Ruth begged Jack to take the fall for their husbands. Their daughters would never marry if their fathers went to jail, they told their brother. Jack only had sons, and thus, they believed, less to lose. Whatever the details, when the papers reported the arrests, only Jack was on trial.

Jack's attorney had advised him to plead guilty, promising that he could get Jack a good deal. But the trial was held not in St. Paul, as the lawyer had expected, but in Minneapolis, that hotbed of antisemitism. The family story is that a need to make an example of the Jews was both the reason for their arrest and for what happened next, but it's difficult to prove.

"What does that diary say? Read it aloud," Etta says that day in her bedroom. I hadn't been expecting this. I do as I am told. As I speak, my great-grandmother's looping blue script springs off the page and into the room.

"The day to be remembered. I shall never forget. We went to hear the trial, first we went to the wrong building. Later when we found the right place it was packed with people. I had an awful sick feeling. After listening to the sentence all went black before me and I fainted, next thing I knew I was in a cab going home. I nearly lost my mind from grief."

"I didn't know this," Etta says, shock drawing her blue eyes wide. "I've never heard this before. Keep reading."

I read page after page until the afternoon light leaves us. Within weeks, Jack was fined $800 and sent to Leavenworth Penitentiary for an eighteen-month sentence, leaving behind his twelve- and fourteen-year-old sons. Ruth wrote in her diary that every time she looked at her nephews, she cried.

When my throat goes dry from reading, I look up to see Etta staring at me, her nostrils flared in a way that is familiar—it's the exact expression my mom has when she is on the defensive, readying for a fight. The same expression, I've realized, I make, too.

"I don't want you to write this part."

I remind her that this wasn't happening in a vacuum. That what happened had to do with antisemitism, with how hard it was for them to get other work. I remind her that, for my generation, for my brother and cousins, the fact that our relatives were bootleggers isn't a shanda but something to be a little bit proud of. This was a bad law and our ancestors stuck it to the man.

Etta doesn't roll her eyes at me, but her voice does.

"They still broke the law. It was the worst time in our family. Don't write about it."

The sounds of the construction outside, of the air-conditioning coming through the ceiling vent, of the trees moving against the house, all of it stops. Time slips off the bed and oozes onto the floor. The bed between us grows as wide as the prairie. We sit together in silence for a long time.

Back home in Portland, I find it hard to do any writing at all. For months, I am stuck. I understand Etta's love for her parents and uncles. I understand why revealing this story of illegal activity complicates the official family story of hard work and good deeds. But to keep it cloaked feels uncomfortably similar to the way America fails to teach a more complete history of Indigenous land dispossession and genocide.

The award-winning historian Richard White confronted a similar dilemma when writing about his own family in *Remembering Ahanagran: A History of Stories*. In the book, he describes how his mother despaired about his inclusion of some malicious gossip. "Why is it necessary to tell these things? 'Have mercy,'" she told him. He responded, "If I edit out what might be offensive to my family . . . how can I have any standing to give offense to anyone's family? Do I take out everything that might give anyone offense?"

I call Judge Abby for advice. After listening to me, she pauses for a long minute before answering. By not telling a full story, she tells me, I'm not only absolving my family, I'm absolving the systems that put us in a position where bootlegging was our best option. If we keep secrets, we don't understand the past, and so, we don't have the opportunity to take responsibility and share the fault.

I keep thinking about it. I keep having trouble writing. On a cool, overcast day a few weeks before the Jewish New Year would wind around again, Rabbi Benjamin and I take a walk in his neighborhood, leaves crunching under our feet. He reminds me that these fears and concerns of mine are not new, they had plagued me since I first set down to write this book. He tells me again what he has been telling me all along: be compassionate and be honest. This has been a key piece of the Jewish approach to making amends for nearly one thousand years.

The twelfth-century Sephardic philosopher and rabbi Moses ben Maimon, known as Maimonides, arguably one of the most prolific and influential Jewish scholars, wrote a ten-chapter Laws of Repentance, which codifies a playbook for repairing relationships. Of the six steps he directs the person who has caused harm to take, an apology doesn't occur until step five. First, he writes, we must stop doing the harm. Next, confess as specifically as possible what harm you have caused and, ideally, say this truth out loud in public.

Rabbi Danya Ruttenberg, in her book *On Repentance and Repair: Making Amends in an Unapologetic World*, details how Maimonides's model helps us today to "envision a way forward." When I call her and ask why it's so important not only to be honest with yourself and the person you've hurt but to say what you've done in public, she tells me, "'cause you've got to own your stuff, man. It's accountability."

A few weeks later, during a bris that I watch over Zoom, one of my cousins texts me that he's found a stash of old letters from Aunt Rose. What I read gives me the final nudge I need to move forward with this story.

"I really feel that a family should not be raised up not knowing the truth as I feel it's not right," Rose wrote to my grandmother Pauline in 1963. "The truth does come out, no matter how long ago. As the old saying is, 'oil always comes to the top of water.' As my mother [Faige Etke] always used to say to me, 'we are never too old to learn, no matter how old we are and we have to be able to always take the bitter with the sweet.'"

To me, the Jewish involvement in bootlegging and the reality that some of them, like Jack, got caught shows that they were human. They made mistakes. Knowing this about them makes it possible for me to judge myself with more compassion, without the expectation of living up to these picture-perfect ancestors who only ever worked hard and prayed to God and posed for photographs in flattering clothing.

Jack's life didn't end at Leavenworth. After getting out early on good behavior, he resumed training guide dogs for the blind, taking what had been a hobby and making it a life's work. In the end, he helped more than a thousand people, including scores of war veterans, a U.S. senator, and a woman who was not only blind but deaf. These good deeds earned him a presidential pardon from Harry Truman in 1952. Jack's two sons, decorated war heroes, became a doctor and a lawyer and lived lives filled with good work.

And yet, due to Jack's arrest and jail time and the associated debts from legal fees, he lost the thing he had used repeatedly to build his wealth: in 1938, while he was still in jail, his wife, Gen, sold 2,360 acres of their land on Jew Flats to Jack's youngest brother, Louie, the one gangsters pushed down the elevator shaft. That same year, possibly due in part to a fine for his involvement with bootlegging, Issie and Rose couldn't pay the taxes on their land. They defaulted on a federal farm loan, of which more than $5,800 remained to be repaid. After what Etta remembers as the worst fights of her parents' marriage, Jake agreed to bail out his in-laws and pay their taxes and the interest on the loan. The cost was huge: all of Jack's, and Rose and Issie's, land on Jew Flats, including Faige Etke and Harry's homestead, was transferred to Ruth and Jake. For years, Rose and Jack argued that they had put so much into the land they deserved to have it back, but Jake never released them from their debt. They never owned a piece of Jew Flats again. For Rose, this loss throbbed like a bad bruise until the end of her life.

I don't want to diminish the pain they felt about losing their land. I know it was awful. But what was about to happen to the White Bulls and hundreds of other Lakota, the ways their land would be taken, puts Jack's and Rose's losses in perspective.

9

A TRIPLE THREAT

Doug White Bull was born in 1943 on the banks of the Missouri River into a family rich in both children and land. Rich because they had enough, and rich because they had so much to lose. The youngest of eight brothers and three sisters, Doug grew up playing in the giant cottonwoods that clustered along the banks. The trees were so wide, "like this," he says, holding his hands far apart. "You'll never see trees like that here again." Deer and other animals frequented the forests, and his dad, a good hunter, could feed his family when there was nothing else to eat.

Their land, Doug likes to say, was eight miles south of nowhere. When he lived there, on the banks of the Missouri, he'd never heard the word "bored" in his life. In summer, he'd swim the river and fish for walleye and catfish from its banks. He and his siblings would catch wild gophers, rabbits, and sometimes even baby skunks and turn them into pets. He'd run barefoot across the tawny buttes that rose above their house. A voracious reader, he sprinted through all his sisters' stashed books: first the Bobbsey Twins, then the paperback Westerns, then the romances. When he was very young, the White Bulls had dozens of cows and horses, and his dad, Jacob, the World War I vet, would put up hay and a big garden every year. They'd pick wild fruits and berries that grew along the riverbanks, and all summer long, Doug's mom, Julia, canned—insurance for the long winters.

Some spring and summer nights, Jacob would sit on a big rock behind

Doug (right) with his sister Rita White Bull on the
old land near the Missouri River, circa 1946.

the house and play his violin. The sound of Mozart or Beethoven would
echo up and down the river, threading the leaves of the cottonwoods as the
sun slid away. Doug, watchful of his dad's dark moods, would sit out of
sight, his back against a corner of the house, listening to Jacob make that
violin sing. "Oh," Doug remembers, "that was good."

Life wasn't perfect. Jacob, haunted by his time in the Great War and
other more local traumas, drank too much. There was always enough food,
but there was always concern that there might not be enough. Their frame
house had no running water or electricity. The nearest hospital was forty
miles of dirt road and gumbo, that heavy clay soil, away. Despite the lack
of roads, social workers found their way to the house, demanding Doug
and his siblings enroll in federal boarding schools. In those schools, Doug
spent the worst days of his life. Throughout Doug's childhood, this place
of rolling hills and wide trees, this land the United States had allotted to

his grandparents and parents, this definition of home, became as endangered as the buffalo.

With the nation on the brink of yet another war, the federal government was looking to take the money it had promised, by treaty, to spend on Native Nations and spend it instead on empire building. The latest American offer to "free" Indian Country was, in reality, the old dish of Indigenous land dispossession and assimilation that it had been serving cold for more than a century. In the thick of Doug's youth, when Indigenous peoples in America were living with roughly fifty-five million acres, less than 4 percent of the land with which they'd lived only a century earlier, Congress set out to take the rest using dams, bus tickets, and the law in a series of policies known as the Pick–Sloan Program, Relocation, and Termination. Without land, the thinking went, Native Americans could be pushed into the melting pot where their sense of culture and identity would fully dissolve.

Spin the helix, and these federal assimilationist policies of the 1940s and '50s are doubly problematic: in this same era when the United States viewed Indigenous land rights and sovereign status based on ethnicity as suspect, the country helped establish Israel as a Jewish state to which any Jew, worldwide, could emigrate. That my family helped with this Zionist cause but not with the plight of the Lakota is an inconsistency worth sharing. That Ruth was expanding our family's landholdings at the exact time that the Lakota were continuing to lose theirs is another.

WHEN JULIA WHITE BULL WAS PREGNANT WITH DOUG, A QUICK SPRING thaw far to the north in Montana melted the ice-clogged Missouri River. Below their house, the river rose with a roar. Its muddy water carried haystacks, old homesteader shacks, and deer swimming desperately toward shore. Downriver, in southern South Dakota and Nebraska, water flooded the banks. Six people died, and Omaha's roads, buildings, and other infrastructure incurred $8 million in damage. Over the next two years, the river flooded several more times, ruining farmers' crops and wrecking more houses and cities, running up a price tag of more than $100 million.

The public demanded relief and help. The solution, cooked up by a federal engineer who had earned esteem by building roads in war-torn Europe but had near zero experience with flood control, was to build five giant earthen dams, among the largest in the world at the time. These would turn the Missouri into a series of lakes that, ostensibly, could be controlled. The project, known as the Pick–Sloan plan, would bring power and irrigation to thousands and would reshape the entire Missouri River basin, every river, every creek. To prevent flooding in large cities, other places upriver would need to flood. The destruction of land would be borne almost entirely by reservation communities. Dam locations that would have affected majority-white towns such as Pierre, Bismarck, and Williston were reconsidered and relocated to instead submerge the prime waterfront lands of three of the five Lakota reservations created by the Great Sioux Agreement, as well as four other reservations along the river.

Using the authority afforded to him by America being at war and the resultant need to develop power to run its factories, President Franklin D. Roosevelt quietly signed off on the Pick–Sloan Missouri Basin Program in 1945. This skirted the spine of what was legal. Even though the *Lone Wolf* decision allowed the United States to take Indigenous lands, Indigenous Nations were still supposed to be consulted and reimbursed—a point that exactly one congressman pointed out, a point that the remaining five hundred and thirty ignored. It would take another four years before the Lakota and other impacted Nations realized the full effect the dams would have on their land and their citizens. By then, there was scant opportunity for true consultation. By then, the U.S. Army Corps of Engineers had already spent approximately $65.5 million of the taxpayer's money to start preliminary construction.

The Bureau of Indian Affairs declared that the flooding of the Missouri was, in fact, good news for the Lakota. As the agency wrote in a report, without access to fertile bottomlands where they could hunt and forage, where they could exist without relying on agriculture, they would be disconnected from the one thing keeping them from "merging with the total population" and evolving beyond their "primitive status." In 1953, the then-director of the bureau insisted that the dams would expedite that old idea of cultural evolution and "lead the Indians toward more and more assimilation and integration."

The Lakota themselves saw the situation a bit differently.

The impact of the Oahe Dam "cripples the entire reservation popula-tion," Louis Thief, an enrolled citizen of Standing Rock who lived in the same area as the White Bulls, said to a 1955 congressional hearing. He likened the flooding of the land, what he called "the best place," to an atomic bomb that "will explode and hurt us."

More than six decades later, historian Nick Estes, a citizen of the Lower Brule Sioux Tribe, whose reservation was also flooded by a Pick–Sloan dam, clarified Thief's assertion.

"The Pick–Sloan dams were a twentieth-century Indigenous apoca-lypse," he wrote in *Our History Is the Future*. "[It] was a new round of dispossession, a new round of enclosure, that used the most precious resource—water—as its weapon to eliminate and destroy nations and the land on which they depended for life."

And in the midst of this latest trial, the Lakota faced another federal attack on their rear flank. This one wasn't only a threat to their land and welfare but to their very existence as a Nation.

IN THE WAKE OF WORLD WAR II, CONGRESS WAS LOOKING TO CUT FEDERAL spending in the face of rising inflation. Cold War conservatives replaced the New Dealers and aimed their sights at social programs, with the Indian Bureau at the top of its list. Almost every Jewish bureaucrat at a high level at the Department of the Interior fled the scene during this era, and many of the reforms implemented during the thirties and early forties fell victim to anemic funding and intentional bureaucratic molasses. The Indian Claims Commission, for example, created to be a place where both Indigenous peo-ple and Indigenous Nations could seek redress for harmful federal policies, considered only 12 percent of the 850 claims on its docket within its first decade and awarded less than 2 percent of the requested compensation.

As early as 1947, Republicans in Congress were asking the Bureau of Indian Affairs for a list of Native American Nations that no longer needed federal financial support. The rhetoric was thick on freedom, thin on input from Indigenous people, and coated with racist overtones.

"The Indian population is no longer a pure ethnic group. Rather, it represents a mélange of 'full bloods' and people of mixed ancestry," read a 1949 report by the Hoover Commission, a group of twelve white men chaired by former president Herbert Hoover and appointed by President Harry S. Truman to recommend budget cuts. It called for "complete integration" of Indians "into the mass of the population as full, tax-paying citizens."

Based on the Hoover Commission's suggestions, Congress and President Truman set out to craft a series of laws that would eliminate the Bureau of Indian Affairs and erase reservations, turning all Indigenous land in America, roughly more than fifty-five million acres, into private property. Like the Allotment Act, like the Competency Commissions, this new effort, known today as Termination, aimed to dismantle centuries-old government-to-government relationships between the United States and Native Nations.

This would both save money and make money. By converting reservations into land that could be sold and taxed, some of the last remaining undeveloped property in America could be grazed, farmed, drilled, logged, and paved. Indigenous lands contained 20 percent of America's energy resources and huge swaths of uncut forests.

It's unsurprising that Republicans loved Termination, given how much money was on the line. To sell this to their Democratic colleagues, conservatives cloaked the policy in the language of civil rights and tyranny.

"Do-gooders," said E. Y. Berry, a South Dakota congressman and leading Termination advocate, "condemn segregation in the South, they themselves are demanding that the American Indian be segregated, that he be placed on a reservation." These reservations, he continued, with lands held communally by Indigenous Nations, were "as ungodly as Communist Russia."

Ignoring the 374 treaties that Native American Nations had signed in which the United States government promised to provide schools and hospitals in exchange for land—what the writer Louise Erdrich likens to paying rent—those in favor of Termination labeled Indigenous dependence on such services as loafing.

"They want all the benefits of the things we have, highways, schools, hospitals, everything that civilization furnished, but they don't want to help pay their share of it," said Senator Arthur Watkins, a Utah Republican who championed Termination. A Mormon who believed that it was his religious duty to assimilate and convert brown-skinned people, Watkins likened his Termination legislation to the Emancipation Proclamation.

Despite being a clear subversion of sovereign-nation status, these arguments, delivered during the heart of the Cold War to an American population largely uneducated about the history of Indigenous Nations and their unique rights, found purchase. In 1953, Congress passed House Concurrent Resolution 108, which declared its intention to abolish the federal relationship with all Native Nations. At last, proponents cheered, America would be out of the Indian business. Passing with bipartisan support within two months of introduction, the law had effectively no opposition. Legislation passed two weeks later allowed for the transfer of all services previously provided by the federal government to states. Of course, most states had nothing close to the infrastructure or budgets to provide adequate health care, education, and policing to Indigenous communities in the first place.

This affront to Native American sovereignty sparked widespread activism throughout the Indigenous community. A new kind of Indigenous warrior emerged, one who recognized the need to use the skills of the oppressors to fight for the survival of Indigenous people and culture in courtrooms, in newspapers, and at the ballot box. These men and women would slow down and ultimately overturn Termination, and yet, one of the oldest and most vaunted Mnicoujou Lakota warriors would take no part in this battle. In 1947, Joseph White Bull died at the approximate age of ninety-eight.

ON AN OVERCAST DAY IN THE SPRING OF 2021, DOUG AND I ARE DRIVING IN my rental car, trying to find Joseph White Bull's gravestone, but we are lost, for the third time in as many hours.

"Did we pass a house?" Doug asks me, his eyes shaded by his black felt fedora. At his side is a gold-handled cane. I tell him there's a butte on the left. Cell service sucks on much of Standing Rock and Cheyenne River, and my phone isn't working. Knowing this might happen, I'd brought an actual map, but I can't make sense of it. I'm entirely dependent on Doug's memory.

"You've gone too far," he says, irritated. "Turn around."

After issuing this directive and telling me parts of an old story, he falls asleep, suddenly, chin on chest, mouth open. He's thirsty because I forgot to pack water. He's hungry because I didn't know that there is nowhere to get food on this part of the reservation, no restaurants, no gas stations, no grocery stores. I drive the spine of green hills that drop like curtains on either side of a narrow red road. I see only my sweaty palm prints on the steering wheel.

By this point, it has been almost two years since I first met Doug. Since then, we've been speaking regularly on the phone for an hour or more at a stretch and meeting when the constraints of the pandemic have made it possible. At seventy-seven, he's almost entirely blind, his sight reduced to shadow and outline. I didn't know then that it could get any worse, though of course it could.

More than a year into the COVID-19 pandemic, death has cut a wide swath across both the Standing Rock and Cheyenne River reservations, like it has across Native American communities nationwide. Indigenous people in the United States had infection rates more than three and a half times that of white populations during the first months of the pandemic. The disparity is stark: I personally don't know a single person who has died from the coronavirus, but a Lakota friend on Cheyenne River has lost seventeen friends and family members to the disease. The high rates of diabetes in Lakota communities—in large part the result of starch-, sugar-, fat-, and cholesterol-rich foods provided as federal food rations—has put people here at high risk.

There are so many funerals happening during my visit that there's a run on star quilts, the traditional Lakota blankets that cover coffins. People are calling quilters on distant reservations, desperate for their spares. Everyone I interview and visit with has at least one if not two funerals to attend within a week. These are not all deaths from COVID. Some are the result, most people say, of the stress of living during a pandemic. Doug's oldest son, Chicky, has died of a heart attack; his wake will be the next day. I stare at Doug in the seat beside me, his body held by the seat belt, and tighten my grip on the wheel.

Eventually, far below us, I see Cherry Creek, its blue water shining like a compass needle. Back on track, we soon reach the town of Cherry Creek near the southwestern corner of the Cheyenne River Reservation, where Joseph spent most of the final years of his life. When we go to the wrong cemetery on the wrong side of town, a young man in a beat-up van rolls down his window. When I introduce Doug, the young man kindly offers to lead us to the right place. "Is that the famous basketball coach?" he asks me as he jumps out of his rig to open the cemetery gate for us. The young man has been here a lot lately, he tells me. He has buried four people out here this past week alone.

Doug is unsteady on his feet. He now stumbles sometimes as he walks, but he gets down on one knee beside Joseph's gravestone and speaks to him in Lakota. I turn my recorder off and look away, listening to the birdsong, smelling the willows along the banks of the creek.

To the end, Joseph White Bull had fought the forces of assimilation. He kept his hair long, braided with blue calico. He wore moccasins. When children would pass his house on the way to school, he'd wave and speak to them in Lakota, often wearing his eagle-feathered war bonnet. Outside his log cabin was a tipi and a Chevrolet he never learned to drive.

The stories I've heard and read about him tell me that, like Doug, he cared about self-sufficiency. When Joseph went deaf in his old age, he bought a "speaking trumpet," complete with tube attachment, from the Sears catalog. He never had running water or indoor plumbing. Like Doug, he was known for his quick wit and his love of a practical joke. And he never quit pushing for justice over the taking of the Black Hills and the slaughter of the buffalo. "Always a champion of the cause of his people," wrote a newspaperman a few years before Joseph died. Another called him "a hero out of Homer."

Back in the car, Doug sighs, deep in thought. As we drive away, he tells me, "Many things happened in my life, I feel he was there watching out for me. I'm very proud to be related to Grandpa Joe. He lived a really great life."

With Joseph White Bull's death in 1947, one of the last living connections to the pre-reservation era was severed. How strange he might have found it, after everything he had endured as a young man that forced him onto the reservation and coerced him to stay there under threat of death, that now, under a program called Relocation, the United States would push his descendants to move away.

BY THE EARLY 1950S, A POSTER WITH PHOTOS OF A CHICAGO BEACH WAS as commonplace on reservations throughout the Northern Plains as snow and mud. STUCK IN YOUR TEEPEE? read one flyer pinned to the wall in a reservation grocery store. A WAY OUT THROUGH RELOCATION SERVICES FOR A HEAP-A-LOT OF LIVING.

This was the new and improved, modern version of assimilation and the third federal program, after Termination and the federal dams on the Missouri River, that threatened Lakota existence during Doug's childhood. The feds had changed their mind. No longer would they try to turn Indigenous people into lovers of private property through agricultural enterprise. There was, they said, simply not enough land left for every Native American to become a farmer. This was largely the result of the allotment policies of fifty years earlier that had, intentionally, failed to set aside enough land for future generations and instead sold more than half of the Standing Rock and Cheyenne River reservations to non-Indigenous farmers. Rather than attend to the legacy of such harms, the solution, cooked up by the same people working to terminate Native Nations entirely, was to remove able-bodied Indigenous people from the reservations and send them to cities. There, the bureaucrats suggested, they'd not only learn to be American but would fill labor shortages in an industrialized postwar economy.

The brains behind what would be called the Voluntary Relocation Program was Dillon S. Myer, a man whom a former interior secretary called "Hitler and Mussolini rolled into one." During World War II, Myer had been head of the War Relocation Authority, which forced more than one hundred thousand people of Japanese descent away from their homes and businesses into rural internment camps, where armed guards in towers and barbed wire fences constrained their freedom. When President Truman put Myer at the helm of the Bureau of Indian Affairs in 1950, Myer filled the ranks with staff that had worked to imprison Japanese Americans, including one who'd been called "the great mover of people." Myer touted Indian Relocation in the same manner that Watkins touted Termination, as a program of "liberation" that would help Indigenous people escape reservations, which Myer compared to "large detention camps." Under Myers's command, the agency would weaponize not only freedom but science.

In reams of reports, the BIA used soil health and overpopulation as justification for sending the Lakota away. The land itself, it wrote, had become unsustainable, too anemic to support all the people living on reservations in the Dakotas and throughout the country. The bureaucrats failed to mention that, by the 1950s, white people, not Lakota, were monopolizing reservation lands. On Standing Rock, Lakota had access to only 17 percent of the reservation; on Cheyenne River, that rate was closer to 20 percent. The U.S. Interior Department leased the rest to non-Native ranchers. Yet, there were no reports about moving white people away.

In 1953, under Myers's supervision, the BIA sent staffers onto reservations nationwide armed with slideshows, scripts, or shiny brochures. Their purpose was to recruit young men and women of working age, strapping in mind and body and able to speak English, to move to Los Angeles, Denver, or Chicago—cities with large populations and year-round work. Distributed on every reservation in the Dakotas, the slideshows depicted Native Americans working in stores, happily answering phones, going to church, playing basketball, it even showed sisters working side by side on an assembly line. The shows ended with pictures of Lake Michigan glimmering not unlike the Missouri River. The difference, it claimed, was that Lake Michigan belonged "to everybody," with beaches that, unlike on the Missouri, were "free for everybody to use."

BIA field staff were instructed to tell success stories about Relocation, according to an agency handbook. Helpfully, it described what exactly success meant: "the purchase of a home, or a car, or telling of a job promotion." The BIA denied widespread rumors that it had quotas of Indigenous people to enlist for Relocation, but there was certainly pressure to recruit. One employee later confessed that his bosses threatened to shut down his office if he didn't convince more people to go on Relocation. By 1956, the agency had a "goal" (not a "quota") to relocate no less than five thousand people within the year.

The pressure was even greater on those working to relocate people from the reservations about to have their land flooded by dams on the Missouri. A BIA report from 1951 (a year before Relocation became an official program), describes how dramatic the effect of the Oahe Dam would be on the Lakota, how the remaining reservation land would be insufficient for everyone then living there to be successful ranchers. The report recommended that "those who are physically and psychologically qualified for life away from the reservation" be placed in "industrial employment." Once again, the bureaucrats spun a harm as if it were a benefit, as other BIA reports pointed to the "opportunity" presented by the flooding of reservations. As Nick Estes wrote, "put plainly, the dams would speed up termination and relocation."

From what I've read and been told, it seems that most people went on Relocation for the same reasons my own family left Russia: it was the best bad option and provided hope of a safer, better life.

By the 1950s, Native Americans living on reservations in the Dakotas were making about $950 a year, while whites in those states made an average of nearly $4,000. In 1957, nearly three fourths of all Indigenous households in South Dakota received relief or welfare payments for at least part of the year.

While many of my relatives who had served in World War II were eligible, like tens of thousands of other GIs, for federal loan assistance to buy a home, Native American veterans living on reservations were virtually excluded from the program. The racism in nearby cities was pervasive, making it hard for them to get jobs off the reservation. In 1954, Herschel V. Melcher, the mayor of Chamberlain, South Dakota, wrote to Senator Francis Case that "if they [Lakota] come in here it will be necessary to declare an open season on Indians. . . . We do not intend to let an Indian light around here at all. We do not want to live with them and we see no reason why we should, we don't want them in our schools, the hospital is plenty."

Throughout the state, there were signs on storefront windows reading INDIAN TRADE NOT WANTED. If you were Indigenous, finding a place to rent off the reservation was often impossible. The opportunity for young Lakota to move to a place so big that no one would care if you weren't white had a certain appeal. Over the following two decades, an estimated 750,000 Native Americans would grab those one-way bus tickets and move to the big city.

THREE OF DOUG'S OLDER BROTHERS SIGNED UP, EXCITED FOR THE CHANCE at a new start in Chicago, but what they found there wasn't exactly what the slideshow had promised.

"Having grown up in the country, it was hard to be around so many people," Doug's nephew Frank says about his parents' time in Chicago. Maybe they, like other new Indigenous arrivals, felt small in the shadow of the tall buildings, the noise of traffic overwhelming. Maybe they, like others, had never been anywhere as busy as the bus station.

Upon arrival, the Bureau's Relocation Office had given them a couple hundred bucks to last until they could find work. Like other new arrivals in cities nationwide, they were offered a modicum of help, from an "overworked and undermanned staff," in the form of lessons on how to use a city map, open a bank account, buy food at a grocery store, and get a telephone.

Frank's mom found administrative work. But the money, says Frank, was barely enough to live on. Most Native Americans in Chicago had job experience in farming and no more than an eighth-grade education, which didn't qualify them for great jobs.

Doug's brothers joined a throng of Indigenous men and women waiting in long employment lines. The prize at the end was usually not an office job but day labor, work that was short term and low paid. Run by middlemen who would take up to 20 percent of an already slim check, the day-labor market was later likened by one BIA employee to slave labor. Overall, Relocation was, in the words of a future commissioner of the BIA, "essentially a one-way ticket from rural to urban poverty."

In an effort to speed the rate of assimilation, the agency often placed Native Americans in apartments far away from one another, repeating the history of the Indian Agents spreading Indigenous land allotments miles apart. This was especially notable in Chicago, a place that, like Sioux City and St. Paul, was characterized by its ethnic neighborhoods. The Irish, the Italians, and the Poles all dominated various parts of town where people of shared backgrounds helped one another, set each other up in business, and gave each other loans. Isolated in high-rises, many Lakota went without the support that people like my ancestors had repeatedly relied upon as new arrivals.

Doug tells me it was loneliness, as much as a thin paycheck, that drove one of his brothers to seek comfort in Chicago's Indian bars. Even when that brother left the city and returned to Standing Rock, the shadow of alcoholism followed him home. This wasn't an unusual story.

The BIA measured the success of the relocated not on how happy they were, or how successful they'd become at their jobs, or how well their children did at school, or any marker that truly indicates a person's satisfaction. Instead, the agency measured its success on whether people stuck around. This marker, like so much about the BIA, quickly became political.

The bureau claimed that no more than 30 percent of those who went on Relocation returned to reservations. Indigenous rights groups claimed it was closer to 90 percent. (After a few years, the agency stopped collecting data, explaining that it gave critics of the program ammunition to shut it down.) Those who stayed formed pan-Indigenous communities and support groups, sent their children to college, and chased a version of the American dream similar to the one my family followed. By 1963, approximately a third of all Standing Rock citizens lived away from the reservation; on Cheyenne River, that percentage was about 40 percent. Today, more than two thirds of all Indigenous people in the United States live not on reservations but in cities.

But for those Lakota who didn't stay, the home they returned to wasn't the one they'd left.

DURING THE YEARS THAT DOUG'S BROTHERS WERE IN CHICAGO, THE U.S. Army Corps of Engineers, working from the plans that had been signed off on in 1945, turned the Missouri River into a series of dammed reservoirs.

Completed in the 1960s, the Pick–Sloan Program destroyed more Indigenous land than any other public-works project in American history, diminishing Indigenous lands in the Dakotas by 6 percent. That is the equivalent of the United States losing both Montana and Idaho.

The lakes formed by the dams flooded more than 205,000 acres on the eastern edges of the Standing Rock and Cheyenne River reservations. Among the flooded plains was the Lakota's most valuable land, including fields and more than 90 percent of forestlands on Cheyenne River.

The large rocks on which Doug and his family once sat to watch the river and feel its cool breeze were submerged. All of that was gone. Gone were the cottonwoods and the ash and the oak. Gone were the chokecherries and the buffalo berries, the gooseberries, the currants, and the plums. Gone were the timbers Lakota used for building and for fence posts. Gone was the kindling and logs for cookstoves and woodstoves, the main source of heat for more than four hundred families. Gone was the wild game and native fish that the White Bulls and others had long counted on. Gone were the wild mint, wild onion, honey, the oak and red willow used for ceremony. Entire towns, including Kenel, where three generations of White Bulls had lived, were drowned and rebuilt miles away in a slapdash style.

On a hot day in the summer of 1959, some white men hired by the government loaded the White Bulls' two-story frame house onto a flatbed, bulldozed a road where there'd never been one, and hauled Jacob and Julia's home thirty miles west. When they arrived at the new location, the rifles and guns that had been hanging on their wall were gone, just one more theft on top of everything else.

The dams destroyed more than 550 square miles of Indigenous lands in the Dakotas, forcing more than nine hundred Native American families to move. On Cheyenne River, 30 percent of all reservation denizens were forced to relocate. The equivalent percentage for the entire U.S. would be if everyone in New York, Texas, and California was forced inland. That's the same as the estimated percentage of how many Jews left the Pale of Settlement and came to America at the turn of the twentieth century.

With uncharacteristic terseness, Doug refers to this era as simply "another horrible time for our tribe." The full impact of the Oahe Dam on both the Cheyenne River and Standing Rock reservations has been described by economists, a group not known for hyperbole, as "an irreplaceable loss." One Tribal Leader called it "the gutting of our reservation." The legacy of this period is a gash that runs deep, the healing prevented by an ongoing sense of loss.

For most people, their new homes, far from the shores of Lake Oahe, were much more desolate places, where, as one elder put it, even "the jackrabbit carried a box lunch." Unable to plant gardens or raise their own animals, many Lakota became dependent on United States Department of Agriculture commodity foods. The highly processed foods—canned meat and vegetables—were high in sugar, starch, salt, and fat, delivering an "Insulin Holocaust," in the words of one Muscogee Creek artist. After the forced resettlement caused by the Oahe Dam, the rate of diabetes skyrocketed across the reservations.

The economic loss to the Lakota on the Cheyenne River and Standing Rock reservations has been estimated as the equivalent of nearly $1.5 billion today. In the 1950s, Congress compensated those two communities with the equivalent of less than 20 percent of that value. The Lakota on Cheyenne River, for example, received around $22 an acre. Some non-Indigenous ranchers living downstream received as much as $200 an acre from the Army Corps for their flooded land, according to a 1957 article in Sioux Falls' *Argus Leader*. The relatively low price the United States paid the Lakota is further clarified by a 1963 contract from the Department of the Interior that I found at my aunt Etta's house, made out to my great-grandmother Ruth. For an easement to run a transmission line from the Oahe Dam across Jew Flats, the agency paid Ruth approximately $24 an acre, and unlike the White Bulls' flooded property, her land could still be accessed by the family and used to graze cattle.

Not only was the $22 an acre what Doug calls "peanuts," it was also restricted. Many Lakota could use the money only if they participated in specific educational and economic programs. Much of these funds, to help "rehabilitate" those Lakota who'd been resettled, were set aside as loans for cattle and farming equipment. On Cheyenne River, a $4 million investment in new cattle and equipment helped "only a handful" earn a living as ranchers, wrote historian Michael L. Lawson in *Dammed Indians*. For most, including the White Bulls, starting over as commercial ranchers was impossible on their new land.

Instead, Doug's older brothers would work from spring through late fall in construction, spending the rest of the year unemployed and living, as Doug puts it, "on handouts." As a teenager, when Doug was home in the summer or on vacation from boarding school, he would wake up in a cold sweat, thinking *I can't be like my brothers.* Sometimes he'd wake to loud fights or conversations between his mom and brothers, their worries about money coming through the thin wall. It was one of those nights that Doug decided to become a teacher, to have a regular paycheck.

"If I'd known, of course, I'd be signing up to remain in poverty, I would've picked something else," he jokes.

Though Congress had promised that the dams would bring cheap

Doug's parents, Julia (Red Fish) and Jacob White Bull, after the flood, 1960s.

hydropower, flood control, and irrigation, those benefits—clearly extended to white communities in the southern portion of the Missouri River— haven't come through for the Lakota. Despite the dams, there continue to be floods on the Cheyenne River Reservation. Though the Oahe Dam's generators produce enough electricity for 259,000 homes, people on the Cheyenne River and Standing Rock reservations get only a fraction of their power from the dams, according to Tribal government officials, what amounts to a few dollars a month off their electric bill.

There are official histories of the Pick–Sloan dams published by the Department of the Interior, the National Park Service, the Bureau of Reclamation, and the U.S. Army Corps of Engineers. There are entire chapters on the birth of soil mechanics and the evolution of federal marketing agreements, but the cost of the projects to Native Americans merits barely a single paragraph.

THE TRIPLE THREAT OF RELOCATION, TERMINATION, AND THE MISSOURI River dams was contained by an uprising of Indigenous activism. Though the impacts were devastating, it could've been worse. Ironically, it was the reality of Relocation, of Native Americans from all over the country living together, that gave rise to some of the nation's first Pan-Indian groups, such as United Native Americans, the American Indian Movement, and the National Indian Youth Council. Working across Indigenous communities, these organizations ensured that America didn't entirely renege on its treaty obligations and that the Termination era was short-lived.

In 1961, around seven hundred Indigenous people representing sixty-four Nations, including many Lakota, met to create a political agenda. Their Declaration of Indian Purpose was a mission statement to combat Termination and other land takings, such as those caused by the Pick–Sloan dams.

"When our lands are taken for a declared public purpose, scattering our people and threatening our continued existence, it grieves us to be told that a money payment is the equivalent of all the things we surrender. Our forefathers could be generous when all the continent was theirs. They could cast away whole empires for a handful of trinkets for their children. But in our day, each remaining acre is a promise that we will still be here tomorrow. Were we paid a thousand times the market value of our lost holdings, still the payment would not suffice."

Back in South Dakota, Lakota activists organized to combat the state legislature's efforts to rob Indigenous peoples of their sovereign status (unlike that of many states at the time, the South Dakota constitution required that federal action such as Termination be approved at the state level). At the time, the state legislature of South Dakota was composed entirely of white Christians and was hugely pro-Termination, with an eye on the millions of acres of Indigenous land, and the oil and gas under that land, that could become available. In 1963, Lakota volunteers collected more than twenty thousand signatures, successfully forcing a statewide referendum on state legislation that would terminate all tribes in South Dakota without Lakota consent. Over the following seventeen months, Lakota activists used the media to sway public opinion, convincing whites to consider the expense of educating and policing Lakota Country. In 1964, 77.6 percent of voters rejected Termination. The Lakota lands had been saved.

"It remains the single most stunning political upset in U.S.–Native relations in the twentieth century," wrote Dakota historian Edward Charles Valandra in his 2006 book, *Not Without Our Consent*.

Not every Indigenous Nation had such success. By 1968, the United States had turned nearly 1.4 million acres of Indigenous land into private property and terminated 113 Indigenous communities across the country, revoking their sovereign status. After many legal battles, Indigenous activists have been able to reverse most of that loss, though not all of it. To this day, twenty-seven Nations that were terminated have no land, and many more have reclaimed only a relatively small amount of their traditional landholdings. Twenty-four Indigenous Nations in the United States are "considered extinct."

But for the Lakota, the activism launched during the Termination era would carry over into all manner of efforts, such as the fights to reclaim the Black Hills, and to receive more federal compensation for the dire losses caused by the Pick–Sloan dams. Similar to the Black Hills case, the fight for "flood money," as peopled called it, was rife with political machinations and lawsuits, interagency bickering, and stalemates. But after decades of effort, Lakota leadership and attorneys working on their behalf compelled Congress to cough up more money. In 1992, Congress appropriated $90.6 million to Standing Rock, and in 2000, it appropriated $290.7 million to Cheyenne River.

While these victories were significant, the way this money was delivered was, once again, dripping in paternalistic overtones. Rather than giving the money to the Lakota immediately, the settlement amounts were placed in the U.S. Treasury, where the money was left to accrue interest for a decade. Only the interest earned on the initial settlements was awarded to the Lakota. The original sums remain in a federal bank today. As before, that money is restricted; it can't be given directly to individuals but must be granted to an educational, social, or economic program approved by the secretary of the interior.

"Congress determined we were once again hosed over," says Les Ducheneaux, an elder on Cheyenne River whose father, Frank, was Tribal Chairman in the 1950s and had worked to negotiate the earlier settlement.

In 2007, the Standing Rock Sioux Tribe used money from its general fund to cut checks for those members whose land had been flooded, giving them money without funneling it through a federal program. Doug received $5,000. He told *The Bismarck Tribune*, "This is still just a pittance, but at least it's something."

For all the ways the Pick–Sloan Program hurt the White Bulls, there was one significant way it helped. Money from the original Oahe Dam settlement in the fifties created a program that helped Doug pay for college. Unlike so many of his peers, who never returned to their communities, Doug wanted to teach Lakota students living on reservations, hoping he might offer someone a more compassionate education than he'd had at boarding school.

In a forty-year career, Doug taught and coached hundreds of students across four different Lakota reservations. He never yelled, his former students tell me. He was the kind of coach and teacher you wanted to impress, whom you wanted to make proud. Due in large part to Doug's activism and influence, the South Dakota High School Activities Association, which oversees sports in the state, created a permanent spot on its board for a Native American member, increasing Lakota children's representation and welfare. In his retirement, Doug served on the Standing Rock school board for twelve years, pushing for a more standardized and rigorous approach to teaching Lakota language. December 20, 2019, was, by order of the governor of South Dakota, Doug White Bull Day, recognizing him for, among other things, "his leadership and the work he did in Tribal communities, where he continues to spread hope and encouragement," according to the official proclamation.

ONE DAY, DOUG, MYSELF, AND ONE OF DOUG'S FORMER STUDENTS, JEFF McLaughlin, drive out to visit what's left of the place where Doug grew up on the edge of the Missouri River. There aren't any roads to get there. Up and down over buttes, we off-road in an old minivan that Jeff calls his "vuck." "It's a truck and van, get it?" he asks me with a quick, shy smile. Jeff, like many former students, calls Doug *lekshi*, Lakota for uncle. When Jeff was in high school, Doug was his cross-country coach. One night before a meet, Jeff asked Doug if he could spend the night at Doug's house to get a good night's sleep and a ride to the race early the next day. Jeff was supposed to stay the weekend; he stayed the rest of the year. So many kids did this at the White Bulls' that Doug and his wife, Joyce, eventually built bunk beds in the basement so there were enough places for everyone to sleep.

As we near the cutbank far above the deep-blue water, red chokecherries and wild plum cluster in the folds and creases of the land. When we reach the grassy slope where Doug used to run barefoot with his sisters, I ask him how it feels.

"Feels great, feels like home," he says closing his eyes under the bright sun.

Swallows swoop through the sky, the air is filled with birdsong and the buzz of insects and the river and the wind. But for the moment, I'm not noticing any of that. I'm distracted by our effort to touch the past.

An old cemetery, fenced off and thick with chokecherry, has survived the flood. While it had been slated for removal, the water never got that high, and the feds, by neglect or delay, left it alone. Deep inside the thicket of wild plants are gravestones of Doug's relatives, and he is determined to visit. Getting there will require this blind old man, who relies on his cane as if it were a third limb, to do the equivalent of bushwhacking.

Doug, wearing his Green Bay Packers jacket and a yellow polo shirt, beige pants, and dark shoes, follows Jeff through the dense weeds and roots. "I think I found a new place to have a keg party," Doug jokes. "Cops wouldn't dare come out here."

I explain to Doug where to put his foot and how to hold on to my arm and Jeff's arm. I'm embarrassed to share this part, but it's what happened: on the audio file, you can hear my voice asking if this is a good idea, cautioning Doug to be careful. Jeff quietly helps Doug step over the wire fence, gets a camp chair out of the van, and sets it up in the shade in case Doug needs a break.

I should've known better. By this point, I knew a lot of Doug's stories, especially his greatest hits, such as the time he, as a teenager, ran a fifty-mile race, finishing with bloody feet. I knew that, when the school district told him there was no money for his track and cross-country teams, he bought a bingo set and raised the money himself, making enough to send his team throughout the state with proper shoes and warm meals. I knew about his time at boarding school, where he was repeatedly hit and kicked by his teachers, sometimes with a wooden board across his bottom for the crime of speaking Lakota or not making his bed correctly. I knew that he'd survived all that and become a straight-A student anyway.

Not a person given to giving up, Doug slowly but steadily traverses the weedy expanse from the van to the graves deep in the middle of the cemetery. He never slows down, never complains. Standing as close as we can get to the old stones, the words in the marble etched in Lakota, I read the inscription aloud to Doug, and he translates: "Here was Mary White Bull, who died May 18, 1902, at the age of four."

The shade of the chokecherry makes patches across our faces. As Doug takes a moment to contemplate the graves, I'm struck again by the weight of his loss, of what has been taken from him and his family to ensure a specific brand of American progress.

There's a debate, described in the Talmud, between two rabbis, over what should be done if it's discovered that a house, or even a palace, was built using a stolen beam as part of its foundation. One rabbi says the entire building must be demolished so that the beam can be returned to its original owners. The other rabbi, the far more pragmatic, says the building can remain standing if the full value of the beam is repaid. Both rabbis make clear that, as soon as it is known that the beam was stolen, those living in the house must do something, they must make amends.

"Our country was built on a stolen beam," Rabbi Sharon Brous of Los Angeles famously said in a 2017 sermon. To ignore this history and the legacy of this history diminishes the legitimacy and the power of this house, of this nation. Building without a solid foundation inevitably leads to collapse, wrote Rabbi Sholom Noach Berezovsky. A Holocaust survivor, born not far from Kapulye, he understood the societal danger of theft and denialism.

The money that has come to the Lakota was arguably never a fair trade for what was taken, rarely a deal negotiated without some degree of coercion. And the losses compound one another: the flooding of Doug's childhood home, here on the banks of the Missouri, built on the taking of his father's land, and his grandfather's land, and his father's before that. And what of everything else that was stolen? The years Doug spent in fear at boarding school, the state-mandated destruction of Lakota language, religion, and culture? What payment can be made to replace such a loss?

AFTER DOUG FINISHES SPEAKING TO THE DEAD, AFTER WE SLOWLY AND steadily walk out of the shade and back to the "vuck," Jeff drives a little ways south, to where his ancestors once lived, on the banks of the Missouri not far from the White Bulls. Jeff has been working for twenty years to convince the Tribal Council to demand that the United States return these lands, seized during the flood, to his family and the other families who once lived along the river. He'd like to create a place where his relatives can live intentionally and in the tradition of their ancestors.

"Look at that," he says, nodding to what looks, to me, like a few scattered

Doug White Bull on his family's former land,
May 2016.

logs. Jeff cuts the engine, and we get out to investigate, while Doug rests
in the front seat. It turns out the logs are a tipi frame, fallen in a storm.
Using a crude pully and rope getup, Jeff and I try to raise the poles. The
wood is heavy, we're on a hill, and my upper-body strength has never been
anything to brag about. We keep almost getting the frame to rise before it
collapses again. At one point one of the logs smacks Jeff in the head, but
he keeps assuring me we can do it. Before too long, we do, the poles held
in place, balanced by the weight they place on one another.

10

❊❊❊❊❊

OH TO BE A JEWISH
ROCKEFELLER

I n the late 1940s, as plans to flood the reservations nearby were under way, Louie Sinykin, youngest child of Faige Etke and Harry, was back on Jew Flats chasing ambition and security. He—like the federal dam builders, like his parents and siblings—believed that humans can control nature and make it profitable. For the previous two decades, Louie had bounced back and forth between the ranch and St. Paul, where he went to college, worked for his older relatives in their pharmacies and liquor stores, and, later, sold life insurance. Life had delivered Louie a toll: his first wife died of cancer, he'd broken his back when mobsters pushed him down that elevator shaft, and he'd never completed his degree. Now in his forties, he wasn't the lawyer his parents had hoped he'd become, but with four kids and a second wife, Louie, a consummate optimist, was certain he would soon fulfill Faige Etke's dreams. At last, Jew Flats would turn the Sinykins into millionaires.

Pooling in pockets of deep sand beneath the ranch was oil. Louie's original source for this intelligence was likely not a geologist or a petroleum engineer but his neighbor and best friend, who'd spent a summer in the 1920s working on an oil rig. Energy companies punched so many test wells in western South Dakota over the next few decades that, on certain maps, the state appeared to have a bad case of measles. But after the companies drilled down as far as 3,508 feet and hit nothing but "dry holes,"

Louie Sinykin, on the left in the dark suit jacket, and
his children Bill and Diane, pictured in front, at a
Dakota oil well, 1948.

Dakota oil didn't seem commercially viable. Louie Sinykin, unfazed by this
corporate opinion, proceeded to do another classically American thing: his
own research.

In August 1948, when the summer sun was slathered across the wide
sky, Louie took his wife and kids on a two-week road trip to tour potential
oil prospects in the Dakotas. Both of Louie's children who are still alive
today were too young to remember this "vacation," but it wasn't exactly
the stuff of childhood dreams. Through the heat, they drove more than
928 miles, crisscrossing gravel and dirt roads to visit wells and drill rigs,
where they all got out of the car and posed for photos. With the windows
down, dust settled in a fine layer across Louie's dark suit jacket, his fedora,
and the blond hair of his daughter's doll. At each county seat, he stopped
to pull records of existing oil leases. At each small town, Louie would blow

into the local newspaper office, cigar in mouth, fedora in hand, "like a cy-clone," in the words of one editor, spreading the news he wanted to be fact.

"The largest potential oil and gas field in the North American contin-ued [*sic*] lies in the Dakota basin beneath North and South Dakota according to Louis A. Sinykin," wrote the *Mandan Daily Pioneer* on August 10.

"The biggest boom in the history of the oil industry is slated for west-ern South Dakota by 1950," Louie told the *Rapid City Journal* on August 13. "[He] maintains the first commercial flow tapped by some wild-catter in this area will bring 'a rush eclipsing the scramble for gold in the days of '76.'"

"Sinykin maintains it is perfectly feasible now to drill 12,000 feet or more to tap the 'black gold' believed lying deep in the Dakota basin," ran the *Pennington County Currant* on August 18.

Louie Sinykin is "confident that there is oil in this area," wrote the *Chamberlain Register* on August 19. "Having plenty of money at his dis-posal, he plans on doing considerable test drilling."

This "plenty of money" was not, in fact, his own. Louie had gone bank-rupt at some point (no one alive can remember when or why), and according to his letters, he couldn't get a bank loan. The oil company he would soon organize would be funded entirely by my great-grandparents and other immi-grant Jews, many of them friends and relatives living in St. Paul. Like Louie, not one of them, as far as I can tell, had experience in the energy business.

Over the course of his life, Louie gave himself many titles: insurance salesman, rancher, oil man, South Dakota booster, promoter. He hit the rodeo circuit as a young man and wasn't half bad, making it to the National Saddle Bronc riding competition in 1919. When a local newsman dubbed him "Bronco Lou," the nickname stuck for the rest of his life. His neigh-bors on the prairie called him other names, too: shyster, Lou the Jew, or simply, the Jew. For Louie, and for all those other immigrant Jews still not quite as secure in their status as they'd like, black gold was a passport, proof of how far they'd come from the shtetl. Making a million dollars would shake off the recent shanda caused by bootlegging, and it would prove Faige Etke right; she always believed that the minerals in the South Da-kota ground would make the state rich.

Louie, unlike his five older siblings, unlike his parents, seems to have been more aware of the entangled history between our family and the Lakota. He always told his children that it was important to "support the Indians." And yet, due in large part to the times in which he lived, Louie didn't understand that, without meaning to, his actions could create a new slate of problems and pain for his Lakota neighbors.

FOR MUCH OF MY LATE TWENTIES AND EARLY THIRTIES, I WAS WRITING regular pieces for national magazines about oil and gas development throughout the western United States. I would put on my thrift-store boots and either a hard hat, if I was visiting a well rig, or a soft expression, if I was sitting at a kitchen table. The good stories, the ones that paid, were bad news: how the unmitigated effects of energy extraction were harming the environment, public health, and, at times, even the local economy.

Underground minerals are often connected, ignoring any property lines on the surface. When problems occur in drilling operations, they can cause toxic substances to leak into soil, drinking water, and air, causing contamination even for those living far away from oil and gas wells.

Over the course of my career, I've seen plenty of cases in which faulty drilling operations ruined people's lives. There was the time methane from a well seeped into a creek, fizzed like soda pop for half a mile, and scores of frogs and trout went belly-up. There were the families that could light their lemonade on fire after drilling operations beyond their property lines went wrong and natural gas flooded their water wells. There was the smell of rotten eggs that gave me, and the photographer I was with, not to mention the people who lived nearby, an instant headache. There was the woman who told me, "We drink bottled water, but the air is everywhere we go."

When I learned about my family's oil and gas company, I thought of the Cheyenne River, approximately thirteen miles north of the Sinykin ranch, which feeds the Missouri River, which feeds the Mississippi. I thought about how the air coming off Jew Flats was the same air in the Black Hills, in the Cheyenne River and Standing Rock reservations. Such environmental concerns, what economists call *externalities*, weren't on any of my relatives' minds seventy years ago.

"Now it's oil oil oil . . . we talked oil until 3 a.m.," wrote my great-grandmother Ruth in her day diary on November 7, 1953. For the next several days, she, Louie, and the other Sinykin siblings stayed up into the wee hours, visiting in Ruth and Jake's living room with a Texas oilman. Two days later, it was still "talk, talk, talk oil."

By this point, Louie, with the help of his siblings, in particular Ruth and Jake, had turned his dream of becoming the next Rockefeller into something with edges and sides. The Dakota Basin Oil Company, with Ruth Kozberg as president, was established by a team of Jewish lawyers in St. Paul and incorporated in September 1951 with approximately seventy "investors" (read: friends and family), with shares sold at $100 (today's equivalent of a little more than $1,000). Most investors, including my grandparents and my great-aunts and great-uncles, had several shares. The money was used to buy the rights to drill on and around Jew Flats, and the word was out: "There's not a man from Pierre to Deadwood that don't know Louie and his oil leases," one South Dakota "oilman" told Ruth.

Louie pored over newspapers and industry journals, cutting articles and pasting them, and related correspondence, into a notebook that, of course, being a Sinykin, he kept all his life. (It's now in his granddaughter's garage.) From his clippings, it's clear he took meetings with various petroleum geologists, including one at the University of Minnesota, who wrote a follow-up letter saying, "The letters and reports in your scrap-book indicated to me that your hope for success could not be dismissed as a 'pipe-dream.' . . . That conclusion has been strengthened subsequently by reference to geologic maps and meager geologic reports on the area. There is absolutely no reason to reject at this time the possibility of finding oil under Pennington County."

At Louie's behest, three additional geologists had come out to Jew Flats and confirmed the presence of oil after consulting seismographic reports and something called "oil charts of the strata" deep below Jew Flats. By 1953, with Ruth and Jake's money, Louie had expanded the Sinykin ranch to more than five thousand acres, now encompassing all the land and underground minerals of the original Jew Flats. In addition, he'd leased the mineral rights from his neighbors and friends for a total of roughly thirty thousand acres.

At night, by kerosene lamp, Louie and his son, Bill, who was around nine at the time, would pore over section maps, outlining in red which property to lease next. The house still had no running water or electricity. There were snakes in the root cellar and no heat upstairs. My cousins rode to school on winter mornings huddled under buffalo robes in a horse-drawn milk wagon. No wonder Louie was desperate to believe what he'd told the newspapers. On those nights, he and Bill huddled around the section maps as if they were fire, and the hope that things were about to change, that their circumstances could flip, was palpable.

"I can't ever remember going hungry, but I can remember money always being very tight," says Bill Sinykin, now eighty and living in Utah. Bill, whose email handle is "wildbill," is excessively polite and kind, and his memories of his dad, even the less flattering ones, are often cut with a laugh. "It could be middle of winter, and Dad would go out to promote this whole oil thing. He was just so enamored with it." At this, Bill laughs, remembering how, in the cold, the old International truck wouldn't reliably start unless his dad set it on the top of a draw, popped the clutch, and pushed it down a steep hill, racing after it across the prairie. "Obviously, if the oil hit, it would mean a good deal of money, and so that was exciting."

This doesn't sound all that different from how Doug talks about the underground potential on Standing Rock. "We would've been an oil-rich Nation; it's oil like they have in Saudi Arabia." But federal policies of the past ensured that Native Americans weren't just excluded from the opportunities available to settlers, but that the process by which oil and gas was extracted on reservations would often cause them harm.

THE HISTORY OF OIL AND GAS EXTRACTION ON INDIGENOUS LAND IS A story of "economic rape," says Roger Fragua, one of the country's foremost experts in Native American energy, who is enrolled in the Pueblo of Jemez. "The history of energy extraction has been one of legal theft with the industry and the United States government in collusion."

In 1891, Congress—which, at the time, was treating the reservations more like colonies than sovereign Nations—determined that the minerals beneath Indigenous lands were being wasted. As a corrective, it allowed private companies to lease and drill for black gold and other riches. Technically, the consent of a Native Nation was required, but that technicality was often overlooked. Indigenous communities were rarely consulted or given any say about the terms of development. When they were, oil men were sometimes known to prey on their ignorance.

"There is a dangerous and flammable and explosive substance lurking beneath your land," wrote one oil company to the Ute Mountain Utes in the early 1900s. "We will gladly remove it for you."

In 1916, Congress negated the need for even a rubber stamp from Indigenous leadership, enabling companies to drill and mine on Native lands simply with permission from the Office of Indian Affairs. Subsequent laws allowed states to tax Indigenous Nations on the royalties they received from oil and gas, diminishing their income. During this era, Congress deemed that federal officials, rather than Tribal governments, would determine how Nations should use the money earned from oil and gas development on reservations. Sometimes, a Nation's royalty earnings sat in the federal treasury collecting interest that the Indian Office used to pay for its telephone lines and employee salaries. This during a time when many Native Americans were literally starving.

One Arapaho Councilman wrote to Congress in 1911, "Probably God has made the Indians just like the white man, and I do not understand why the government did not ask us if they could use this money."

Federal policy allowed oil and gas companies to self-report the amount they pumped, which led to widespread abuse. Court documents have revealed that, for decades, operators working on Indigenous lands lied about the amounts they extracted and greatly underpaid royalties to Native Nations. Lawsuits and newspaper investigations in the 1980s revealed that this honor system had allowed the theft of at least $5.8 billion in royalties.

"It's as if I were to go into a restaurant and order steaks and dessert and a big bottle of wine, and then I stopped at the cashier and said, 'I had a hot dog today,'" Fragua, the Indigenous energy expert, told me when I was reporting on such abuse for *Indian Country Today*. "There is no other business where that practice would be acceptable."

By the time the Dakota Basin Oil Company had formed in the 1950s, oil and gas had been discovered on both the Cheyenne River and Standing Rock reservations. This was something very much on the minds of state and federal lawmakers interested in Termination legislation. Among the first Indigenous Nations that Congress stripped of their sovereign status were those in the Northern Plains and Oklahoma, where the land was rich in minerals like oil and gas.

"Nothing revealed the hypocrisy of the termination movement more than the taking of Indian resources during this period," wrote journalist Marjane Ambler in her book about Indigenous energy, *Breaking the Iron Bonds*. "Termination proponents emphasized that they wanted Indian tribes to be self-sufficient, but while saying this, they took away the means for the tribes to be so."

From this vantage, the Lakota living on the Cheyenne River Reservation were lucky: the minerals drilled there in the fifties and sixties went dry quickly. The lack of production may have lessened the desire of state voters to adopt Termination legislation. It also may explain why, when Louie was tirelessly searching the state for oil, leasing as many minerals in the region as possible, he didn't cross the Cheyenne River to lease oil rights on the reservation. In light of the damage that drilling can cause to both the environment and communities, this is something of a relief. I'd guess, from what I think I know about Louie, that if he knew the science of potential health and environmental risk, he'd be glad he never tried to drill on the reservations either. For he not only counted himself as having Lakota friends—according to his daughter, he claimed the entire Lakota Nation as distant kin.

WHEN LOUIE HAD FIRST RETURNED TO THE RANCH BACK IN 1935, WHEN land was cheap and he was snapping up abandoned homesteads for the price of back taxes to expand the family ranch, he was moving in a cloud of grief. His first wife, Florence, had died of cancer. He had left his baby girl with Ruth and, licking his wounds out on the prairie, may have found his way, more often than not, to bars in Rapid City and elsewhere. It was there that he made friends with Lakota men, who, by then, were allowed to leave the reservation. Many of them lived in a sort of shantytown on the edge of Rapid City.

"Dad learned to speak Lakota. He thought they were just like us," says my cousin Diane, Louie's daughter, who has inherited her father's warmth and optimism. "They taught their kids the same traditions we do. They had the same rituals. He thought they were like the lost tribe."

This could be true. Or not—my cousin Bill doesn't remember their dad ever saying such a thing. But regardless of whether Louie believed it, plenty of other Americans, some of them Jews, had noticed certain similarities between Jews and Lakota that, at a cursory glance, could make a pattern. Both Jews and Lakota elevate the importance of the number seven. Both traditionally would change the name of someone who was gravely ill as a means of avoiding death. Both cultures have language and customs that highlight the deep value of family interconnectedness and filial responsibility.

And yet, the leap to seeing those similarities as evidence that Indigenous peoples in the United States are a lost tribe of the Jews is deeply problematic, as it has been used for centuries to justify land-taking and oppression. As early as the mid-seventeenth century, settlers and missionaries in the Americas wielded the theory that Native Americas descended from ancient Israelites to justify conversion and assimilation. In 1830, Joseph Smith, founder of the Church of Jesus Christ of Latter-Day Saints, wrote in the Book of Mormon that ancient Israelites were the original inhabitants of the American continent. In the nineteenth century, people searched for evidence to make such theory fact: settlers in Ohio unearthed Hebrew-inscribed stones amid ancient Indigenous burial mounds, others in Massachusetts claimed to have found tefillin, Jewish prayer cases, in an area locals called "Indian Hill." (All such "evidence" was eventually exposed as hoaxes.) By 1920, more than sixty essays, pamphlets, and books had been published in the European and American popular press arguing for a connection between Jews and Indigenous peoples in the Americas.

"The theory that Americans are of Jewish descent has been discussed more minutely and at greater length than any others," reads the late-nineteenth-century book *Native Races of the Pacific States of North America* (which proceeds to spend twenty-five pages discrediting the theory).

Let me be as clear as possible: this Lost Tribe theory is a myth. Not only has it been repeatedly discredited by historians for generations, the way it has been manipulated as a thinly veiled assault on Indigenous land and people makes it dangerous. That said, I think I understand why it could've had a lasting appeal for people like Louie. If immigrant Jews were, in fact, tied to America's original inhabitants, then they were no longer in exile but had, at last, come home. For Jews, this theory has always been as much about belonging as it is about land.

As one Orthodox rabbi wrote in his newspaper, *The Occident*, in the mid-nineteenth century, Native Americans descended from ancient Jews, who had "penetrated into the distant wilds" of America before the Vikings or the Pilgrims and "had been there on the plains where the buffalo's hoof makes the soil ring with his measured tread." In this telling, Jews weren't immigrants; they were the true, original Americans. This idea of indigeneity had been around for several decades: in 1825 another influential Jewish leader bought an island near Niagara Falls and called it "Ararat," a Jewish homeland where not only Jews but their "lost tribesmen," Indigenous people in the Americas, could form their own nation. Clearly, it didn't take.

And yet, what compelled many Jews to keep embracing this theory into the twentieth century was their inherited fear of exile. Jewish organizations continued to uphold land as a claim on belonging and a hedge against antisemitic attack.

"Too often is the charge heard that the Jew has neither inclination nor aptitude to toil or to till. The Jewish farm class . . . refutes that charge," reads the 1943 book *Our Jewish Farmers*. "In rediscovering the satisfaction of life on the soil, their ancient tradition, they have also rediscovered themselves. Jewish farmers are growing in numbers, adding to their acreage, and prepared in times of war as in times of peace to make their fullest contribution to the basic economy of this blessed land of hope and opportunity."

Though, by this point, there were around ninety thousand Jewish farmers, they represented only 2 percent of the total American Jewish population. Without that proximity to landownership, Jews looked more like outsiders, less like real Americans.

For Louie, the idea that he might be related, on some level, to his Lakota neighbors would've been a powerful tonic. Around the age of four, he'd left Kapulye with Faige Etke and had very few memories of life there. He was so taken with the state of South Dakota that, when he visited out-of-state friends and relatives in the 1950s, he'd show a thousand feet of film he'd helped take of the Black Hills, the Badlands, and his ranch. According to him, more than five hundred people had watched his movies, and he'd personally convinced more than ten couples to honeymoon in the Black Hills. A salesman as much as he was ever anything else, Louie was also a card-carrying extrovert who never forgot a name and who could talk to anyone. But belonging, like so much else, exists on a spectrum. For all of Louie's ardor for the prairie, many of his neighbors didn't claim him as one of their own.

"Bronco Lou," circa 1919.

A few years ago, I spent an early morning at Wall Drug, the famous South Dakota roadside attraction, visiting with a group of locals who regularly gather there over coffee and donuts before heading out to work their ranches. Not one of them told me about the WPA dam that Louie fought to have built in 1937 on Jew Flats, something that brought critical jobs during the height of drought, when many neighbors were struggling to feed their kids. Not one of them remembered the lobbying that Louie did at the state legislature in the early '40s on behalf of ranchers and farmers.

One old-timer told me that Louie's dream of oil set him apart from the many ranchers who didn't want to be bothered with outsiders on their land. Other ranchers in the area worried that drilling operations would hurt their cattle. Another one told me there had been rumors of gangsters visiting Louie, the thinking being, "He's a Jew, so maybe he's with the mafia."

Over time, I spoke with more locals. One echoed the sentiment of several, telling me, "being Jewish didn't alarm anybody," and both Louie and Diane insisted they never felt any antisemitism while living on Jew Flats. But it certainly made them different in the eyes of at least some people. Once, when I asked an old-timer if he remembered my uncle, he said, "Oh, you mean the Jew?" Another neighbor said his dad dreaded Louie's visits, as they often involved requests for money or proposals to sell or buy equipment that usually stalled. "We figured his family didn't want him in Minneapolis, and that's why they kept him out here," that same neighbor told me.

Being an outsider doesn't always feel great, but it often leads to greatness. For so many successful people, it has fueled tenacity and verve. In Louie's case, I believe this longing to fit in was part of his drive to become an oil tycoon, a drive that leads our story to a hot summer day in either 1952 or '53, when Louie's dreams of grandeur hung in the balance.

AT LAST, THE LONG-PLANNED-FOR DAY HAD ARRIVED: A FORTY-FOOT RIG was drilling pipe into the prairie north of the house to determine whether there was, in fact, oil pooling under Louie's land. There weren't peanuts and refreshments, and people throughout the county didn't gather by the hundreds to watch, as they had when drillers came to the area in the 1930s, but Louie's son Bill was there, and he remembers that it was thrilling. He and his brother had ridden their horses up to watch, and his parents and younger sister all gathered around. I'd guess Louie was smoking a cigar and wearing his black fedora. To run the seismic tests, to create sound waves that bounce off underground strata, the drillers set off dynamite deep down the hole. Bill and his brother Larry's horses spooked and ran for home. Everyone felt like they were surfing the solid ground, as if their world had come off its axis for a moment, and everything could be rewritten.

No one still living saw the test results and, interestingly, Louie didn't paste them into his scrapbook, but family lore is that they proved Louie right. There was, in fact, oil deep underground. If they drilled ten-thousand-feet deep, farther down than anyone in the area had yet drilled, they'd hit black gold.

But oh, poor Louie. Drilling is always expensive, and to drill that deep would cost more than the Dakota Basin Oil Company had in reserve. Undaunted, Louie went off to raise investment. What my family and their friends didn't know, because they were immigrants with no experience in the oil business, was that when you lease rather than buy a mineral right, every month that passes without drilling, the company must pay the landowners rent. By 1955, the Dakota Basin Oil Company was in the red. The St. Paul attorneys managing the Dakota Basin persuaded Atlantic Refining Company to buy up the lease interests for $70,000.

For my great-grandparents and some of their siblings, for my grandparents and great-aunts and great-uncles who had put money into the company, this was not such a big loss, at least not for long. Half of the original owners of the Dakota Basin Oil Company, those family members included, reinvested their earnings from the sale to Atlantic, and added enough to bring each investment to $1,000. With $70,000, their attorney went out and bought (rather than leased) the mineral rights to sixteen parcels in North Dakota and one in Montana from farmers who had most likely either been homesteaders on former Indigenous land or had bought their land from such homesteaders. For years, nothing happened, no one drilled or made a cent. But when the oil embargo of the seventies hit, they did at last drill, and they did okay; based on what Etta remembers, my grandparents might have made close to $1,000 a year for a couple decades.

Louie himself made almost nothing. He'd done all the organizing and begging and lobbying, but he'd been broke when the company was founded and did not own a single share of the Dakota Basin Oil Company. It had never been his intention to sell the leases without drilling.

At first, Louie doubled down and set out to make a new energy company all on his own. In 1956, he and Ruth leased the ranch to his neighbor, and Louie's family moved to Rapid City for the kids to attend high school. Louie set out to drum up business. The following spring, he was telling the papers that new test wells would be drilled on Jew Flats any day.

The new venture didn't take. None of his relatives or friends were willing to invest. He still couldn't get a bank loan. In failure, he was dejected and depressed. His marriage soured. The spasm in his back, the result of that fall down the elevator shaft during the bootlegging days, had worsened until Louie was in almost constant pain. By 1960, he was begging Ruth and Jake for money. "I am not well but got no money to go to Mayo Clinic or Battle Creek for I need medical attention the sooner the better," wrote Lou on Sinykin Family Oil Co. letterhead. "I need money to pull over the winter months all ranch rental money gone = we are financial in bad shape."

He once swore he would never sell the ranch in South Dakota, but facing a winter with no money, he looked into selling the two-story house on Jew Flats where he'd brought home his bride and babies. He closed the letter with the desperate, "Please write if you can help me buy this house. Please, Louie."

It didn't happen. Sooner than expected, because death almost always comes sooner than we'd like, my great-grandfather Jake died, suddenly, on Yom Kippur in 1962, of complications from ruptured varicose veins in his esophagus. It was, says Etta, a terrible shock, and no one was ever quite the same. Within a few years, Ruth began to suffer from dementia. She may have already been in the early stages on the day her three daughters came to her house on a mission. They sat their mother down in the living room, the scene of countless happy gatherings, and told Ruth it was time to sell the land. Maybe it was to be expected, but the talk between mother and daughters didn't go well.

"Never sell the land," were Faige Etke's dying words. "I'll never sell, I'll never move," wrote Louie in one of his famously long letters. It was "the good Earth" to Rose and to Ruth. Even though Ruth hadn't lived in South Dakota for more than four decades, she'd regularly vacationed in the Black Hills. She and Jake had spent thousands of dollars to keep the ranch afloat.

"We were sitting down, and we were talking to my mother, and she got furious at us," Etta tells me one day over the phone. "She said to Pauline, 'You were the Jewish princess,' and then she pointed to Betty and said, 'You had the biggest mouth, you were the big talker.' She pointed at me, and said, 'You were the Indian, you washed the floors.' And I always felt she really described us. She really knew who we were."

When I ask Etta why her mother got so mad at them, she slides directly into another story about how much her mother loved the land, as if to say the connection is obvious, as if to say she understood her mother's anger. "It was like we were cutting off a part of her life. The land was really a part of them. Owning it made them feel they were a part of America, that they lived in a free country."

By 1965, Ruth had signed the paperwork selling the bulk of the ranch to Louie's best friend, who was a neighbor and the descendant of the German immigrants who had originally homesteaded beside them. The $142,240 was split between Louie and Ruth, according to a family letter. Two years later, my grandmother and her sisters signed papers giving them legal guardianship for their mother. Three years after that, they sold their final parcel of South Dakota, Jake's homestead, what the papers had once called one of the best ranches in the county. The deed of sale leaves the amount unspecified, and while it's impossible to say whether any of the money that Ruth received was passed directly to my grandmother Pauline, and then to my mom, and then to me, some of that money, in one way or another, eventually became part of my inheritance.

In the years leading up to these sales, there were twenty-one-page letters back and forth between the Sinykin siblings. There were family meetings and other meetings with attorneys and land speculators. There was all manner of family mishigas ("drama") about who exactly owned the land and who stood to benefit from its sale. That's the thing about land, whether it's nations or relatives who love one another: it's rarely enough. I will spare you the heartbreaking details. If you're fortunate enough to be part of a family with shared property, you can imagine. The bottom line is that there were hard feelings, there were secrets and misdeeds, and in the end, I don't think it was anything close to fair. My uncle Jack was so furious about how it all went down that, according to one of his grandsons, he didn't speak to Louie for years.

LIKE ANY GOOD WESTERNER, LOUIE HAD LEARNED SOMETHING ABOUT reinvention. Throughout the years of back-and-forth over the land sale, his dreams of becoming the next Rockefeller slipping away, Louie, that eternal optimist, jumped at the chance to have a bit part in a deep cut of American mythmaking.

In the early 1960s, Debbie Reynolds, John Wayne, and John Ford came to Rapid City to film the star-studded epic *How the West Was Won*. The movie would go on to earn eight Oscar nominations, including Best Picture, and would win for Best Story and Screenplay. While it was panned by *The New York Times*, *Variety* called it "as vivid as anything ever put on celluloid."

Louie offered his services to the director as a professional settler consultant. What that means is that he and his kids hung around the set and got hired as extras. Louie's speaking part was ultimately cut from the still-bloated, almost three-hour film, but plenty of lines remained that sent a certain message home.

In voice-over, Spencer Tracy narrates views of mountain majesty and tells the audience that the West was won by pioneers and settlers. To clarify, he states, "The land had to be won, won from nature and from primitive man." That struggle climaxes on screen in the scene in which Louie has his cameo. In the fourth of the film's five subsections, a railroad man has laid track through Arapaho territory, breaking an earlier treaty promise. The Arapaho respond by spurring a herd of buffalo to stampede through the railroad's outpost. The racing animals flatten the emblems of civilization, a water tower and a windmill, but soldiers run the Arapaho off, and the railman gets the money quote: "The Arapahos will have to change, too, and if they don't, they're finished."

Sweeping orchestral music accompanies a chorus that closes the film with the line, "Here it is, the beautiful promised land, we won't forget them and how the West was won." Lacking any measure of nuance, the picture on screen at that moment is an aerial shot of the Hoover Dam.

Twenty years later, I myself acted in a related piece of American fairy tale, the children's play *How the West Was Really Won*, with the chorus line "the only thing that doesn't change is change." The play, though billing itself as revisionist, hits the same basic plot points of the movie: the hardships of pioneer life, the gold rush, the Civil War, and the building of the railroads. (Clearly related to Ruth and Etta, I kept the 1982 school-play program in a box all these years. The line between historian and pack rat is paper thin.)

At first, it seemed remarkable that Louie and I would both participate in these related American legends, but I've learned that it isn't such a coincidence. Since it was first published in 1980, the script for the play has been sold more than fifty thousand times, and it is still staged by several elementary schools every year.

All I remember about my fleeting acting career is my outfit: a yellow "country" dress, bonnet, and my hair in braids. Less clear is how the play may have shaped my ideas about American history. We sang the following lines ("sadly," as instructed by the script) from the perspective of "the Indians":

"The white man is coming with iron horse and track. I no longer rise with the dawn. The warrior will play farewell on his flute. My people will perish. We soon will be gone."

That song was a real earworm. I can still sing it to this day. What meaning did I make from those lines? Were we meant to believe that Indigenous people no longer existed in America? Both the play and the movie repeatedly mention the free land on offer in the West, but neither explain that this free land had already been home to tens of thousands of Native

Americans. By "winning the West," the movie and the play make clear, white people prospered.

In that sense, they weren't wrong. Today, white Americans own 95 percent of private farmland in the United States. More than a quarter of American adults, as many as 92 million people, descend from the estimated 1.6 million homesteaders who had received free land by the time the program ended. Relatively few of them are Black, Indigenous, or people of color. These homesteader descendants can potentially link their "property ownership, upward mobility, economic stability, class status, and wealth directly to one national policy [the Homestead Act]," writes sociologist Thomas M. Shapiro, in *The Hidden Cost of Being African American: How Wealth Perpetuates Inequality.*

Even though the oil business didn't hit for Louie and my relatives, in a way, Faige Etke's kids followed through on her directive to make a million off the land: throughout the time my ancestors owned a piece of South Dakota prairie, Faige Etke and Harry, their children, and sons-in-law took out twenty-nine mortgages. The estimated total amount of those mortgages and land sales, adjusted for inflation, comes to $2,406,224. That money helped Faige Etke's children start businesses, move, buy homes, and get ahead, away, far away, from the shtetl. Our family today has a deep roster of doctors, lawyers, entrepreneurs, artists, writers, and academics. Most of us own houses. Some of us own second houses. I can't think of a single family member who didn't go to college.

Knowing what I now know, the dominant narrative of the Sinykins is less one of landownership than one of movement. Yes, the ranch gave my family a fresh start and a sense of belonging in a new country. But I believe that what was more important to the arc of the family's history was how the land allowed us to leave, how it provided the financing to make our way in America. What I have truly inherited is an instinct to survive, to be prepared to ditch a beloved place when faced with opportunity or threat. To flee is more Jewish than to stay. It echoes a certain John Wayne–style attitude of independence and self-sufficiency.

"Ghost towns and dust bowls, like motels, are western inventions," wrote Wallace Stegner, who was born and raised on homesteads and ranches throughout the West, and himself believed he was shaped by the motion of the Western mind.

Throughout my childhood, my parents often talked about leaving the United States and moving somewhere like New Zealand, which shone in their imaginations as having both professional opportunity and a more compassionate society. That it never happened, that, instead, we stayed in Seattle throughout my childhood and moved only once, a distance of a few miles, didn't fail to underscore the point. The thing is to keep an eye on the horizon. The ranch remains both a source of pride and, as my cousin Herbie once put it, "one bitchy place to live," one more place that we survived.

Our leaving, however, did nothing to restore the balance of power on the prairie. When we sold the ranch, we sold it to another family descended from European immigrants. Though it doesn't appear ever to have been officially researched, it's estimated that a relatively small percentage of the land that Congress took from Indigenous Nations and made available to white settlers under the Homestead Act has been returned to or purchased by its original inhabitants.

ON A HOT AUGUST DAY IN 2003, FIFTY-FIVE YEARS AFTER LOUIE TOOK HIS family on that summer road trip chasing dreams of oil, an assortment of Sinykin descendants took a different sort of road trip through western South Dakota. The sky was bright blue, and around seventeen of us loaded into a chartered bus and drove from Rapid City, where we were staying in a nice hotel, out to the ranch. On the way there, Louie's son Larry stood in front telling us the history of Jew Flats.

It was our fourth official family reunion in thirty years. Like at the others, there were dinners and singing and labored-over presentations of family history. Afterward, there would be a memorial scrapbook album, a group photo, and a VHS tape for order. The thing about my family that endures is the sense that everyone counts. This isn't by accident but by intention.

In 1963, my aunt Rose wrote to my grandmother and her sisters that Faige Etke and Harry had raised their children to "be close, to do things for others as much as you can. Love your brothers and sisters. And never break or tear yourself away from one another. I remember that since I was a little girl! That's why our family stuck together all those years no matter what happened . . . I do hope you will always sisters stick together and that it could go too generations on. I pray."

In this way, we may have exceeded Faige Etke's wildest dreams.

I have third cousins, descendants of Ruth's brothers and sisters, that I visit regularly. I never use the word *honey* as much as when I'm with my mom's family; it serves as a sort of shorthand for connective tissue. We show up for one another: attending b'nai mitzvahs, dancing at weddings, and throwing dirt on the graves of the dead. When someone is sick or ailing, everyone seems to know about it, and then there are calls, and often there is a food delivery. The rejoicing in one another's simchas, the mourning for the losses, this is what connects us. It has very little to do with land.

On that trip out to the ranch, most of us were going for the first time. None of us were locals. We came by airplane from western and midwestern cities like Salt Lake, Los Angeles, Phoenix, Minneapolis, and Seattle. No one in the family worked as a rancher or a farmer.

When we rolled up a gravel road, the bus stopped near an old cottonwood on the original homestead of one of the Sinykins' closest neighbors. To this day, their family refers to the land they bought from my family, and continue to ranch, as Jew Flats or the Jew Estate.

I remember there were hot dogs and coleslaw under the old tree. Old-timers, people my cousins grew up with, brought food to share, and we chatted. I walked around with my mom's old Nikomat camera taking pictures of farming equipment and trucks rusting in the yard. I wore my hair in braids. My polyester Wrangler pants were something ironic I had purchased at a thrift store. Some of my cousins wore cowboy hats. This was not too long after I had been to Pine Ridge and had tried to win favor with that Oglala Lakota hemp grower by mentioning that my family were once ranchers in South Dakota, but it was far before I made any serious connection between this land and the Lakota.

At the end of the afternoon on the day I first visited Jew Flats with my relatives, we all piled into the chartered bus, the tinted windows and air-conditioning a balm after the heat of the prairie sun. I sat beside Etta as she told me family secrets and took notes in my reporter's notebook with the slim binding at the top. Eventually, I would learn these stories by heart. Eventually, I would become so close to Etta that I would strive to live my life in a way that honored the lessons behind her stories: keep a positive outlook, keep your family close, be generous with your food and home and time, give back to your community.

On that day we left the ranch, I remember my head was bent toward Etta's as we drove slowly down the dirt road, Jew Flats behind us covered in a haze of dust kicked from the large tires. We stopped at Wall Drug on the way back to Rapid City, drank the free ice water, bought rabbits' feet, T-shirts, and tchotchkes, and posed for pictures like the tourists we had become.

Etta Fay Orkin holding the book she authored
for the 125th anniversary of the Adath Jeshurun
Congregation synagogue, Minneapolis, 2009.

EPILOGUE

※※※※※

AN AMERICAN INHERITANCE

In America, we are raised on stories that teach us that life moves in a straight line, with history safely behind us. After spending time in Native American communities, after reading ancient Jewish texts, after learning about the entangled realities of white immigrants and Indigenous Nations, I now believe that the past is threaded to today like string through a seam. Look closer, and the string itself contains many strands: to pull on one is to expose a complex weave.

Every year, Doug's nephew Frank White Bull gets a check in the mail from the U.S. Department of the Interior for six cents. This is income from the .000001 acres of Tribal land he has inherited from Lakota relatives.

"That's about a tablespoon of dirt," says Doug, shaking his head. He's sitting at Frank's sister's dining room table in Kenel, the rebuilt town above the Missouri River. The undeveloped hills and buttes behind the house glow the color of a dark bruise in the dim evening light. Frank has inherited several small parcels from various relatives, but because his acreage, like most Lakota property, is still held in trust by the federal government and administered by the Bureau of Indian Affairs, he doesn't have much control over it.

"It's tough, what can we do with this land?" asks Frank, leaning back on his stool. At fifty-six, Frank has been around long enough to earn his skepticism. A former Standing Rock Tribal Councilman and a veteran of the military police who worked at Guantanamo, his eyes take me in across the table for the stranger I am. He wears glasses and a goatee and keeps his hair in a long ponytail. "We're fractionated Indians."

When Congress created the Allotment Act and doled out individual parcels to Native Americans, it determined that, after the allottee died, land ownership would be divided among their heirs. Here's where it gets confusing: it wasn't the land itself that would be divided, but instead the land title or ownership. With every generation, the number of people owning an interest in the same property title has splintered exponentially, leading to what is called fractionation. Such fragmentation has made the land, owned by hundreds of thousands of Indigenous individuals, unusable; to do anything with a particular parcel, which in some cases is co-owned by more than two thousand heirs, requires the agreement of those owners who control a majority of the fractionated interests. Due to Relocation, many people who own Tribal land have lived off-reservation for generations, meaning that often co-owners don't know each other. Today, the United States leases allotted acreage on behalf of more than 243,000 landowners who own a combined 2.5 million slivers of interest in 5.6 million acres of land. The slim checks people like Frank receive in the mail help contextualize the joke from the hit television show *Reservation Dogs*: "We're Indian. We don't own land."

"Fractionation is a physical manifestation of the shadow of poor government policies in Indian Country," says Remi Bald Eagle, Mnicoujou Lakota and the Intergovernmental Affairs Coordinator for the Cheyenne River Sioux Tribe. "Fractionation is one of the ways you can physically look at something to see the damage that was done. You can see the harm on a map."

Exacerbating the dysfunction of fractionated land is another legacy of federal policy. Remember, after the Indian Agents allotted Native people property, any leftovers were offered for free, or practically free, to white settlers. Today, non-Indigenous people own more than half of the Cheyenne River Reservation and more than two thirds of Standing Rock, and reservation ownership maps look like checkerboards. The splintering of contiguous Indigenous land makes it difficult for many Native Nations to use their property in ways that honor traditional and contemporary economies. Most of these non-Indigenous landowners also lease fractionated lands, which helps explain why, today, more than 80 percent of all the money made through agriculture on the Standing Rock Reservation, and more than 65 percent on the Cheyenne River Reservation, is made by non-Natives. Nationwide, that statistic is closer to 87 percent.

The mixed jurisdiction of Indigenous and non-Indigenous landownership on reservations isn't only a problem for economic development, it's also a security risk. In many cases, federal law prohibits Tribal police and Tribal Courts from arresting and prosecuting nonmembers who break the law on reservations. This loophole "creates lawlessness and impunity for criminals," Elizabeth Reese, a professor at Stanford Law School and a citizen of the Nambé Pueblo, told NPR. For Native American women, such lack of safety protocols is particularly dangerous: four out of five report having been victims of violent crime, and 96 percent of their attackers were non-Native.

Over the past decade, as part of a broader effort to mitigate such problems, Indigenous Nations have been buying individual land parcels to consolidate their landholdings into larger chunks. Using money obtained through the 2009 settlement of the Cobell lawsuit—the massive court case that exposed a century of federal mismanagement of Indigenous bank accounts—Indigenous Nations have acquired more than 2.8 million acres and consolidated about a million fractional interests. But it's not entirely good news.

Due to the legacy of the Allotment Act, even the land successfully consolidated by Native Nations isn't actually controlled by them. It remains held in trust by the federal government. That means if a Nation wants to do anything with its land or the minerals underground, it needs federal approval. If you have come this far in this book, you know that trusting the Bureau of Indian Affairs requires amnesia. Plus, most of the participants, at least on Cheyenne River, aren't willing sellers, says Bald Eagle.

"If I'm a grandma and my daughter is in rehab, and I've got all eight of her kids in my Tribal housing unit, and I've got propane for a hard winter and eight kids to clothe, feed, and take to the hospital seventy miles away, can I really say no to this? If I'm addicted to meth and I get an offer,

I'm going to take it," says Bald Eagle. "Land buyback is preying on people of this reservation that have no choice but to sell."

Tribal members have come to Bald Eagle's office begging him to buy their land, so they don't feel compelled to take part in the buyback program. Others have cried when considering what to do and only signed out of fear that their grandchildren won't survive the winter without the money to pay for heat.

Because the buyback program doesn't fix the underlying problem of fractionation, it has been compared to a Band-Aid on a gaping wound. The program, which ended in 2022, converted around 40 percent of fractionated land titles belonging to Indigenous individuals into land owned by Native Nations. With every subsequent generation, the land that remains with individuals will continue to split exponentially, diminishing options and opportunities.

A lack of good reservation jobs means that the brightest and most ambitious young people leave, draining their communities of potential. Those who do return, usually taking jobs for far less money than they could make elsewhere, are often hamstrung by what Doug calls "the self-destruct element." He and others tell me repeatedly how those with big ideas, who are doing well, are often viewed with suspicion in their communities. Seen as outsiders, they don't get promoted or elected.

"It's the crab in the bucket business, where one starts to get out and another one pulls him down," says Les Ducheneaux, Mnicoujou Lakota elder. The journalist Isabel Wilkerson explains this dynamic as inherent to America's caste system, which is so insidious, so unseen, that those who exist in the marginalized classes, such as Indigenous people, are often unknowing actors in this play. Though caste in the United States often uses race to diminish those with darker skin, lateral oppression, or discrimination against one's own group, minimizes people on a basis of culture and tradition—on whether, for example, a person lives on a reservation or can speak their native language.

"Casteism can mean seeking to keep those on your disfavored rung from gaining on you, to curry the favor and remain in the good graces of the dominant caste, all of which serve to keep the structure intact," writes Wilkerson in *The New York Times*, referencing her book *Caste*. "No ethnic or racial category is immune to the messaging we all receive about the hierarchy, and thus no one escapes its consequences."

Lakota who live on reservations in North and South Dakota rank among the least employed and poorest people in the country. On Standing Rock and Cheyenne River, the median per capita income is less than $11,000. That's less than half the average income made by people who live across the Missouri River, off the reservation. Poverty is a key predictor of health, and Pine Ridge and other Lakota reservations hold the unfortunate distinction of being home to the lowest life expectancy rates in the United States. These stark numbers are why Doug repeatedly tells me Standing Rock is "a rural ghetto."

This reality isn't shaped only by the legacy of former federal policies but also by the way we teach and talk about the history of American dispossession of Indigenous lands. *What are the stories we tell, and what are the stories we don't tell, and why?* This project started with those questions. The answer is the knot at the top of the thread that links the past to today.

ON HER DAY OFF, DOUG'S NIECE JANET WHITE BULL LOVES TO RIDE HER Harley into the wide, empty roads that slice the Great Plains. A few years ago, on one such ride through North Dakota, she came upon a stone column with a statue of an American soldier at the top, a trumpet forever at his lips. A veteran herself, Janet is patriotic—the leather vest she wears on these rides has patches of Old Glory and others that honor the military— but this monument at Whitestone Hill didn't fill her with pride.

Carved into the granite at the statue's base is a dedication to twenty soldiers who were killed IN BATTLE WITH SIOUX INDIANS, but Janet knew what had really happened: in 1863, American soldiers ambushed a camp of nearly four thousand Sihasapa and Húŋkpapȟa Lakota and Ihanktonwan, killing between one hundred and three hundred, most of them children and elders.

"That was a massacre, and they're still calling it a battle," Janet says one morning as she serves Doug, who calls himself part shark, a breakfast of eggs and toast and spam. Gospel is on the radio, and sunlight filters through the curtains. "Why aren't they taking down these statues like we're taking down the ones of Robert E. Lee?"

An audit conducted in 2021 of nearly all fifty thousand public monuments, statues, and memorials throughout the country found them to be, overall, "badly misleading and out of balance." Of the 916 that mentioned pioneers, only 15 percent also referenced the terms Native American, Indian, or Indigenous. There are fifty-three monuments memorializing white settlers or soldiers who were murdered by Indigenous people but only four for Indigenous people killed by whites. Historians estimate that Native Americans account for nearly 70 percent of those who died during the pre-reservation era, the time commonly known as "the Indian Wars."

"Monuments are not facts on a pedestal, they are versions of a story, a statement of power and presence in public," says Paul Farber, director of Monument Lab, the nonprofit that conducted the audit. "In the places that have been spaces of dispossession, displacement, and broken treaties, what's left behind is myths."

This mythologizing of the past for political purposes isn't just a relic of history, it's breaking news. NORTH DAKOTA HOUSE PASSES BAN ON CRITICAL RACE THEORY IN SCHOOLS led *The Bismarck Tribune* in mid-November 2021. Passing in a landslide and signed into law the following day, the bill, according to its sponsor, keeps children safe, because learning about systemic racism in America is "insidious."

Months earlier, South Dakota governor Kristi Noem had cut more than half of all references to Indigenous Nations and citizens from history textbooks and curricula in her state, saying she wants to give students "a patriotic education." She's in good company: nationwide, half of all states fail to mention a single Indigenous person in their K–12 history curriculum, and of those that do, nearly 87 percent of the time they don't teach anything about Indigenous people living in the United States after 1900.

The poet and essayist Hanif Abdurraqib describes this sort of erasure this way: "Power, when threatened, pulls an invisible narrative from the clouds that only others in power and afraid can see."

Judge Abby likes to say Indians picked the wrong superpower: they're invisible. Although Indigenous-led efforts are starting to change that with award-winning television shows and movies written, directed, and acted by Indigenous artists, media coverage of Native Americans remains scarce. There are approximately thirteen independent (non-Native-government owned) news organizations in the United States that have a desk dedicated to covering the more than 574 federally recognized Indigenous Nations.

I've written so much in these pages about the Nazis. I'll return to them here for the last time, because their descendants have arguably worked harder to face the past than Americans. Unlike the United States, Germany has paid reparations to its Holocaust victims. Germany has a national law that requires its secondary schools to teach the Holocaust. These reparations and these lessons are deserving of great critique, as they're far from perfect, but at least they do exist.

Rather than monuments to Nazis and statues of Hitler, Germany is marked by small brass plaques that detail the names, birth dates, and dates of deportation of Holocaust victims, indicating the last location where they lived before being taken away or killed. There are at least seventy thousand of these "stumbling stones" in more than twelve hundred cities and towns across Europe.

"Each four-inch square recalls an ordinary human being, in the midst of her life, who was deported and murdered with little notice and no protest from the other ordinary human beings who surrounded her every day. The terror was here," writes Susan Neiman in *Learning from the Germans*. Rather than celebrate the past, as do our American monuments to the Confederacy, Indigenous genocide, and land dispossession, "they are designed to evoke shame."

German students who complain about the attention given to the Holocaust point to America and Israel as reasons their country's response is overblown. What was done to the Jews, they say, according to a 2005 *Frontline* report, wasn't any different from what Americans did to Indigenous people and what Israelis do to the Palestinians.

Unlike Australia and Canada, nations that, like the United States, have histories of Indigenous land theft accessorized by assimilation and genocide, America has failed to undergo any process of national truth-telling, reparation, or reconciliation, let alone any real public amends. (Like Germany's efforts at reconciliation, the efforts of Australia and Canada have been uneven and controversial but, again, at least they exist at all.)

"The world's quietest apology" is how some Indigenous leaders describe America's one federal attempt to say sorry for centuries of land theft and attempted genocide. Tucked into unrelated legislation, called the 2010 Department of Defense Appropriations Act, the official acknowledgment and apology was signed by President Barack Obama on a Saturday; he didn't read it out loud. The press weren't invited and neither was a single representative from a Native American Nation. While it "recognizes that there have been years of official depredations, ill-conceived policies, and the breaking of covenants by the Federal Government regarding Indian tribes," it fails to mention the word *genocide*. The final lines are particularly chilling:

DISCLAIMER.—Nothing in this section—

(1) authorizes or supports any claim against the United States; or

(2) serves as a settlement of any claim against the United States.

The Oglala Lakota poet Layli Long Soldier, author of *WHEREAS*, a collection of work that powerfully responds to this non-apology, told journalist Krista Tippett, why, in part, it took months before she'd heard about the resolution. "It was so quiet, and there really was not a lot of risk taken in how it was delivered. . . . It's so carefully crafted. I mean, my goodness, these guys are poets. . . . Even the phrasing of 'the arrival of Europeans opened a new chapter for Native People'—that's crazy."

This failure to acknowledge the past, this scripted amnesia, tears away the scabs of history, giving rise to a different sort of persistent harm.

* * * * *

AT A WHITE BULL FAMILY GATHERING IN NOVEMBER 2021, OVER PLATES
of ham, baked beans, and fry bread, Doug's nephew Frank stood up and
shared an awful story that surprised no one, which, I guess, is why everyone laughed. Not too long ago, Frank was on a date at a restaurant in Bismarck. More than an hour away from the Standing Rock Reservation,
Bismarck is the closest place to go to the movies or the mall. While he and
his friend were eating, Frank overheard two white men at a nearby table
referring casually to "savages." As in, "those savages who killed Custer."
Frank, because he was on a date, held his tongue and his fist.

Such racism is so pervasive in the Dakotas that pretty much every Lakota I interviewed for this book had a story of overt bigotry. There were
the students whose classmates called them racial slurs that don't merit repeating. There were those who recounted the common practice called
"dooring," in which the non-Indigenous open the passenger door of their
moving cars to try to hit Lakota walking on the side of the road. A huge
white sign outside a bar just north of Pine Ridge, still bedazzled with more
than fifty buffalo skulls, read NO INDIANS ALLOWED until 1953. Posters that
read NO INDIANS OR DOGS ALLOWED hung in South Dakota businesses into
the 1970s. It's weird to brag about what western state is the most racist, and
there are several quality contenders, but many Native American sources
nominate South Dakota, including one who referred to it as "the Mississippi of the North." In 2009, five white kids drove through Rapid City
(commonly known throughout Lakota Country as "Racist City") shooting
Indigenous people with BB guns. In 2015, a beer salesman dumped beer on
Indigenous students at a hockey game, shouting, "Go back to the reservation." In 2022, the owners of a hotel and bar in Rapid City announced that
they could not "allow a Native American to enter our business."

Throughout a forty-minute drive across Standing Rock one morning,
as dawn seems to break the sky into shards, Doug tells me story after story
of being attacked by non-Natives in the white border towns that ring and
dot the reservation. At the end, I realize these stories were instructive: he

warns me not to tell anyone in such towns about my book project, about the fact that I've been spending time with Lakota people. "You're a woman, traveling alone," he says as he gets out of the car. "You need to be careful."

These are anecdotes, and perhaps easily dismissed, but the following facts reveal the true depth and width of racism in the Dakotas. Native Americans are 9 percent of South Dakota's population but accounted for at least 37 percent of those killed by law enforcement officers between 1999 and 2020, a rate two and a half times the national average and the highest rate of police killings in any state, according to the Centers for Disease Control and Prevention. Indigenous youth in South Dakota are four and a half times more likely than their white peers to be incarcerated, making it, again, a state with one of the highest racial disparities nationwide. Lakota children have been far more likely than their white peers to be removed from their parents and put in foster care: between 2010 and 2017, more than one thousand Lakota children in South Dakota's Pennington County (home to Jew Flats) were taken from their families and placed, disproportionately, in non-Indigenous homes, a violation of federal law, according to a lawsuit filed and won by the American Civil Liberties Union. And while, as of this writing, 65 percent of missing persons in South Dakota are Indigenous, their cases are rarely prioritized or solved.

Locals who live in Wall, a town still populated primarily by descendants of homesteaders, looked at me with genuine concern when I told them I was headed the next day to Pine Ridge. "You be careful down there," one told me. "We never go down there. We never need to go that way."

One old woman, born in 1919 not far from Jew Flats, told me that, no, she never saw any "Indians" when growing up on the prairie, and no, they never bothered anybody in the neighborhood, but she did grow up afraid of them, having heard stories about "them scalping whites." That her paternal grandmother was Cherokee didn't seem to change her perspective. The Lakota, she said, "feel that they still own this land, and they think they own the Black Hills, too, but really they have been paid for it. And they have maybe been mistreated or feel that they were, but I don't think there's hard feelings anymore."

It's instructive to remember that there were two roads leading to

Kapulye, one for the Jewish side, one for the Christian, and that these roads ran in parallel, effectively separating Jews from their neighbors.

It's instructive to consider the way many Israelis think about Palestinians. Israeli peace activist Rami Elhanan says, "[Arabs] were objects to be feared, because, if you didn't fear them then they would become real people. And we didn't want them to be real people, we couldn't handle that."

Racism, like antisemitism, eradicates responsibility for those who don't look or pray like you do. The writer Dara Horn, in her essay collection *People Love Dead Jews*, explained antisemitism as "a conspiracy theory, and one appeal of conspiracy theories is that they absolve their believers of accountability, replacing the difficult obligation to build relationships with the easy urge to destroy."

Here again is the thread in the seam: Our failure to teach American history in its full and nuanced complexity leads to ignorance, which saps empathy and allows racism and hatred to flourish, which keeps our caste system in place, which keeps marginalized people poor and disenfranchised, which allows the dominant class to maintain a historical narrative that is inaccurate in its simplicity. How to stop this cycle of harm?

THE FIRST TIME I MEET LES DUCHENEAUX, THE MNICOUJOU ELDER FROM the Cheyenne River Reservation, he's raking a fenced field to prepare for the Sun Dance he'll lead the following month. His long brown hair is in braids. His bright eyes belie his age. Ducheneaux, seventy-four, came to Lakota religion later in life—he, like most people of his generation, went to boarding school and was raised on Christianity. For the past several decades, however, he has been living on what people here call "the red road," living as a modern traditionalist, his mind-set steeped in ancient Lakota values. For many years, he managed the Cheyenne River Sioux Tribe's buffalo herd, and he's now teaching Lakota culture and language in the local schools. But the work he has done to help his people has been repeatedly frustrated by his wasicu neighbors, who don't only fail to support Lakota self-empowerment, but don't acknowledge how their ancestors treated his people.

"The most important thing that's happening is their refusal to recognize their history," says Les a year and a half after we first met. Outside, through the window of his dining room, is a sweat lodge, and beyond it is the blue water of Lake Oahe. "They need to come here and say, 'We really screwed you over, and we can't give you all the land back, but we're here now, and we're going to do everything in our power to make sure you succeed.' They should ask, 'How can we help?' Not, 'Hey I've got a plan to straighten everything out.' That's paternalistic. But come here with an open mind and open heart and an open pocketbook, because everything costs money nowadays."

When Native and non-Native people talk together about their shared history of trauma and loss, they build common ground, says Faith Spotted Eagle, a politician, activist, and Ihanktonwan elder from the Yankton Sioux Tribe. "The Native people's objective is to heal. The non-Native's objective is to come out of denial." What she calls "freedom from denial" is much more powerful than guilt, she says, and allows non-Indigenous people to step toward repair.

When I first met Judge Abby, she told me the reason I should go out and study Jewish teachings about repair and healing is that justice works best when grounded in one's own culture. These traditional models were usually developed over generations in small communities, places with nowhere to hide, where a lack of anonymity pressured people to create moral societies. Village people, she told me, don't steal from the village, because it's not tenable. "Our ancestors worked much harder than we do on values, and those values weren't grounded in greed."

The years of study I did with Rabbi Benjamin have impressed upon me that, from our earliest written texts, Jewish scholars have insisted we have a moral obligation to pursue justice, to repair the world, to take responsibility for our part. I've returned, repeatedly, to the famous philosopher Maimonides's Laws of Repentance, and his time-tested strategy for making things right. Here is a modern breakdown of his six steps:

First: Stop doing the harm. Second: Confess as specifically as possible what harm you have caused and, ideally, say this truth out loud in public. Third: Begin the work of transforming yourself from a person capable of causing such harm to one who isn't. (In ancient days, people changed their names. Today, it might mean therapy.) Fourth: Make financial restitution that reflects the size of the harm. Fifth: Apologize in a way that doesn't necessarily anticipate being forgiven but that makes clear to the victim that you have heard them, and that you understand how you have caused them pain. Finally: When you face the opportunity to cause the same sort of harm, make different choices.

This idea isn't very far from what Lakota elders have explained to me about how their communities would traditionally repair. They would talk it through until everyone was satisfied. Sometimes this process was helped by collective ceremony, by taking a sweat together, or smoking the canunpa so that their words were carried to the Creator and, in this way, made holy.

It also isn't very different from the process recommended by the leading research in restorative justice: listen to those who you've harmed, assure them you understand what they've been through, ask what they need and how you can help them, and make a financial restitution.

After I'd known Doug for several years, I asked him what he thought my family might do to step toward repair. He didn't answer me directly, he didn't tell me exactly what to do, that's not his way. Instead, he told me again about the ongoing efforts to buy private land in the Black Hills and put it in trust for all Lakota.

In response, my family and I have started a fund with the Indian Land Tenure Foundation, an Indigenous-led nonprofit organization that has been around for decades working to help Native Nations buy back their lands, and this includes the Lakota efforts to purchase private land in the Black Hills. We aim to work toward donating $1.1 million, the amount, adjusted for inflation, that my family received as mortgages on our "free" land in South Dakota. This is our piece of the stolen beam. I share this here because, unlike tzedakah, or charitable giving, which is most valuable if done anonymously, my tradition tells me that amends should be made publicly. Ours is just one model among many. Throughout the country, many Indigenous Nations and organizations are leading reconciliation efforts with the descendants of settlers.

As the great-granddaughter of homesteaders, my distance to the hurt caused by federal land policies is shorter than that of someone who arrived in this country last week or whose ancestors were brought here against their will on slave ships. But all of us who are non-Indigenous and living in America today are benefiting from stolen land and broken treaties: the real estate the United States took from Indigenous Nations is the foundation of our cities, our highway systems, our railroad lines, and the industrial agriculture we eat. The sale and leasing of former Native lands funded public universities that have offered low-cost tuition to millions of Americans. Many of us have access to cheap power from hydroelectric dams that flooded Indigenous lands. Throughout its history, up to this moment, the United States has made choices to benefit settlers at the detriment of Native Americans. The harm is ongoing.

"Now is the time for people to come forward and take responsibility for their one tiny thread of this much larger story, which is how everybody in this country has benefited from the murder and theft of Indians," Judge Abby told me recently. "Climate change should make us realize we're all in this together, and you can't keep doing wrongs to people or places. If we don't repair our relationships with one another, if we don't get on the same page, we can't move forward, we can't survive."

Some things can never be healed—children were murdered and abused, families were torn apart—but as Judge has told me so many times, that doesn't mean we don't try. As Rabbi Benjamin likes to remind me, Rabbi Nachman of Bratzlav, who lived centuries ago, famously said, "If you believe breaking is possible, believe fixing is possible."

TWENTY YEARS AFTER MY FIRST TRIP TO PINE RIDGE, I FIND MYSELF again in a truck with a Lakota buffalo rancher. This time, I'm with Fred DuBray, a relative of Doug's, and Doug, who is sitting in the back seat. This time, I'm on the Cheyenne River Reservation, and I know exactly how to get from here to Jew Flats. This time, there is no weed. This time, I'm well aware of how much I still don't know.

Outside the truck, the buffalo stare with their dungeon eyes, their breath rising to the white, flat sky. They walk slowly toward us, and then they stop and crowd together, tails swinging. It's a cold March afternoon, just days before everything will shut down due to the pandemic. Fred tells me that, if I'm quiet, maybe the buffalo will talk to us. Long minutes pass while we wait and watch. Fred laughs, mostly to himself. Then he tells me that buffalo and Lakota people are the same, they're cautious around strangers.

"All the elders tell me that the only language they understand is Lakota," says Doug.

"Seems like that's the case," says Fred, and he leans out the open window to say a few words. The language is soft to my ears, as though water has smoothed its rough edges.

When Fred was growing up, this was his family's cattle ranch, but around thirty years ago, he transitioned the herd to buffalo.

"Our culture won't survive without the buffalo. The herds are our university, where we gain knowledge," says Fred, explaining that the animals taught his ancestors where to live, what plants to eat, and even how to relate to one another. Throughout the day, Fred repeatedly shares examples of how buffalo and Lakota are alike. They're tough. When penned in, constrained by too-tight quarters, they become agitated and take it out on one another. They like to live in small family groupings, and then, at certain seasons, the entire herd gathers. They have ritual: Fred and his wife once watched an entire herd line up to stop and sniff a dead calf; it went on for hours. Except for breeding season, females run the show. They hate to be alone.

"Put this guy by himself, and he'll go crazy," Fred chuckles, nudging Doug.

"I am by myself," says Doug.

"That's why you're crazy," laughs Fred.

The two of them, related through the marriage of their siblings, laugh easily and are quick to tease, but there's a current of serious talk that runs through the day. For Fred and Doug, as for Les Ducheneaux and so many other Lakota, the return of healthy buffalo populations to the prairie is critical to the recovery of their people on every level, something too important to wait for the limping gait of American justice.

Rebounding buffalo populations enable Indigenous people to practice ceremonies reliant on the animals. The Cheyenne River Sioux Tribe, which has its own herd and meat-processing plant, considers buffalo meat a key aspect of food security, providing it to those in quarantine, for school lunches, elder meals, and at funerals.

Because buffalo are what biologists call a keystone species, an animal critical to the survival of other animals and native plants, their recovery helps the entire ecosystem. This is especially important in the face of climate change: Because the animals are better adapted to the drought-prone Plains than cattle, buffalo seek water less frequently, leading to less trampling near streams, meaning that the soil and water of these critical areas have a better chance of withstanding a warming climate.

"I draw strength from knowing that each buffalo is an opportunity for an elder to hold the hand of a child and tell the story of how this resource was taken away from us and how, through lots of efforts and lots of cooperation and lots of belief, this animal was returned to us, so we now can live as close to the way our ancestors did," says Troy Heinert, executive director of the InterTribal Bison Council and a Sicangu Lakota buffalo rancher from South Dakota's Rosebud Reservation. "Buffalo were near extinction, and now those numbers are rebounding. The Lakota people, we've had to be resilient as well."

The Lakota are one of around eighty Native Nations that have a collective herd of more than twenty thousand buffalo on Indigenous land throughout the country. The dark-brown humps that now dot the prairie are one of the most obvious signs of a movement of resilience and recovery across Indigenous America. In the more than fifty years since my family sold off the last bits of Jew Flats, Indigenous Nations and citizens have harnessed Tribal sovereignty to work toward reclaiming all the aspects of Lakota religion and culture that America spent more than a century trying to diminish. Doug once told me that it took a hundred years for the Lakota to learn how to be a new kind of warrior, to use American education and courts to fight for their people and make their own change. In a direct retort to the centuries of effort to diminish the role of women in Indigenous societies, many of these modern-day warriors are female, comprising the majority of

Indigenous attorneys throughout the country, and holding leadership positions on Tribal Councils, agencies, and organizations. I once asked a source, a Tribal Councilwoman, why it appeared as though the vast majority of national nonprofits dedicated to Native America were run by women. She shrugged and said simply, "Because we've been the most oppressed."

THE INDIGENOUS ACTIVISM THAT EMERGED IN THE FACE OF THE TERMI-nation era led Congress to begin to reject its genocidal and assimilationist policies of the past. In 1975, Nations became empowered to run their own schools, leading to the closure of most federal boarding schools. In 1978, it stopped being illegal for Indigenous people to practice traditional ceremonies, religious practices, and spirituality. That same year, Congress passed the Indian Child Welfare Act, legislation intended to stop social-service agencies from removing Native children from their homes and reservations—something that had happened to as many as one third of Indigenous families. In 1990, it became illegal to steal or sell the bones from Native American graves.

Today, Indigenous Nations run their own schools, courts, and hospitals. Some Nations run their own energy companies. For the first time ever, after years of Indigenous lobbying and effort, Congress is considering legislation that would allow Indigenous Nations to comanage federal lands, such as national parks and forests (though Indigenous leaders consider this an important step, for many it's a far cry from the goal of returned land).

Today, American policy, at least officially, is focused on respect for Tribal sovereignty and self-determination. For the first time, the Department of the Interior and the National Parks Service are both led by Native Americans. It's increasingly common to hear world leaders, scientists, and activists say that Indigenous traditional knowledge is key to surviving climate change.

The modern battleground for Native rights is no longer the prairie but the courtroom, where Nations are fighting for their freedom to act as the sovereigns they are, as designated by federal treaty. Though the protests over the Dakota Access Pipeline are no longer front-page news and the Oceti

Sakowin camp where hundreds of activists spent months has long since been dismantled, attorneys for the Cheyenne River Sioux Tribe have proven, in court, that the pipeline permit process was flawed, a significant blow to federal authority.

That lawsuit is one of dozens currently testing the boundaries of how far the Lakota and other Indigenous Nations can expand their power. It won't be easy. Over the past forty years, the U.S. Supreme Court has ruled against Indigenous Nations and their interests in nearly 75 percent of cases. Federal Indian Law professor Matthew L. M. Fletcher, a member of the Grand Traverse Band, describes this trend as "an institutional bias against tribal interests." And yet, the needle does move: sixteen years after FBI agents first raided Lakota hemp fields on Pine Ridge, the Oglalas won a lawsuit in federal court recognizing their right to plant the crop. Lakota hemp is now used in health food products sold in all fifty states.

In the face of a mostly anemic legal arena, many Indigenous communities are doing what they can—looking for ways to improve things at the local level. One such example: on the Cheyenne River and Standing Rock reservations, by Tribal law, all schools must teach the Lakota language and Lakota culture. At the high school in Fort Yates, on Standing Rock, sick children can certainly have Tylenol, but they can also be treated with traditional medicine, like bear root and sage. There are multiple efforts at various stages of the planning process to build traditional Lakota villages, where elders care for infants, and everyone speaks Lakota, grows traditional foods, and is governed, as they were in the past, by designated leaders who represent each tiyospaye.

But until the United States drops its paternalistic attitude toward Indigenous people, stops controlling their land, acknowledges the past, and truly apologizes, it will be hard to fully heal, Fred DuBray tells me on that cold March day at his buffalo ranch. We've come inside to warm up, and Fred has a pot of buffalo soup on the stove. Once again, he and Doug are talking about Holocausts, both the one in Europe and the one here. Fred, like Doug, feels, on a personal level, the failure of the world to acknowledge what happened in America while it condemns Germany.

"People say all these things like 'Indian people need to move on. That was the past. That wasn't me that did that. That was my ancestors. You can't be blaming me.' You can't move on when you have those kinds of realities," says Fred, setting a bowl of soup in front of Doug, who tucks into the food for a while before speaking.

"Every treaty the United States made with Natives, once they got their foot in the doorway, they kicked us out. They lied. And now we've just got these little bitty reservations. A pittance of what we'd have had if the federal government had lived up to their word. I get really angry sometimes, and I control myself, but the only thing I can do is cry," says Doug. Just like the first day I met him, he connects the past to the reality he sees in his community. "We're in a poverty area here, and everyone is looking every day for their next meal, making sure their kids have shoes. It's the bottom rung of Maslow's Hierarchy."

Fred promises that whatever ails Doug will be fixed by the soup, and I wish that were true. In the coming years, Doug will develop heart disease. Like so many people his age, he will have a series of injurious falls. His eyesight will worsen until he becomes officially blind. He will avoid COVID, but his grandson will not, surviving one of the worst cases the doctors in Bismarck had seen. Doug's family will urge him to move to assisted elder housing, but he will refuse, wanting his community, wanting his freedom. "I have one foot in the grave and another on a banana peel," he'll tell me, laughing it off.

Every time we speak, he will teach me something, remind me of what I should be asking. And after all this time, his perspective has filtered into mine, changing me.

Outside Fred DuBray's sliding glass door is Lake Oahe, its silver edges licking at the brown ground like long tongues. When Fred was a child, this was a river; today, the lake serves as a daily reminder, another one, of how the past doesn't stay put, it keeps changing the world.

Before the three of us sat down to eat at Fred's kitchen table, I snapped a picture from the deck. My kids might stare at this photograph someday, much the way I've stared at so many old photos taken by my ancestors. If they do, they'll see a frozen lake, brown hills, and a white circle of sky. But if they have asked enough questions, if we have taught them well, they'll look at the picture and see everything else: Deep under the ice are the stumps and remains of a thick forest of cottonwoods and pine drowned by the flood caused by the federal dams. The brown hills fold onto themselves, places to hide from federal agents, if you were Doug's and Fred's ancestors, or to wait out a blizzard, if you were mine. Missing from the lens are flocks of birds thick in the sky. Missing are the native plants, the waist-high grasses waving in the wind. Up on a southern hill, at the very edge of the frame, is a scene unimaginable to Faige Etke, to Ruth, or to Louie: there is a buffalo herd. From here, with enough distance, the animals' dark-brown backs, bent toward the ground, look just like seeds.

AUTHOR'S NOTE

In the winter of 2022, Rabbi Benjamin Barnett and I led a class for members of our synagogue here in Portland to extend a conversation that the two of us had been having for several years. As mentioned, at the urging of Judge Abby, to learn how I might respond to the history of federal land policies that helped my ancestors at great cost to their Lakota neighbors, Rabbi Benjamin and I had met regularly to study Jewish texts. We wanted to understand what our culture teaches about how to repair a harm, even one we didn't directly commit but have benefited from.

The class was full of smart and thoughtful people. Many of them, like many Jews in this country, descend from immigrants who arrived in America penniless and never had the luck to receive free land. Because of the specifics of their own family histories, they saw the treatment of Indigenous Nations as a societal issue—it upset them but wasn't at all personal. When Rabbi Benjamin and I suggested that they had, in fact, benefited from this history, some of them bravely shared that they felt defensive and struggled to see that this had anything to do with them. By the end of the six-week class, I think most of them saw their place in America in a new way.

Some came to understand that broken treaties cleared the way for the land, roads, and infrastructure where they lived. Others, who grew up in western and midwestern cities, realized that their families may have profited from the cheap labor force created by federal boarding schools and the Relocation program. Some participants learned how the land-grant universities they'd attended could offer relatively cheaper tuition because those schools were funded by the taking of Indigenous lands. Others came to understand how the cheap hydropower they use to heat their homes and run their computers was created by dams that flooded and displaced Indigenous communities.

There are a lot of ways we can each measure our own distance to the taking of Indigenous land. If you feel compelled, after reading this book, to educate yourself about what has happened and what is happening to your Indigenous neighbors, I hope the following information will be helpful.

Indigenous-led movements such as #LandBack and organizations such as the Indian Land Tenure Foundation are working to reclaim ancestral homelands for Native Nations throughout the United States. Not only are they raising money for such efforts, they're also raising awareness through public campaigns and school curricula. The Native Governance Center, a nonprofit, urges those who make land acknowledgments to put action behind their words by offering a donation to a local Indigenous Nation or a nonprofit that supports Native Americans.

Some descendants of settlers are taking steps toward reconciliation over this unjust history of Indigenous land theft. Churches, farmers, landowners, and local governments in California, Nebraska, Virginia, Oregon, British Columbia, and Ontario have donated some or all of their land to local Nations. Jewish farmers, drawing for inspiration from shmita, the Torah's teaching that only God can truly own land, deliver free produce to elders and donate percentages of their earnings to local Indigenous communities. At least one homesteader descendant has donated a portion of the earnings made from the sale of her family's homestead to a local Native Nation. Several Indigenous Nations throughout the country have created land taxes, through which those who live on former Indigenous lands can pay a voluntary annual fee in acknowledgment and gratitude. The Duwamish Tribe's Land Tax in Seattle has more than twenty thousand participants. The Lisjan in the Bay Area, who don't have a reservation, have acquired several acres, which include sacred ancestral burial sites, due to their Shuumi Land Tax.

Professor Margaret Jacobs, a descendant of settlers, and journalist Kevin Abourezk, a member of the Rosebud Sioux Tribe, are tracking such acts of reconciliation at their website, reconciliationrising.org. They've found that the key to success is to follow the lead of Indigenous voices. Apologies and actions by local governments and individual citizens to the Indigenous Nations that live and lived where cities now stand are, they write, "significant and meaningful." They're also pragmatic: to wait for federal leadership on this issue is to delay justice indefinitely. It's possible that Congress could be spurred to action if enough citizens lead by example. This happened in Australia in the late 1990s, when activists there created "Sorry Books"—available in public spaces such as libraries, churches, and schools—that provided settler descendants the opportunity to apologize to the Indigenous people of Australia when their government refused to do so. The books were so popular that more than half a million people signed them, inspiring other grassroots projects and activism that eventually pushed the Australian government to take real action.

One place to start is to investigate the ways your family and you yourself have benefited from the history of American dispossession of Indigenous lands. A guide for taking these initial steps to find yourself in this story can be found at the back of this book, in the Resources for Further Research section.

ACKNOWLEDGMENTS

This entire book can be read as a land acknowledgment to the Lakota Nation. However, I wrote the vast majority of it not on Lakota land, but in my attic in Portland, Oregon, on the traditional village locations of the Multnomah, Kalapuya, Molalla, Wasco, Cowlitz, Clackamas, Kathlamet, and Chinook. These Nations each have a unique history and a unique set of contemporary circumstances, and yet, like the Lakota, they, too, have been harmed by both the history and the legacy of federal land theft and state-sanctioned attempted genocide. My friends and sources from Indigenous communities have taught me that it's important for action to accompany land acknowledgments. I'll be donating a portion of the proceeds from this book to Seeding Justice, an Indigenous-led nonprofit that funds Oregon-based Native organizations and communities. I'll also be donating another portion to the InterTribal Buffalo Council for their work to restore the buffalo to Lakota Country.

To write a book such as this, especially in the midst of a global pandemic, is to risk seeing far too much of your own mind for days, months, and years at a stretch. Fortunately for me, a huge host of people ensured that I didn't do this alone.

This book was championed from the first by my wonderful agent, Jessica Papin. Thank you for loving this idea and believing I could pull it off. Every writer should be so lucky to have such an advocate in their corner.

Thank you to everyone at Viking Penguin, particularly to Gretchen

Schmidt for understanding exactly what I was trying to do here and for the many conversations that helped improve the thinking behind my sentences. And to Terezia Cicel for fighting to inherit this project—thank you for your great questions, your careful eye, and your excellent editing. Special shout-out to the publicity, marketing, and production teams. I'm so grateful for your hard work on this project.

For the gift of not only critical sources of funding but all manner of intangible support, thank you to the Whiting Foundation, the Fund for Investigative Journalism, the Regional Arts and Culture Council, and Art/Lab. The Sitka Center for Art and Ecology provided me (twice!) with not only a place of my own to write but an inspiring view.

For over a year, the pandemic prevented me from doing any in-person research. I'm so grateful to the following people who ensured that my reporting didn't suffer a meaningful pause. Diana Pevak, researcher extraordinaire, deserves all the praise for her work at the Pennington County Register of Deeds office, pulling my family's mortgages and deeds so that I could analyze the value of our land. Sam Herley, curator of the University of South Dakota Oral History Center, provided me with an hour of each of the following graduate students' time per week: Mikayla Kappenman, Victoria Tobin, and Jill Swanson—thank you for helping me retrieve and organize interviews with Lakota people from decades before I was born, adding an important layer of depth to this project. During this time, our public library closed its interlibrary loan office for nearly two years—thanks to Jessica Wyse for enabling me access to the books I needed when I needed them, not to mention talking me through all manner of complicated ideas.

I couldn't have written this book without the twenty years I first spent reporting in the American West, and during that time having the opportunity to consider how federal policies have shaped the lives of both homesteader descendants and Native Americans. Thank you to the publications that sent me into rural places, recorder in hand, and paid for me to get there and back: *High Country News*, *InvestigateWest*, *The Nation*, *Indian Country Today*, *Ms.*, *Orion*, and *Salon*.

My dear friend Alicia Jo Rabins once said that if you are in conversation with someone throughout the length of a project, that person becomes a sort of colleague, regardless of whether you share an office or a boss. Throughout the past five years, the following writers have helped me to think this book better and write this book better, talking through concepts, structure, and the ethics of writing about both my own family and people of another culture. Alicia, Lee van der Voo, and Margot Kahn Case: you are the colleagues of my dreams, thank you for editing early drafts and for all the phone calls and walks in the rain. Apricot Irving and Krissy Clark: thank you for being there at critical moments, picking me up and getting me going again. To David Wolman, whose instincts are impeccable, I owe you endless beers for setting me on the path. To Sierra Crane Murdoch, your guts and tenacity are an inspiration. And to my fellow Whiting winners, in particular to Catherine Moore, Sangu Iyer, and Lorelei Lee, our regular Zoom calls and texts got me through some sticky parts of this process, I'm so grateful to you all.

I spent a lot of years wondering if I, as a white lady, could or should write a book about Lakota people. Thank you to Brett Shelton, Les Ducheneaux, Wayne Ducheneaux, Abby Abinanti, Fred DuBray, Remi Bald Eagle, Jodi Rave Spotted Bear, Se-ah-dom Edmo, Chuck Hudson, Matt Fletcher, and Wenona Singel for your encouragement and guidance. What I didn't anticipate, but probably should have, is how fraught it is to write about one's own community. The following Jewish scholars, rabbis, and all around menschen gave generously of their time and wisdom: Andy Bachman, Eddy Portnoy, Jonathan Friedmann, Danya Ruttenberg, Joshua Rose, Shoshana Gugenheim Kedem, Toba Spitzer, David Koffman, and Benjamin Barnett. Thanks to all of you for helping me write this book with nuance, complexity, and sensitivity.

So many archivists, librarians, scholars, Lakota elders, family members, and writers provided invaluable help and guidance. I could fill the pages of a second book with just the names of all the people I spoke to, whose books I read, who were excessively patient with my excessive questions. To anyone I fail to mention here, I hope I've told you in person how grateful I am. In particular, I owe a great debt to Tawa Ducheneaux, Michael Moore, Donovin Sprague, Anne Lucke, Cris Stainbrook, Josh Meisel, Jonathan Friedmann, Alisha Babbstein, Kate Dietrick, Mark Hirsch, Haley Aguirre, Fred Hoxie, Richard Edwards, Margaret Jacobs, Mikal Eckstrom, Roberta Newman, Cody White, and Stephan Pevar. Big extra thank you to the good people at both Illuminative and the Native American Rights Fund for ensuring my Indigenous terminology was as accurate as possible.

Ena Alvarado and Mikal Eckstrom: fact-checkers of my dreams. Oh my goodness thank you times a million for saving me from myself.

To Katey Linkus and Meg Gibson, thank you for caring for my kids and making sure we could see the kitchen counters. I love you guys.

Both Judge Abby and Rabbi Benjamin deserve an extra round of applause. Judge, you have changed the way I see the world. In so many ways both small and profound, your mentorship and guidance have gently nudged me to be more compassionate, more generous. Rabbi Benjamin, the learning we have done together has been so rich and has led me to understand and appreciate our culture and the living nature of our traditions in profound ways. Thank you both.

It is an uncomfortable thing to be written about, and perhaps even more nerve-racking to have one's family described in ink. I owe an enormous debt to Doug White Bull for trusting me to tell this story. It's not overstatement to say that knowing you has changed my life. I am forever formed by the perspective you've shared. Thank you also to so many members of the White Bull family for your help and kindness.

And to all Sinykins near and far: there's not really a word quite wide or deep enough to convey my gratitude. So many of you shared letters and photographs and handed-down stories about our family. Thank you for trusting me. I especially want to thank Cathi Oskow for sharing her notes from her 1983 interviews with Jack and Marvin Sinykin; Aviva Oskow for coming with me to South Dakota; and Cathy Siegel for her genius genealogy research skills. Auntie Etta, what a gift it has been to listen to your stories and learn from you. I couldn't have written this book without your care and holding of our family history. I'm forever grateful for you.

And last but certainly never least: to my closest people, the ones who I couldn't have done this without, who believed in me and kept me going: my parents, Sandra and Sterling Clarren; my brother, Jonathan Clarren; all my Eastmans, Winters, and Esmers; and so many dear friends near and far, thank you. To my darling kids, Jude and Louie, it's a joy and privilege to be your parent. And most importantly, to Greg—you make everything better.

NOTES

vii *He [Rabbi Tarfon] used to say*: Pirkei Avot 2:16 (The William Davidson Talmud), Sefaria. Available at www.sefaria.org/Pirkei_Avot.2.16?lang=bi.

PROLOGUE

1 **Twenty-two years ago:** Reporting trip by the author to South Dakota, fall 2001. Resulting article: Rebecca Clarren, "Seed in the Ground," *High Country News*, March 4, 2002.

2 *This American Life* **comic:** Jessica Abel and Ira Glass, *Radio: An Illustrated Guide* (Chicago: WBEZ Alliance, 1999).

3 **many other immigrants:** It doesn't appear that anyone has investigated exactly how many of the nation's homesteaders were immigrants. That said, in a phone interview on November 22, 2022, Jonathan Fairchild, historian for the National Park Service's Homestead National Historical Park, told me that he thought 10 percent of homesteaders may have been immigrants. "About the Homestead Act," National Park Service, www.nps.gov/home/learn/historyculture/abouthome steadactlaw.htm.

3 **One such story:** Author's phone interviews with Etta Orkin, July 2019 and May 2020; Diane Small, November 2018; and Marcia Goldman, December 12, 2018. This was a story I knew from growing up, that my mother, Sandra Clarren, told.

3 **Another selection from our:** Nancy Sinykin, phone interview with the author, July 8, 2019. Since none of them arrived with birth certificates, the Sinykins often changed their birth dates to suit their needs. For example: Rose gets her homestead in 1913, but if her birth date is correct on the family tree that Etta created in 1977 (when Rose was still alive and weighing in on such things), Rose was born in 1894 and, therefore, only nineteen at the time.

5 **In 2017, I found:** Reporting trip by the author to the Yurok Reservation, California, September 2017. Resulting article: Rebecca Clarren, "Judge Abby Abinanti Is Fighting for Her Tribe—and for a Better Justice System," *The Nation*, November 30, 2017.

CHAPTER 1: BEYOND THE PALE

11 **when my great-great-grandfather:** According to paperwork filed with a notary in Ramsey County, Minnesota, in 1945, Harry swore that he was born in 1859. According to the "Proof of Testimony" filed on his homestead, he was born in 1862. His obituary also states that he was born in 1862 ("Former County Resident Dies," *Rapid City Journal*, August 30, 1945).

11 **It was unseasonably hot:** Irena Grosfeld, Seyhun Orcan Sakalli, and Ekaterina Zhuravskaya, "Middleman Minorities and Ethnic Violence: Anti-Jewish Pogroms in the Russian Empire," *Review of Economic Studies* 87, no. 1 (2020): 289–342. More on the economic downturn: Great Britain, Foreign Office, *Reports from Her Majesty's Consuls on the Manufactures, Commerce, &c., of Their Consular Districts, Part VII* (London: Harrison and Sons, 1881). Page 542 begins a section on Odesa for the year 1880.

11 **Months earlier, terrorists:** John Doyle Klier and Shlomo Lambroza, eds., *Pogroms: Anti-Jewish Violence in Modern Russian History* (Cambridge: Cambridge University Press, 2004), 19. I. Michael Aronson, *Troubled Waters: Origins of the 1881 Anti-Jewish Pogroms in Russia* (Pittsburgh: University of Pittsburgh Press, 1990). John Klier, *Russians, Jews, and the Pogroms of 1881–1882* (Cambridge, UK: Cambridge University Press), 2011.

11 **Harry Sinykin, drawing:** Etta Orkin, phone and in-person interviews with the author, September 2018 to November 2022. Cathi Oskow's 1983 interviews with Jack Sinykin (Harry's son) and Marvin Sinykin (Harry's grandson). I interviewed Cathi (Etta's daughter and my cousin) while she related her notes from those taped conversations, December 16, 2020.

11 **If he was armed:** Sophie Trupin, *Dakota Diaspora: Memoirs of a Jewish Homesteader* (Lincoln, NE: University of Nebraska Press, 1988). For other accounts of Jews not having anything but boiling water with which to defend themselves, see: Linda Mack Schloff, *And Prairie Dogs Weren't Kosher: Jewish Women in the Upper Midwest Since 1855* (New York: Lantern Books, 1996). It's worth noting that there are accounts of some Jews having guns during these violent clashes.

12 **The looting of Jewish shops:** Klier and Lambroza, *Pogroms*.

12 **On a cold September day in 2018:** Etta Orkin, interview with the author, Minneapolis, September 25, 2018. Omeljan Pritsak, "The Pogroms of 1881," *Harvard Ukrainian Studies* 11, no. 1/2 (1987): 8–43.

14 **To be a Jew is to live:** Campbell Robertson, Christopher Mele, and Sabrina Tavernise, "11 Killed in Synagogue Massacre; Suspect Charged with 29 Counts," *New York Times*, October 27, 2018, www.nytimes.com/2018/10/27/us/active-shooter-pittsburgh-synagogue-shooting.html. Jon Haworth, "Dozens of Graves in Jewish Cemetery Defaced with Swastikas, Offensive Graffiti," ABC News, November 15, 2022, www.abcnews.go.com/US/dozens-graves-jewish-cemetery

-defaced-swastikas-offensive-graffiti/story?id=93325341. Thea DiGiammerino and Mark Pratt, "Mass. Man Indicted in Investigation into Fires Set at Jewish Institutions in 2019," Associated Press and NBC10 Boston, February 16, 2022, www.nbcboston.com/news/local/mass-man-indicted-in-investigation-into -fires-set-at-jewish-institutions/2646678. For more on this, read: Dara Horn, *People Love Dead Jews: Reports from a Haunted Present* (Washington, DC: National Geographic Books, 2022).

14 **my mother told me:** My mother, Sandra Clarren, has no memory of this conversation.

14 **As early as the second century:** Eli Barnavi, ed., *A Historical Atlas of the Jewish People: From the Time of the Patriarchs to the Present* (New York: Knopf, 1992).

15 **Here, Jews were:** Author's phone interviews with Natan Meir (Judaic studies professor, Portland State University), August 31, 2022; Eddy Portnoy (academic adviser at YIVO Institute for Jewish Research), undated; and Jonathan Dekel-Chen (professor of Jewish history, Hebrew University of Jerusalem), September 13, 2022.

There were periods when Jews were allowed to buy land, but they were both rare and brief, such as from 1862 to 1864, when, in the Minsk region, Jews could buy land from Russian noblemen. Some wealthy Jews were also able to make agreements with non-Jewish leaseholders who officially owned the land but allowed Jews to hold the lease. For more on this see: Judith Kalik, "Movable Inn: The Rural Jewish Population of Minsk Gubernia from 1793 to 1914," in *Movable Inn* (Poland: De Gruyter Open, 2018).

15 **twenty-five-year stints:** Olga Litvak, *Conscription and the Search for Modern Russian Jewry* (Bloomington, IN: Indiana University Press, 2006).

15 **According to family lore:** Etta Orkin, interview with the author, July 2019. Letter to Etta Orkin, February 15, 1977, from a cousin whose mother lived in Russia until 1908 and "tells stories of the Tsar's soldiers looking for boys for the army, and how they hid in the hay when the soldiers came."

15 **When Tsar Alexander II:** Klier and Lambroza, *Pogroms.*

15 **"They beat us with the ruble":** Aronson, *Troubled Waters*, 72.

16 **the new tsar, Alexander III:** Alexander III was so terrified that he, too, would be killed, he was known to routinely check under his bed for hiding assassins, Klier and Lambroza, *Pogroms*, 31.

16 **Throughout the following year:** Klier and Lambroza, *Pogroms*, 143.

16 **a nearby village:** Fanny Smith Landman (cousin), interview with Etta Orkin, 1977. This was the town of Romanova, another shtetl in the Slutsk region of what is today Belarus. Fanny estimates that Romanova and Kapulye were ten miles apart.

16 **Enter Faige Etke:** We have a copy of their ketuba, a Jewish wedding contract, printed in Hebrew and Yiddish.

18 **They were relatively wealthy:** Etta Orkin, interview with the author, September 25, 2018. Jack Sinykin, interview with Cathi Oskow. Etta Fay (Kozberg) Orkin, *Etta and Harry's Megillah*, 1977. Jack Sinykin's file from Leavenworth Penitentiary says, on page 6, "they rented a modern eight room house in Russia in town and lived on a marginal economic level."

18 **Kapulye, a town:** I'm using this spelling out of deference to my aunt Etta, who said this was the spelling her mother used. The following are also accurate: Kapolia, Kapylia, Kopulia, Kapulia, Kapolye. In Polish, it's Kopyl. On contemporary Belarussian maps, it's Kapyl. Other sources of information about Kapulye: "The Jewish Community of Kapyl," ANU—Museum of the Jewish People. Also: "Nathan Feinstein's Story. Info on Kapulye (Jewish Shtetl) aka Kopyl, Belarus," YouTube, posted December 7, 2014, www.youtube.com/watch?v=lo6Wjz0LB-8. Finally, the organization Jewish Genealogy has collected Yizkor (Memorial) Books that were written by groups of former residents to document Jewish communities that were destroyed in the Holocaust. The collection on the Jewish Genealogy website for Kapulye can be found here: www.jewishgen.org/yizkor/slutsk /slu473.html.

19 **S. Y. Abramovitsh, one of the greatest:** S. Y. Abramovitsh, "Dos vintshfingerl," (1865). Abramovitsh (also known as Mendele Mocher Sforim) set this story, the title of which translates to "The Magic Ring," in Kabstansk, his version of Kapulye. In the introduction to Abramovitsh's *Tales of Mendele the Book Peddler* (New York: Random House, 1996), Dan Miron writes, "Kabstansk is the quintessentially poor, helpless Jewish community." For more about Abramovitsh, see: "Abramovitsh, Sholem Yankev," The YIVO Encyclopedia of Jews in Eastern Europe, www.yivoencyclopedia.org/article.aspx/abramovitsh_sholem_yankev.

19 **two parallel roads:** Jewish Genealogy's Yizkor Books. Jack Sinykin, interview with Cathi Oskow.

19 **Actual danger persisted, too:** Etta Orkin's notes from her interview with Fanny Smith Landman, 1977. Fanny's father was Faige Etke's brother Yisroel. It's not clear from the interview that any specific person in my own family was actually raped, just that this generally happened.

19 **brothers drank lye:** Rich Sinykin, phone interview with the author, August 12, 2019. Peggy Schaeffer (granddaughter of James Zilboorg, Faige Etke's brother), phone interview with the author, April 23, 2021.

19 **these "May Laws":** Klier and Lambroza, *Pogroms*, 41. Herman Rosenthal, "May Laws," JewishEncyclopedia.com, www.jewishencyclopedia.com/articles/10508 -may-laws.

20 **Harry's younger brother Sam:** Rich Sinykin interview. SS *Taormina* manifest, New York, August 14, 1891.

20 **chaotic Lower East Side:** Barnavi, *A Historical Atlas of the Jewish People.* Kenneth Libo and Irving Howe, *We Lived There Too: In Their Own Words and Pictures— Pioneer Jews and the Westward Movement of America, 1630–1930* (New York: St. Martin's/Marek, 1984). Karen Brodkin, *How Jews Became White Folks and What That Says about Race in America* (New Brunswick, NJ: Rutgers University Press, 1998).

20 **NO DOGS. NO JEWS:** Naomi W. Cohen, *Encounter with Emancipation: The German Jews in the United States, 1830–1914* (Ann Arbor: University of Michigan, 1984), 250.

20 **self-styled German Jews:** Oscar Handlin, "Our Unknown American Jewish Ancestors," *Commentary* 6 (1948): 104. Handlin observes that Yiddish- or German-

speaking Jews in the United States before 1880 were often recognized, or even referred to themselves, as "German." Germany didn't unify as a nation until 1871. This label had more to do with signaling wealth, status, and having Americanizing aspirations than with geography. Jonathan Friedmann, of the Jewish Museum of the American West, explains many of these "German" immigrants hailed from Galicia, Posen, Prussia, Bavaria, Bohemia, Alsace, Holland, or beyond.

See also: Norton B. Stern and William M. Kramer, "The Major Role of Polish Jews in the Pioneer West," *Western States Jewish Historical Quarterly* 8, no. 4 (1976).

"A New Surge of Growth," Immigration and Relocation in U.S. History—German, Library of Congress, www.loc.gov/classroom-materials/immigration /german/new-surge-of-growth: "Antisemitic violence in Germany and Austria-Hungary drove thousands of German Jews to emigrate. German Jews during this period were, by and large, proud of their German culture; they generally chose to speak German instead of Hebrew or Yiddish and lived together with Catholics and Lutherans in German American communities."

"From Haven to Home: 350 Years of Jewish Life in America," Library of Congress, www.loc.gov/exhibits/haventohome/haven-century.html: "In the first half of the nineteenth century, Jewish immigrants come mostly, though not exclusively, from Central Europe. In addition to settling in New York, Philadelphia, and Baltimore, groups of German-speaking Jews made their way to Cincinnati, Albany, Cleveland, Louisville, Minneapolis, St. Louis, New Orleans, San Francisco, and dozens of small towns across the United States. During this period there was an almost hundred-fold increase in America's Jewish population from some 3,000 in 1820 to as many as 300,000 in 1880."

20 **The answer cooked up:** Leonard George Robinson, *The Agricultural Activities of the Jews in America* (New York: American Jewish Committee, 1912).

21 **The Homestead Act of 1862:** A good introduction to the act can be found at: "About the Homestead Act," National Park Service, www.nps.gov/home/learn /historyculture/abouthomesteadactlaw.htm.

21 **had deep roots:** Jonathan Dekel-Chen, "(Mostly) Everything You Wanted to Know about Jewish Farming History but Didn't Know Who to Ask," Zoom lecture, Cultivating Culture: A (Virtual) Gathering of Jewish Farmers, January 30, 2022.

21 **This movement, dubbed Am Olam:** Violet Goering and Orlando J. Goering, *Jewish Farmers in South Dakota: The Am Olam* (Pierre: South Dakota State Historical Society, 1982).

21 **"a worse hell":** Leo N. Levi, a B'nai B'rith official from Texas. Ava F. Kahn, *Jewish Life in the American West* (Washington, DC: ICS Publications, 2004), 45. See Kahn also for more on the Industrial Removal Office.

21 **Beginning in 1901:** Jewish Agricultural Society, *Jews in American Agriculture: The History of Farming by Jews in the United States* (New York: Jewish Agricultural Society, 1954).

22 **Galveston Movement, funded by:** Edward Allen Brawley, "When the Jews Came to Galveston," *Commentary*, April 2009. Writer Calvin Trillin writes about

his family's sponsorship by the Galveston plan in: Calvin Trillin, *Messages from My Father: A Memoir* (New York: Macmillan, 1997).

22 **He'd heard that a number of Jews:** Michael J. Bell, "'True Israelites of America': The Story of the Jews of Iowa," *Annals of Iowa* 53 (1994), 99. Sioux City, Iowa Jewish Federation Newsletter, November 15, 1968. There are several official histories of the Jews of Sioux City: Simon Glazer, *The Jews of Iowa* (Des Moines, IA: Koch Brothers, 1904). Bernard Shuman, *A History of the Sioux City Jewish Community, 1869 to 1969* (Sioux City, IA: Jewish Federation, 1969). Susan Marks Connor, ed., *I Remember When . . . Personal Recollections and Vignettes of the Sioux City Jewish Community, 1869–1984* (Sioux City, IA: Jewish Federation, 1985).

22 **(A brief public service announcement):** The birthplace of Ashkenazi Jewry was western Germany, a region called the Rhineland-Palatinate. For information about the cultural background of American Jews, see: "Race, Ethnicity, Heritage and Immigration among U.S. Jews," Pew Research Center, May 11, 2021, www .pewresearch.org/religion/2021/05/11/race-ethnicity-heritage-and-immigration -among-u-s-jews.

23 **Sam became a peddler:** Hasia R. Diner, *Roads Taken: The Great Jewish Migrations to the New World and the Peddlers Who Forged the Way* (New Haven, CT: Yale University Press, 2015). My description of Sam is from an interview with his descendent Richard Sinykin: "He started out as a peddler with a pack on his back."

23 **a midwife, Faige Etke:** Jack Sinykin, interview with Cathi Oskow. Orkin, *Megillah*.

24 **There are stories that we:** Sandra Clarren, conversations with the author, June 2019 and July 2022. Jack Sinykin, interview with Cathi Oskow: "Harry had bad temper, unhealthy, rupture from pogrom, bad asthma."

24 **Harry arrived in America:** My cousin Cathy Siegel is a genius at finding historical documents, and she found Harry's ship manifest on Ancestry.com. It has him leaving for New York on November 3, 1895. His name upon arrival was Hirsch Chait, but his half brothers had the last name Sinykin, and the family story is that they convinced him to adopt it, too. His Declaration of Intention for becoming a citizen was filed on October 27, 1896, in Minnehaha County, South Dakota. His oath to support the Constitution and renounce the tsar of Russia was signed on August 2, 1897, also in Minnehaha County.

24 **"Kids in Europe":** Jack Sinykin, interview with Cathi Oskow.

25 **Even non-citizen immigrants:** Trina Williams Shanks, "The Homestead Act of the Nineteenth Century and Its Influence on Rural Lands" (CSD Working Paper No. 05–52, Center for Social Development, Washington University, St. Louis, 2005).

26 **"untouched by human toil":** Trupin, *Dakota Diaspora*, 2.

26 **"fertile prairie" for millennia:** Some Indigenous people prefer the term "time immemorial" to describe the longevity of their Nations, but that is also a legal term that simply indicates a time before colonization (literally: before the memory of the law).

26 **When Jack arrived:** Jack Sinykin, interview with Cathi Oskow. Sioux City Public Museum archivist Haley Aguirre did many searches on my behalf in old Sioux City directories.

27 **A new wave:** Klier and Lambroza, *Pogroms*. Trupin, *Dakota Diaspora*.

27 **She packed up:** Diane Small, phone interview with the author, March 2, 2019. Orkin, *Megillah.* For more general information about what people packed and brought, see: Schloff, *And Prairie Dogs Weren't Kosher.*

27 **For days, they traveled:** Some details sourced from "Via Antwerp. The Road to Ellis Island," an exhibit created by the Red Star Line Museum, Antwerp, Belgium, displayed at Ellis Island Immigration Museum, New York, 2016. SS *Manitou* manifest, Antwerp to Boston, November 1, 1906 (found by my cousin Cathy Siegel). Details about Aunt Rose's eye infection: Rosalind Smith Friedman, interview with Etta Orkin, 1977.

28 **"nice white tablecloths":** Etta Orkin, phone interview with the author, July 2019.

28 **some critical revision:** Letter by Jake Kozberg, kept in a safe-deposit box in Minneapolis and then in my parents' basement. Letter to Harry Sinykin from Mr. Smith (president of the Granite City Bank of Dell Rapids, SD), May 20, 1908, stating "you owe us amounting to $296.62."

28 **from the Pale, came to America:** "Jewish Immigration to America," YIVO Institute for Jewish Research, https://immigrationusa.yivo.org/exhibits/show/immigrationstories/home.

28 **Upon landing, they:** Rabbi Toba Spitzer, phone interview with the author, October 21, 2020. Brodkin, *How Jews Became White Folks.*

28 **In 1941, the Nazis:** Rabbi Andy Bachman, phone interview with the author, June 26, 2019. Rabbi Bachman is a descendant of Kapulye Jews and has been involved with the placing of Holocaust Memorials there and throughout Belarus. The memorial marker erected in honor of those who were killed reads, in part, "2,965 Jews from Kopyl ghetto were brutally murdered here in 1942," www.belarusmemorials.com/memorials/minsk/kopyl. See also: Yahad In-Unum, "Execution of Jews in Kopyl," The Map of Holocaust by Bullets: www.yahadmap.org/#village/kopyl-kapyl-minsk-belarus.922.

More than six hundred thousand, or 90 percent, of Belarusian Jews were killed in the Holocaust, as described in: Judith Matloff, "The Last Shtetl Jews of Belarus," *Forward*, October 4, 2010.

29 **Thanks in part:** Orkin, *Megillah.* Etta Orkin, interview with the author, Minneapolis, September 25, 2018.

CHAPTER 2: THE HOLOCAUST AT HOME

31 **the United States was bent:** Suzan Shown Harjo, *Nation to Nation: Treaties Between the United States and American Indian Nations* (Washington, DC: NMAI and Smithsonian Books, 2014). An untitled article that ran in *The Black Hills Weekly Journal*, January 25, 1884, states, "The Sioux lands, capable of supporting a great population if opened to settlement and cultivation lie utterly unproductive and valueless. The reserve is a great obstacle in the way of development of the natural resources of the country, a barrier in the way of railroads and a hindrance to the establishment of such commercial relations as should at this day connect Western Dakota with the cities of the east."

31 **In the winter of 1880:** "Old Indian Warrior Still Lives in Past," *Argus Leader*, September 17, 1943. "Dakota Prairie Buffalo Hunt Recalled by Chief White

Bull," *Rapid City Journal*, December 30, 1936. Joseph White Bull, *Lakota Warrior*, trans. and ed. James H. Howard (Lincoln: University of Nebraska Press, 1998), 2–4. Stanley Vestal, *Warpath: The True Story of the Fighting Sioux Told in a Biography of Chief White Bull* (Lincoln: University of Nebraska Press, 1934), 233–40. The dates on this are a little tricky. I use the winter of 1880, because that's what White Bull recalled in both of the above newspaper stories. In *Lakota Warrior*, he describes such a hunt when he was thirty-one years old. If his birth year was indeed 1849 (the date that is most commonly given), then this is the same hunt, but in certain census counts and other documents, his birth year is listed as 1843 or 1850. In *Warpath*, he recounts another buffalo hunt that happened "sometime later" than August 1882.

31 **Joseph White Bull went hunting:** In historical documents written by white people, he is often called "Lazy White Bull." This is a mistranslation of his Lakota name, Pte San Hunka, which means "leading in the head White Bull" but was erroneously misconstrued with the word for lazy in Lakota, *hunkesini*, per the South Dakota State Historical Society.

32 **White Bull was broad shouldered:** These details come primarily from: White Bull, *Lakota Warrior*, and Vestal, *Warpath*. White Bull appears in the federal census in 1900 and 1910, as well as South Dakota's census in 1905, 1915, and 1925. See also: "Indian Chief Is Very Vain," *Sioux City Journal*, November 4, 1906. "White Bull Is for Peace," *Sioux City Journal*, November 2, 1906. "A Hero Out of Homer," *Salt Lake Tribune*, April 22, 1934.

32 **required to carry:** Vestal, *Warpath*, chap. 23.

32 **animals massed together:** Untitled article, *Black Hills Weekly Pioneer*, September 18, 1880.

33 **"By the time we had skinned":** White Bull, *Lakota Warrior*, 3–4.

33 **the American bison would be decimated:** Larry Barsness, *Heads, Hides, and Horns: The Complete Buffalo Book* (College Station: Texas A&M University Press, 2013). Barsness writes that, by the fall of 1883, buffalo in the Dakotas were decimated to "about 1,000 head" (131–32). "By 1902 the 635 buffalo alive in 1890 had decreased to an estimated seventy-two in the United States and twenty-five in Canada."

33 **the trail White Bull most likely took:** James D. Osburn, Ken R. Stewart, and Lonis R. Wendt, *Fort Pierre–Deadwood Trail: Then & Now* (Wasta, SD: Cheyenne River Press, 2008).

33 **I first meet Joseph White Bull's grandson:** Doug White Bull, interview with the author, McLaughlin, SD, June 3, 2019.

33 **the oldest living descendant:** Lakota track family structure differently than most other Americans. For example: traditionally in Lakota culture, while your mother's brother is called uncle, your father's brother is called father. I've seen White Bull family trees that depict Joseph White Bull as the direct ancestor of Doug. I've also been told by members of the family that, as far as they can tell, it's more likely that Joseph was the brother of Doug's biological great-grandfather or grandfather. The question of who is related to famous chiefs such as White Bull or Sitting Bull has become political in some cases. While many Lakota have told me that the richest person in their culture is the one with the most relatives, there are certain

people who claim to be related to Joseph White Bull but insist he has no descendants on Standing Rock.

34 **Doug has diabetes:** Dawn W. Satterfield, John E. Shield, John Buckley, and Sally T. Alive. "So That the People May Live (Hecel Lena Oyate Ki Nipi Kte): Lakota and Dakota Elder Women as Reservoirs of Life and Keepers of Knowledge about Health Protection and Diabetes Prevention," *Journal of Health Disparities Research and Practice* 1, no. 2 (2007): 2. Lakota are overrepresented nationally in diabetes, heart disease, and obesity.

34 **Within the first year of the pandemic:** Katherine Leggat-Barr, Fumiya Uchikoshi, and Noreen Goldman, "COVID-19 Risk Factors and Mortality among Native Americans," *Demographic Research* 45 (2021): 1185–1218, www.medrxiv .org/content/10.1101/2021.03.13.21253515v2.full-text. Nina Lakhani, "Exclusive: Indigenous Americans Dying from Covid at Twice the Rate of White Americans," *The Guardian*, February 4, 2021, www.theguardian.com/us-news/2021 /feb/04/native-americans-coronavirus-covid-death-rate.

34 **"When we had the buffalo":** Doug White Bull, phone interview with the author, January 20, 2020.

35 **Papers published in:** Donna L. Feir, Rob Gillezeau, and Maggie E. C. Jones. *The Slaughter of the Bison and Reversal of Fortunes on the Great Plains* (working paper 30368, National Bureau of Economic Research, 2022). Richard H. Steckel and Joseph M. Prince, "Tallest in the World: Native Americans of the Great Plains in the Nineteenth Century," *American Economic Review* 91, no. 1 (2001): 287–94.

35 **In the 1700s:** "Where the Buffalo Roamed," National Park Service, last updated December 5, 2022, www.nps.gov/gosp/learn/nature/where-the-buffalo-roamed .htm.

35 **the top lands of the ranch:** Visit by the author to South Dakota, February 2019.

35 **"The [buffalo] would come":** Doug White Bull, phone interview with the author, September 2019.

35 **ride and breed horses:** For more about the introduction of horses to Indigenous people living on the Great Plains, see: Emil Her Many Horses, ed., *A Song for the Horse Nation: Horses in Native American Cultures* (Wheat Ridge, CO: Fulcrum Publishing, 2006).

35 **lip of Lake Superior:** Josephine Waggoner, *Witness: A Húŋkpapȟa Historian's Strong-Heart Song of the Lakotas* (Lincoln: University of Nebraska Press, 2013), chap. 12. Luther Standing Bear, "Buffalo Hunt," in *Stories of the Sioux* (Lincoln: University of Nebraska Press, 1988). Susan Bordeaux Bettelyoun and Josephine Waggoner. *With My Own Eyes: A Lakota Woman Tells Her People's History* (Lincoln: University of Nebraska Press, 1999). Donovin Sprague (Mnicoujou Lakota, professor of American Indian studies and history at Sheridan College), interview with the author, June 2019; Steve Vance (historic preservation officer for the Cheyenne River Sioux Tribe), phone interview with the author, February 2021.

35 **a tiyospaye, a group of families:** Pekka Hämäläinen, *Lakota America* (New Haven, CT: Yale University Press, 2019), 17. Brett Shelton (Oglala Lakota, attorney for the Native American Rights Fund), phone interview with the author, October 3, 2018.

36 The handful of American explorers: "Great Desert" found in: Stephen Harriman
    Long, *The Northern Expeditions of Stephen H. Long: The Journals of 1817 and 1823
    and Related Documents* (St. Paul: Minnesota Historical Society Press, 1978).

36 In 1842, the first pioneer train: Edward Lazarus, *Black Hills/White Justice: The
    Sioux Nation versus the United States, 1775 to the Present* (Lincoln: University of
    Nebraska Press, 1999), chap. 1.

36 "Covered wagons were stringing": Waggoner, *Witness*, 461.

37 hailed by President James Polk: Mark Hirsch (historian at the Smithsonian's
    National Museum of the American Indian), interview with the author, Wash-
    ington, DC, May 21, 2019. We spoke while viewing the museum's "Nation to
    Nation" exhibit.

37 instruments of Manifest Destiny: John L. O'Sullivan, "The True Title," *New
    York Morning News*, December 27, 1845, described in Julius W. Pratt, "The Origin
    of 'Manifest Destiny,'" *American Historical Review* 32, no. 4 (1927): 795–98.

37 born into a powerful family: Vestal, *Warpath*, 6. Again, White Bull's birth year
    isn't reconciled in the historical record. That said, it's most commonly stated as 1849.

37 "God sees you": This quote comes from Vestal's interview notes with White Bull,
    found in Box 106, Folder 44, Walter Stanley Campbell Collection, Native Amer-
    ican Manuscript Collections, Western History Collections, University of Okla-
    homa, 17–19. They are slightly different than the words published in *Warpath* but
    are close to those on page 232. To see more of Vestal's notes from his interviews
    and his correspondence with Joseph White Bull, look up Walter Stanley Camp-
    bell (Vestal was his pen name) in the Native American Manuscript Collections
    of the Western History Collections at the University of Oklahoma.

38 a series of treaties: The Fort Laramie Treaty of 1851 (aka Horse Creek Treaty),
    Fort Laramie Treaty of 1868, and the Black Hills Act of 1877. For more details, see:
    Charles J. Kappler, ed., *Indian Affairs: Laws and Treaties*, vol. 7 (Washington, DC:
    Government Printing Office, 1904).

38 crippled by miscommunication: Suzan Shown Harjo, "'The Indians Were the
    Spoken Word:' An Interview with N. Scott Momaday," in *Nation to Nation*, 115.
    Abby Abinanti, interview with the author, November 2019. Arwen Nuttall,
    "Language and World View at the Horse Creek Treaty," *Nation to Nation*, 113.

38 On a September morning: The Treaty location is just to the east of the Wyoming–
    Nebraska border. Raymond J. DeMallie, "The Great Treaty Council at Horse
    Creek," *Nation to Nation*, 88–111. "Fort Laramie Treaty of 1851 (Horse Creek
    Treaty)," National Park Service, www.nps.gov/articles/000/horse-creek-treaty
    .htm. Nick Estes, *Our History Is the Future: Standing Rock versus the Dakota Access
    Pipeline, and the Long Tradition of Indigenous Resistance* (New York: Verso Books,
    2019), 15.

39 capturing enemy horses: Her Many Horses, ed., *A Song for the Horse Nation*, 9–10.

39 live *with* the land: Wayne Ducheneaux II (Mnicoujou Lakota of Cheyenne River,
    executive director of the Native Governance Center), phone interview with the
    author, August 10, 2022.

39 approximately sixty million acres: Phone interview with Steve Fullmer, park
    ranger, Fort Laramie National Historic Site, National Park Service, August 31,
    2022, confirmed this acreage. Land set aside by treaty wasn't determined by acre-

age but by geographic description. This leaves a lot to interpretation, and experts disagree about the exact land mass involved. I'm using the best available data, sourced by historians who use GIS maps. Joshua Jerome Meisel (Haskell Indian Nations University), email exchange with the author, September 14–15, 2022. Claudio Saunt, email exchange with the author, September 8–16, 2022. Saunt is the author of *Unworthy Republic: The Dispossession of Native Americans and the Road to Indian Territory* (New York: W. W. Norton & Company, 2020).

40 **Lakota women, who had powerful status:** Julie Collins, "The Status of Native American Women: A Study of the Lakota Sioux," *Drake University Social Science Journal* (2005), www.drake.edu/media/departmentsoffices/dussj/2006-2003 documents/StatusCollins.pdf. Kathleen A. Ward, "Before and After the White Man: Indian Women, Property, Progress, and Power," *Connecticut Public Interest Law Journal* 6 (2006): 245. Estes, *Our History Is the Future*, 82. Ella Cara Deloria, *Speaking of Indians* (Lincoln: University of Nebraska Press, 1998), 39, on traditional gender roles in Dakota culture: "Woman had her own place and man his; they were not the same and neither inferior nor superior."

40 **a completely different narrative:** Harjo, *Nation to Nation*, 108–9, depicts two different Winter Counts with pictures of peace made with the Crows. Hirsch, interview.

40 **The peace guaranteed:** Harjo, *Nation to Nation*, 88.

40 **scores of violent interactions:** Stanley Vestal, *New Sources of Indian History, 1850–1891: The Ghost Dance and the Prairie Sioux; A Miscellany*, vol. 7 (Norman: University of Oklahoma Press, 2015).

40 **White Bull came of age:** Joseph White Bull, *Lakota Warrior*, trans. and ed. James H. Howard (Lincoln, NE: University of Nebraska Press, 1998).

40 **A gold strike:** I've seen reports that gold was discovered in Montana as early as 1853, but the first big strike was in 1862. For more on this, see: "Boom and Bust: The Industries That Settled Montana," Digital Public Library of America, https://dp.la/exhibitions/industries-settled-montana/mining.

41 **"Kill every buffalo":** Barsness, *Heads, Hides, and Horns*, 126.

41 **Their efforts at extinction:** Waggoner, *Witness*, 3.

41 **photographs of buffalo skulls:** For more information about the photo pictured here, read: Leroy Barnett, "Buffalo Bones in Detroit," *Detroit in Perspective*, Winter 1975.

41 **indiscriminate death zones:** Doug Smith (senior biologist, Yellowstone National Park), phone interview with the author, January 2020.

41 **"The whole country":** Bettelyoun and Waggoner, *With My Own Eyes*, 65.

42 **"living on bark":** Charles E. DeLand, "Sioux Wars," *South Dakota Historical Collections*, vol. 15 (1930). For more on the Lakota's response to this eradication: Jeffrey Ostler, "'They Regard Their Passing as Wakan': Interpreting Western Sioux Explanations for the Bison's Decline," *Western Historical Quarterly* 30, no. 4 (1999): 475–97.

42 **The movie *Dances with Wolves*:** *Dances with Wolves*, directed by Kevin Costner (Orion Pictures, 1990), www.imdb.com/title/tt0099348.

42 **"They came upon a scene":** Doug White Bull, phone interviews with the author, November 2019 and January 29, 2020.

42 **I ask Doug:** For source of unemployment rate: *Public Witness Hearing—Tribal Programs: Day 2, Afternoon Session, Before the House Appropriations Subcommittee on Interior, Environment, and Related Agencies: Concerning the FY 2020 Budget for the BIA, BIE and HIS*, 116th Congress (March 7, 2019) ("Testimony of Ira Taken Alive, Vice-Chairman for the Standing Rock Sioux Tribe"): www.congress.gov /116/meeting/house/109014/witnesses/HHRG-116-AP06-Wstate-TakenAliveI -20190307.pdf.

About teen suicide: Matthew Green, "The Youth Activists Behind the Standing Rock Resistance (with Lesson Plan)," KQED, May 23, 2017: www.kqed.org /lowdown/27023/the-youth-of-standing-rock%20from%202017; Jodi Rave, "Suicide Rate for Tribal Youth Extremely High," *Lincoln Journal Star*, July 8, 2005, https://journalstar.com/special-section/news/suicide-rate-for-tribal-youth -extremely-high/article_faa42db5-7a6c-5cde-98b8-4e630beea08b.html.

42 **Lakota beat the U.S. Army:** Donovin Sprague, interview with the author, Cheyenne River Reservation, June 4, 2019. Lazarus, *Black Hills/White Justice*.

42 **resulting Fort Laramie Treaty:** Raymond J. DeMallie "'Scenes in the Indian Country': A Portfolio of Alexander Gardner's Stereographic Views of the 1868 Fort Laramie Treaty Council," *Montana: The Magazine of Western History* 31, no. 3 (1981): 42–59. Treaty with the Sioux Indians, U.S.–Sioux, April 29, 1868, 15 Stat. 635. Estes, *Our History Is the Future*, 107–9. As part of the treaty terms, Lakota who wished to live on the Great Sioux Reservation would receive federally provided daily rations of a pound of meat and a pound of flour for four years. Those who wanted to continue to hunt in the unceded territory beyond the reservation wouldn't receive such a ration. A few thousand traditionalists, including Sitting Bull and Crazy Horse, chose to live as they always had and as far as possible from the Agency where federal representatives had been installed on the reservation to dole out rations and religion.

43 *wasicu*, **or fat-taker:** E. Deloria, *Speaking of Indians*, 77 and 120. Also Estes, *Our History Is the Future*, 97. Steve Vance, interview with the author, February 8, 2021. Vance adds that the definition might also have to do with how many more words are required to get one's point across in English than in Lakota, so it can also be interpreted as "mouthy."

43 **done making treaties:** Mark Hirsch, "1871: The End of Indian Treaty-Making," *American Indian* 15, no. 2 (Summer/Fall 2014): www.americanindianmagazine .org/story/1871-end-indian-treaty-making. There were a number of treaties that were signed but never ratified by Congress. Only 368 were ratified between 1778 and 1868.

43 **nearly four hundred treaties:** Claudio Saunt, "The Invasion of America," Aeon .com, January 7, 2015, www.aeon.co/essays/how-were-1-5-billion-acres-of-land -so-rapidly-stolen.

For a complete list of Indian Land Cessions in the United States from 1784 to 1894, see this from the Library of Congress: www.memory.loc.gov/ammem/amlaw /llss_browse.html. See also: Harvey Rosenthal, *Their Day in Court: A History of the Indian Claims Commission* (Kent, OH: Kent State University, 1976). Jameson Sweet quote is from: Robert Lee and Tristan Ahtone, "Land-Grab Universities," *High Country News*, March 30, 2020.

43 **paved with gold**: I realize this sounds like a cliché, that it's hard to fathom anyone really thought this, but Etta tells me her father, my great-grandfather, Jake Kozberg, really believed this.

43 **the United States was in the worst debt**: Matt Phillips, "The Long Story of U.S. Debt, from 1790 to 2011, in 1 Little Chart," *The Atlantic*, November 13, 2012, www.theatlantic.com/business/archive/2012/11/the-long-story-of-us-debt-from-1790-to-2011-in-1-little-chart/265185. That article includes a link to an annual Treasury report with data from the time period at issue.

44 **"The Great Spirit gave us this land"**: Stanley Vestal, *Sitting Bull: Champion of the Sioux: A Biography* (Norman: University of Oklahoma Press, 1989), 102. Sitting Bull said this to Pierre-Jean De Smet, a Flemish Catholic priest, in May 1868.

44 **In the summer of 1874**: Lazarus, *Black Hills/White Justice*, 72. I have not been able to pin down how many reporters were there.

44 **"Does the treachery and blood-shedding"**: John M. Carroll and Lawrence A. Frost, eds., *Private Theodore Ewert's Diary of the Black Hills Expedition of 1874* (Piscataway, NJ: Consultant Resources Incorporated, 1976), 463.

44 **Custer's expedition spent weeks**: Carroll and Frost, *Private Theodore Ewert's Diary*. Waggoner, *Witness*, 326. Lazarus, *Black Hills White Justice*.

45 **Red Cloud countered**: Jeffrey Ostler, *The Lakotas and the Black Hills: The Struggle for Sacred Ground* (New York: Viking, 2010), 128.

45 **changed the rules**: This is why the Agreement of 1877 is often referred to as the "Sell or Starve Treaty."

45 **President Ulysses S. Grant had pledged**: Peter Cozzens, "Ulysses S. Grant Launched an Illegal War Against the Plains Indians, Then Lied about It," *Smithsonian*, November 2016, www.smithsonianmag.com/history/ulysses-grant-launched-illegal-war-plains-indians-180960787.

45 **operating under bad intelligence**: Peter Cozzens, phone interview with the author, August 31, 2022.

45 **soldiers never made it**: Luther Standing Bear, *My People, the Sioux* (Lincoln: University of Nebraska Press, 1975), 83. Vestal, *Warpath*. Letter from Harold W. Schunk (superintendent of Cheyenne River Reservation) to Will G. Robinson (State Historical Society of South Dakota), February 18, 1957, in which Schunk recalls White Bull telling him that "as soon as the battle started it was nothing but confusion and dust which lasted in the neighborhood of one-half hour." Also, see: David Treuer, *The Heartbeat of Wounded Knee: Native America from 1890 to the Present* (New York: Riverhead Books, 2019).

46 **Calls for revenge**: Oliver Knight, *Following the Indian Wars: The Story of the Newspaper Correspondents among the Indian Campaigners* (Norman: University of Oklahoma Press, 1993), 235, 246.

46 **Four months after Custer's defeat**: Vestal, *Warpath*, 224–27.

47 **Over the next six months**: Russell Freedman, *Indian Chiefs* (New York: Holiday House, 1987). Richmond Clow, "General Philip Sheridan's Legacy: The Sioux Pony Campaign of 1876," *Nebraska History* 57, no. 4 (1976): 460–77, https://history.nebraska.gov/wp-content/uploads/2017/12/doc_publications _NH1976PonyCampaign.pdf. Forrest W. Daniel, "Dismounting the Sioux," *North*

Dakota History: Journal of the Northern Plains 41, no 3. James McLaughlin, *My Friend the Indian* (Boston: Houghton Mifflin, 1910), 275. McLaughlin writes, "The disarmament was complete so far as the agency Indians were concerned."

48 **Under threat of imprisonment:** Found in Vestal's notes from his interviews with Joseph White Bull: "Four years after they've been at the agency, WB went on a deer hunt," and "this was the first time the Indians were allowed out."

48 **"Every tent seemed to be silent":** Waggoner, *Witness*, 134.

48 **According to the testimony:** Testimony of elders who were at the 1876 meeting, from 1911 meeting, Cherry Creek, SD (provided by Rami Bald Eagle). Details about commissioners' return to DC: Ostler, *The Lakotas and the Black Hills*; Lazarus, *Black Hills/White Justice*.

49 **"And that," White Bull told:** Vestal, *Warpath*, 228.

49 **a Paiute man in Nevada named Wovoka:** He was also known as Jack Wilson.

49 **This Ghost Dance:** E. Deloria, *Speaking of Indians*, 80–83; Louis S. Warren, *God's Red Son: The Ghost Dance Religion and the Making of Modern America* (London: Hachette UK, 2017). Louis S. Warren, email exchange with the author, August 29, 2022. Warren explained that the Lakota originally called the practice "the Spirit Dance," but it was mistranslated as the Ghost Dance and the press took that name and went with it. For more on the Ghost Dance in the Dakotas and Wounded Knee, see: James M. Robinson, *West from Fort Pierre: The Wild World of James (Scotty) Philip* (Los Angeles: Westernlore Press, 1974), 459–560. W. C. Vanderwerth and William R. Carmack, eds., *Indian Oratory: Famous Speeches by Noted Indian Chiefs*, vol. 110 (Norman: University of Oklahoma Press, 1979), 244–48.

49 **In 1884, the Department:** Department of the Interior, *Regulations of the Indian Department* (Washington, DC: Government Printing Office, 1884).

50 **white ceremonial shirts:** The possible source of the belief that the Ghost Dance shirts were impervious to bullets likely came from Wovoka, who had held public demonstrations of his power in the 1880s. In one, he asked his brother to shoot him with a shotgun that he'd secretly loaded with dust and sand. His shirt was riddled with holes, but he was unharmed. He later told a government agent of his demonstration, "That was a joke." This from: Warren, *God's Red Son.*

50 **Some articles inaccurately:** Rani-Henrik Andersson, *The Lakota Ghost Dance of 1890* (Lincoln: University of Nebraska Press, 2008). For more on why white settlers feared Ghost Dancers: Philip Joseph Deloria, *Indians in Unexpected Places* (Lawrence: University Press of Kansas, 2004), 27.

50 **soldiers swarmed Lakota Country:** Cozzens, interview.

51 **As Sitting Bull's wife:** Bettelyoun and Waggoner, *With My Own Eyes*; Waggoner, *Witness*; and Stanley Vestal, *New Sources of Indian History, 1850–1891: The Ghost Dance and the Prairie Sioux; A Miscellany, Civilization of the American Indian*, vol. 7 (Norman, OK: University of Oklahoma Press, 2015).

51 **dynamics of colonization:** Paulo Freire, "Pedagogy of the Oppressed," in *Toward a Sociology of Education* (London: Routledge, 2020), 374–86. For additional thoughts on these dynamics, see: Vine Deloria, *We Talk, You Listen: New Tribes, New Turf* (Lincoln: University of Nebraska Press, 2007), 38: "There is a tendency to overlook the obvious renegades, Indians who were treacherous and would have been renegades had there been no whites to fight. . . . If the weak points of each

minority group's history are to be covered over by a sweetness-and-light interpretation based on what we would like to think happened rather than what did happen, we doom ourselves to decades of further racial strife."

51 **his people fled:** Sprague, text exchange with author, March 2, 2023.

51 **More than a century later:** Sprague, interview. "Journey to Wounded Knee," signage, Badlands National Park, www.hmdb.org/m.asp?m=62104.

51 **my cousin Aviva and I:** Aviva Oskow is Etta Orkin's granddaughter and my second cousin.

52 **Ghost Dancers found neither:** James Emery, *Oyate Radio Program*, University of South Dakota Radio, Vermillion, SD: KUSD, June 1969, South Dakota Oral History Center, American Indian Research Project (AIRP 520). In this radio appearance, Emery read an interview with Paul High Back, who fled with Spotted Elk, aka Big Foot. Lazarus, *Black Hills/White Justice*, 115. Waggoner, *Witness*, 224.

52 **All night, they heard:** Dean S. Nauman, ed., *The Vanishing Trails Expedition—16 Years* (Wall, SD: Vanishing Trails Committee, 1976).

53 **The several hundred:** Though many archival and contemporary sources wonder whether the presence of the Seventh was intentional and a planned opportunity for revenge, leading historians suggest it was likely simple coincidence, as the regiment was stationed at Fort Riley, Kansas, only a few hundred miles south of Pine Ridge. Jerome Greene, email exchange with the author, August 30, 2022. For more on Wounded Knee, see: Jerome A. Greene, *American Carnage: Wounded Knee, 1890* (Norman, OK: University of Oklahoma Press, 2014).

53 **"Shoot 'em down":** The following oral histories are part of the South Dakota Oral History Center's American Indian Research Project (AIRP) and housed at the University of South Dakota: Robert C. Norman, interview conducted by Reuben Nelson, September 8, 1963 (AIRP 095). Emery, *Oyate Radio Program* (AIRP 520). James Holy Eagle, interview conducted by Don Doll, July 5, 1991 (AIRP 2171). Pete Lemley, interview conducted by Dr. Ray Lemley, 1959 (AIRP 542). William Sitting Bear, interview conducted by Dr. Joseph Cash, 1971 (AIRP 728). Charles Little Dog, interview conducted by George Nielsen, 1971 (AIRP 730). Elijah Broken Leg, interview conducted by George Nielsen, 1971 (AIRP 739).

For a look at how the press reported on the events at Wounded Knee at the time: Kevin Abourezk, "From Red Fears to Red Power: The Story of the Newspaper Coverage of Wounded Knee 1890 and Wounded Knee 1973" (master's thesis, University of Nebraska–Lincoln, 2012).

54 **this image posted:** www.nativewomeninfilm.com/american-holocaust-when-its-all-over-ill-still-be-indian-2.

54 **L. Frank Baum, the author:** A. Waller Hastings, "L. Frank Baum's Editorials on Sioux Nation," Northern.edu, Northern State University, 2007, https://diogenesii.files.wordpress.com/2012/12/baum.pdf. Tim Giago, "The Man Who Called for the Extermination of the Lakota," *HuffPost*, May, 22, 2014. Giago is the founder of the Native American Journalists Association.

54 **received the Medal of Honor:** P. Deloria, *Indians in Unexpected Places*, 34. Legislation was introduced in Congress in 1938, and again for four consecutive Congresses into the early forties, to compensate the heirs of those killed or wounded at Wounded Knee with $1,000. It was never passed. That from: Vine Deloria, ed.,

Of Utmost Good Faith (New York: Simon & Schuster, 1971), 165. For information on Medals of Honor: www.army.mil/medalofhonor/history.html. For information on the two people from South Dakota who received Medals of Honor, see the Congressional Medal of Honor Society website: www.cmohs.org/recipients /page/1?conflicts[]=world-war-ii&state_accredited_to[]=44.

54 **A bill currently:** Remove the Stain Act, S.1073, 117th Cong. (2021): www.congress .gov/bill/117th-congress/senate-bill/1073/text?r=4&s=1.

54 **History textbooks published:** *American History: Reconstruction to the Present, Guided Reading Workbook* (Boston: Houghton Mifflin Harcourt, 2017).

54 **By that time:** Jeffrey Ostler, "Genocide and American Indian History," *Oxford Research Encyclopedia of American History* (Oxford, UK: Oxford University Press, 2015): www.doi.org/10.1093/acrefore/9780199329175.013.3. For decimation of the buffalo: Barsness, *Heads, Hides, and Horns: The Complete Buffalo Book* (Fort Worth, TX: Texas Christian University Press, 1985). For decimation of Native peoples: David J. Hacker and Michael R. Haines, "American Indian Mortality in the Late Nineteenth Century: The Impact of Federal Assimilation Policies on a Vulnerable Population," *Annales de démographie historique* 2, no. 110 (Paris, France: Cairn/Softwin, 2005): 17–29, www.cairn.info/revue-annales-de-demographie -historique-2005-2-page-17.htm.

55 **none other than Adolf Hitler:** John Toland, *Adolf Hitler: The Definitive Biography* (New York: Anchor, 1992), 702. James Q. Whitman, *Hitler's American Model* (Princeton, NJ: Princeton University Press, 2017). Susan Neiman, *Learning from the Germans: Confronting Race and the Memory of Evil* (London Allen Lane, 2019).

55 **One January day:** Doug White Bull, phone interview with the author, January 2019.

CHAPTER 3: JEWFACE ON THE FRONTIER

57 **On a hot summer day:** The Buffalo Bill show came to Sioux City in 1899, 1901, and 1908. I don't have a ticket stub or other hard evidence that my family members attended these shows, but it's hard to imagine they missed them. Even though Faige Etke and Harry had moved more permanently to the homestead by January 1908, many of their children remained in Sioux City until the following year or two, and there was much back-and-forth.

The best details about individual Buffalo Bill shows are found in the local paper. Here's a sampling of the news articles I pulled on the Sioux City Buffalo Bill shows: "Col. Cody Gets Big Crowds," *Sioux City Journal*, August 28, 1908 ("10,000 people saw the show yesterday afternoon, the seats being well filled, and another large audience greeted the performers last night"). "Old Settlers with Show," *Sioux City Journal*, August 15, 1908. "Buffalo Bill Is in Town," *Sioux City Journal*, August 5, 1901. "Fought at Wounded Knee," *Sioux City Journal*, August 8, 1901.

Booklets from the years in question were provided by the Buffalo Bill Center of the West, Cody, Wyoming: William Frederick Cody, *Buffalo Bill's Wild West and Congress of Rough Riders of the World*, 1901. William Frederick Cody, *Buffalo Bill's Wild West, Historical Sketches and Daily Review*, 1908.

57 **dozens of half-naked Lakota:** "Each year, between seventy-five and one hundred

Indian people, often recruited from Pine Ridge or other South Dakota reservations, joined the show." Philip Joseph Deloria, "Representation," in *Indians in Unexpected Places* (Lawrence: University Press of Kansas, 2004), 69.

57 **actors rode bareback:** For discussion of how the show portrayed Indigenous Americans: L. G. Moses, "Wild West Shows, Reformers, and the Image of the American Indian, 1887–1914," *South Dakota History* 14, no. 3 (1984): 193–221.

57 **and Indian-killer himself:** Brooklyn Museum, *Buffalo Bill and the Wild West* (Pittsburgh: University of Pittsburgh Press, 1981). Published in conjunction with an exhibition of the same title, organized by and presented by the Brooklyn Museum, November 21, 1981–January 17, 1982. Cody himself had served as a buffalo hunter and scout during the Indian Wars; he boasted that he killed 4,280 buffaloes while working as a hunter for the Kansas Pacific Railroad. He participated in seventy-one or seventy-two fights between whites and Indians. In the great rush to avenge Custer's death, Cody spent the summer fighting Plains Nations as part of the Fifth Cavalry, killing a Cheyenne named Yellow Hand. This "first scalp for Custer," as he put it, adorned his *Wild West* programs and the outsides of his theaters for years. (The reality, as reality usually is, was more nuanced and complex.) Despite the damage done by these shows and the myth they created about Native Americans, Buffalo Bill himself was reportedly good to the Lakota in his employ. He offered them some of the only jobs they could get off the reservation at the time. For more on this: Luther Standing Bear, *My People, the Sioux* (Lincoln: University of Nebraska Press, 1975).

57 **spectacle, the *Wild West* show:** Richard White and Patricia Nelson Limerick, "The Frontier in American Culture," in *The Frontier in American Culture* (Berkeley: University of California Press, 1994). Paul Fees, "Wild West Shows: Buffalo Bill's Wild West," Buffalo Bill Center of the West (2016).

59 **a story of American exceptionalism:** P. Deloria, *Indians in Unexpected Places.*

59 **The Sinykin kids:** Advertisement for Martin's in the *Sioux City Journal*, November 7, 1908.

59 **"Yonkle, the Cow-Boy":** Baylor University's France G. Spencer Collection of American Popular Sheet Music has both "Yonkle, the Cow-Boy Jew" and "I'm a Yiddish Cowboy (Tough Guy Levi)" in their entirety: https://digitalcollections -baylor.quartexcollections.com/Documents/Detail/yonkle-the-cow-boy -jew/72988; https://digitalcollections-baylor.quartexcollections.com/Documents /Detail/im-a-yiddish-cowboy-tough-guy-levi/70527.

60 **One such act, Jordan & Harvey:** Joe Laurie, *Vaudeville: From the Honky-Tonks to the Palace* (New York: Henry Holt, 1953). Laurie calls Jordan & Harvey "one of the first Jewish comic acts." *The Philadelphia Inquirer* (November 1, 1907) called them "two very popular Hebrew impersonators." In 1911, the showbill for *Jordan and Harvey* from New South Wales described them as "originators of Hebrew Comedy, Fun Without Offensiveness. . . . A laugh a second for twenty minutes." They likely came through Sioux City multiple times but were at least there for the week of April 19, 1908, at the Orpheum Theatre. I'm grateful to retired professor Richard Poole for sharing his unpublished paper, "Ancient Voices, Improbable Venues: Yiddish Theatre in Sioux City, Iowa, 1908–1919."

60 **This was Jewface:** For more about Jewface in general, the YIVO Institute for

Jewish Research has a great entry at: www.yivo.org/Jewface. To take a deeper dive, watch this lecture by YIVO historian Eddy Portnoy and *New York Times* cultural critic Jody Rosen: YIVO Institute for Jewish Research, "Jewface: 'Yiddish' Dialect Songs of Tin Pan Alley (Exhibition Opening)," November 24, 2015, www.youtube .com/watch?v=agbGHITZIN8. More on Jewish vaudeville can be found in: J. Chris Westgate, *Staging the Slums, Slumming the Stage: Class, Poverty, Ethnicity, and Sexuality in American Theatre, 1890–1916* (New York: Springer, 2014). Harley Erdman, *Staging the Jew: The Performance of an American Ethnicity, 1860–1920* (New Brunswick, NJ: Rutgers University Press, 1997). Douglas Gilbert, *American Vaudeville: Its Life and Times* (New York: Dover Publications, 1940), 287–92.

61 **Central Conference of American Rabbis:** Eddy Portnoy, interview with the author. Multiple editorials that ran in *Jewish Comment*: May 9, 1913; September 26, 1913; October 24, 1913; available at YIVO.

61 **says Jody Rosen:** Jody Rosen, interview with the author, February 17, 2020. Author interview with Eddy Portnoy, YIVO office in New York, November 2019.

61 **the album *Jewface*:** *Jewface*, compilation, Reboot Stereophonic Records RSR 006, 2006, compact disc. Teri Gross, "'Jewface' and Jody Rosen," *Fresh Air*, National Public Radio, January 2, 2007, www.npr.org/templates/story/story.php?storyId =6710022.

61 **a Pocahontas-like daughter:** "The myth and trope of Pocahontas provided an enduring vehicle for whites' sexualization of Native American women and reigns as one of the dominant subthemes of white men's narrative of colonizing America," found in: David S. Koffman, *The Jews' Indian: Colonialism, Pluralism, and Belonging in America* (New Brunswick, NJ: Rutgers University Press, 2019), 11. See also: Richard Godbeer, "Eroticizing the Middle Ground: Anglo-Indian Sexual Relations Along the Eighteenth-Century Frontier," in *Sex, Love, Race: Crossing Boundaries in North American History*, ed. Martha Hodes (New York: New York University Press, 1999), 91–111.

61 **When Jews dressed up:** Erdman, *Staging the Jew*. Historian Rachel Rubinstein adds that "Jewish writers and performers could use travels 'among Indians' to theatricalize, disguise, and Americanize themselves all at once," in Rachel Rubinstein, *Members of the Tribe: Native America in the Jewish Imagination* (Detroit: Wayne State University Press, 2010). P. Deloria, *Indians in Unexpected Places*.

61 **In the 1930 movie *Whoopee!*:** Michael Rogin, *Blackface, White Noise: Jewish Immigrants in the Hollywood Melting Pot* (Berkeley: University of California Press, 1996), 151.

62 **Indigenous people had lived for millennia:** A 1924 Sioux City Directory writes, "The spot where the city was later to be placed was a favorite spot for the Indians to camp. It afforded fuel and fresh water, as well as protection from the cold winds of the plains. The camp sites have become giant factories, jobbing houses and office buildings."

62 **Indigenous population was almost nonexistent:** A town directory from 1915 (provided by the Sioux City Public Museum), which doubled as both phone book and enticement to out-of-towners, boasted of having a population that was 99 percent white. In 1900, the U.S. Census counted not a single "Indian" in the city. It's possible that members of the nearby Omaha Tribe or Winnebago Tribe

worked at meatpacking plants during this time in a more transient way that didn't get culled by the census. These workers would have lived in the same lower-class neighborhood as the Sinykins, and it's possible that Harry may have met some of them while working at the meatpacking plant. Based on interviews with Haley Aguirre (Sioux City Public Library archivist), November 2020.

62 **Joseph White Bull himself came:** "Indian Chief Is Very Vain," *Sioux City Journal*, November 2, 1906; "White Bull Is for Peace," *Sioux City Journal*, November 4, 1906.

62 **Reverend Dr. Marilyn van Duffelen:** Marilyn van Duffelen (vicar, St. Paul's Indian Mission Episcopal Church, Sioux City), phone interview with the author, November 19, 2020.

62 **the local press:** I gleaned this information by digging through newspapers.com using the search terms "Sioux," "Indians," and "Lakota" between 1902 and 1908. It's my original reporting but should not be seen as definitive. A sampling of the articles I found, all from the *Sioux City Journal*: "Progress of the Indian, Civilization Claiming the Red Man as Its Own," June 24, 1906; "The Future of the Indian: Outlook for the Aboriginal American Not Good," April 16, 1905; "How to Play Indian," April 5, 1903; "A Friend of the Red Man, Ex-Senator Henry L. Dawes," March 12, 1903; "The Indian Still an Indian: His Essential Characteristics Remain Unmodified, Leads a Simple, Idle Life," January 31, 1904; "Progress of the Noble Red—Sioux Indians Do Well Under New System—Are Learning to Work," July 18, 1907.

63 **Isabel Wilkerson in her 2020 book** *Caste*: Isabel Wilkerson, *Caste: The Origins of Our Discontents* (New York: Random House, 2020), 229.

63 **bastion of racist thought:** Frederick E. Hoxie, *A Final Promise: The Campaign to Assimilate the Indians, 1880–1920* (Lincoln: University of Nebraska Press, 2001), 95.

63 **"Suspicion, jealousy, and hatred":** Ida Jacobs, "The Jews of Des Moines: Their Progress and Prospects," *Reform Advocate*, December 14, 1912.

63 **Jewish-owned businesses in Sioux City:** Susan Marks Connor, ed., *I Remember When . . . Personal Recollections and Vignettes of the Sioux City Jewish Community, 1869–1984* (Sioux City, IA: Jewish Federation, 1985), 22.

64 **"our people will not patronize a Jew":** C. J. Rich, "History of Leeds," 1934, 23, unpublished, provided by the Sioux City Public Museum.

64 **cartoon depicting a hook-nosed man:** *Sioux City Journal*, July 31, 1905, cartoon.

64 **Sam Sinykin and his brothers:** "To Rent," *Sioux City Journal*, August 5, 1905. Describes Mr. S. Sinykin as "one of our leading merchants." Throughout 1906, the local papers ran ads from their new "Sinykin Bros." store in Sioux City.

65 **"one of the cutest and funniest stories they told":** Etta Orkin, interview with the author, September 24, 2018. Also related by Jack Sinykin, interview with Cathi Oskow.

65 **in East Bottoms:** Haley Aguirre, phone interview and email exchange with author, November 13–18, 2020. Additional information: Haley Aguirre, "History at High Noon: South Bottoms," lecture at Sioux City Public Museum, November 15, 2019, www.youtube.com/watch?v=sSbQHqgpXww.

65 **Jews were often robbed:** "There were pool halls and gambling houses and bars, where, according to an article that ran in the *Sioux City Journal* in 1893, 'Reubens

and Isaacs,' a Jewish slur, were regularly robbed, the police turning a blind eye," from an unpublished essay provided to the author by Richard Poole, professor emeritus of theater and speech communication at Briar Cliff University, Sioux City, Iowa.

65 **Harry's condition had improved:** Jack Sinykin, interview with Cathi Oskow.

66 **Under his direction:** "Cudahy to spend $300,000," *Sioux City Journal*, March 29, 1905. Haley Aguirre determined that Cudahy's main engineer on the project was named Carter. Carter is who Harry worked for, per Jack Sinykin, interview with Cathi Oskow.

66 **It took six months:** Etta Orkin, interviews with the author, September 2018– November 2022.

66 **the story of exile:** Eli Barnavi, ed., *A Historical Atlas of the Jewish People: From the Time of the Patriarchs to the Present* (New York: Knopf, 1992).

67 **"Exile proves to be the rule":** Arnold Eisen, "Exile," in *20th Century Jewish Religious Thought*, eds., Arthur A. Cohen and Paul Mendes-Flohr (Lincoln: University of Nebraska Press, 2010), 221.

67 **late 1907 or early 1908:** I have no letters or other documentation of when exactly they moved from Sioux City to their 160 acres north of Wall in Eastern Pennington County, South Dakota, land that, before 1889, had belonged to the Great Sioux Nation. According to records I received from the National Archives, Harry and Faige Etke were living on their land full time starting in January 1908. It seems like bad sense to make such a move in the winter, and according to the experts I consulted on this question, including the historians Richard White and Eric Zimmer, it was common for settlers to take their time filing their official paperwork while actually squatting on the land much earlier.

CHAPTER 4: "KILL THE INDIAN . . . SAVE THE MAN"

69 **"I was taken to school":** Sarah Buffalo, interview with Steve Plummer, Bridger, SD, June 29, 1971, South Dakota Oral History Center, American Indian Research Project (AIRP 719), University of South Dakota.

69 **They most likely wouldn't see:** Native American Rights Fund (NARF), "Trigger Points: Current State of Research on History, Impacts, and Healing Related to the United States' Indian Industrial/Boarding School Policy," Boulder, CO, 2019, www.narf.org/nill/documents/trigger-points.pdf.

69 **Upon arrival at the Rapid City Indian School:** Scott Riney, *The Rapid City Indian School, 1898–1933* (Norman: University of Oklahoma Press, 1999); NARF, "Trigger Points." For original sourcing of these attitudes about the capacities of Indian students, see U.S. Department of the Interior, *Report of the Commissioner of Indian Affairs to the Secretary of the Interior, 1907* (Washington, DC: Government Printing Office, 1907), 20–22.

70 **recalled Silas Condon:** Silas Condon, interview with Steve Plummer, 1971, South Dakota Oral History Center, American Indian Research Project (AIRP 714), University of South Dakota. Condon says he was born in 1900 and was expelled in 1916 after going to school there for eleven years, hence I'm assuming he went to school there when he was five.

70 **Congress passed legislation:** Brenda J. Child, *Boarding School Seasons: American Indian Families, 1900–1940* (Lincoln: University of Nebraska Press, 1998).

70 **Indian Industrial Schools:** David Wallace Adams, *Education for Extinction: American Indians and the Boarding School Experience, 1875–1928* (Lawrence: University Press of Kansas, 1995). Also: Denise K. Lajimodiere, *Stringing Rosaries: The History, the Unforgivable, and the Healing of Northern Plains American Indian Boarding School Survivors* (Fargo: North Dakota State University Press, 2019).

70 **The year my family:** "Indian Appropriations," *Black Hills Weekly Journal*, December 18, 1908.

70 **more than one hundred thousand Indigenous children:** Data on the number of children and even the number of schools is evolving as nonprofits such as the Native American Rights Fund and the National Native American Boarding School Healing Coalition, among others, have filed Freedom of Information Act requests. In June 2021, Interior Secretary Deb Haaland announced the Federal Indian Boarding School Initiative. Read more on these efforts and their findings at: "Federal Indian Boarding School Initiative," Indian Affairs, U.S. Department of the Interior, www.bia.gov/service/federal-indian-boarding-school-initiative. Also: "Resources," National Native American Boarding School Healing Coalition, https://boardingschoolhealing.org/education/resources.

70 **(This strategy of forced assimilation):** Canons 59 and 60, Fourth Council of Toledo, 633 CE. David M. Freidenreich, "Jews, Pagans, and Heretics in Early Medieval Canon Law," in *Jews in Early Christian Law: Byzantium and the Latin West, 6th–11th Centuries*, eds. John Tolan, Nicholas de Lange, Laurence Foschia, and Capucine Nemo-Pekelman (Turnhout, Belgium: Brepols, 2014), 73–91.

70 **a concentration camp:** Doug White Bull, interview with the author, August 13, 2021.

71 **When Sarah Buffalo:** Riney, *The Rapid City Indian School*, chap. 5.

71 **the use of corporal punishment:** Samuel Torres (deputy chief executive officer, Native American National Boarding School Healing Coalition), interviews and email exchange with the author. Torres's dissertation, which details such abuse, is: Samuel B. Torres, "Beyond Colonizing Epistemicides: Toward a Decolonizing Framework for Indigenous Education" (PhD dissertation, Loyola Marymount University, 2019).

71 **A recent federal report:** Bryan Newland, "Federal Indian Boarding School Initiative Investigative Report," United States Department of the Interior, 2022.

71 **theory of unilinear evolution:** Lewis Henry Morgan, *Ancient Society: Or, Researches in the Lines of Human Progress from Savagery, through Barbarism to Civilization* (London: Macmillan & Company, 1877).

71 **used to justify Nazism:** Richard Weikart, *From Darwin to Hitler: Evolutionary Ethics, Eugenics and Racism in Germany* (New York: Springer, 2016).

71 **Brigadier General Richard Henry Pratt:** Here's the full quote from Pratt: "A great general has said that the only good Indian is a dead one, and that high sanction of his destruction has been an enormous factor in promoting Indian massacres. In a sense, I agree with the sentiment, but only in this: that all the Indian there is in the race should be dead. Kill the Indian in him, and save the man."

71 **"to turn the Indian from a child into a man"**: Theodore Roosevelt, *Report of Hon. Theodore Roosevelt Made to the United States Civil Service Commission, Upon a Visit to Certain Indian Reservations and Indian Schools in South Dakota, Nebraska, and Kansas* (Philadelphia: Indian Rights Association, 1893), 8. For more on Teddy Roosevelt's views of Indians, see: Alysa Landry, "Theodore Roosevelt: 'The Only Good Indians Are the Dead Indians,'" *Indian Country Today*, June 28, 2016, updated September 13, 2018, www.indiancountrytoday.com/archive/theodore-roosevelt-the-only-good-indians-are-the-dead-indians.

71 **By the early 1880s**: Adams, *Education for Extinction*, 20: "In 1882, Secretary of the Interior Henry Teller reckoned that 'over a ten-year period the annual cost of both waging war on Indians and providing protection for frontier communities was in excess of $22 million, nearly four times what it would cost to educate 30,000 children for a year.'" Also: Native American Rights Fund, "Let All That Is Indian within You Die!" *NARF Legal Review* 38, no. 2 (2013): "It was, in fact, simply too expensive to enter into an extended campaign of genocide on the heels of an expensive Civil War. It was estimated that the annual cost to maintain a company of United States Cavalry in the field was $2,000,000. Whatever the standards of humanity, the economics augured for assimilation as the preferred alternative."

71 **By weaponizing not only education**: Frederick E. Hoxie, *A Final Promise: The Campaign to Assimilate the Indians, 1880–1920* (Lincoln: University of Nebraska Press, 2001).

72 **Suddenly, Western senators**: Richard White, *Railroaded: The Transcontinentals and the Making of Modern America* (New York: W. W. Norton & Company, 2011). White writes, on page 24, that the United States gave railroads east and west of the Mississippi more than 131 million acres, the equivalent of a small country or an entire American state. "The government did not actually own much of this land; it belonged to Indians. But Indian ownership had never proved much of an obstacle to congressional schemes. Indeed, the very fact that it belonged to Indians initially seemed an asset in financing western railroads."

73 **a particular stock of settler**: James B. Hedges, "The Colonization Work of the Northern Pacific Railroad." *Mississippi Valley Historical Review* 13, no. 3 (1926): 311–42.

73 **the chronology of federal land grabs**: Fort Laramie Treaty of 1851: Establishes the Great Sioux Reservation, reserving approximately 60 million acres for the Lakota.

Fort Laramie Treaty of 1868: Reiterates the definition of the Great Sioux Reservation, but tells Lakota to stop getting in the way of the railroads. Lakota land is reduced to approximately 26.4 million acres, with an additional approximate 30 million acres set aside as hunting lands, intended to be held open only until there are no longer enough buffalo to "justify" a hunt.

1871: Congress abolishes treaty making.

The Act of 1877: Takes 7.3 million acres of the Black Hills away from the Great Sioux Reservation, plus all of the reserved hunting lands, diminishing Lakota lands in the Dakotas to 20.3 million acres.

For more on this: Alan L. Neville and Alyssa Kaye Anderson, "The Diminishment of the Great Sioux Reservation: Treaties, Tricks, and Time," *Great Plains Quarterly* (2013): 237–51.

73 "The white man has": Cong. Rec. 1495 (1889) (statement of Rep. Byron M. Cutcheon), www.govinfo.gov/content/pkg/GPO-CRECB-1889-pt2-v20/pdf/GPO -CRECB-1889-pt2-v20-14-2.pdf.

73 called the Great Sioux Agreement: Herbert T. Hoover, "The Sioux Agreement of 1889 and Its Aftermath." *South Dakota History* 19, no. 1 (1989): 56–94.

73 "Three Stars" aka Crook, offered him $200 cash: Stanley Vestal, original notes from his interviews with Joseph White Bull, Box 105, Folder 28, Walter Stanley Campbell Collection, Native American Manuscript Collections, Western History Collections, University of Oklahoma.

74 (There is a bigger story): Frederick E. Hoxie, "From Prison to Homeland: The Cheyenne River Indian Reservation before WWI," *South Dakota History* 10, no. 1 (1979): 1.

74 Crook leaned on fear: Josephine Waggoner, *Witness: A Húŋkpapha Historian's Strong-Heart Song of the Lakotas* (Lincoln: University of Nebraska Press, 2013), 302.

75 the General Allotment Act (you may know it as the Dawes Act): An Act to Provide for the Allotment of Lands in Severalty to Indians on the Various Reservations (General Allotment Act or Dawes Act), Statutes at Large 24, 388-91, NADP Document A1887, www.archives.gov/milestone-documents/dawes-act#transcript.

75 The idea was: Gail Landsman, "The Ghost Dance and the Policy of Land Allotment," *American Sociological Review* 44, no. 1 (1979): 162–166.

75 Married women were entirely excluded: For more on the ways Indigenous women, and Lakota women in particular, were excluded from the Allotment Act and other policies during this time, read: Patricia C. Albers, "Sioux Women in Transition: A Study of Their Changing Status in Domestic and Capitalist Sectors of Production," in *The Hidden Half: Studies of Plains Indian Women*, eds. Patricia C. Albers and Beatrice Medicine (Lanhan, MD: University Press of America, 1983), 175. Also: Christina G. Mello, "Gender and Empowerment: Contemporary Lakota Women of Rosebud," *McNair Scholars Journal* 8, no. 1 (2004): 6.

75 "take pity on my women": Sarah Deutsch, "Coming Together, Coming Apart: Women's History and the West," *Montana: The Magazine of Western History* 41, no. 2 (1991): 58–61. The white anthropologist mentioned is Alice Fletcher. You can find more about her from the Library of Congress: "Alice Cunningham Fletcher (1838–1923)," Biographies, Library of Congress, www.loc.gov/item /ihas.200196222.

75 The guts of the law: Vine Deloria, ed., *Of Utmost Good Faith* (New York: Simon & Schuster, 1971), 52–63.

76 "Indian's Emancipation Proclamation": Edward Lazarus, *Black Hills/White Justice: The Sioux Nation versus the United States, 1775 to the Present* (Lincoln: University of Nebraska Press, 1999), 108.

76 newspapers hailed such policy: *The Black Hills Journal*, January 25, 1884: "The question of civilizing the Indians and bettering their condition would be to a great extent solved by the allotment of land to them. This action would break up the tribal relations, which have ever been the chief obstacles in the way of their progress and improvement of their condition." "The Sioux Agreement," *New York Times*, August 7, 1889 (on the Great Sioux Agreement): "The opening of the reservation will be of general benefit. . . . The Indians will receive many millions of

dollars, the interest on which, added to their annuities, will give them many of the comforts of civilization, while the land they retain is more than they need, and will rapidly grow in value."

76 **"a huge form of affirmative action for white people":** Ann E. Tweedy, "Unjustifiable Expectations: Laying to Rest the Ghosts of Allotment-Era Settlers," *Seattle University Law Review* 36 (2012): 129.

77 **deemed by President Grant:** Ulysses S. Grant, "Second Annual Message to Congress," December 5, 1870, American Presidency Project, www.presidency.ucsb.edu /documents/second-annual-message-11. Despite the official ouster of Jews from such jobs, at least a few Jews did work as Indian Agents and subagents for the government. For example, President Grant selected Dr. Herman Bendell, a Jewish physician from New York, as superintendent of Indian Affairs for the Arizona Territory. Solomon Bibo, a Jewish trader, became governor of the Acoma Pueblo. Bibo was reportedly favored by the Acoma, in part because he didn't proselytize and took time to learn their language and culture. He even married into the Acoma. There are other examples like this. See: M. L. Marks, *Jews Among the Indians: Tales of Adventure and Conflict in the Old West* (Chicago: Benison, 1992).

77 **"choosing sides for touch football":** Vine Deloria, *Custer Died for Your Sins: An Indian Manifesto* (Norman: University of Oklahoma Press, 1988), 106.

77 **Charles Hall, a missionary:** Rev. and Mrs. Harold W. Case, *100 Years at Fort Berthold: The History of Fort Berthold Indian Mission, 1876–1976* (Bismarck, ND: Bismarck Tribune, 1977).

77 **The loss of such religious practice, particularly:** Jeffrey Ostler, *The Lakotas and the Black Hills* (New York: Viking, 2010), chap. 5.

77 **Christian patriarchy, with its focus:** Beatrice Medicine, *Learning to Be an Anthropologist and Remaining "Native": Selected Writings* (Champaign: University of Illinois Press, 2001), 155.

77 **the punishment was jail:** Professor Michael Moore of Sitting Bull College tipped me off to the existence of old Department of the Interior arrest books housed at the State Historical Society of North Dakota in Bismarck. I found two old, leather-bound books for Standing Rock Agency, Indian Police Court Records from 1895 and 1892. The Interior Department, without the consent of Congress, created "Regulations of the Indian Department" starting as early as 1884. The regulations included rules against practicing traditional culture or religion. See: U.S. Department of the Interior, *Regulations of the Indian Department with An Appendix Containing the Forms Used* (Washington, DC: Government Printing Office, 1884); U.S. Department of the Interior, *Regulations of the Indian Department with An Appendix Containing the Forms Used* (Washington DC: Government Printing Office, 1904).

77 **its civilization efforts:** "Superintendent's Annual Narrative and Statistical Reports from Field Jurisdictions of the Bureau of Indian Affairs, 1907–1938," digitized by the National Archives and Records Administration.

78 **As Joseph White Bull said:** Joseph White Bull and Susie Her Blanket (his wife), interview conducted by the South Dakota Emergency Relief Administration, Cherry Creek, SD, October 22, 1935. Under the heading "Social Interest," the administration's notes say, "M and W were members of the Congregational Church but M stated he held religious services in his own home."

78 (Included among those ceremonies): Louis S. Warren, *God's Red Son: The Ghost Dance Religion and the Making of Modern America* (London: Hachette UK, 2017), 369.

78 As of today, churches own: Data set created for the author by Robert Lee, Domesday Database, americandomesday.org (publication pending). The database includes only thirty states but comprises the majority of lands where the United States redistributed Native lands to churches and others.

78 In 1990, the Catholic Church: "Bureau of Catholic Indian Missions Property Descriptions and Notes by State," 1990, provided by Mark Thiel, Marquette University Archives. See also: Mary Annette Pember, "The Catholic Church Siphoned Away $30 Million Paid to Native People for Stolen Land," *In These Times*, July 7, 2020. Pember's investigation details other ways the Catholic Church accrued Indian land.

78 the Episcopal Church makes money: Phone interview with Cleve Her Many Horses, director of Tribal Land Enterprise for the Rosebud Sioux Tribe and former BIA superintendent, March 1, 2023.

79 "It has been said of missionaries": V. Deloria, *Custer Died for Your Sins*, 101.

79 "Kindly old missionaries were really land agents": V. Deloria, ed., *Of Utmost Good Faith*, 169.

79 Lakota ranchers were producing: These details come from both archival newspapers (such as: "The Indian Problem," *Argus Leader*, November 23, 1901) and also from an unpublished report, housed at the Newberry Library, prepared by historian Fred Hoxie for the court case *United States v. Dupris*. Frederick E. Hoxie, *Jurisdiction on the Cheyenne River Indian Reservation: An Analysis of the Causes and Consequences of the Act of May 29, 1908* (undated manuscript), app. 81, at 5, prepared for *United States v. A Juvenile*, 453 F. Supp. 1171 (D.S.D. 1978), vacated, *Dupris v. United States*, 446 U.S. 980 (1980) (on file with author).

80 "easiest Indians in the country": 57 Cong. Rec. 4803 (1902) (Agreement with Indians of Rosebud Reservation).

80 the Indian Office leased: Good information about the Bureau of Indian Affairs' leasing of Indigenous lands can be found in: Janet A. McDonnell, *The Dispossession of the American Indian, 1887–1934* (Bloomington: Indiana University Press, 1991). Also: Peter Iverson, *When Indians Became Cowboys: Native Peoples and Cattle Ranching in the American West* (Norman: University of Oklahoma Press, 1994).

80 Joseph White Bull, alone: Details from this event come from a number of sources: Stanley Vestal, original notes from his interviews with Joseph White Bull, Box 105, Folder 28, Walter Stanley Campbell Collection, Native American Manuscript Collections, Western History Collections, University of Oklahoma. Stanley Vestal, *Warpath: The True Story of the Fighting Sioux Told in a Biography of Chief White Bull* (Lincoln: University of Nebraska Press, 1934), 241–42. Joseph White Bull, interview with the Indian Rights Association, in *The Twenty-Second Annual Report of the Executive Committee of the Indian Rights Association* (Philadelphia: Office of the Indian Rights Association, 1904). Harvey Eagle Horse (Lakota elder), interview with the author, Cheyenne River Sioux Tribe Cultural Preservation Office, May 2021. Eagle Horse, a retired policeman, remembers the jail at the old Agency as having a cement floor, brick walls, bars, and a window.

81 meant as punishment: Conjecture from: Steve Vance, interview with the author,

February 20, 2021. Vance grew up listening to elders in his community of Cherry Creek tell stories about White Bull.

81 **(This dual system of rights):** James Q. Whitman, *Hitler's American Model* (Princeton, NJ: Princeton University Press, 2017), 38, 67–68.

81 **covering the lease agreement:** "The Leasing Question," *Argus Leader*, January 10, 1902. "Bishop Hare's Protest," *Argus Leader*, January 15, 1902. "Protest Is Vain," *Argus Leader*, January 20, 1902. "Immense Range Is Leased from the Indians by Cattlemen," *Lead Daily Call*, February 8, 1902. "Maj. Hatch Talks, Says Cheyenne Indians Favor the Land Leases," *Argus Leader*, February 12, 1902. "Major Ira A. Hatch, Indian Agent at Cheyenne River Has Gone to Washington," *Rapid City Journal*, February 18, 1902. "Decision on Indian Leases," *Argus Leader*, February 4, 1902. "Leasing of the Cheyenne Reservation Is All Settled," *Black Hills Union*, March 21, 1902. "Over 200 Miles of Wire Fencing Is Planned," *Argus Leader*, March 27, 1902. "No Trouble Over Trail," *Argus Leader*, October 11, 1902. (Untitled), *Rapid City Journal*, February 18, 1902.

82 **"feel that the 'Great Father'":** "Superintendent's Annual Narrative and Statistical Report from Field Jurisdictions of the Bureau of Indian Affairs," Cheyenne River, 1913; and Standing Rock, 1914.

82 *Lone Wolf v. Hitchcock*: *Lone Wolf v. Hitchcock*, 187 U.S. 553 (1903), www.supreme .justia.com/cases/federal/us/187/553. Argued October 23, 1902. Decided January 5, 1903. Oyez.org, the Supreme Court's online archive, has great information on the case at www.oyez.org/cases/1900-1940/187us553.

82 **the population of western South Dakota:** Iverson, *When Indians Became Cowboys*, 40: "The West River population mushroomed from 57,575 in 1905 to 137,687 in 1910 . . . more than 81,000 people registered for the 10,000 parcels offered at Cheyenne River and Standing Rock."

83 **The United States passed a series:** Donovin Arleigh Sprague, *Cheyenne River Sioux, South Dakota* (Mount Pleasant, SC: Arcadia Publishing, 2003), 61. Frederick E. Hoxie, "From Prison to Homeland: The Cheyenne River Indian Reservation before WWI," *South Dakota History* 10, no. 1 (1979): 1, 165.

83 **Congress continued to extend:** J. Patterson, "By the Mouth of the Moreau: The Legal History of the Cheyenne River Sioux Nation," University of Tulsa College of Law, 77 (unpublished, housed at the National Indian Law Library).

83 **Much of the best farmland:** This claim comes from interviews with Fred DuBray, Doug White Bull, and others on the Cheyenne River and Standing Rock reservations.

84 **"going up and down hills":** Reporting trip by the author to South and North Dakota, May 2021.

84 **Indian Agents intentionally:** Michael Moore (Sitting Bull College), interviews with the author. I looked up all their original allotments in the Department of the Interior's General Land Records Office. Joseph White Bull's original allotment of 640 acres, allotted May 31, 1907, is N1/2 Section 27, W1/2 Section 23, Township 21 North and Range 30 East. His son George's allotment, allotted October 3, 1907, is in Section 24 and 25, Township 21 N and Range 25 E (each range unit is approximately six miles wide). Jacob's allotted land, allotted June 26, 1908, 160 acres, NE1/4 Section 27, T 19 North and Range 23 East.

84 **A 1909 map:** "The Only Authentic and Up-to-Date Map of the Standing Rock and Cheyenne River Indian Reservations, 36 x 25" (St. Paul, MN: Great Sioux Reservation Information Bureau, September 1909), https://sddigitalarchives.contentdm .oclc.org/digital/collection/p15914coll3/id/1303/rec/13.

84 **98 percent of the land:** I'm indebted to Josh Meisel, Haskell Indian Nations University professor of geography, for his help crunching these numbers. Some of this is also found in: Neville and Anderson, "The Diminishment of the Great Sioux Reservation," 237–51.

84 **1.5 million families:** Trina Williams Shanks, "The Homestead Act: A Major Asset-Building Policy in American History," *Inclusion in the American Dream: Assets, Poverty, and Public Policy* (2005), 20–1.

84 **"This land is your land":** When Woody Guthrie wrote "The Land Is Your Land," in 1940, it was meant as a piece of social commentary and a criticism of private property. For more on this: Nick Spitzer, "The Story of Woody Guthrie's 'This Land Is Your Land,'" NPR 100, NPR.org, February 15, 2012, www.npr.org/2000 /07/03/1076186/this-land-is-your-land.

On the Twitter eruption after President Joe Biden's inauguration on January 20, 2021: Al Donato, "Jennifer Lopez's 'This Land Is Your Land' Performance Criticized for Colonial Themes," *HuffPost*, January 22, 2021, www.huffpost.com/archive /ca/entry/jlo-indigenous-inauguration_ca_60086d18c5b6ffcab969d69d.

Examples: Nick Estes (@nickwestes), "The inauguration began by JLO singing a song celebrating stolen land and Indigenous genocide," Twitter, January 20, 2021, 11:55 a.m., www.twitter.com/nickwestes/status/1351936515585179649.

Rebecca Nagle (@rebeccanagle), "For the record. This Land is Your Indigenous Land," Twitter, January 20, 2021, 1:57 p.m., twitter.com/rebeccanagle/status /1351967075070324736.

Nick Estes is an award-winning Lakota historian. Rebecca Nagle is a citizen of Cherokee Nation and the host of the award-winning podcast *This Land.*

84–85 **the Wakpá Wašté:** Sprague, *Cheyenne River Sioux, South Dakota,* 7. For how it was easily forded: Gayloa Proutek, "Cherry Creek: The Oldest Continuously Inhabited Town in SD," in *South Dakota's Ziebach County: History of the Prairie* (Dupree, SD: Ziebach County Historical Society, 1982).

85 **Newspapers published throughout:** Ann E. Tweedy, "Unjustifiable Expectations: Laying to Rest the Ghosts of Allotment-Era Settlers." *Seattle University Law Review* 36 (2012): 129.

86 **"care very little":** Hoxie, *Jurisdiction of the Cheyenne River Sioux Indian Reservation.*

86 **"Everyone knew what was happening":** Abby Abinanti, interview with the author, August 23, 2022.

87 **Jews have spent centuries:** Rabbi Benjamin Barnett, interviews with the author, in person, over Zoom, and by phone, conducted between September 2, 2019, and October 2022.

CHAPTER 5: LITTLE SHTETL ON THE PRAIRIE

89 **My blue shadow:** Reporting trip by the author to the Dakotas, February 2019.
89 **around thirty Jewish families:** To derive the roster of Jew Flats residences, I con-

sulted Anne Haber Stanton, *Deadwood's Jewish Pioneers* (Prairie Hills Publishing, 2019), family documents, and then pulled the land records from the U.S. General Land Office for all possible residents. I reached out to families and interviewed those I could and also read many volumes of local histories of the county, some of which mentioned these families and their children. References to the Jews of Jew Flats are hard to find, though Susan Marks Connor's *I Remember When* mentions that "some thirty Jewish families did make a try at homesteading in western South Dakota in the early 1900s." The historian Eric Zimmer writes of Jew Flats that there were twenty couples and eighteen single men, in: Eric Zimmer, Art Marmarstein, and Matthew Remmich, "Fewer Rabbis Than U.S. Senators: Jewish Political Activism in Twentieth Century South Dakota," in *The Plains Political Tradition: Essays on South Dakota Political Culture*, vol. 3, ed. Jon K. Lauck, John E. Miller, and Donald C. Simmons Jr. (Pierre: South Dakota State Historical Society Press, 2018), 112–39. Also see: "The Jews of South Dakota," *Heritage of the Great Plains*, vol. 16 (Bloomington: Indiana University, 1983). And a small mention in: Matthew B. Schwartz, *Jews in America: The First 500 Years* (Eugene, OR: Wipf and Stock Publishers, 2019), 253.

89 **place as Jew Flats:** Author's interviews with locals from 2019 to 2022. Sometimes called "Jew Flat" (as found in "Spouting Off," *Rapid City Journal*, December 15, 1963) and sometimes called "the Jew Estate."

89 **Despite proximity, my ancestors:** "Aside from the fact that the reservation is just across the Cheyenne River, no Indian life exists in Haakon County." From: Pioneer Club of Western South Dakota (Midland, SD), *Pioneers of the Open Range* (Midland, SD: Pioneer Club of Western South Dakota, 1965). Mikal Brotnov Eckstrom, "Probationary Settlers and Indigenous Peoples in the American West: American Jews and American Indians, 1850–1934" (dissertation, University of Nebraska–Lincoln, 2018), ETD collection for University of Nebraska–Lincoln, AAI10840891. Mikal Eckstrom, interviews with the author, June 2020.

90 **the official documents:** According to the records I received from the National Archives and Records Administration, Harry filed a claim with the Land Office in Quinn, South Dakota, on January 25, 1908. When he filed his Final Proof to claim his Homestead in 1913, he swore an affidavit that he "first established actual residence upon this land" on January 25, 1908. However, family lore indicates he had been out on the prairie living in a cave for at least several years prior to filing this claim.

90 **Inside the bundles:** Diane Small (daughter of Louie Sinykin), interviews with the author, November 2018, March 2019, February 2020, May 2020, May 2021, and November 2021. See also: Diane Small and Etta Orkin, "Women of Jew Flats," 17th Annual West River History Conference, 2009. I admit it seems questionable that they would have shlepped a writing desk and piano all the way from Russia, but this is the story I've been told.

90 **an "Earthly Paradise":** "All Aboard for Pennington County," *Sioux City Journal*, March 15, 1908.

91 **what I know:** "Sinykin, who still shudders when he recalls his 1908 trip to their fresh sod shanty in South Dakota," from: "Isolated, 5,500-Acre Dakota Ranch Is Operated by Jewish Family," *National Jewish Post and Opinion*, October 10,

1958. Other details from: Etta Fay (Kozberg) Orkin, *Etta and Harry's Megillah*, 1977, and author interviews with most every single living grandchild and great-grandchild of Harry and Faige Etke.

91 **good news about soddies:** "Life in a Sod House: More Information," Smithsonian Institute: https://amhistory.si.edu/ourstory/activities/sodhouse/more.html.

91 **the prairie in all seasons:** Paula Nelson, *After the West Was Won: Homesteaders and Town-Builders in Western South Dakota, 1900–1917* (Iowa City: University of Iowa Press, 1986), 34.

92 **"End of the World":** Letter from Rose Sinykin to Pauline Bernstein, Etta Orkin, and Betty Rappaport, 1963, author's collection.

92 **immigrants, many of them:** Bill Bielmaier, phone interview, May 2022. Ruby Gabriel, *It's More Than a Place . . . West River* (Chamberlain, SD: Register Lakota Printing, 2012).

92 **"It was one bitchy place":** Herbie Marsh, phone and in-person interviews with the author, January 2020. Etta Orkin, "Wrong-Way Marsh," phone interview with the author, March 2020.

93 **Her hobbies were:** Fanny Smith Landman, interview with Etta Orkin.

93 **Blood seeps through:** Julie Rappaport and Aimee Orkin, phone interview with the author, February 20, 2019.

93 **slapped their daughters:** Chanel Dubofsky, "Daughter Got Her Period? Slap Her," *Jewniverse*, September 2, 2015, www.jta.org/jewniverse/2015/daughter-got-her-period-slap-her. Haley Winters, "Jewish Girls Get Slapped on Their First Menstrual Cycle," USC Digital Folklore Archives, April 27, 2012, https://folklore.usc.edu/jewish-girls-get-slapped-on-their-first-menstrual-cycle. Carol Cott Gross, "My Mom Slapped Me When I Got My Period," *Kveller*, June 13, 2017, www.kveller.com/my-mom-slapped-me-when-i-got-my-period.

94 **the rules of the Homestead Act:** For a great source to learn more about the act and homesteading in general, see: Richard Edwards, Jacob K. Friefeld, and Rebecca S. Wingo, *Homesteading the Plains: Toward a New History* (Lincoln: University of Nebraska Press, 2017). Professor Edwards clarified for me: the 1862 Homestead Act doesn't mention anything about the need to improve the land or specific measures required. The General Land Office issued periodic circulars clarifying their expectations. The verbiage "improve" comes from the 1895 circular.

94 **By the spring following:** Orkin, *Megillah*. Also: Sinykin Homestead records, National Archives and Records Administration.

95 **Settlers liked to say:** Nelson, *After the West Was Won*, 40.

95 **undammed and undiverted:** Less than 0.5 percent of farms in South Dakota were irrigated in 1910. For more on South Dakota farms, visit the State Agricultural Heritage Museum, South Dakota State University: www.sdstate.edu/south-dakota-agricultural-heritage-museum.

95 **Hail the size of baseballs:** *South Dakota's Ziebach County*, 39. Data for Pennington County, South Dakota, (home to Jew Flats between 1910 and 1920) from the National Oceanic and Atmospheric Administration's "Climate at a Glance County Time Series," www.ncei.noaa.gov/access/monitoring/climate-at-a-glance/county/time-series. I also pulled a huge amount of information about the early days of homesteading in western South Dakota from a series of county "memory books."

There are a number of these, but see: *Eastern Pennington County Memories*, 1965, American Legion; *Haakon Horizons*, 1982. For details about stem rust: Gwen McCausland (director, South Dakota Agricultural Heritage Museum, South Dakota State University), interview and email exchange with the author, September 2020. McCausland contacted plant scientists on my behalf.

96 **"enough to starve"**: Rich Smith, interview with the author, February 2019.

96 **"move here with trauma"**: Cathy Park Hong, *Minor Feelings: An Asian American Reckoning* (New York: One World, 2020), 34.

96 **"What H.S. did"**: Letter, "Facts to Attorney," typed but undated, written, it seems, by my great-grandfather Jake Kozberg, Harry's son-in-law (and first cousin), probably in 1930.

96 **Harry did love Faige Etke**: Etta Orkin, notes from a 1976 interview with her uncle, Jack Sinykin. Full quote from Jack: "Grandpa had temper—but went thru [*sic*] a lot of misery—blow up—She had a timing when to discuss things—She knew how to handle him—stress and pressure caused him to be that way but he did love her."

97 **a wonderful life**: *Eastern Pennington County Memories*. Orkin, *Megillah*. Etta Orkin, interviews with the author, June 2022, August 2021, July 2019. Sinykin family photographs, author's collection.

98 **an "expert rider"**: Small and Orkin, "Women of Jew Flats."

98 **"a bunch of horse thieves"**: Linda Carney, interview with the author, April 30, 2021. Bruce Cohne, email exchange with the author, March 7, 2019. Cohne wrote that his father, Ben, Faige Etke's oldest grandson, "did mention riding with a posse after horse thieves." Search of newspapers at the Library of Congress using the terms "horse thieves," "South Dakota," and "1905–1920."

98 **"horse stealing seems to be an epidemic"**: (Untitled), *The Bad River News*, December 15, 1910.

98 **more than one hundred thousand settlers**: Nelson, *After the West Was Won*, xiv. That many of them were immigrants is evident in reading the county memory books from the "West River" area.

98 **"thick as the stars"**: *Eastern Pennington County Memories*, 295.

98 **built the shacks**: Almost all claim shacks were ten feet by twelve feet, because that was the total lumber that one team of horses and a wagon could haul. Timbers were rare on the prairie, and most people had to bring their boards from Fort Pierre, approximately eighty miles away. Audio recording of Fanny Cohne, undated, author's collection.

99 **"they loved it"**: Etta Orkin, interviews with the author, May 2022, August 2021, July 2019.

100 **farm communities composed of**: Ava F. Kahn, ed., *Jewish Life in the American West* (Washington, DC: ICS Publications, 2004), 115. As early as 1837, thirteen Russian Jewish families created a farming settlement in upstate New York called Shalom. Data of the number of Jewish farmers varies somewhat based on the source, but estimates hover consistently between twenty-five thousand and thirty-seven thousand people during this era. Additional information on Jewish farmers can be found in: Jewish Agricultural Society, *Jews in American Agriculture* (New York: Jewish Agricultural Society, 1954). Also: Leonard George Robinson,

"The Agricultural Activities of the Jews in America," *The American Jewish Year Book* 1912–1913, ed. Herbert Friedenwald (Philadelphia: The Jewish Publication Society of America, 1912), 21–115; Gabriel Davidson, *Our Jewish Farmers: The Story of the Jewish Agricultural Society* (New York: L. B. Fischer, 1943).

100 **By 1912, there were an estimated twenty-five thousand:** Robinson, "Agricultural Activities of the Jews in America," *American Jewish Year Book* vol. 14, 76–78, www.ajcarchives.org/main.php?GroupingId=10045.

100 **one thousand Jews were homesteaders:** Schloff, *And Prairie Dogs Weren't Kosher*, 47. This is an estimate only for the years between 1882 and 1910.

100 **a sliver of Dakota settlers:** Data courtesy Professor Trina Shanks, now at the University of Michigan, and shared with the author by Richard Edwards, director emeritus, Center for Great Plains Studies, University of Nebraska.

100 **JAIAS offered grants:** The Jewish Agricultural and Industrial Aid Society, *Annual Report for the Year 1910* (New York: Jewish Agricultural and Industrial Aid Society, 1909), quote found on page 24, 1908 loan information on page 22. All JAIAS annual reports from 1901 to 1919 are available at https://catalog.hathitrust .org/Record/007863493.

100 **the first agricultural schools:** Jonathan Dekel-Chen, phone interview with author, September 13, 2022.

100 *The Jewish Farmer*: Samples of the publication can be found at the National Library of Israel. Here's one example that YIVO's Eddy Portnoy translated on my behalf: https://www.nli.org.il/en/newspapers/ydfarm. Subscriber numbers are found in the JAIAS annual reports.

100 **any of these loans:** In April 2019, Professor J. Sanford Rikoon (author of "Jewish Farm Settlements in America's Heartland," in *Rachel Calof's Story: Jewish Homesteader on the Northern Plains*, ed. J. Sanford Rikoon [Bloomington: Indiana University Press, 1995], 106–128) kindly went through his original research of those settlers who received funds from the JAIAS, and no one with my family's last name showed up on the lists.

100 **$24,000 in mortgages:** Throughout the pandemic, when I couldn't travel there myself, Rapid City–based researcher Diana Pavek spent countless hours at the Pennington County Office of Deeds pulling every single mortgage associated with the legal descriptions of the land owned by Jew Flats homesteaders. I also pulled files from the Haakon County Office of Deeds (Jew Flats straddles both counties). Documents, and the resulting spreadsheets, author's collection.

100 **praised by reporters:** Nelson, *After the West Was Won*, 22–23, 134, 170.

100 **Carrie Ingalls, whose older sister:** "Carrie Ingalls Swanzey," Keystone Historical Museum, www.keystonehistory.com/index.php/cultural-innovators/carrie-ingalls. Additional information provided by emails to the author from Julie Hedgepeth Williams, author of *Little Newspapers on the Prairie: The Frontier Press Career of Carrie Ingalls* (Keystone, SD: Keystone Area Historical Society, 2019).

101 **free to worship:** "The Sinykin Family," *Eastern Pennington County Memories*, 374. Orkin, *Megillah*.

102 **free to educate:** "The Calloways and Quinn," *Eastern Pennington County Memories*. Lou Calloway remembered of their Jewish neighbors, "Their children were bright and the parents wanted them educated so two schools were established in

two homesteaders houses . . . we each had a couple of adult pupils who wanted to learn more English."

102 **couldn't speak or read English:** "There were Yiddish newspapers instructing their readership which symbols to look for and to mark those with an *X*, assuming that many couldn't yet read English," Eddy Portnoy, interview with the author, August 2022. Eddy Portnoy, *Bad Rabbi: And Other Strange but True Stories from the Yiddish Press* (Redwood City, CA: Stanford University Press, 2017).

103 **to bury their dead:** Paula Rodenas (descendent of Louis Kronick, a Jew Flats settler and distant cousin of the author), phone interview with the author, September 2020. Paula Rodenas, "The Legend of Uncle Louis," author's collection. Rodenas writes that Kronick "befriended the local Sioux Indians. He helped them round up horses, make whiskey and bury their dead."

103 **enough to fear them:** Marcia Goldman, phone interview with the author, December 12, 2018. Etta Orkin, phone interview with the author, November 28, 2022. Etta stressed the point that "they were terrified of the Indians. They thought they were out to get them."

103 **"women were scared":** Clara Josephine Roseth and the Stanley County Historical Society, "The Marrington Story," *Prairie Progress in West Central South Dakota* (Midwest Beach, 1969), 454. *Eastern Pennington County Memories*, 164. Henry and Lea Fine, "North Dakota Memories," *Western States Jewish Historical Quarterly* 9, no. 4 (July 1977).

103 **"Indian is fair game":** Letter from Superintendent Thomas J. King to Walter Huddleston, March 5, 1912, filed with "Response to Circular 612," Special Series A, Box 1, Records Group 75, National Archives.

104 **a segregated prairie:** Mikal Eckstrom, phone interviews with the author, June 2020–October 2021.

104 **"the matter of Americanization":** Phil Freshman and Linda Mack Schloff. *In America "People Were Free": Four Personal Accounts of Immigration and Settlement* (Minneapolis, MN: Upper Midwest Jewish History, 2004), 62–63. The usage of *reverend* or *minister* was so common during this era that even many Jewish Orthodox clergymen adopted the titles.

104 **the 1942 novel *Jewish Cowboy*:** Isaac Raboy, *Jewish Cowboy*, trans. Nathaniel Shapiro (Westfield, NJ: Tradition Books, 1989), 127. Originally published in Yiddish in 1942 as *Der Yiddisher Cowboy*.

104 **"disdained honest toil":** Debra Shein, "Isaac Raboy's *Der Yiddisher Cowboy* and Rachel Calof's *My Story*: The Role of the Western Frontier in Shaping Jewish American Identity." *Western American Literature* 36, no. 4 (2002): 359–80.

104 **in elementary school, "Lou the Jew":** Diane Small, interviews with the author, September 2019 and April 2021.

105 **conflating Lakota with Cossacks:** David Koffman, interview with the author, August 2020.

105 **"This is our inheritance":** Eula Biss, *Notes from No Man's Land: American Essays* (Minneapolis, MN: Graywolf Press, 2018), 161.

106 **the dead weight:** My thinking on this was heavily influenced by: Edmund De Waal, *The Hare with Amber Eyes: A Family's Century of Art and Loss* (New York: Macmillan, 2010).

106 **driest periods of the century:** Pennington County, South Dakota, Precipitation Data from the National Centers for Environmental Information, www.ncei.noaa .gov. Other sources of information about the drought of 1911 come from: Nelson, *After the West Was Won*; Harry Sinykin's Homestead Claim paperwork, National Archives; and *Eastern Pennington County Memories*, especially page 327.

106 **And so, an exodus:** Jim Sherman, interview with the author, July 2019.

107 **"find a self-respect":** Shein, "Isaac Raboy's *Der Yiddisher Cowboy* and Rachel Calof's *My Story*." More from Shein: "When [Jewish homesteaders in North Dakota] eventually exchange their lives in the rural West for a future in an area with a greater Jewish population, we do not read such outcomes as failures . . . rather, we understand that their choices are positive, motivated by the self-awareness gained by their period of separation."

107 **returned to Sioux City:** Haley Aguirre, email message to the author, June 23, 2020. Aguirre, searched the 1912 city directory with the list I gave her of Jew Flats residents. Here's a sampling: "Louis Kronick, horses and mules; Harry Margolin, clerk for a coal, wood, and junk dealer; Isaac Rivin, peddler; Isaac Udansky, salesman for J. H. Bolstein's saloon; Louie Baker, butcher; Abraham Kozberg, peddler." Also, see: Rodenas, "The Legend of Uncle Louis."

107 **title to new land:** Nelson, *After the West Was Won*, 131–32; Cris Stainbrook (president, Indian Land Tenure Foundation), interview with the author, May 2022.

108 **their best years yet:** "Homestead Entry, Final Proof, Testimony of Witness," Department of the Interior, signed by Harry Sinykin, February 24, 1913, received from the National Archives and Records Agency, author's collection.

108 **received his own cattle brand:** State of South Dakota certificate for cattle brand. No. 8109, signed August 26, 1914, author's collection.

108 **from the Sears catalog:** Jack Sinykin, interview with Etta Orkin, 1976.

108 **the marriage plot:** Steve Felix (Rose and Issie's grandson), phone interview with the author, May or June 2021. Gordon Siegel (Rose's great-nephew), phone interview with the author, April 2021. Herbie Marsh, phone and in-person interviews, January 2019. Etta Orkin, interview with the author, December 2019. According to the *Deadwood Daily Pioneer-Times* (July 28, 1914), Jake would continue to visit his 160-acre farm on Jew Flats where he not only had "excellent and plentiful" crops but also "fine herds of cattle and horses." I learned that there were three synagogues in St. Paul in 1915 from: "St. Paul Historic Context Study, Synagogues and Religious Buildings: 1849–1950," St. Paul Heritage Preservation Commission, 2001. "Will Marry Bride's Sister," *Lead Daily Call*, August 7, 1915. "Account of the Wedding," *Lead Daily Call*, August 28, 1915.

109 **honeymoon on Jew Flats:** "Mr. and Mrs. Jake Kozberg," *Lead Daily Call*, September 28, 1915. "Arrivals on the Late Pierre Train Last Night," *Lead Daily Call*, August 27, 1915.

CHAPTER 6: IN DI SHVARTSE BERG

111 **a giant hole—the Homestake Mine:** Steven T. Mitchell, *Nuggets to Neutrinos: The Homestake Story* (Bloomington, IN: Xlibris, 2009): "over the next century [1877–1977], would yield more gold than any other mine in the western hemi-

sphere." The 311,020-ounces figure comes from researchers at the Black Hills Mining Museum who based their calculations on the Homestake Mine's 1915 Annual Report. The mine was initially staked by Fred and Moses Manuel, Jewish brothers, in 1876, per: Al Alschuler, "The Colmans and Others of Deadwood, South Dakota," *Western States Jewish Historical Quarterly* 9, no. 4 (July 1977).

111 **Lead and its nearby sister city, Deadwood:** Irma Klock, *Lead City—Restless Gold Camp* (self-published, 1983), collection of the author. "City of Lead, 1876–1981," copied and shared by the Black Hills Mining Museum. "Mill and Main Streets Paved," *Lead Daily Call*, December 21, 1908. "Deadwood—Thrifty, Orderly, Progressive," *Lead Daily Call*, March 25, 1915. Ad for hotel with "steam heat, electric lights," *Lead Daily Call*, May 22, 1915. "The A & F Café," *Lead Daily Call*, December 11, 1915. Mention of trolley between Deadwood and Lead, *Lead Daily Call*, October 26, 1915. Additional information culled by research volunteers Sharon Chadwick and Diane Monday at the Black Hills Mining Museum. Rick Mills (South Dakota State Railroad Museum), interview with the author, Hill City, South Dakota, October 1, 2020.

112 **this land was illegally occupied:** "Black Hills, Radical Members of Sioux Nation Favor Armed Force," *Lead Daily Call*, July 25, 1904. "Was a Great Success," *Lead Daily Call*, September 21, 1912.

112 **the Lobby Liquor House:** "Notice of Dissolution," *Lead Daily Call*, October 9, 1912 (notes that Jacob Kozberg and Chris Crosby are now owners of "Lobby Liquor House"). "Lobby Liquor House," ad in *Lead Daily Call*, November 11, 1913 ("all wines at 5¢ per Glass"). "Notice," *Lead Daily Call*, July 22, 1914 (Jake becomes the sole proprietor of Lobby Liquor House). *Sanborn Map*, Lead, SD, October 1915.

112 **called Ruth *tsuker pushkele*:** Postcard from Dov Shapiro to Ruth Sinykin, sent in 1908, translated by Roberta Newman, August 2020.

112 **He complained in:** Letter from Jake Kozberg to Faige Etke Sinykin, September 30, 1914, translated by Roberta Newman, November 2021.

113 **was a mucker:** Dave Reddick (former miner and current treasurer of Black Hills Mining Museum), interview and tour with the author, Black Hills Mining Museum, Lead, SD, July 8, 2020.

113 **"use your head":** Etta Orkin, interview with the author. Photo of Jake Kozberg and other miners at Old Abe mine entrance, back of photo dated "circa-1908."

114 **the halcyon days:** Letter from Ruth Kozberg to Pauline Kozberg, February 24, 1933, "There was no happier woman living than I was when Dad and I were first married." Letter from Ruth to Jake Kozberg, January 8, 1916.

114 **their own friends:** Correspondence between Ruth Sinykin and friends. Photographs of Ruth and Jake Sinykin and various friends at picnics and dinner parties. Notices in the local paper of dinner parties. All author's collection.

115 **"prominent businessmen of Lead":** *Deadwood Daily Pioneer-Times*, September 15, 1916. Jake also continues to be noted for his successful ranch: "Mr. Kosberg [*sic*] has one of the best stocked and one of the finest cultivated ranches this side of the Missouri," *Deadwood Daily Pioneer-Times*, June 3, 1916.

115 **heightened social status:** William Toll, "The Jewish Merchant and Civic Order

in the Urban West," in *Jewish Life in the American West*, ed. Ava F. Kahn (Seattle: University of Washington Press, 2002), 83–112.

115 **"Jews were mining the miners"**: Ann Haber Stanton, interview with the author, February 11, 2019. Ann Haber Stanton, *Jewish Pioneers of the Black Hills Gold Rush* (Mount Pleasant, SC: Arcadia Publishing, 2011). Stanton, *Deadwood's Jewish Pioneers*. Pam Monsky, "Jewish Deadwood? One Family's Summer Vacation," *Jewish Press*, August 6, 1999. Tom and Nyla Griffith, "The Jewish Traveler, Deadwood," *Hadassah Magazine*, August/September 1999. Ann Haber Stanton, "When Deadwood Was Jewish," *The Forward*, May 9, 2015.

115 **exiling Native Americans to reservations**: Toll, "The Jewish Merchant and Civic Order," mentions Trinidad, Colorado, and Prescott, Arizona, as places Jews were having economic success by the 1870s. Both of these towns, as with Lead and Deadwood, were mining communities that had recently displaced local Indigenous peoples to reservations. "Native Americans and Spaniards," in "Las Animas County," *Colorado Encyclopedia*, https://coloradoencyclopedia.org/article/las-animas -county#Native-Americans-and-Spaniards.

115 **one ethnic group of many**: South Dakota Department of the Census, *Third Census of South Dakota, Taken in the Year 1915* (Pierre: South Dakota State Archives, 1915), 26–27, table V. Donald Toms, *The Flavor of Lead: An Ethnic History* (Lead, SD: Lead Historic Preservation Commission, 1992).

115 **Jake's naturalization hearing**: "Fourteen Up for Naturalization," *Deadwood Daily Pioneer-Times*, September, 16, 1913.

115 **with their Torah**: "The Deadwood Jewish community used a Torah that had been shipped over from Germany in 1888," from: Eric Zimmer, Art Marmarstein, and Matthew Remmich, "Fewer Rabbis Than U.S. Senators: Jewish Political Activism in Twentieth Century South Dakota," in *The Plains Political Tradition: Essays on South Dakota Political Culture*, vol. III, ed. Jon K. Lauck, John E. Miller, and Donald C. Simmons Jr. (Pierre: South Dakota State Historical Society Press, 2018): 112–39. "Jewish Day of Atonement," *Deadwood Daily Pioneer-Times*, October 1, 1911, which mentions that Rabbi Harry Kosberg [*sic*], Jake's brother, will lead Yom Kippur services. "Jewish Services," *Deadwood Daily Pioneer-Times*, October 3, 1911, mentions that "between seventy-five and eighty people" gathered for services and that Ted Sinykin and others "gave in Hebrew the 'Kol Nidrei' the most beautiful prayer known to the Jews."

116 **snowballs at "the Chinamen"**: Toms, *The Flavor of Lead*, 125–27.

116 **they were educated**: Etta Orkin, interview with the author, June 2020.

116 **Jewish men created**: Stanton, *Deadwood's Jewish Pioneers*. Stanton, *Jewish Pioneers of the Black Hills Gold Rush*; ad for The Model Furniture Store, Joe Seelig proprietor, *Lead Daily Call*, January 26, 1915. "[Jack] Sinykin . . . now stock solicitor for the Hill City Mining and Development C.," (untitled note), *Philip Weekly Review*, December 10, 1914.

116 **one third of all the buildings**: Estimate by Ann Haber Stanton, based on decades of research, from an interview with the author and her self-published book: *An Unbroken Chain: Deadwood's Jewish Legacy*. Published in conjunction with an exhibition of the same title, organized by and presented by the Adams Museum,

Lead, SD, 1999. The exhibit included a walking tour of Deadwood with buildings that were occupied or owned by Jewish businesses.

116 **for political power:** Again, from Stanton, *Deadwood's Jewish Pioneers*. My great-
grandfather was installed as a trustee in the Fraternal Order of Eagles, Lead,
No. 246: "Eagles Install," *Lead Daily Call*, January 14, 1914.

116 **less Jewish and more:** Jonathan Freidmann (Jewish Museum of the American
West), phone interview with the author, November 3, 2020. Found on microfilm
at the South Dakota State Historical Society: 1915 Census card for 'Jack Kosberg': Occupation: Saloon Keeper, Birthplace: Norway, Ancestry: Norwegian,
Town: Lead."

117 **considered "lesser people":** Reddick, interview and tour, July 8, 2020. Research
volunteers at the Black Hills Mining Museum shared that they had no official
records of Homestake hiring an Indigenous person. Despite these records,
Homestake certainly did hire Native people on occasion. Doug White Bull and
others have told me of Lakota friends who worked in the mines. Also mentioned
in this memoir: Diane Wilson, *Spirit Car: Journey to a Dakota Past* (St. Paul: Minnesota Historical Society, 2008), 71–72.

117 **measure their distance:** This teaching can be found in Deuteronomy 21. Rabbi
Toba Spitzer, "Slavery and Its Atonement: Priestly Concepts for Confronting
Racism," Yom Kippur Sermon, 5778, Congregation Dorshei Tzedek, West New-
ton, MA, September 29, 2017.

118 **For many thousands of years:** Linea Sundstrom, *Storied Stone: Indian Rock Art
in the Black Hills Country* (Norman: University of Oklahoma Press, 2004). Mike
Hilton (Black Hills National Forest), phone interview with the author, November
2020. U.S. Department of Agriculture, "Black Hills National Forest Cultural
Resources Overview," 1996. Michael Catches Enemy, "Traditional and Naturally
Significant Places Process Primer for the Oglala Sioux Tribe" (master's thesis,
St. Cloud University, 2019). Also: Austin A. Buhta, Rolfe D. Mandel, and L. Adrien
Hannus, "The Archeology, History, and Geomorphology of the Ray Long Site
(39FA65), Angostura Reservoir, Fall River County, South Dakota." Archaeolog-
ical Contract Series 254. Prepared by the Archaeology Laboratory, Augustana
College, Sioux Falls, SD. Prepared for the Bureau of Reclamation, Dakotas Area
Office, Rapid City, SD (2012). There's archaeological evidence that humans have
been coming to the Black Hills for centuries, but whether these people were the
Lakota is somewhat controversial. Many Indigenous Nations claim a deep and old
connection to the Hills. Some non-Indigenous historians think the Lakota didn't
come to the area until the 1700s. Others say the Lakota would travel to the Hills
during certain seasons and that they did so for centuries earlier than the 1700s.

118 **they call the He Sapa:** James Sanovia, "HES Seminar: James Sanovia 'Lakóta
GeoSpatial Applications of the Black Hills Area: Makówapi Wítaya,'" Boise
State College of Innovation and Design, September 28, 2020, www.youtube.com
/watch?v=WznqM2wwwVU.

118 **When Joseph White Bull was a child:** Richard Stone, *First Encounters: Indian
Legends of Devils Tower* (Belle Fourche, SD: Sand Creek Publishing, 1982).

118 **the sacred home:** John G. Neihardt, *Black Elk Speaks* (Woodstock, IL: Dramatic
Publishing, 1996), 16. Many of the oral histories from the South Dakota Oral

History Center's American Indian Research Project, housed at the University of South Dakota, touch on the sacredness of the Black Hills for the Lakota, including: Arthur Amiotte, interview conducted by George Nielsen, 1971 (AIRP 724); Charles Kills in Water, interview conducted by George Nielsen, 1971 (AIRP 2187); and Billy Mills, interview conducted by Don Doll, 1991 (AIRP 2156).

118 **stars are "the holy breath":** Ronald Goodman, *Lakota Star Knowledge: Studies in Lakota Stellar Theology* (Mission, SD: Sintte Gleska University, 1992).

118 **in his book *Legends of the Lakota*:** James LaPointe, *Legends of the Lakota* (San Francisco: Indian Historian Press, 1976), origin legend from page 13. Alternate version: James R. Walker, "How the Lakota Came Upon the World [excerpt]," in *The Sun Dance and Other Ceremonies of the Oglala Division of the Teton Dakota* (Anthropological Papers of the American Museum of Natural History, vol. 16, 2), 1917, 181–82, www.nativecairns.org/projects/leap/lakota-emergence/lakotaemergence narrative.html. Also, an oral recitation of the story: Sina Bear Eagle, "Lakota Emergence Story," Wind Cave National Park, National Park Service, 2016, www.nps.gov/wica/learn/historyculture/the-lakota-emergence-story.htm. Mike Catches Enemy (Cultural Liaison, Oglala Sioux Tribe), phone interview with the author, September 17, 2020.

120 **structure of the language:** Author's phone interviews with Jhon Goes In Center, September 20, 2020; Doug White Bull, October 9, 2020; and Brett Shelton, May 2021.

120 **Yiddish, the language:** Madeleine "Mindl" Cohen, phone interview with the author, Yiddish Book Center, June 16, 2021. Dara Horn, email message to the author, June 2, 2021. Michael Wex, *Born to Kvetch: Yiddish Language and Culture in All Its Moods* (New York: St. Martin's Press, 2007). Benjamin Harshav, *The Meaning of Yiddish* (Berkeley: University of California Press, 1990).

120 **jars of Israeli soil:** Eddy Portnoy, email exchange with the author, April 22, 2022.

120 **called it "God's Country":** *Lead Daily Call*, February 26, 1914, Jake Kozberg "is glad to be back in 'God's Country.'"

121 **Lakota leaders were protesting:** Jeffrey Ostler, *The Lakotas and the Black Hills* (New York: Viking, 2010). Also: Edward Lazarus, *Black Hills/White Justice: The Sioux Nation versus the United States, 1775 to the Present* (Lincoln: University of Nebraska Press, 1999).

121 **Joseph White Bull's father:** Stanley Vestal, *Warpath: The True Story of the Fighting Sioux Told in a Biography of Chief White Bull* (Lincoln: University of Nebraska Press, 1934), 232.

121 **councils to discuss:** Ostler, *The Lakotas and the Black Hills*. Transcript of "Convention Held from January 27–February 1, 1911, at Cherry Creek, SD," provided by Remi Bald Eagle, intergovernmental affairs coordinator for the Cheyenne River Sioux Tribe. Richmond L. Claw, "A New Look at Indian Land Suits: The Sioux Nation's Black Hills Claim as a Case for Tribal Symbolism," *Plains Anthropologist* 28, no. 102 (1983): 315–324.

121 **The eager Ralph Hoyt Case:** Lazarus, *Black Hills/White Justice*.

121 **no need for such justice:** John R. Brennan, "The Truth About the Black Hills Treaty," *Lead Daily Call*, March 1, 1911. Brennan served as president of Rapid City's first city council and as superintendent of the Pine Ridge Reservation. "In-

dians Holding Council Over Hills Treaty of 1876," *Black Hills Weekly*, February 20, 1914.

121 **Black Hills to homesteaders:** Norman Hollow (former Tribal Chairman of the Fort Peck Reservation), interview conducted by Don Doll, 1992, South Dakota Oral History Center, American Indian Research Project (AIRP 2169), University of South Dakota.

122 **another long fight:** Lazarus, *Black Hills/White Justice*, chap. 7.

122 **sculptor Gutzon Borglum:** "1925: Federal and state legislation authorizes carving of memorial in Black Hills. Borglum quits Stone Mountain project and goes to SD. Chooses Mount Rushmore as site," Mount Rushmore National Memorial Brochure and Guide from National Parks Service, obtained by the author while visiting the site, July 2020. Nick Estes, "The Battle for the Black Hills," *High Country News*, January 1, 2021, www.hcn.org/issues/53.1/indigenous-affairs-social-justice-the-battle-for-the-black-hills. Estes reports that "By 1923, Borglum was a trusted Klan insider who served on the Kloncilium, the highest decision-making body, second only to the Grand Wizard." See also: Diane Bernard, "The Creator of Mount Rushmore's Forgotten Ties to White Supremacy," *Washington Post*, July 2, 2020, www.washingtonpost.com/history/2020/07/03/mount-rushmore-gutzon-borglum-klan-stone-mountain.

About the family lore that Louie and Jack befriended Borglum: This may be true, but the photos we have of them climbing on the side of Rushmore as it's being carved, and later photos of them posing in front of the completed faces, have them posing not with Gutzon Borglum but, I believe, with his son, Lincoln Borglum (the archivists I consulted at the National Park Service also believe this is Lincoln: www.nps.gov/moru/learn/historyculture/lincoln-borglum.htm). For more on Lincoln and Gutzon Borglum and the carving of Mount Rushmore: Lincoln Borglum, *My Father's Mountain: Mt. Rushmore National Memorial and How It Was Carved* (Rapid City, SD: Fenwinn Press, 1965).

123 **"The Shrine to Hypocrisy":** Sean Newcomb, "Bush at Mount Rushmore: 'The Shrine of Hypocrisy,'" *Indian Country Today*, August 11, 2004, updated September 12, 2018, www.indiancountrytoday.com/archive/bush-at-mount-rushmore-the-shrine-of-hypocrisy. Tim Giago, "Means Called Mount Rushmore the 'Shrine of Hypocrisy,'" *Native Sun News Today*, August 19, 2021: www.nativesunnews.today/articles/means-called-mount-rushmore-theshrine-of-hypocrisy.

123 **delays and setbacks:** Fred Barbash, "58 Years Later, Sioux Legal Claim Still in Court," *Washington Post*, April 28, 1980, www.washingtonpost.com/archive/politics/1980/04/28/58-years-later-sioux-legal-claim-still-in-court/0f21cb1d-c374-47db-89ac-cb18bc3ff311.

123 **"ripe and rank case":** *United States v. Sioux Nation of Indians*, 448 U.S. 371 (1980), https://caselaw.findlaw.com/us-supreme-court/448/371.html. Dan Lewerenz (Native American Rights Fund), phone interview with the author, May 2, 2022.

124 **Indigenous legal organizations:** Native American Rights Fund, www.narf.org/about-us.

124 **"We are like the Jews":** William Greider, "The Heart of Everything That Is," *Rolling Stone*, May 7, 1987, www.rollingstone.com/politics/politics-news/the-heart-of-everything-that-is-101503.

124 **the longest ongoing legal case:** A few of the many news stories on this: Ruth
Hopkins, "Reclaiming the Sacred Black Hills," *Indian Country Today*, June 28,
2014, updated September 12, 2018, www.ictnews.org/archive/reclaiming-the
-sacred-black-hills. James Giago Davies, "History: Stealing Lakota Land," *Native Sun News Today*, April 3, 2019, www.nativesunnews.today/articles/history
-stealing-lakota-land. Tim Giago, "The Black Hills Award Approaching 1 Billion
Dollars," Indianz.com, March 22, 2022, www.indianz.com/News/2022/03/22/tim
-giago-sioux-nation-refuses-payout-for-stolen-land. Alex Williams, "Tim Giago,
Native American Newspaperman, Is Dead at 88," *New York Times*, July 28, 2022,
www.nytimes.com/2022/07/28/us/tim-giago-dead.html.

125 **Black Hills continue to make America rich:** "The Black Hills Gold Rush," *Black
Hills Visitor* magazine, October 15, 2019, www.blackhillsvisitor.com/learn/history
/the-black-hills-gold-rush. "Timber Sustainability on the Black Hills National
Forest," U.S Forest Service, Black Hills National Forest, U.S. Department of
Agriculture, www.fs.usda.gov/detail/blackhills/landmanagement/resourcemanage
ment/?cid=fseprd731012. Abby Wargo, "Outdoors Industry Harvests Millions
of Dollars from Black Hills National Forest," *Rapid City Journal*, April 3, 2021,
updated May 8, 2021, www.rapidcityjournal.com/news/local/outdoors-industry
-harvests-millions-of-dollars-from-black-hills-national-forest/article_f50e265c
-3726-5272-b846-d75d18a31504.html. Cyle Clark, "Tourism Brings in Billions
of Dollars to South Dakota," KEVN Black Hills FOX, October 26, 2022, www
.blackhillsfox.com/2022/10/26/tourism-brings-billions-dollars-south-dakota.
A National Park Service report from 2022 showed that tourists visiting sites run
by the Park Service (as opposed to state parks and towns) generated $231.6 mil-
lion in 2021.

125 **politicians have championed:** Lazarus, *Black Hills/White Justice*, 419. "Could
President Obama Settle the Black Hills Question?" *Argus Leader*, August 30,
2009: www.turtletalk.blog/2009/08/30/could-president-obama-settle-the-black
-hills-question. Les Ducheneaux, interview with the author, November 15, 2021.

125 **rally at Mount Rushmore:** Stephen Groves and Darlene Superville, "President
Trump to Give Speech at Rushmore Amid Virus, Protests," KSL-TV, July 3,
2020, www.ksltv.com/440761/president-trump-to-give-speech-at-rushmore-amid
-virus-protests. Nick Estes, "The Battle for the Black Hills," *High Country News*,
January 1, 2021, www.hcn.org/issues/53.1/indigenous-affairs-social-justice-the
-battle-for-the-black-hills.

126 **history as the honeypot:** Author reporting trip to South Dakota and road trip in
nearby states, July 2020.

126 **is Hebrew Hill:** "Hebrew Hill (Mt. Zion)," Historical Marker Database, March 13,
2023, www.hmdb.org/m.asp?m=27070.

126 **"not cowardly interlopers":** Jerry Klinger, "Deadwood, South Dakota and the
Jews," *Jewish Magazine*, November 2006, www.jewishmag.com/108mag/deadwood
/deadwood.htm. To read the three historic markers erected by the Jewish Society
for Historic Preservation, see: "Deadwood, South Dakota Jews and the Frontier
Gold Mining Town," Jewish American Society for Historic Preservation, www
.jewish-american-society-for-historic-preservation.org/sdakotawyoming/dead
woodsouthdakota.html. There are about ten such signs scattered throughout

the American West: www.jewish-american-society-for-historic-preservation.org
/mdpa/glendaleoregon.html.

126 **Jewish settlers is "agenda driven":** Jonathan L. Friedmann, phone interview with
the author, November 2020. Joel Gereboff and Jonathan L. Friedmann, eds.,
Jewish Historical Societies: Navigating the Professional-Amateur Divide (Lubbock:
Texas Tech University Press, forthcoming).

127 **"no depictions of Lakota":** Hannah Marshall, conversation on Zoom with the
author, February 4, 2022. Author's notes from visits to the Days of '76 Museum,
Adams Museum, and Deadwood History, Inc. (all in Deadwood, SD), towns of
Deadwood and Lead, SD, the Black Hills Mining Museum, Lead, South Dakota,
and the Mount Rushmore National Memorial, Keystone, SD, July 7–10, 2020.

127 **Little Bighorn Battlefield National Monument:** Author's visit to Little Bighorn
National Monument, Crow Agency, MT, July 7, 2020. Dana Dupris, interview
with the author, May 13, 2021.

128 **There are Custer counties:** "Our View: Done with Oñate," *Durango Herald*, June 25,
2020, www.durangoherald.com/articles/our-view-done-with-onate.

128 **"But this is our land":** Juliana White Bull-Taken Alive, interview with the author, July 10, 2020.

129 **DESTROYED BOOZE read:** "Destroyed Booze," *Weekly Pioneer-Times*, July 26, 1917.

129 **North Western Railway's freight station:** The freight station is a wing of the passenger station where they would store and dispatch baggage, mail, and merchan-
dise brought in by the train, per author's phone interview with Rick Mills at the
Hill City Railroad Museum, October 1, 2020.

129 **South Dakota's bone-dry law:** Chuck Cecil, *Prohibition in South Dakota: Astride
the White Mule* (Charleston, SC: The History Press, 2016). "Chris Crosby Sells
Out," *Lead Daily Call*, February 5, 1917, article tells of Ted and Sol leaving.

129 **leapt to embrace Prohibition:** Jill E. Martin, "'The Greatest Evil': Interpretations
of Indian Prohibition Laws, 1832–1953." *Great Plains Quarterly* 23, no. 1 (2003):
35–53. U.S. Department of the Interior, *Report of the Commissioner of Indian Affairs to the Secretary of the Interior, 1909* (Washington, DC: Government Printing
Office, 1909). Ten of twenty-one questions in the Annual Reports from 1916 to
1917 concerned Lakota access to alcohol. Cecil, *Prohibition in South Dakota*, 12.

129 **little trouble finding hooch:** Doane Robinson, interview with the Sioux Falls
Argus Leader, 1936, as quoted in Cecil, *Prohibition in South Dakota*. Robinson
describes how enforcement of Indigenous Prohibition laws didn't work. Paula
Rodenas, phone interview with the author, September 2020.

130 **The Anti-Saloon League, a national:** J. C. Jackson, "The Work of the Anti-
Saloon League," *Annals of the American Academy of Political and Social Science* 32,
no. 3 (1908): 12–26. Brad Japhe, "The Anti-Semites Who Pushed Prohibition on
America," *Daily Beast*, July 20, 2021, www.thedailybeast.com/the-anti-semites
-who-pushed-prohibition-on-america.

130 **were foreign born or the children:** "Volume 4: Occupation Statistics," *Thirteenth
Census of the United States, Taken in the Year 1910* (Washington, DC: Government
Printing Office, 1914). Also: "Volume 1: General Report and Analysis," *Thirteenth
Census of the United States, Taken in the Year 1910* (Washington, DC: Government
Printing Office, 1913), chap. 7, "Country of Birth of the Foreign-Born Population."

By 1910, 80 percent of saloon keepers and brewery workers were either immigrants or the children of immigrants.

130 **a soft-drink emporium:** (Untitled), *Lead Daily Call*, August 22, 1917.

130 **a $1,000 mortgage:** Author's collection.

130 **all signs pointed east:** Letters from Ted Sinykin to Jake Kozberg, January 8, 1916. Jack Sinykin, who had been working for his brother Ted's liquor distribution company, also left the Black Hills for St. Paul at this time, according to the *Deadwood Daily Pioneer-Times*, July 8, 1917. "Mr. and Mrs. Jake Kozberg left on the Northwestern for Minneapolis and St. Paul where they will make their future home," *Lead Daily Call*, August 22, 1917.

CHAPTER 7: THE ARROW FOR THE PLOW

133 **stage a mini-play:** "Ritual on Admission of Indians to Full American Citizenship," U.S. Department of the Interior, 1918, from the Major James McLoughlin Papers, on file with the North Dakota Historical Society. This script was provided to me by Sitting Bull College professor Michael Moore. See also: Janet McDonnell, "Competency Commissions and Indian Land Policy, 1913–1920," *South Dakota History* 11, no. 1 (1980): 21–34. Major McLaughlin aided Lane in the creation of the script.

133 **the white sky:** The average weather on this day in Pierre, South Dakota, historically, is 17 to 28 degrees. Temperature data for the city does not go back to 1916.

134 **free to sell their land:** Janet A. McDonnell, *The Dispossession of the American Indian, 1887–1934* (Bloomington: Indiana University Press, 1991).

134 **these Last Arrow ceremonies:** Frederick E. Hoxie, *A Final Promise: The Campaign to Assimilate the Indians, 1880–1920* (Lincoln: University of Nebraska Press, 2001), 180–81: "The press covered similar proceedings at the Crow, Shoshone, Coeur d'Alene, Fort Hall, Sisseton, Fort Berthold, and Devil's Lake agencies." I collected a number of news clips outlining these mini-plays in the Dakotas; here's a sampling: "To Treat Indian as Brother," *Dakota Farmers' Leader*, May 21, 1915, which notes that the Indian is "to be treated as a brother, instead of as a child . . . the present secretary of the interior is saying to the Indians: 'I believe that your ability, intelligence, resourcefulness and energy is equal to that of your white brother, and only because you have not had the opportunity he has had to develop are you behind. You will now be given citizenship and find that you are able to care for your family.'" "Full Citizenship for Many Sioux Indians," *Sioux County Pioneer*, October 15, 1915. "Indians Are Made Citizens," *Sisseton Weekly Standard*, November 10, 1916. "Their Last Arrow," *The Dickinson Press*, December 29, 1917.

134 **President Woodrow Wilson (whose signature):** Hoxie, *A Final Promise*, 108: "Wilson rejected the idea that the federal government had a special responsibility to oversee and encourage Indian progress."

135 **the Burke Act:** "Land Tenure History," Indian Land Tenure Foundation, https://iltf.org/land-issues/history.

135 **"pulverizing engine to break up":** President Theodore Roosevelt, "1901 State of the Union Address," December 3, 1901. From the American Presidency Project, www.presidency.ucsb.edu/documents/first-annual-message-16.

135 **the taking of their land:** Peter Iverson, *When Indians Became Cowboys: Native Peoples and Cattle Ranching in the American West* (Norman: University of Oklahoma Press, 1994), 58: "Despite protestations the government would have issued to the contrary, there can be no escaping one conclusion: Washington did more to hinder than to help the evolution of Indian cattle ranching."

135 **volunteer in the U.S. Army:** Doug White Bull, phone interview with the author, January 7, 2021, and in-person interviews with the author, May 2021.

136 **By becoming a soldier:** This perception comes from many interviews I conducted with Indigenous people throughout America when I was working on a series for *InvestigateWest* about Indigenous Nations and their citizens, but there are, of course, any number of reasons why an individual might join the U.S. military. For more on this, please see: "Why We Serve: Native Americans in the United States Armed Forces," National Museum of the American Indian, www.americanindian.si.edu/why-we-serve. For more details about those who served in World War I: Olivia B. Waxman, "'We Became Warriors Again': Why World War I Was a Seemingly Pivotal Moment for American Indian History," *Time*, November 23, 2018, www.time.com/5459439/american-indians-wwi.

137 **These Competency Commissions:** Calico Ducheneaux, "'Incompetent Indians': Some Things Never Change," video presentation, Center for Indian Country Development Research Summit, December 10, 2021, provided by Cris Stainbrook. See also: Janet McDonnell, "Competency Commissions and Indian Land Policy, 1913–1920," *South Dakota History* 11, no. 1 (1980).

137 **a "forced fee patent":** Kim J. Gottschalk, "The Federal 'Forced Fee' Policy Era—A National Disgrace," *Indian Law Support Center Reporter*, 1985, available at the National Indian Law Library.

137 **Most people had no choice but to sell:** "As a result of this unauthorized action of the Government, many [veterans] found themselves obliged either to mortgage or dispose of their property in order to meet the tax levies and to prevent their lands from being sold for taxes." 74 Cong. Rec. H3411–3414 (January 28, 1931).

138 **converted his land:** Jacob White Bull, fee patent 718354, issued November 11, 1919. The 160 acres on the Standing Rock Reservation was originally allotted June 26, 1908. Found on the Bureau of Land Management's General Land Office Records website: www.glorecords.blm.gov.

138 **"He couldn't pay no taxes":** Doug White Bull, phone interview with the author, March 16, 2021.

138 **"'That's just legalized stealing'":** Fred DuBray, interviews with the author, in person, March 11, 2020; by phone, September 30, 2022. For a view on land takings from this era more specific to Pine Ridge, see Robert J. Gay, "The 1910 Theft of Bennett County," presentation, 19th South Dakota History Conference, Oglala Lakota College, April 10, 1987.

139 **Oklahoma's Quapaw Nation:** Ducheneaux, "Incompetent Indians."

139 **sold or mortgaged:** "1913 Cheyenne River Agency Annual Report," *Cheyenne River 1910–1922*, M1011-016. These reports have been digitized and can be found at the National Archives (1910–1922): https://catalog.archives.gov/id/155863425; (1923–1935): https://catalog.archives.gov/id/155864476.

139 **"Give me your tired":** Emma Lazarus, "The New Colossus," 1883, www.nps.gov

/stli/learn/historyculture/colossus.htm. Rose arrived with Faige Etke, Ruth, and Louie in Boston, not New York, but this is the way the story was told: she could see the statue far off in the distance as they arrived.

139 **overtly about race:** "Indian Commissioner Sells a Declaration of Policy, October 15, 1917," *Documents of United States Indian Policy*, ed. Francis Paul Prucha (Lincoln: University of Nebraska Press, 2000), 213–15.

140 **nearly 780,000 acres:** Gottschalk, "The Federal 'Forced Fee' Policy Era."

140 **"given their freedom":** Hoxie, *A Final Promise*, 182.

140 **50 percent Indigenous ancestry:** American Indian History Timeline, Indian Land Tenure Foundation, 2018, www.iltf.org/wp-content/uploads/2016/11/American -Indian-History-Timeline_small.pdf. The timeline is an excellent source of information for the history of Indigenous people in the United States in general.

140 **popular magazine *The Outlook*:** McDonnell, *The Dispossession of the American Indian*, 104–5.

140 **ten thousand pages of annual reports:** "Annual Report from Lower Brule Reservation Superintendent, 1919." "1913 Cheyenne River Agency Annual Report."

140 **"the final disposition":** Peter Iverson, *When Indians Became Cowboys: Native Peoples and Cattle Ranching in the American West* (Norman: University of Oklahoma Press, 1994), 69.

141 **"let them suffer":** Hoxie, *A Final Promise*, 184.

141 **"squandered [rather] than as swindled":** Philip Joseph Deloria, *Indians in Unexpected Places* (Lawrence: University Press of Kansas, 2004), 150–51.

141 **Subsequent laws allowed these:** Cris Stainbrook, phone interview with the author, December 15, 2022. The Indian Reorganization Act of 1934 tackled a piece of this, but, for many reservations, it took individual acts of Congress for the land status to be changed. This is ongoing, with Congress passing one such law as recently as 2020.

141 **anything to remedy:** In 1987, the Native American Rights Fund brought a case (*Nichols v. Rysavy*) to federal court on behalf of a number of Indigenous landowners who had lost their land after the government had forced it into fee patent status. The brief: *Nichols v. Rysavy*, 809 F.2d 1317, available at the National Indian Law Library. Kim Gottschalk (attorney for the Native American Rights Fund), phone interview with the author, March 18, 2021. For more on the case and the issue of fee patent claims in South Dakota, see: LeAnn Larson LaFave, "South Dakota's Forced Fee Indian Land Claims: Will Landowners Be Liable for Government's Wrongdoing," *University of South Dakota Law Review* 30 (1984): 59. For a more recent discussion: Wenona T. Singel and Matthew L. M. Fletcher, "Power, Authority, and Tribal Property," *Tulsa Law Review* 41 (2005): 21.

141 **Nowhere in the country:** In South Dakota alone, there were more than 3,300 such forced fee patents issued, which could exceed three hundred thousand acres of land (Larson, "South Dakota's Forced Fee Indian Land Claims"). "No state has more identified forced fee claims than South Dakota" (74 Cong. Rec. H3411–3414, January 28, 1931).

141 **same dry sky:** "Historical Drought Conditions in Pennington County, SD," National Integrated Drought Information System, Drought.gov: www.drought.gov /historical-information?state=south-dakota&countyFips=46103&dataset=1

&selectedDateUSDM=20101102&selectedDateSpi=19220401&dateRangeSpi =1921-19300.

141 **delinquent taxpayers in 1921:** Paula M. Nelson, *The Prairie Winnows Out Its Own: The West River Country of South Dakota in the Years of Depression and Dust* (Iowa City: University of Iowa Press, 2005), 6.

141 **special banks and special credit:** Sara M. Gregg, "From Breadbasket to Dust Bowl: Rural Credit, the World War I Plow-Up, and the Transformation of American Agriculture," *Great Plains Quarterly* (2015): 129–66. See also: Raymond J. Saulnier, Harold G. Halcrow, and Neil H. Jacoby, *Federal Lending and Loan Insurance* (Princeton, NJ: Princeton University Press, 1958); John R. Brake, "A Perspective on Federal Involvement in Agricultural Credit Programs," *University of South Dakota Law Review* 19 (1974): 567.

142 **Not one of these loans:** The author's phone interviews and emails with the following agricultural historians, December 8–9, 2022: Albert Way (editor of *Agricultural History*), Tom Okie (agricultural historian at Kennesaw State University), William Bauer (director, American Indian and Indigenous Studies at University of Nevada, Las Vegas), Rani-Henrik Andersson (author of *Lakhota: An Indigenous History*), and Richard Edwards (former director, Center for Great Plains Studies). None of them had ever heard of Indigenous landowners receiving such loans. Cris Stainbrook, emailed message to the author, June 2, 2021: "My understanding of the relationship between USDA and Indian farmers and ranchers [is that it] was, for the most part, nonexistent until sometime in the mid-20th century."

142 **These "real-photo postcards":** Luc Sante, *Folk Photography: The American Real-Photo Postcard, 1905–1930* (Portland, OR: Verse Chorus Press, 2009).

142 **According to Lakota archivists:** On my earliest reporting trips to the Dakotas for this project, Cheyenne River Reservation historian Donovin Sprague and Michael Moore, history professor at Standing Rock's Sitting Bull College, both identified the man in the photo as Joseph White Bull. Tawa Ducheneaux, the librarian at Oglala Lakota College, helped identify that the pipe bag isn't the one that typically appears in other photos of Joseph White Bull. Steve Vance, historic preservation officer for Cheyenne River, also noted this. The vast majority of people whom I have interviewed and shown the photograph to on the Cheyenne River and Standing Rock reservations (including most of Doug's relatives) believe this is indeed Joseph White Bull, but there are those who disagree.

143 **his time in Cherry Creek:** According to census records and research done by Lynelle White Bull, Doug's niece, Joseph White Bull traveled back and forth between Cherry Creek, on the Cheyenne River Reservation, and Little Eagle, on Standing Rock, where his brother One Bull lived. Stories about White Bull in Cherry Creek: Marilyn Runs After (Lakota elder), interview with the author, May 19, 2021. Marilyn was "the oldest person in Cherry Creek" and had memories of White Bull from her childhood. Harvey Eagle Horse and Russell Bennoist (Cheyenne River elders), interviews with the author, May 13, 2021. According to a history of Cherry Creek (Gayla Piroutek, "Cherry Creek: The Oldest Continuously Inhabited Town in SD"), Tommy Condon served as an interpreter at the town market. Tommy Condon was a neighbor of my ancestors and shows up in family letters and photographs. Jack's daughter-in-law, Nancy Sinykin, once told me

that Jack used to go to dances on the reservations and that he would come through when he was a "traveling store." I could never verify any of that, as the elders from Cherry Creek connected to the store had all died by the time I looked into it.

143 **had no land to sell:** No land to sell because Joseph White Bull's land remained in trust, under the administration of the superintendent.

143 **"It can be tempting":** Martha A. Sandweiss, "Seeing History: Thinking about and with Photographs." *Western Historical Quarterly* 51, no. 1 (2020): 1–28.

145 **"Bossing Indians Around":** Robert McCarthy, "The Bureau of Indian Affairs and the Federal Trust Obligation to American Indians," *Brigham Young University Journal of Public Law* 19 (2004): 1.

145 **routinely declined requests:** Thomas Biolsi, *Organizing the Lakota: The Political Economy of the New Deal on the Pine Ridge and Rosebud Reservations* (Tucson: University of Arizona Press, 1992), 16.

145 **eradication of female power:** Patricia Albers, *The Hidden Half: Studies of Plains Indian Women* (Lanham, MD: University Press of America, 1983).

145 **waiting for their funds:** McDonnell, *Dispossession of the American Indian*, chap. 5, "Leasing."

145 **Elouise Cobell, a banker herself:** For more about Elouise: Greg Hanscom, "A Banker Battles to Hold the Government Accountable," *High Country News*, August 3, 1998, www.hcn.org/issues/135/4329. To learn more about what her case revealed, see: Stephanie Woodard, "Big Government Gone Wild—How the U.S. Helps Outside Interests Plunder Indian Land," *In These Times*, October 15, 2016, www.stephaniewoodard.blogspot.com/2016/10/big-government-gone-wildhow -us-helps.html.

146 **The delay in payments:** E. D. Mossman, *Report to the Members of the Visiting Congressional Committee Regarding the Standing Rock Indian Agency, Fort Yates, North Dakota*, 1925.

146 **having great success:** Iverson, *When Indians Became Cowboys*.

146 **The money Lakota made:** *Survey of Conditions of the Indians in the United States: Hearings before a Subcommittee of the Committee on Indian Affairs*, U.S. Senate, 71st Cong., July 1929 (Washington, DC: Government Printing Office, 1929), South Dakota, parts 7 and 8; North Dakota, part 9. See also: Mossman report, 1925. Joseph White Bull, interview with the South Dakota Emergency Relief Administration.

146 **By 1920, Lakota ranchers:** Iverson, *When Indians Became Cowboys*, 68–69: Red Eagle is the man who said the benefits were "very small, not enough to bother with." The other quote comes from James Red Cloud, grandson of Chief Red Cloud: *Complaint of the Pine Ridge Sioux: Hearings before the Committee on Indian Affairs*, U.S. House, 66th Cong. 2nd Sess., April 6, 1920 (Washington DC: Government Printing Office, 1920).

147 **practically no cattle owned by Lakota:** Iverson, *When Indians Became Cowboys*. "Superintendent's Annual Narrative and Statistical Report from Field Jurisdictions of the Bureau of Indian Affairs, Cheyenne River, 1924." Joseph White Bull, interview with the SDERA. For details about how leasing allotted land was disastrous on Pine Ridge Reservation, see: Paul Robertson, *The Power of the Land: Identity, Ethnicity, and Class among the Oglala Lakota* (London: Routledge, 2018). Robertson

writes of the leasing done against the will of the Oglalas: "the whole history of the land could be boiled down to the fact that white people wanted it."

147 **Due to the double-barreled impact:** Lewis Meriam, *The Problem of Indian Administration. Report of a Survey Made at the Request of Honorable Hubert Work, Secretary of the Interior, and Submitted to Him, February 21, 1928* (Washington, DC: Government Printing Office, 1928), chap. 10, "General Economic Conditions." U.S. Department of the Interior, *Report of the Commissioner of Indian Affairs to the Secretary of the Interior, 1920* (Washington, DC: Government Printing Office, 1920), 171.

147 **At a federal hearing:** *Survey of Conditions of the Indians in the United States: Hearings before a Subcommittee of the Committee on Indian Affairs*, U.S. Senate, 70th Cong., 2nd Sess. Pursuant to S Res. 79, A Resolution Directing the Committee on Indian Affairs of the United States Senate to Make a General Survey of the Condition of the Indians of the United States, vols. 7, 8, and 9 (Washington, DC: Government Printing Office, 1929).

147 **titled "The Problem of Indian Administration":** Meriam, *The Problem of Indian Administration*, chap. 1, "Summary of Findings and Recommendations."

148 **"one of the most destructive":** David E. Wilkins, *Documents of Native American Political Development: 1500s to 1933* (Oxford: Oxford University Press, 2009), 232.

148 **90 million acres of:** "National Park Service Acreage Reports," National Park Service, www.nps.gov/subjects/lwcf/acreagereports.htm. "Land Tenure History," Indian Land Tenure Fund, https://iltf.org/land-issues/history.

148 **Over the course of three days:** "Semi-Centennial of the Battle of the Little Big Horn, Custer's Last Stand, On the Battlefield—Crow Agency, Mont. June 24, 25, 26, 1926," Burlington Route flyer.

148 **afraid for their lives:** Stanley Vestal, *Warpath: The True Story of the Fighting Sioux Told in a Biography of Chief White Bull* (Lincoln: University of Nebraska Press, 1934), 251.

149 **On the day of the reenactment:** "There are thousands of Indians camped near the battlefield in the great Indian village of modern times. Virtually every tribe of the west can be found," from: "Custer Fight Anniversary Dawns," *Sheridan Post-Enterprise*, June 25, 1926. Joseph White Bull, interview with the South Dakota Emergency Relief Administration (SDERA). *The Custer Semi-Centennial Ceremonies, 1876—June 25-26—1926* (Casper, WY: Casper Printing & Stationery, 1926), provided by the Historical Society of Montana in Helena. A great source of analysis of the ceremony is found in: Douglas C. McChristian, "Burying the Hatchet: The Semi-Centennial of the Battle of the Little Bighorn," *Montana: The Magazine of Western History* 46, no. 2 (1996): 50–65.

149 **happiest days of his life:** Vestal, *Warpath*, 1934, 255. Here's the full quote: "I asked, 'What was the happiest day of your life?' Then a smile broke over his strong features. He smacked his lips and answered: 'It was the day I was honored above all Indians. I was a great man that day. Ever since, I have thought that the happiest day of my life.'"

150 **Little Bighorn Days festival:** "Little Bighorn Days," Big Horn County Historical Museum and Visitor Center, www.bighorncountymuseum.org/little-bighorn-days. Sierra Crane-Murdoch, "Reviving Custer: Re-enactment and Revision at the Little Bighorn," *High Country News*, January 2, 2013.

150 **a hate crime:** Stephanie Woodard, "Veterans Administration Powwow Fiasco: Custer Reenactor Participates in Color Guard," *Indian Country Today*, June 2010, www.stephaniewoodard.blogspot.com/2011/10/veterans-administration-powwow -fiasco.html.

150 **"When I was in Pierre Indian School":** Doug White Bull, interview with the author, September 6, 2022.

CHAPTER 8: A SHANDA

151 **On a wretched day:** This story was handed down from my cousin Marcia Goldman, whose mother, Helen, Rose's daughter, grew up on the prairie. Marcia Goldman, phone interview with the author, December 12, 2018. According to state records, during the months of July and August 1923, there was an epidemic of anthrax in thirty-five of sixty-six counties throughout South Dakota. Dustin Oedekoven (South Dakota state veterinarian), phone interview with the author, June 22 or 23, 2021.

151 **On that awful day:** I don't know how many cows they had. They were ranching about two thousand acres by that point, though some of it was in corn and other crops. Most people in western South Dakota need approximately thirty acres per animal. So it wouldn't have been more than one hundred cows, and I'd guess it was closer to fifty, but it's hard to say.

151 **and torched them:** Anthrax is caused by spores that live underground and can persist in dead animals. Even to this day, the main way to contain the spread of the disease is by eradicating the spores with fire and then preventing their exposure to air by burying them deep underground. Oedekoven, phone interview, June 2020. Norm Geigle (Pennington County rancher), phone interview with the author, June 25, 2021.

152 **A short list:** Handwritten document of remembrances by Helen Marsh, undated. Steve Felix, phone interview with the author, May or June 2021. Cathy Siegel, email message to the author, December 8, 2022. The story about Fanny and Abe leaving because of the tornado comes from: Diane Small and Etta Orkin, "Women of Jew Flats" (17th Annual West River History Conference, 2009), which states that there had also been a prairie fire that torched the house. I left that detail out because none of Fanny and Abe's surviving grandchildren or great-grandchildren have ever heard about the prairie fires, though most of them had heard about the tornados.

152 **By then, Faige Etke's children:** Etta Fay (Kozberg) Orkin, *Etta and Harry's Megillah*, 1977. Letter from Jake Kozberg, undated: "In the year 1923 I have two letters from Mrs. Rose Moskowitz of Grandstone, So Dak imploring her sister Ruth to move her mother out from the farm or she will die out there fighting with her father . . . when their mother was out there she would not eat any meat because it was not kosher." Letter from Rose Sinykin to Ruth Kozberg, September 22, 1923: "I am worried, mother she has her headacke [*sic*] today. She sure goes through enouf [*sic*] in her life." Letter from Moshe Y. Zilboorg (Faige Etke's brother) to Ruth Kozberg about Faige Etke after her death: "She made her livelihood with great difficulties . . . she sometimes didn't eat enough." Lack of electricity or running

water from: Bill Sinykin, phone interview with the author, November 2021. Harry and Faige Etke sold their land to Louie, Rose, and Issie in May 1923, and it appears that was when they moved to St. Paul, where Jack and Jake had bought an apartment building for Harry to manage. According to the undated letter from Jake, "the reason for doing that was all on account of JL's mother [Faige Etke] so she would not suffer any longer on the wild prairie."

153 **While Aunt Rose struggled:** Letters of Rose Sinykin, including one to Ruth Kozberg, September 22, 1923, in which Rose writes that she doesn't have money to pay for her children's clothing.

    Travel: Photographs of Ted, Fanny, Cele, Pauline, Faige Etke, and Ruth camping and sightseeing in Yellowstone National Park, undated, likely around 1919. Photos from a road trip that Fanny, Ruth, and Pauline took to Idaho, circa 1919. Letter from Ted Sinykin to Ruth Kozberg, addressed to the Battle Creek Sanitarium, Battle Creek, Michigan, March 1, 1930. Letter from Jack Sinykin to Ruth Kozberg, addressed to Mexico City, Mexico, March 7, 1928. Telegram from Jake Kozberg to Ruth Kozberg, addressed to the Breakers Hotel, Miami Beach, Florida, April 17, 1929. Letter from Ruth Kozberg to Jake Kozberg, postmarked "Habana Cuba," April 10, 1929. Family letters, telegrams, and diary entries from March and April 1929. Ruth Kozberg, diary entry, March 1930: she and Louie are at Battle Creek Sanitarium. Photographs of Ruth Kozberg posing nude at Battle Creek, also posing at an airport, April 1930. Photographs of Pauline Kozberg and the pony from Jack, family in Cuernavaca on horses, and smoking cigarettes while visiting the Zilboorg cousins in Mexico City, family collection.

    Wealth: Ruth bought Faige Etke a fur coat from Rubin Fur Co. for $315 in 1924, noted in undated letter by Jake Kozberg. Pauline Kozberg, diary entry, September 8, 1930: "Got an electric stove." Mentions of "the girl," a maid or nanny, in diaries of both Pauline and Ruth Kozberg throughout the 1920s and early '30s.

    Philanthropy: Clipping, source unknown, about Ruth Kozberg, chairman of the Women's League of Temple Aaron, November 1, 1929. Faige Etke wired $68 to people in Romanova, Slutzkavo Uezda, September 8, 1925.

    Jack Sinykin: Letter from Jack Sinykin to Ruth Kozberg in Mexico, March 7, 1928, notes that he's showing dogs and won first prize. Pauline Kozberg, diary entry, September 9, 1931: "Went to horseshow with Uncle Jack . . . Minnesota Joan owned by Uncle Jack won 5th prize." "Our Hotel," St. Paul Hotel, www .saintpaulhotel.com/our-hotel/history. Author's visit to St. Paul Hotel, June 2021.

154 **On the books:** Ideal Leather Manufacturing Company, owned by Jake Kozberg and his nephew Max Kozberg as early as 1927. Based on a letter dated March 11, 1937, they had the land in South Dakota and also owned several buildings in St. Paul. Letter to Jake in 1924 states that the value of his land in St. Paul is $1,800, and the buildings are valued at $6,800. Drug-and-cosmetics companies: La Salle Co. and Cinderella Cosmetics.

154 **Wholesale drugstores made their own:** Ad for the La Salle Co., *Star Tribune*, December 21, 1922: "This concern manufactures such well known products as White Bear Washing Compound, Evaporato, Eden Shampoo, Eden Hair Tonic, and other popular items." Later, they started the Cinderella Cosmetics Company, ads and details listed below.

154 **Congress passed the Volstead Act:** Also called the National Prohibition Act, it implemented the Eighteenth Amendment, prohibiting "the manufacture, sale, or transportation of intoxicating liquors," and became law on October 28, 1919. More on the act and links to original documents can be found at the National Archives: www.archives.gov/education/lessons/volstead-act.

155 **a "rum ring":** "Druggists Held in Liquor Raids; Big Plot Seen," *Star Tribune*, September 17, 1922. "Million Dollar Liquor Ring Is Officers' Claim," *La Crosse Tribune*, September 17, 1922. "Former Lead Men in Toils of Enforcement Officers, *Lead Daily Call*, October 6, 1922. "La Salle Drug Company Exonerated," *American Jewish World*, October 13, 1922.

155 **Jack's older brother Ted:** Swee-Tone ads, "Perfume: A Prohibition-Era Mystery," *Minnesota History*, Winter 2015–2016. The Minnesota Historical Society has a number of items in its collections that were used by bootleggers during these years. Sondra Reierson and Tom Braun (Minnesota Historical Society), Google Meet interview with the author, February 18, 2021.

155 **Within three years, this perfume:** "Link Twin Cities to Rum Ring," *Minneapolis Tribune*, February 11, 1930. This article and other stories about the case indicated that this was part of a "nation-wide syndicate headquartered in Chicago . . . the list of those indicted was notable for the entire absence of names known in Chicago gangland, all of those named being officials of the various companies or their employee."

Daniel Sinykin (Ted's great-grandson), interview with the author, September 3, 2019.

To find out if there was a connection between my relatives and the Chicago mob, I went through every telegram my grandfather Ben Bernstein and my grandmother Pauline (Ruth and Jake's daughter) received on their wedding day in April 1946 (the telegrams had been kept, of course, and were in a box in my parents' basement). I then shared the names of the senders with Joe Kraus (author of *The Kosher Capones: A History of Chicago's Jewish Gangsters* [DeKalb: Northern Illinois University Press, 2019]) in a phone interview on April 26, 2021. One or two people who wrote to my grandparents shared last names with some of the "Kosher Capones," but that doesn't really mean anything. I also searched old family letters for Chicago addresses or notable correspondence and never found anything. Bottom line: I never found any clear connection between my ancestors and the mob.

155 **Another cousin, a former Jew Flats:** "Grabs Booze Runners but U.S. Man is Hurt," *Argus Leader*, May 9, 1919. "Seven Bandits Raid St. Paul Dwelling, Get $4,000 Loot," *Duluth Herald*, August 2, 2021.

156 **According to family lore, trucks:** Bill Sinykin, phone interview with the author, August 19, 2021. This story was told to Bill by his father, Louie Sinykin, a Jew Flats homesteader, and also by the man who owned the farm and who showed him the underground vats in the 1970s.

157 **One day, my aunt Etta, myself:** Author's driving tour of St. Paul with Etta Orkin, Cathi, Noah, and Aviva Oskow, June 11, 2021. Shabbat dinner that evening at Cathi and Craig Oskow's house.

157 **"they lived Jewish lives":** Etta Orkin, two phone interviews with the author, one

undated, the other March 2021. Etta insists that she experienced antisemitism only once while growing up and that she "never really suffered from antisemitism."

157 **the nation's capital of antisemitism:** Minneapolis's reputation as the nation's capital of antisemitism is traced to: Carey McWilliams, "Minneapolis: The Curious Twin," *Common Ground*, Autumn 1946, 61–65. The accusation has been widely repeated since then. Laura Weber, former editor of *Minnesota History*, recently published a reexamination of McWilliams's article and its legacy: Laura Weber, "'Minneapolis: The Curious Twin': A Reexamination, *Middle West Review* 8, no. 2 (2022), 59–75. See also: Michael Gerald Rapp, *An Historical Overview of Anti-Semitism in Minnesota, 1920–1960—With Particular Emphasis on Minneapolis and St. Paul* (Minneapolis: University of Minnesota, 1977).

158 **the Woman's Christian Temperance Union had:** Erin M. Masson, "The Woman's Christian Temperance Union, 1874–1898: Combatting Domestic Violence," *William & Mary Journal of Women and the Law* 3 (1997): 163.

158 **was the Anti-Saloon League:** Daniel Okrent, *Last Call: The Rise and Fall of Prohibition* (New York: Simon and Schuster, 2010).

158 **Henry Ford, a major financial supporter:** Marni Davis, *Jews and Booze: Becoming American in the Age of Prohibition* (New York: New York University Press, 2012), 158.

158 **makers and purveyors of booze:** Ofer Aderet, "The Wind That Shook the Barley for Polish-Jewish Spirit Makers," *Haaretz*, April 14, 2014, www.haaretz.com /jewish/premium-when-jews-ran-poland-s-spirit-biz-1.5245087.

158 **Jews had managed as much as two thirds:** Davis, *Jews and Booze*, 73: "According to one estimate, 50,000 Jews managed taverns in the Russian Polish countryside at partition, and an 1870 census revealed that Jews operated 190,000 taverns, in addition to 89 percent of the distilleries and 74 percent of the breweries, in Kiev and provinces to the West." Also: Joel Haber, "The Forgotten History of Jews in the Alcohol Industry," *The Nosher*, July 7, 2020.

158 **"the Jewish Lake":** Jenny Hendrix, "'Prohibition' Tells Changing Story of Jews in America," *Forward*, October 4, 2011, www.forward.com/culture/143791/pro hibition-tells-changing-story-of-jews-in-americ.

158 **Even rabbis got in:** Davis, *Jews and Booze*; Okrent, *Last Call*. "Application to Procure Wine for Sacramental Purposes and Like Religious Rites," U.S. Internal Revenue, Treasury Department, Form 1412-Revised May 1920, completed by Rabbi Philip Kleinman, Temple Aaron Congregation, to the La Salle Company. I have copies of these forms from March 7, 1923 (50 gallons kosher port) and September 27, 1922 (200 gallons port and sherry).

159 **President Calvin Coolidge:** The full quote: "Restricted immigration is not an offensive but purely a defensive action. It is not adopted in criticism of others in the slightest degree, but solely for the purpose of protecting ourselves. We cast no aspersions on any race or creed, but we must remember that every object of our institutions of society and government will fail unless America be kept American." Calvin Coolidge, "Accepting the Republican Presidential Nomination, August 14, 2024," in C. Bascom Slemp, *The Mind of the President* (Garden City, NY: Doubleday, Page & Co., 1926), www.coolidgefoundation.org/quote/quotations-i.

159 **In keeping with this tenor, Congress:** More than two million Jews, mostly from

Eastern Europe, arrived in the U.S. between 1880 and 1924. During that period, some twenty million total immigrants came to the U.S. from central, southern, and eastern Europe. The Chinese Exclusion Act of 1882 is an infamous earlier example of racism and targeted discrimination in U.S. immigration policy. David S. Koffman, *The Jews' Indian: Colonialism, Pluralism, and Belonging in America* (New Brunswick, NJ: Rutgers University Press, 2019), 127.

159 **the Immigration Act of 1924:** Also known as the Johnson–Reed Act, it completely barred all immigration from Asia and created quotas for immigrants from elsewhere. Per the Office of the Historian at the U.S. Department of State: "The most basic purpose of the 1924 Immigration Act was to preserve the ideal of U.S. homogeneity," www.history.state.gov/milestones/1921-1936/immigration-act.

160 **passed the Indian Citizenship Act:** Indian Citizenship Act, U.S. Statutes at Large, 43:253 (1924). Nick Estes, *Our History Is the Future: Standing Rock versus the Dakota Access Pipeline, and the Long Tradition of Indigenous Resistance* (New York: Verso Books, 2019), 219: "the Indian Citizenship Act, which unilaterally imposed citizenship upon all individual Indigenous peoples without consent."

160 **Hitler argued that America's exclusion:** James Q. Whitman, *Hitler's American Model* (Princeton, NJ: Princeton University Press, 2017), 46.

160 **Indian New Deal:** Vine Deloria, ed., *The Indian Reorganization Act: Congresses and Bills* (Norman: University of Oklahoma Press, 2002).

160 **Felix S. Cohen, an Interior lawyer:** Koffman, *The Jews' Indian*, chap. 5.

161 **For my aunt Rose:** Letter from Rose Marsh (formerly Moskowitz) to Pauline Bernstein, September 23, 1963.

162 **had never liked the ranch:** Quotes from letters of Rose Marsh. For more details about what life was like for women ranchers on the Plains during this time, see: Paula M. Nelson, *The Prairie Winnows Out Its Own: The West River Country of South Dakota in the Years of Depression and Dust* (Iowa City: University of Iowa Press, 2005). For more on childbirth for Jewish homesteaders on the prairie, see: Rachel Calof, *Rachel Calof's Story: Jewish Homesteader on the Northern Plains*, ed. J. Sanford Rikoon (Bloomington: Indiana University Press, 1995). While Rose's first two children were born at home, her third child, Libby, was born in a hospital.

162 **By 1930, Rose and Issie:** Herbie Marsh, interview with the author, January 2020. Steve Felix, interview. Bill Sinykin, interview with the author, May 2022.

162–63 **the Cinderella Cosmetics Company:** Ad for Cinderella Cosmetics featuring actress Grace Hayes, *Star Tribune*, November 14, 1927. "2,000 See Star Open New Building," *Minneapolis Star*, October 7, 1930, about the opening of the Cinderella Building; guests included the mayors of both Minneapolis and St. Paul. "Sinykin Opens New Building," newsclip in family files, October 3, 1930.

164 **Such wealth built:** Letter from Jake Kozberg to Ruth Kozberg, September 1930. Pauline Kozberg, diary entry, June 20, 1931: her dad is diagnosed with catarrhal jaundice. Pauline Kozberg, diary entry, June 21, 1931: "Mother took sick with nerves. Uncle Lou is out of the hospital. He went to a resort. There has been a great deal of family trouble lately." Pauline Kozberg, diary entry, March 11, 1932: "What an Awful day! One has to go on smiling no matter how bad one feels." This follows an argument between her parents, and her mother leaving for Battle

Creek. Letter from Ruth Kozberg to Pauline Kozberg, February 24, 1933, describing her "constant worry" for the past seven years. Pauline Kozberg, journal entries, May 3–June 2, 1933: "Life is just hell around home lately and that is business trouble and all my father's fault . . . Mother has to put up with so much . . . we're going through bankruptcy all because of my father."

164 **in 1931, Faige:** Faige Etka Sinykin obituary, clipping from family files, August 28, 1931. Obituary mentions that she was a member of "the Ladies Auxiliaries of the Hebrew Institute, the Jewish Home for the Aged, the Chesed Shel Emes, Hadassah, Sheltering Home for Children and the Hebrew Free Loan Society. During her residence in St. Paul, she devoted much time to charitable undertakings."

165 **Faige Etke died of:** State of Minnesota Certificate of Death, August 24, 1931.

165 **"she died of a broken heart":** Etta Orkin, phone interview with the author, March 2021.

165 HER DEEDS DO PRAISE HER: Etta Orkin, phone interview with the author, February 2021, on Faige Etke's good deeds.

165 **a Torah in her name:** Invitation for the dedication of a Sefer Torah at the St. Paul Hebrew Institute, St. Paul, Minnesota, November 1, 1931, author's collection.

166 **In the late afternoon:** Reporting trip by the author to Minneapolis, June 2021.

166 **biggest illicit liquor case:** "Trio Added to 7 Seized in Raids Two Weeks Ago, *Star Tribune*, April 24, 1936. "25 Are Accused of Conspiracy to Divert Alky," *Minneapolis Star*, February 20, 1937. "15 Admit Guilt in Liquor Plot," *Star Tribune*, March 7, 1937. "12 in 'Alky Ring' Handed Terms," *Minneapolis Tribune*, March 23, 1937. Ruth Kozberg, diary entries, February 19–April 15, 1937. "U.S. Penitentiary, Leavenworth Inmate Case Files, Inmate: J. L. Sinykin (#50794)," National Archives and Records Administration.

168 **historian Richard White confronted:** Richard White, *Remembering Ahanagran: A History of Stories* (Seoul: Ewha Womans University Press, 2003).

168 **I call Judge Abby:** Abby Abinanti, phone interview with the author, August 17, 2021.

169 **Rabbi Benjamin and I take a walk:** Benjamin Barnett, conversation with the author, late August 2021.

169 **Laws of Repentance, which codifies:** Rabbi Moses ben Maimon is also referred to as Rambam. His Mishna Torah, Repentance can be found on Sepharia, www.sefaria.org/Mishneh_Torah,_Repentance?tab=contents. Danya Ruttenberg, *On Repentance and Repair: Making Amends in an Unapologetic World* (Boston: Beacon Press, 2022). Danya Ruttenberg, phone interview with the author, January 28, 2022.

169 **"I really feel":** Letter from Rose Marsh to Pauline Bernstein, 1963.

170 **Jack's life didn't end:** Harry S. Truman pardons Jack Sinykin, September 6, 1952, from the collection of Nancy Sinykin. Guide dog information: "Sinykin, Guide Dog Pioneer, Dies," undated, collection of Etta Orkin; "'Seeing Eye' Dog Arrives to Aid Sightless," *St. Paul Pioneer Press*, December 2, 1934. Nancy Sinykin, phone interview with the author, July 8, 2019. Interview of Jerry Sinykin by Linda Schloff, March 6, 2006, part of the World War II Veterans Oral History Project housed at the Upper Midwest Jewish Archives, University of Minnesota.

170 **he lost the thing:** Sinykin deeds, author collection. Letter from Rose Marsh to Pauline Bernstein, Betty Rappaport, and Etta Orkin, September 29, 1963. Letter from Louie Sinykin to Ruth Kozberg and others, February 16th, 1964. Steve Felix, interview with author.

CHAPTER 9: A TRIPLE THREAT

171 **Doug White Bull was born:** Doug White Bull, in-person and phone interviews with the author, November 2019–December 2022. For a look at how important the land was to another family and the impact of the river on their lives, see: Lanniko L. Lee, Florestine Kiyukanpi Renville, and Karen Lone Hill, *Shaping Survival: Essays by Four American Indian Tribal Women* (Lanham, MD: Scarecrow Press, 2006).

173 **roughly fifty-five million acres:** The careful reader will notice that this is a sizeable increase in landholdings since 1934. The reason being that, under the 1934 Indian Reorganization Act, Indigenous Nations had the authority to purchase lands abandoned by settlers by paying the back taxes. This was essentially the same process that my uncle Louie and great-grandmother Ruth used, in some cases, to expand our family's ranch. Data provided by historian Claudio Saunt, email message to the author, September 15, 2022, and found in "Indian Lands Under Jurisdiction of Bureau of Indian Affairs, 1881 to 1953," 83rd Congress, 2nd Sess., Serial Set Vol. No. 11808, Session Vol. No. 44, H. Doc. 320.

173 **When Julia White Bull:** Doug White Bull, phone interview with the author, October 4, 2021.

173 **water flooded the banks:** Michael L. Lawson, *Dammed Indians: The Pick–Sloan Plan and the Missouri River Sioux, 1944–1980* (Norman: University of Oklahoma Press, 1994), 7. Michael Lawson (historian), Zoom interview with the author, October 1, 2021.

174 **The destruction of land:** The west side of the river, where the reservations were, was also home to basically all of the river's tributaries. The east side, home to mostly non-Indigenous communities, had bluffs that served as natural protection from the rising waters caused by the dam. This is why almost all of the flooding caused by the man-made lakes occurred on the west side, on the side of the river home to reservations. Indigenous citizens have repeatedly echoed what historians such as Lawson and Estes write—that Indigenous communities bore the brunt of the impact from the dams. Nick Estes, *Our History Is the Future: Standing Rock versus the Dakota Access Pipeline, and the Long Tradition of Indigenous Resistance* (New York: Verso Books, 2019).

174 **Using the authority:** Lawson, *Dammed Indians*, 19: "[Roosevelt] quietly authorized the army's nine-foot navigation channel as part of the Rivers and Harbors Act of 1945." Representative Francis H. Case, a South Dakotan Republican moderate, "was the only politician who voiced concern about the issue of how the army intended to acquire Indians [the] lands it would need for its main-stem projects." As early as November 1943, Case wrote a letter to the Army Corps recommending that, in Lawson's words, "any proposed legislation establish specific authority for the acquisition of Indian lands and for reimbursement to those tribes and

tribal members affected." Case got a response from the acting head of the ACE that his concerns would be "fully considered." Case sharing the exchange with the BIA and heads of Indigenous Nations was the "only known instance in which tribal governments were informed by a federal representative of the possible adverse effects of the Pick–Sloan Plan prior to its enactment."

174 **Bureau of Indian Affairs declared:** The Office of Indian Affairs changed its name to the Bureau of Indian Affairs in 1947.

174 **the agency wrote in a report:** Estes, *Our History Is the Future*, 155.

174 **In 1953, the then-director:** Dillon S. Myer, Commissioner of the Bureau of Indian Affairs, May 1950–March 1953.

175 **1955 congressional hearing:** Unpublished hearing, U.S. Congress, House Subcommittee on Indian Affairs, Committee on Interior and Insular Affairs, 1955, 239–243.

175 **"The Pick–Sloan dams were":** Estes, *Our History Is the Future*, 9–11, 133–141.

175 **In the wake of World War II:** Max Nesterak, "Uprooted: The 1950s Plan to Erase Indian Country," *American Public Media Reports*, November 1, 2019, www .apmreports.org/episode/2019/11/01/uprooted-the-1950s-plan-to-erase-indian -country.

175 **Almost every Jewish bureaucrat:** David S. Koffman, *The Jews' Indian: Colonialism, Pluralism, and Belonging in America* (New Brunswick, NJ: Rutgers University Press, 2019), chap. 5.

176 **1949 report by the Hoover Commission:** *Social Security and Education, Indian Affairs: A Report to the Congress by the Commission on Organization of The Executive Branch of the Government, March 1949*, 81st Congress, 1st Sess., H. Doc. 129 (Washington, DC: Government Printing Office, 1949).

176 **more than fifty-five million acres:** "Indian Lands Under Jurisdiction of Bureau of Indian Affairs, 1881 to 1953," 83rd Congress, 2nd Sess., Serial Set Vol. No. 11808, Session Vol. No. 44, H. Doc. 320.

176 **By converting reservations:** Charles Valandra, *Not Without our Consent* (Champaign: University of Illinois Press, 2006). Charles F. Wilkinson and Eric R. Biggs, "The Evolution of the Termination Policy," *American Indian Law Review* 5, no. 1 (1977): 139–84.

176 **Indigenous lands contained:** Marjane Ambler, *Breaking the Iron Bonds: Indian Control of Energy Development* (Lawrence: University Press of Kansas, 1990).

176 **Republicans loved Termination:** Wilkinson and Biggs, "The Evolution of the Termination Policy," 139–84.

176 **language of civil rights:** Valandra, *Not Without Our Consent*.

176 **Louise Erdrich likens:** Louise Erdrich, *The Night Watchman* (New York: Harper-Collins, 2020), 201.

176 **in favor of Termination:** Nesterak, "Uprooted."

177 **In 1953, Congress passed:** Dean Chavers, "The Bosone Bill: Termination of Indian Treaties," *Indian Country Today*, October 29, 2016, updated September 13, 2018, www.indiancountrytoday.com/archive/the-bosone-bill-termination-of-indian -treaties. H. Con. Res. 108, *Concurrent Resolutions—Aug. 1, 1953*, 67 Stat., www .govinfo.gov/content/pkg/STATUTE-67/pdf/STATUTE-67-PgB132-2.pdf.

177 **affront to Native American sovereignty:** For a general look at the erosion of In-

digenous rights during this era, see: Felix S. Cohen, "The Erosion of Indian Rights, 1950–1953: A Case Study in Bureaucracy," *Yale Law Journal* 62 (1952): 348.

177 **Joseph White Bull died:** "Chief White Bull Alleged Slayer of Custer, Dies," *Jamestown Sun*, July 24, 1947.

177 **we are lost:** Reporting trip by the author to the Dakotas, May 2021, driving between McLaughlin, on the Standing Rock Reservation, and Cherry Creek, on the Cheyenne River Reservation.

178 **COVID-19 pandemic, death:** Erik Ortiz, "As South Dakota Takes Hands-Off Approach to Coronavirus, Native Americans Feel Vulnerable," NBC News, November 25, 2020, www.nbcnews.com/news/us-news/south-dakota-takes-hands -approach-coronavirus-native-americans-feel-vulnerable-n1248868. Jazzmine Jackson, "South Dakota Indigenous Community 'Disproportionately' Affected by COVID-19," Keloland.com, January 19, 2022, www.keloland.com/keloland -com-original/south-dakota-indigenous-community-disproportionately -affected-by-covid-19. "North Dakota Faces World's Deadliest Outbreak, Native Communities Condemn States' COVID Response," *Democracy Now!*, November 18, 2020, www.democracynow.org/2020/11/18/covid_in_indian_country.

This national data, which the Indian Health Service posts on its website, is based on the Center for Disease Control's evaluation of Indigenous communities in twenty-three states but doesn't include data for the Dakotas: www.ihs.gov /coronavirus. Sarah M. Hatcher, Christine Agnew-Brune, Mark Anderson, Laura D. Zambrano, Charles E. Rose, Melissa A. Jim, Amy Baugher, et al., "COVID-19 among American Indian and Alaska Native Persons—23 States, January 31–July 3, 2020," *Morbidity and Mortality Weekly Report* 69, no. 34 (2020): 1166.

178 **seventeen friends and family:** Wayne Ducheneaux II, Zoom interview with the author, January 14, 2021.

178 **The high rates of diabetes:** "American Indians and Alaska Natives have a greater chance of having diabetes than any other US racial group," from: "Diabetes Within American Indian and Alaska Native Populations," Center for Disease Control, www.cdc.gov/healthytribes/native-american-diabetes.html. American Indians/Alaska Natives have diabetes at a rate that is 3.2 times higher than all other races, per the "Disparities" fact sheet from Indian Health Services, www .ihs.gov/newsroom/factsheets/disparities. "A significant racial disparity exists as the prevalence of diagnosed diabetes in Native Americans is 16 percent, compared to 8 percent of whites in South Dakota," *South Dakota Diabetes State Plan, 2018–2020* (Pierre, SD: South Dakota Department of Health, 2018). Salt and fat are primarily responsible for heart disease. Too much starch and sugar will lead to insulin issues and diabetes.

178 **run on star quilts:** Steve Vance and Bruce Brownwolf (elders and historians, Cheyenne River Sioux Tribe), interviews with the author, Eagle Butte, SD, May 13, 2021.

178 **Doug's oldest son:** "Brian 'Chicky' Marshall Sr., 1966–2021," obituary, DRGNews .com, www.drgnews.com/listing/brian-chicky-marshall-sr-1966-2021.

179 **To the end, Joseph:** Marilyn Runs After (Cheyenne River elder), interview with the author, Philip, SD, May 19, 2021. Russell Benoist and Harvey Eagle Horse (Cheyenne River elders), interviews with the author, Eagle Butte, SD, May 13, 2021.

Joseph White Bull and Susie Her Blanket, interview with South Dakota Emergency Relief Administration (SDERA); "Indian Chiefs Revive Talk of Giving Hills to Canada," *Rapid City Journal*, August 10, 1937. "A Hero Out of Homer," *Salt Lake Tribune*, April 22, 1934. And, of course: Joseph White Bull, *Lakota Warrior*, trans. and ed. James H. Howard (Lincoln, NE: University of Nebraska Press, 1998), and Stanley Vestal, *Warpath: The True Story of the Fighting Sioux Told in a Biography of Chief White Bull* (Lincoln: University of Nebraska Press, 1934).

180 **a program called Relocation:** James B. LaGrand, *Indian Metropolis: Native Americans in Chicago, 1945–75* (Champaign: University of Illinois Press, 2002); Donald L. Fixico, *Termination and Relocation: Federal Indian Policy, 1945–1960* (Albuquerque: University of New Mexico Press, 1986). Nesterak, "Uprooted."

180 **not enough land left:** Missouri River Basin Investigations, "Report of Socio-Economic Survey—1951: Standing Rock Indian Reservation, North Dakota and South Dakota," Report 124, Bureau of Indian Affairs (Billings, MT: November 9, 1951). This idea that reservations weren't large enough to support their Indigenous populations was used as justification for the Relocation program nationally: La Verne Madigan, *The American Indian Relocation Program* (Rockville, MD: Association of American Indian Affairs, 1956).

180 **"Hitler and Mussolini":** Lawson, *Dammed Indians*, 98. This was Secretary of the Interior Harold Ickes, appointed by President Franklin D. Roosevelt. From 1942 to 1946, Myer managed ten Japanese American detention camps full of Japanese descendants who were relocated from the West Coast: Azusa Ono, "The Relocation and Employment Assistance Programs, 1948–1970: Federal Indian Policy and the Early Development of the Denver Indian Community," *Indigenous Nations Journal* 5, no. 1 (2004): 27–50.

180 **rural internment camps:** "Prisoners at Home: Everyday Life in Japanese Internment Camps" Digital Public Library of America, https://dp.la/exhibitions/japanese-internment/road-camps/relocation.

181 **program of "liberation":** Azusa Ono, "The Relocation and Employment Assistance Programs."

181 **soil health and overpopulation as justification:** Larry W. Burt, "Roots of the Native American Urban Experience: Relocation Policy in the 1950s." *American Indian Quarterly* (1986): 85–99. Michael Moore (Sitting Bull College), interview with the author, Fort Yates, ND, May 17, 2021. Valandra, *Not Without Our Consent*, chap. 2.

181 **monopolizing reservation lands:** Valandra, *Not Without Our Consent*, chap. 2.

181 **armed with slideshows:** James B. LaGrand, *Indian Metropolis: Native Americans in Chicago, 1945–75* (Champaign: University of Illinois Press, 2002), 66. Later, other cities, such as Minneapolis, Oakland, Cleveland, and Salt Lake City, would be added to the list.

181 **pressure to recruit:** Burt, "Roots of the Native American Urban Experience," 85–99. LaGrand, *Indian Metropolis*, 54.

182 **BIA report from 1951:** Missouri River Basin Investigations, "Report of Socio-Economic Survey—1951."

182 **the bureaucrats spun:** Estes, *Our History Is the Future*, 155.

182 **By the 1950s:** LaGrand, *Indian Metropolis*, 60. See also: "Indians Feel Unwanted in Land of Sitting Bull," *Argus Leader*, June 6, 1957.

182 **GIs, for federal loan:** "No bank will finance a GI bill home loan on tribal land.... That's because the banks can't take back tribal land if the loan defaults." From: Quill Lawrence, "Federal Home Loan Program is Still Failing Native American Veterans after 30 Years," NPR.org, August 25, 2022.

182 **mayor of Chamberlain:** Valandra, *Not Without Our Consent*, 79.

182 **Throughout the state, there:** "A Sioux woman who later moved to Chicago, in part because of the prejudice of rural South Dakota: 'There are signs on the door: "Indians and dogs, not allowed"; "Indian trade not wanted."'... I had always grew up with the idea that we were as good as anybody else. But when I got out there, I found being Indian made you different and being dark, we couldn't hide it. You were treated differently in the store and schools.'" From: LaGrand, *Indian Metropolis*, 29–30; Doug White Bull also has stories of finding it impossible to rent an apartment in the Black Hills when he was going to college there. A white woman even tried to help him and found that, as soon as she mentioned to prospective landlords that the apartment was for a Lakota man and his family, the places weren't available.

183 **an estimated 750,000:** Staff of Senate Committee on Interior and Insular Affairs, 85th Cong., 2nd Sess., *Indian Land Transactions* (Comm. Print 1958), xvii–xxi, 1–17. Reid Peyton Chambers and Monroe E. Price, "Regulating Sovereignty: Secretarial Discretion and the Leasing of Indian Lands," *Stanford Law Review* 26, no. 5 (1974): 1061–64, 1074–75.

183 **Three of Doug's older brothers:** Doug White Bull, phone interviews with the author, March 16, 2021, August 13, 2021, September 14, 2021, October 4, 2021. Frank White Bull (Doug's nephew), interview with the author, Kenel, SD, November 13, 2021.

183 **felt small in the shadow:** Nesterak, "Uprooted."

183 **"overworked and undermanned staff":** Burt, "Roots of the Native American Urban Experience"

183 **Most Native Americans in Chicago:** LaGrand, *Indian Metropolis*, 100–111. American Public Media, "Spotlight on Indigenous Relocation," *Call to Mind*, Minneapolis American Indian Center, Minneapolis, MN, www.calltomindnow.org/spotlight-on-indigenous-relocation.

183 **likened by one BIA employee:** Philleo Nash, a Bureau of Indian Affairs Commissioner from 1961 to 1966 under presidents John F. Kennedy and Lyndon Johnson.

183 **apartments far away:** A report from 1957 acknowledged that observers repeatedly heard Indians complain about being "lonesome because city Relocation Offices will not permit them to live in Indian neighborhoods." From LaGrand, *Indian Metropolis*, 103.

184 **This wasn't an unusual story:** Alfred G. Elgin, Gail M. Thorpe, Edward Mouss, and James Bluestone, *Report on Urban and Rural Non-Reservation Indians: Final Report to the American Indian Policy Review Commission* (Washington, DC: Government Printing Office: 1976).

184 **The BIA measured:** Alan L. Sorkin, *The Urban American Indian* (Lexington, MA: Lexington Books, 1978). Burt, "Roots of the Native American Urban Experience, 85–99. Madigan, *The American Indian Relocation Program.*

184 **Those who stayed:** Missouri River Basin Investigations, "Family Plan and Rehabilitation Programs, Standing Rock Reservation," Report no. 177, Bureau of Indian Affairs (Billings, MT: 1964). Missouri River Basin Investigations, "Evaluation of Livestock Phase, Cheyenne River Rehabilitation Program, South Dakota," Report no. 190, Bureau of Indian Affairs (Billings, MT: 1968). The statistic about Native Americans living in urban areas is often cited and can be found, among other places, on the Indian Health Service's Urban Indian Health Program fact sheet: www.ihs.gov/newsroom/factsheets/uihp.

185 **Completed in the 1960s:** Michael L. Lawson, *Dammed Indians Revisited: The Continuing History of the Pick–Sloan Plan and the Missouri River Sioux* (Pierre: South Dakota State Historical Society, 2009), 286: The total loss to the following impacted Native Nations was more than 340,000 acres: the Three Affiliated Tribes (Mandan, Hidatsa, and Arikara), Standing Rock Sioux, Crow Creek Sioux, Lower Brule Sioux, Cheyenne River Sioux, Yankton Sioux, and Santee Sioux.

185 **That is the equivalent:** I did some math: 6 percent of the United States' landmass is 227,820 square miles. The size of Montana is 147,040 square miles. The size of Idaho is 83,642. The two states together equal 230,682 square miles.

185 **most valuable land:** Robert McLaughlin, *Analysis of Economic Loss Resulting from Lands Taken from the Cheyenne River Sioux Tribe for the Oahe Dam* (Solen, ND: Robert McLaughlin Company, July 1994). Missouri River Basin Investigations, "Problems on the Cheyenne River and Standing Rock Reservations Arising from the Oahe Project," report no. 100, Bureau of Indian Affairs (Billings, MT: February 1950).

185 **On a hot day:** Doug White Bull, phone interviews with the author, October 4, 2021; May 12, 2022; August 9, 2022. While Doug remembers moving in the summer of 1959, most people didn't leave until after that. "In January 1960, 190 Indian families on the Standing Rock Sioux Reservation were evicted from their homes by the United States Army Corps of Engineers. In the midst of a fierce Dakota winter, with temperatures falling as low as thirty degrees below zero, these people were forced to gather all of their possessions and evacuate their land adjoining the Missouri River." From: Michael L. Lawson, "The Oahe Dam and the Standing Rock Sioux," *South Dakota History* 6 (1976): 227–28.

185 **The equivalent percentage:** The total U.S. population (as of this writing) is 329.5 million; one third would be 108.75 million. The population of Texas is 29 million, California is 39.35 million, and New York is 21 million, the three together totaling just shy of 90 million or 27 percent of the total U.S. population. The estimated Jewish population in the Pale in the nineteenth century was 5 million. Around 2 million Jews, roughly 40 percent of the total, left there and came to America during this time. For more on this, see: Richard H. Rowland, "Geographical Patterns of the Jewish Population in the Pale of Settlement of Late Nineteenth Century Russia," *Jewish Social Studies* 48, no. 3/4 (1986): 207–234.

186 **"an irreplaceable loss":** McLaughlin, *Analysis of Economic Loss Resulting from Lands Taken*, 108.

186 **"the jackrabbit carried a box lunch"**: Lawson, *Dammed Indians Revisited*, 102.

186 **dependent on United States**: Red Gates, interview with the author, Fort Yates, ND, March 12, 2020. Amy Jakober, "A 30-Year Journey to Bring Back Bison," *Indian Giver*, November 29, 2019, http://indiangiver.firstnations.org/nl20191206-05. Andi Murphy, "After a Fraught History, Some Tribes Finally Have the Power to Rethink 'Commodity Foods,'" *Civil Eats*, November 1, 2021, www.civileats.com /2021/11/01/after-a-fraught-history-some-tribes-finally-have-the-power-to -rethink-commodity-foods.

186 **an "Insulin Holocaust"**: Daniel McCoy Jr. Art: www.danielmccoyjr.com/about. Rate of diabetes skyrocketing from: Estes, *Our History Is the Future*, 159–60.

186 **The economic loss**: Lawson, *Dammed Indians Revisited*, chap. 11.

186 **Some non-Indigenous ranchers**: "Indians Feel Unwanted in Land of Sitting Bull," *Argus Leader*, June 6, 1957.

186 **paid Ruth approximately $24 an acre**: Contract and grant from U.S. Department of the Interior, Bureau of Reclamation, March 26, 1963, for right-of-way for the Oahe–New Underwood–Stegall Transmission Line, signed by Ruth Kozberg, author collection.

186 **Much of these funds**: Lawson, *Dammed Indians Revisited*, 205.

187 **Doug decided to become a teacher**: Doug White Bull, interview with the author, October 4, 2021.

188 **hydropower, flood control, and irrigation**: Remi Bald Eagle (Cheyenne River Sioux Tribe), phone interview with the author, February 2, 2022; email exchange, June 1, 2022. Lisa Meiman (Western Area Power Administration, Public Affairs), phone interview and email exchange with the author, June 10, 2022. "Hydropower at Oahe," Omaha District, U.S. Army Corps of Engineers, www.nwo.usace.army.mil /Missions/Dam-and-Lake-Projects/Missouri-River-Dams/Oahe/Hydropower.

188 **official histories of the Pick–Sloan dams**: John R. Ferrell, *Big Dam Era: A Legislative and Institutional History of the Pick–Sloan Missouri Basin Program* (Omaha, NE: Missouri River Division, U.S. Army Corps of Engineers, 1993). Barry W. Fowle, ed., *Builders and Fighters: U.S. Army Engineers in World War II*, vol. 870, no. 1–42 (Fort Belvoir, VA: Office of History, U.S. Army Corps of Engineers, 1992). David P. Billington, Donald C. Jackson, and Martin V. Melosi, *The History of Large Federal Dams: Planning, Design, and Construction in the Era of Big Dams* (Denver, CO: U.S. Department of the Interior, Bureau of Reclamation, 2005).

188 **uprising of Indigenous activism**: Estes, *Our History Is the Future*, 170.

188 **"When our lands are taken"**: Michael L. Lawson, "Reservoir and Reservation: The Oahe Dam and the Cheyenne River Sioux," (master's thesis, University of Nebraska at Omaha, 1973), chap. 6, "Conclusion: 'Effects All Bad, Benefits None.'"

189 **Lakota activists organized**: Valandra, *Not Without Our Consent*.

189 **By 1968, the United States**: For a powerful look at the effects of Relocation and Termination, read: Erdrich, *The Night Watchman*. In the afterword of her novel, on page 447, she lists these figures. Though published in 1966 and reflecting somewhat earlier data, Wilkinson and Biggs, "The Evolution of the Termination Policy," finds that by then "approximately 109 tribes and bands were terminated. A minimum of 1,362,155 acres and 11,466 individuals were affected. . . . The total amount of Indian trust land was diminished by about 3.2 per cent."

189 **To this day, twenty-seven Nations:** The number twenty-seven comes from the Indian Land Tenure Fund, which has helped four Nations acquire land since Erdrich's book was published. Cris Stainbrook, phone interview and email exchange with the author, September 2022.

189 **the fight for "flood money":** For a more detailed understanding, I recommend Lawson, *Dammed Indians Revisited*.

190 **"Congress determined we were":** Les Ducheneaux (Mnicoujou Lakota elder), interview with the author, Cheyenne River Reservation, November 2021.

190 **In 2007, the Standing Rock:** "'Long time coming,'" *Bismarck Tribune*, August 10, 2007.

191 **Doug White Bull Day:** Šuŋǧíla Ská (White Fox) Doug White Bull Day, executive proclamation, signed by Kristi Noem, governor of South Dakota.

191 **drive out to visit:** Reporting trip by the author to McLaughlin and Kenel, Standing Rock Reservation, SD, May 15, 2021. Jeff McLaughlin, interview with the author, May 15, 2021.

193 **built using a stolen beam:** Gittin 55a:12, The William Davidson Talmud, www .sefaria.org/Gittin.55a.15?lang=bi.

193 **"Our country was built on a stolen beam":** Rabbi Sharon Brous, "Our Country Was Built on a Stolen Beam: The Call for a National Reckoning," Rosh Hashanah Day 2 Sermon, 5778, IKAR, Los Angeles, CA, September 22, 2017, https://ikar .org/sermons/our-country-was-built-on-a-stolen-beam-the-call-for-a-national -reckoning.

CHAPTER 10: OH TO BE A JEWISH ROCKEFELLER

195 **Life had delivered:** Diane Small, phone interviews with the author, November 2018; March 2, 2019; February 2020; May 2020; April 2021; November 2021. St. Thomas College's 1926 yearbook lists Louie Sinykin as an alternate for the debate team. Ruth Kozberg's diary entries repeatedly and sporadically mention Louie working in Jake's liquor store. "Deceased, Mrs. L. A. Sinykin," newsclip, source unknown, January, 31, 1930, from family archives in Etta Orkin's house.

195 **Louie, a consummate optimist:** Teresa Howell (Louie's granddaughter), email message to the author, October 26, 2021.

195 **Pooling in pockets:** Bill Sinykin, interview with the author, November 2021. Jami (Willuweit) Moon, interview with the author, February 2019. Jeff Klenner (environmental scientist, Minerals and Mining Program, South Dakota Department of Agriculture and Natural Resources), interview with the author, August 18, 2021. I searched through South Dakota State Oil and Gas files of every well drilled during the 1920s. Every single one was described as a "Dry Hole." While the deepest well drilled that decade was 3,508 feet, most were far less deep.

196 **In August 1948:** Within Louie's "Oil Notebook," shared with me by Teresa Howell, are black-and-white photographs of Louie and his children at various oil wells. One clip from the *Rapid City Journal*, date missing, notes, "Sinykin has completed a two weeks [*sic*] tour of potential oil territory in the Dakota basin. . . . Sinykin's wife and family accompanied him on the tour." "Oil Possibilities in

State Considered by St. Paul Man," *Mandan Daily Pioneer*, August 10, 1948. "Wall Rancher Predicts West River Oil Boom," *Rapid City Journal*, August 13, 1948. "Oil Boom Coming Says Louis Sinykin," *Pennington County Currant*, August 18, 1948. "Other Oil Men Checking Possibilities Here," *Chamberlain Register*, August 19, 1948.

197 This "plenty of money": Letter from Louie Sinykin to Ruth and Jake Kozberg, April 11, 1951, author collection. The letter contains much discussion about Louie's creditors and how "they are all excited that I may file bankruptcy again since my time limit is up. It is 7 years since I filed the last time."

197 dubbed him "Bronco Lou": Diane Small, "The Light," self-published biography of Louie Sinykin, author collection.

197 prove Faige Etke right: Jack Sinykin, interview with Cathi Oskow. Jack said, "To her dying day, she said, South Dakota, North Dakota, Montana will be wealthy states, either through oil or coal or something else."

198 important to "support the Indians": Diane Small, email message to the author, October 27, 2022. Diane told me he always said this, but it is not a direct quote from something he himself wrote.

198 For much of my late twenties: A few examples of the magazine stories I wrote over the span of about a decade: Rebecca Clarren, "Unwell," *Mother Jones*, November/December 2008, www.motherjones.com/environment/2008/11/unwell-gas-drilling-chris-lamarca. Rebecca Clarren, "Wyoming's Natural Gas Boom Sees Growing Pains," *Fortune*, June 4, 2007. Rebecca Clarren, "EPA to Citizens: Frack You," *Salon*, May 5, 2006. Rebecca Clarren, "Oil Wells in My Backyard," *High Country News*, March 15, 1999.

198 When problems occur: "7 Ways Oil and Gas Drilling Is Bad for the Environment," Wilderness Society, July 9, 2021, www.wilderness.org/articles/blog/7-ways-oil-and-gas-drilling-bad-environment. An excellent source of information about the health effects associated with oil and gas extraction is: The Endocrine Disruption Exchange, www.endocrinedisruption.org/audio-and-video/oil-and-gas-basics.

199 "Now it's oil oil oil": Ruth Kozberg, diary entry, November 7, 1953.

199 The Dakota Basin Oil Company: For this section, I spoke at length with someone involved with the company who didn't want to be identified. I also had tax returns from my grandparents and legal papers from my great-aunts indicating their shares in the Dakota Basin Oil Company. According to people at the South Dakota Minerals and Mining Program, this sort of homegrown energy company, particularly one created by people with limited oil and gas experience, was incredibly enterprising and rare for the time and the place.

199 "There's not a man from Pierre": Letter from Ruth Kozberg to her daughter Betty Rappaport, May 21, 1950.

199 various petroleum geologists: Letter from W. C. Bell (assistant professor geology and mineralogy, University of Minnesota), to Louie Sinykin, August 26, 1946. A newsclip in Louie's "Oil Notebook" from May 5, 1950, notes that, by then, Louie had thirty thousand acres under his control and was "blocking out approximately ten townships north of Wall and Quinn in cooperation with his neighbors

and hopes to bring in a driller . . . this summer. . . . The rancher says three geologists he has brought to the area confirm magnetometer tests that oil can be found
in that immediate area."

199 **By 1953, with Ruth and Jake's money:** Letter from Ruth Kozberg to Betty Rappaport. Ruth writes of all the oil and gas leases, "the source for all money came
through me." Letter from Louie Sinykin to the Kozbergs, April 1951, about their
"investment here of $16,000." Aside from the thirty thousand acres leased, Ruth
and Jake Kozberg had, with Louie's direction, purchased all the original Jew Flats
homesteads and more. Sinykin Deeds from Pennington County, South Dakota,
collection of the author.

200 **At night, by kerosene lamp:** Bill Sinykin, phone interviews with the author, May
2022, November 2021, and August 2021.

200 **"We would've been":** Doug White Bull, phone interviews with the author, January 7, 2021, and April 7, 2022.

200 **more like colonies:** Marjane Ambler, *Breaking the Iron Bonds: Indian Control of
Energy Development* (Lawrence: University Press of Kansas, 1990). See, especially,
chap. 2, "The Rubber Stamp Era: Early History of Indian Mineral Leasing."

201 **"There is a dangerous":** This came from a letter shared with me by Peter Ortego,
general counsel for the Ute Mountain Ute Tribe, while I was writing an investigative piece about abandoned oil wells on Indigenous lands. The story ran in the
fall of 2018 in *Indian Country Today* and *InvestigateWest* and can be found here:
Rebecca Clarren, "Idle Oil, Gas Wells Threaten Indian Tribes While Energy
Companies, Regulators Do Little," *InvestigateWest*, September 5, 2018, www
.invw.org/2018/09/05/idle-oil-gas-wells-threaten-indian-tribes-while-energy
-companies-and-regulators-do-little. The several graphs that follow that quote
are based on my own research for that story and Ambler, *Breaking the Iron Bonds*.
For more information on the legacy of this, see: Frank Rusco, *Indian Energy Development: Poor Management by BIA Has Hindered Energy Development on Indian
Lands*, GAO-15-502 (Washington, DC: Government Accountability Office,
2015).

202 **oil and gas had been discovered:** R. F. Bretz, L. R. Rice, R. L. Stach, and M. J.
Tipton, *Status of Mineral Resource Information for the Cheyenne River Indian Reservation, South Dakota*, BIA Administrative Report 23 (Washington, DC: Bureau of Indian Affairs, 1976). According to data shared with me by the South
Dakota Department of Agriculture and Natural Resources' Minerals and Mining Program, there were wells that had an "oil show" drilled on Standing Rock
Reservation as early as 1951.

202 **"Nothing revealed the hypocrisy":** Ambler, *Breaking the Iron Bonds*, 20.

202 **When Louie had first returned:** According to news clips, Louie returned to the
ranch in 1936 (see: "Former Resident Returns to Stay," *Rapid City Journal*, September 1, 1936). Letter from Louie Sinykin to Ruth Kozberg, Fred Rappaport, and
Jack Sinykin, February 18, 1964, in which Louie refers to himself as "Manager
of the Family South Dakota Ranch since 1935." The story that he made Lakota
friends comes from his daughter, Diane Small. His son, Bill Sinykin, told me,
"Dad did interact with the Indians." When exactly he made these friendships or

had these interactions is a little hard to say for sure. The "Sioux Addition" wasn't created by Rapid City to house Indian families until 1954 (Jhon Goes in Center, interview; "Indians Housed in Dakota Slum," *New York Times*, June 16, 1962). So, either Diane's dates are a bit off and Louie didn't make friends with Lakota until later, or he made friends closer to the ranch or on the reservations rather than in Rapid City.

203 **a lost tribe of the Jews:** David S. Koffman, *The Jews' Indian: Colonialism, Pluralism, and Belonging in America* (New Brunswick, NJ: Rutgers University Press, 2019) has an extensive list of sources that found connection between Jews and Native Americans, 225–26. See also: Harriet Rochlin and Fred Rochlin, *Pioneer Jews: A New Life in the Far West* (Boston: Houghton Mifflin Harcourt, 2022), 4–5. The American Jewish Archives at Hebrew Union College has the unpublished manuscript of Walter Hart Blumenthal's *In Old America: The Lost Ten Tribes of Israel. Prehistoric Peopling of America: A Bibliographic Survey of the Early Theory of Israelitish Derivation, and the Origin of the American Indians*, American Jewish Archives, manuscript collection (MC) 229, box 1 of 1, Cincinnati, OH, which references scores of additional papers and books written on the topic.

203 **"The theory that Americans":** Hubert Howe Bancroft, *The Native Races of the Pacific States of North America*, vol. 1 (New York: D. Appleton and Company, 1874).

204 **For Jews, this theory:** "What Can Be Done?" *Occident and American Jewish Advocate* 10, no. 9 (December 1852): 418–19. Mordecai Manuel Noah, *Discourse on the Evidences of the American Indians Being the Descendants of the Lost Tribes of Israel: Delivered Before the Mercantile Library Association, Clinton Hall* (New York: J. Van Norden, 1837).

204 **"Too often is the charge":** Gabriel Davidson, *Our Jewish Farmers: The Story of the Jewish Agricultural Society* (New York: L.B. Fischer, 1943), 192–93.

204–5 **around ninety thousand Jewish farmers:** Edward Frank Allen, "Return to the Land," review of *Our Jewish Farmers* by Gabriel Davidson, *New York Times*, May 30, 1943. For more details on Jewish population statistics, see: "U.S. Jewish Population Was 5,199,000 in 1943; Increased During Last Six Years," Jewish Telegraphic Agency, December 18, 1944, www.jta.org/archive/u-s-jewish-population-was-5199000-in-1943-increased-during-last-six-years.

205 **For Louie, the idea:** As I've mentioned before, all birth years are a little unreliable, as we have no birth certificates from Russia. Etta's family megillah has Louie's birth year as 1900, and his obituary has it as 1902.

205 **a thousand feet of film:** "St. Paul Men Take Pictures in State," *Rapid City Journal*, June 23, 1939. "Letter to the editor," *Rapid City Journal*, July 12, 1946. Teresa Howell, email exchange with the author, October 26, 2021.

205 **many of his neighbors:** Reporting trips by the author to the Wall and Philip, South Dakota, areas, February 2019, June 2019, May 2021.

206 **never felt any antisemitism:** "Isolated, 5,500-Acre Dakota Ranch Is Operated by Jewish Family," *National Jewish Post and Opinion*, October 10, 1958. Diane Small, phone interview with the author, March 3, 2019.

206 **At last, the long-planned-for day:** Again, the dates are not solid. Bill Sinykin remembers it was 1953. I have a letter from Louie to Ruth in the spring of 1952

indicating the testing could happen that coming summer. I have no newsclips about it. Bill Sinykin, phone interviews with the author, May 2022, November 2021, August 2021. Letter from Louie Sinykin to Ruth Kozberg, May 6, 1952.

207 **By 1955, the Dakota:** Again, this is all based on correspondence and interviews with the person involved in the Dakota Basin Oil Company who spoke on background. Based on data I pulled from the state oil and gas agency, Atlantic did drill in the Jew Flats area in September and October 1957. When they got to 4,882.5 feet, they found oil, but, according to the state permit file data, "these sections were not considered to be of commercial interest." The well was plugged and abandoned.

207 **sixteen parcels in North Dakota:** Williams County, ND, Recorder's Office database shows that trustees of the Dakota Basin Oil Company had deeds for thirteen sections. The person I spoke with on background said there were additional sections in Divide County, North Dakota. Letter from attorney Linn J. Firestone, March 1, 1994, describing Dakota Basin Oil royalties from income made on wells in North Dakota, Etta Orkin collection.

208 **Louie himself made almost nothing:** Bill Sinykin, interview with the author, November 2021. "Mr. and Mrs. Louis Sinykin and children, formerly of Quinn, have established residence in Rapid City . . . their spread has been leased to Bert Willuweit and Sinykin plans to open an office in Rapid City for oil ventures," *Rapid City Journal*, November 30, 1956. Letter from Louie Sinykin (written on Sinykin Family Oil Co. stationery) to Ruth and Jake Kozberg, February 19, 1960.

208 **He once swore:** Letter from Ruth Kozberg to Betty Rappaport, 1951, author's collection. Ruth writes that Louie said, "Neither Jake Kozberg, Ruth Kozberg or God himself will take it [the land] from me until I die."

208 **my great-grandfather Jake died:** "Former Lead Merchant Dies," *Black Hills Weekly*, October 24, 1962. Etta Orkin, phone interview with the author, May 2022. Etta noted that Louie placed the obituary, and "it wasn't quite right."

209 **By 1965, Ruth:** Deeds for sale of land, author collection. Guardianship paperwork, postmarked December 20, 1967, author collection.

210 **deep cut of American mythmaking:** Bosley Crowther, "'How the West Was Won,' Familiar Saga," *New York Times*, April 1, 1963: www.nytimes.com/1963 /04/01/archives/how-the-west-was-won-familiar-saga.html; "How the West Was Won," *Variety*, December 31, 1961, https://variety.com/1961/film/reviews/how-the -west-was-won-1200420172. "How the West Was Won (1962)," IMDB, www .imdb.com/title/tt0056085. Author's phone interviews with Bill Sinykin, April 29, 2021, and Diane Small, fall 2018.

211 **the children's play:** "Evergreen School presents *How the West Was Really Won*" (the program is undated, but the hand-drawn art is dated 1983). Hope Publishing, email correspondence with the author, December 14, 2021. Lyrics from *How the West Was Really Won* © 1980 Somerset Press (a div. of Hope Publishing Co., www.hopepublishing.com). All rights reserved. Used by permission.

212 **white people prospered:** The latest available data on farmland ownership by race is from: "2017 Race, Ethnicity and Gender Profiles," Census of Agriculture, National Agricultural Statistics Service, U.S. Department of Agriculture, www.nass.usda

.gov/Publications/AgCensus/2017/Online_Resources/Race,_Ethnicity_and
_Gender_Profiles/.

Details about descendants of homesteaders come from Trina Williams Shanks, "The Homestead Act: A Major Asset-Building Policy in American History" (working paper no. 00-9, Center for Social Development, Washington University, St. Louis, MO: 2000), 21–23. 2000.

Using demographic data, Shanks determines that the range of the number of people who descend from homesteaders could be as high as ninety-six million or as low as twenty million. Her median figure of forty-six million was the equivalent, in 2005, of 25 percent of the adults in the United States.

The estimate of the number of original homesteaders who "proved up" comes from: Paul Wallace Gates, *History of Public Land Law Development*, vol. 62 (Washington, DC: Government Printing Office, 1968), 800–801. Gates found that, as of 1968 (the program ran until 1980), nearly three million people filed homestead claims, and, of those, 1.62 million proved up, assuming land ownership.

212 **Relatively few of them:** There were around 3,500 Black homesteaders who proved up and received deeds on approximately 650,000 acres of prairie land (for more on Black Homesteaders, see: "Black Homesteaders," Homestead National Historical Park, National Park Service, www.nps.gov/home/black-homesteading-in-america .htm). Obviously, that's relatively tiny compared to the 1.6 million people total who got free land. I do think it's accurate to say that almost no Indigenous people got free land. The only Indigenous individuals who might have would've been part white or married to non-Natives and living off reservations.

212 **These homesteader descendants:** Thomas M. Shapiro, *The Hidden Cost of Being African American: How Wealth Perpetuates Inequality* (New York: Oxford University Press, 2004), 190.

212 **make a million:** Sinykin and Kozberg mortgages and deeds, collection of the author.

212 **"Ghost towns and dust bowls":** Wallace E. Stegner, *Where the Bluebird Sings to the Lemonade Springs: Living and Writing in the West* (New York: Random House, 1992), xvi.

213 **purchased by its original inhabitants:** Cris Stainbrook, phone interview with the author, December 15, 2022.

EPILOGUE

217 **Every year, Doug's nephew:** Frank White Bull, interview with the author, Kenel, SD, November 13, 2021.

218 **what is called fractionation:** A few good sources of information on fractionation: "Fractionated Ownership of Indian Lands," Tribal Court Clearinghouse, Tribal Law and Policy Institute, www.tribal-institute.org/lists/fractionated_ownership .htm. "What is Fractionation?" Land Buy-Back Program for Tribal Nations, U.S. Department of the Interior, www.doi.gov/buybackprogram/fractionation. "Land Tenure Issues: Fractionated Ownership," Indian Land Tenure Foundation, www .iltf.org/land-issues/issues.

218 **those owners who control a majority:** Federal code dictates that the number of people required to sign off on land deals depends on the number of people involved. So, for zero to five people, you need 90 percent, but, once you get more than twenty people involved, you need 50 percent of the ownership representatives to sign off (not necessarily the same as 50 percent of the owners), per Title 25, Chapter 24, of the Code of Federal Regulations.

218 **"We don't own land":** *Reservation Dogs*, season 1, episode 6, "Hunting," directed and written by Sterlin Harjo, featuring Jon Proudstar, released September 6, 2021, on FX and Hulu. I recognize that the joke isn't directly referring to fractionation, but I think it's still relevant here.

218 **"Fractionation is a physical manifestation":** Remi Bald Eagle, phone interview with the author, January 22, 2022.

218 **Exacerbating the dysfunction:** Michael Moore (Sitting Bull College), interview with the author, June 2019. Information on the percentage that non-Indigenous people earn on reservation agricultural lands comes from: "Agriculture on Native Lands," the Native Land Information System, https://nativeland.info/blog/dash board/usda-census-of-agriculture-for-american-indian-reservations.

219 **it's also a security risk:** Savannah Maher, "Supreme Court Rules Tribal Police Can Detain Non-Natives, but Problems Remain," *Morning Edition*, National Public Radio, June 9, 2021, www.npr.org/2021/06/09/1004328972/supreme-court -rules-tribal-police-can-detain-non-natives-but-problems-remain. Graham Lee Brewer, "Native American Women Face an Epidemic of Violence. A Legal Loophole Prevents Prosecutions," NBC News, June 30, 2021, www.nbcnews.com /news/us-news/native-american-women-face-epidemic-violence-legal-loophole -prevents-prosecutions-n1272670.

219 **buying individual land parcels:** "Land Buy-Back Program for Tribal Nations," U.S. Department of the Interior. See also the "Sales Data" PDF at the same site: www.doi.gov/buybackprogram.

219 **legacy of the Allotment Act:** "Land Tenure History," Indian Land Tenure Foundation.

219 **aren't willing sellers:** Remi Bald Eagle, phone interview with the author, February 3, 2022.

220 **compared to a Band-Aid:** Sierra Crane Murdoch, "A Land Divided: Can a Groundbreaking Settlement Fix a Century of Bad Policy in Indian Country?" *High Country News*, April 4, 2016.

220 **The program, which ended:** The BIA started, pre-buyback, with 2.93 million fractionated interests on 10.6 million acres belonging to Indigenous individuals.

220 **lack of good reservation jobs:** Anecdotally, many people on the Standing Rock and Cheyenne River reservations have told me about the lack of good jobs. The most recent available data from the Federal Reserve Bank of Minneapolis supports this claim: the median household income is $36,406 on Standing Rock and $30,708 on Cheyenne River, compared to $57,652 nationally. Per capita income for Native people is $10,582 on Standing Rock and $10,488 on Cheyenne River, compared to the national average of $30,088. The civilian unemployment rate is 26.4 percent on Cheyenne River and 24 percent on Standing Rock, compared to 6.55 percent nationally. (This data comes from the 2013–2017 American Com-

munity Survey.) Reservation Profiles, Federal Reserve Bank of Minneapolis, www.minneapolisfed.org/indiancountry/resources/reservation-profiles.

220 **"the self-destruct element":** Doug White Bull, phone interview with the author, August 13, 2021. Les Ducheneaux, interview with the author, Cheyenne River Reservation, SD, November 15, 2021.

220 **"Casteism can mean seeking":** Isabel Wilkerson, "America's Enduring Caste System," *New York Times Magazine*, July 1, 2020, updated January 21, 2021, www .nytimes.com/2020/07/01/magazine/isabel-wilkerson-caste.html. Wilkerson's book *Caste* is an excellent source for understanding these issues.

221 **the least employed and poorest:** Reservation Profiles, Federal Reserve Bank of Minneapolis. S1701 Poverty Status in the Past 12 Months, American Community Survey, U.S. Census Bureau, https://data.census.gov/table?t=Poverty&g=050000 0US38085,46031,46041,46137&tid=ACSST5Y2019.S1701. DP03 Selected Economic Characteristics, American Community Survey, U.S. Census Bureau, https:// data.census.gov/table?t=Employment%20and%20Labor%20Force%20Status&g =0500000US38085,46031,46041,46137.

221 **lowest life expectancy:** Laura Dwyer-Lindgren, Amelia Bertozzi-Villa, Rebecca W. Stubbs, Chloe Morozoff, Johan P. Mackenbach, Frank J. van Lenthe, Ali H. Mokdad, and Christopher J. L. Murray, "Inequalities in Life Expectancy Among U.S. Counties, 1980 to 2014: Temporal Trends and Key Drivers," *JAMA Internal Medicine* 177, no. 7 (2017): 1003–11.

221 **"a rural ghetto":** Doug White Bull, phone interviews with the author, January 7, 2021; November 17, 2021; August 9, 2022; November 2019.

221 **Doug's niece Janet White Bull:** Janet White Bull, interview with the author, Kenel, SD, November 14, 2021.

221 **monument at Whitestone Hill:** Whitestone Hill State Historic Site, State Historical Society of North Dakota, www.history.nd.gov/historicsites/whitestone.

222 **An audit conducted in 2021:** "National Monument Audit," National Monument Lab, 2022, www.monumentlab.com/audit. See also: Elizabeth Alexander, "The Big Problem with America's Monuments," CNN.com, September 30, 2021: www .cnn.com/2021/09/30/opinions/big-problem-with-americas-monuments-alexander /index.html.

222 **died during the pre-reservation era:** Marshall Trimble, "How Many People Died During the Indians Wars?" *True West*, June 13, 2018, www.truewestmagazine.com /article/how-many-people-died-during-the-indian-wars.

222 **"Monuments are not facts":** Paul Farber, Zoom interview with the author, April 29, 2022.

222 **mythologizing of the past:** Jack Dura, "North Dakota House Passes Ban on Critical Race Theory in Schools," *Bismarck Tribune*, November 11, 2021, www .bismarcktribune.com/news/local/education/north-dakota-house-passes -ban-on-critical-race-theory-in-schools/article_acbb80e3-a005-595e-8ec4 -aac71b69fc2c.html. Sam Nelson, "Culture War Issue Bills Become Law," *Bismarck Tribune*, November 12, 2021, www.bismarcktribune.com/business/culture-war -issue-bills-become-law-legislatures-special-session-ends/article_982d8263 -c52a-5a9d-8d7c-be51ba390bf8.html.

222 **Months earlier, South Dakota governor:** Levi Rickert, "Under Pressure, S.D.

Gov. Noem Delays Social Studies Standards That Erase Native History," *Native News Online*, September 22, 2021, www.nativenewsonline.net/education/s-d-gov -noem-delays-social-studies-standards-that-erase-native-history.

222 **She's in good company:** Sarah B. Shear, Ryan T. Knowles, Gregory J. Soden, and Antonio J. Castro, "Manifesting Destiny: Re/presentations of Indigenous Peoples in K–12 U.S. History Standards," *Theory & Research in Social Education* 43, no. 1 (2015): 68–101. Alysa Landry, "'All Indians Are Dead?' At Least That's What Most Schools Teach Children," *Indian Country Today*, November 17, 2014, updated September 13, 2018, www.indiancountrytoday.com/archive/all-indians -are-dead-at-least-thats-what-most-schools-teach-children. See also: "Becoming Visible: A Landscape Analysis of State Efforts to Provide Native American Education for All," National Congress of American Indians, 2019, www.ncai.org /policy-research-center/research-data/prc-publications/NCAI-Becoming_Visible _Report-Digital_FINAL_10_2019.pdf.

223 **"Power, when threatened":** Hanif Abdurraqib, *A Little Devil in America: In Praise of Black Performance* (New York: Random House, 2022), 208.

223 **Although Indigenous-led efforts:** The nonprofit Illuminative is working to transform the entertainment industry by advancing "authentic Native stories told by Native peoples." "Pop Culture + Media," Illuminative.org, https://illuminative.org /pop-culture-media.

223 **media coverage of Native Americans:** The Indigenous Media Freedom Alliance (imfreedomalliance.org) is a great source for information about Indigenous media. As of December 2022, it states that, nationwide, there are "less than 12 independent Native media operations." *High Country News* (hcn.org) also has an Indigenous Affairs Desk. This article is a little dated, but still full of solid information: Jodi Rave, "American Indian Media Today," Democracy Fund, November 20, 2018.

223 **about the Nazis:** Susan Neiman, *Learning from the Germans: Confronting Race and The Memory of Evil* (London: Penguin UK, 2019).

223 **German students who complain:** "Holocaust Education in Germany: An Interview," interview with Lars Rensmann (German educator), *Frontline*, May 19, 2005, www.pbs.org/wgbh/pages/frontline/shows/germans/germans/education .html.

224 **Unlike Australia and Canada:** Margaret D. Jacobs, *After One Hundred Winters: In Search of Reconciliation on America's Stolen Lands* (Princeton, NJ: Princeton University Press, 2021), chap. 11.

224 **"world's quietest apology":** Walter R. Echo-Hawk, *In the Light of Justice: The Rise of Human Rights in Native America and the UN Declaration on the Rights of Indigenous Peoples* (Wheat Ridge, CO: Fulcrum Publishing, 2016).

224 **one federal attempt to say sorry:** Rob Capriccioso, "A Sorry Saga: Obama Signs Native American Apology," *Indian Country Today*, January 21, 2010, updated September 18, 2018, www.indiancountrytoday.com/archive/a-sorry-saga-obama -signs-native-american-apology.

224 **"Nothing in this section":** A Joint Resolution to Acknowledge a Long History of Official Depredations and Ill-Conceived Policies by the Federal Government Regarding Indian Tribes and Offer an Apology to All Native Peoples on Behalf

of the United States, S.J.Res.14—111th Cong. (2009), www.congress.gov/bill/111th
-congress/senate-joint-resolution/14/text.

224 **Layli Long Soldier:** Layli Long Soldier, *Whereas: Poems* (Minneapolis, MN: Graywolf Press, 2017). Also find her poems at the Poetry Foundation, www .poetryfoundation.org/poets/layli-long-soldier.

224 **"It was so quiet":** Krista Tippett, "Layli Long Soldier: The Freedom of Real Apologies," *On Being with Krista Tippett* (podcast), March 30, 2017: www.onbeing .org/programs/layli-long-soldier-the-freedom-of-real-apologies.

225 **At a White Bull family gathering:** Reporting trip by the author to the Dakotas, November 14, 2021.

225 **a bar just north of Pine Ridge:** Tim Giago, "Scenic and the Main Street Bars of Rapid City," Indianz.com, November 18, 2019, www.indianz.com/News/2019 /11/18/tim-giago-scenic-and-the-main-street-bar.asp. Nick Estes, "Racist City, S.D.: Life is Violent, and Often Deadly in Rapid City," *Indian Country Today*, September 5, 2014, updated September 13, 2018, www.indiancountrytoday .com/archive/racist-city-sd-life-is-violent-and-often-deadly-in-rapid-city. Evelyn Red Lodge, "Racism Against Native Americans Persists," *High Country News*, September 21, 2017, www.hcn.org/issues/49.17/opinion-racism-against-native -americans-persists. "Native Lives Matter," Lakota People's Law Project, February 2015, www.lakotalaw.org/resources/native-lives-matter.

226 **"need to be careful":** Doug White Bull, interview with the author, Standing Rock Reservation, November 16, 2021.

226 **killed by law enforcement:** Mike Males (senior researcher with the Center on Juvenile and Criminal Justice), email exchange with the author, January 20 and 21, 2022. Males directed me to the Center for Disease Control's Multiple Cause of Death site (https://wonder.cdc.gov/mcd.html), but he wrote that the "CDC numbers are considered undercounts." *The Washington Post* tally finds more police-caused shootings but doesn't separate out Native Americans, www.washingtonpost.com /graphics/investigations/police-shootings-database.

226 **to be incarcerated:** Joshua Rovner (The Sentencing Project), Zoom interview with the author, January 31, 2022. Joshua Rovner, "Disparities in Tribal Youth Incarceration," The Sentencing Project, July 15, 2021, www.sentencingproject .org/fact-sheet/disparities-in-tribal-youth-incarceration.

226 **removed from their parents:** Rebecca Clarren, "A Right-Wing Think Tank Is Trying to Bring Down the Indian Child Welfare Act. Why?" *The Nation*, April 6, 2017, www.thenation.com/article/archive/a-right-wing-think-tank-is-trying-to -bring-down-the-indian-child-welfare-act-why.

226 **missing persons in South Dakota:** Jacob Newton, "Not to Be Forgotten: Missing and Indigenous in South Dakota," Keloland.com, March 30, 2021, www.keloland .com/keloland-com-original/not-to-be-forgotten-missing-and-indigenous -in-south-dakota/?ipid=promo-link-block1.

226 **Locals who live in Wall:** Reporting trip by the author to Jew Flats, February 2019. Reporting trip by the author to the Dakotas, June 2019.

227 **"objects to be feared":** Colum McCann, *Apeirogon* (New York: Random House, 2021), 220–21. Confirmed as an exact quote from Elhanan via email with McCann, February 6, 2022.

227 **"a conspiracy theory"**: Horn, *People Love Dead Jews*, chap. 7, "American Jews, Part Two."

227 **I meet Les Ducheneaux**: Les Ducheneaux, interviews with the author, Cheyenne River Reservation, May 2021, November 2021.

227 **When Native and non-Native**: Faith Spotted Eagle, "Faith Spotted Eagle pt 3 Trauma & Resiliency—Essential Understanding #2," Wo Lakota, September 3, 2013, www.youtube.com/watch?v=bqd_gYAhBII&t=8s.

228 **When I first met**: Abby Abinanti, interview with the author, California, September 2017.

228 **Maimonides's Laws of Repentance**: Ben Maimon, Mishna Torah, Repentance, www.sefaria.org/Mishneh_Torah,_Repentance?tab=contents. See also: Danya Ruttenberg, *On Repentance and Repair: Making Amends in an Unapologetic World* (Boston: Beacon Press, 2022). Danya Ruttenberg, phone interview with the author, January 28, 2022.

229 **leading research in restorative justice**: "Three Core Elements of Restorative Justice," Restorative Justice Exchange, https://restorativejustice.org/what-is-restorative -justice/three-core-elements-of-restorative-justice. Brett Shelton, interview with the author, August 2022.

229 **This is our piece**: Reparations economics is a developing field. I could find no economists who are working on creating calculations for how to determine what might be a fair price for the cost to Native American land and culture. I made this calculation based on a very simple method: simply adding up how much we received in mortgages. The economists I consulted appreciated that this model includes not simply the final sale of land but the mortgages, demonstrating how relatively small amounts of money build wealth over time.

229 **leading reconciliation efforts**: For examples, see Reconciliation Rising (www .reconciliationrising.org) or listen to their eponymous podcast.

230 **benefiting from stolen land**: Jacobs, *After One Hundred Winters*.

230 **former Native lands funded**: Robert Lee and Tristan Ahtone, "Land-Grab Universities," *High Country News*, March 30, 2020.

230 **"Now is the time"**: Abby Abinanti, phone interview with the author, September 12, 2022.

230 **Twenty years after**: Reporting trip by the author to the Dakotas, including visit with Fred DuBray, Cheyenne River Reservation, February 2019.

232 **Rebounding buffalo populations**: Remi Bald Eagle, phone interview with the author, January 20, 2022.

232 **Because buffalo are what**: Kate Wilkins, Liba Pejchar, and Rebecca Garvoille, "Ecological and Social Consequences of Bison Reintroduction in Colorado," *Conservation Science and Practice* 1, no. 2 (2019): e9. Hila Shamon, Olivia G. Cosby, Chamois L. Andersen, Helen Augare, Jonny BearCub Stiffarm, Claire E. Bresnan, Brent L. Brock, et al., "The Potential of Bison Restoration as an Ecological Approach to Future Tribal Food Sovereignty on the Northern Great Plains," *Frontiers in Ecology and Evolution* (2022): 17.

232 **"I draw strength"**: Troy Heinert (executive director of the InterTribal Buffalo Council), phone interview with the author, January 2021.

232 **modern-day warriors are female**: Laura Harris (executive director, Americans

for Indian Opportunity), email exchange with the author, September 16, 2022.
"The Pursuit of Inclusion: Experiences of Native American Women Attorneys,"
National Native American Bar Association, 2015.

233 **The Indigenous activism:** Stephen L. Pevar, *The Rights of Indians and Tribes*, 4th
ed. (New York: Oxford University Press, 2012).

233 **comanage federal lands:** John Echohawk (Native American Rights Fund), phone
interview with the author, March 8, 2022. B. "Toastie" Oaster, "Congress Meets
with Native Leaders to Discuss Co-Management of Federal Lands," *High Country News*, March 9, 2022, www.hcn.org/articles/indigenous-affairs-national-park
-service-congress-meets-with-native-leaders-to-discuss-co-management-of-federal
-lands.

233 **led by Native Americans:** Interior Secretary Deb Haaland is a member of the
Pueblo of Laguna. National Park Service Director Charles F. "Chuck" Sams III
is Cayuse and Walla Walla and is an enrolled member of the Confederated Tribes
of the Umatilla Indian Reservation.

233 **key to surviving climate change:** A few examples: UNESCO has the Local and
Indigenous Knowledge Systems program, aka LINKS, that "promotes local and
indigenous knowledge and its inclusion in global climate science and policy pro-
cesses," en.unesco.org/links. On November 3, 2021, the Wilson Center, a think
tank in Washington, DC, hosted an event to demonstrate ways to incorporate
"Indigenous knowledge into climate decision-making": Shruti Samala, "The
Use of Indigeous Traditional Knowledge in Climate Change Strategies," Wilson Center, www.wilsoncenter.org/event/use-indigenous-traditional-knowledge
-climate-change-strategies. Also: Donna Green and Gleb Raygorodetsky, "Indigenous Knowledge of a Changing Climate," *Climatic Change* 100, no. 2 (2010): 239.

234 **Lakota hemp is now:** Stewart Huntington, "Hemp Planting on the Rise on Pine
Ridge Reservation," KOTA TV, August 2, 2019, www.kotatv.com/content/news
/Hemp-planting-on-the-rise-on-Pine-Ridge-reservation-514669311.html.

234 **at the local level:** Cheyenne River Sioux Tribe, Ordinance No. 66: The Lakota
Language and Culture Education Code of the Cheyenne River Sioux Tribe, September 29, 1994. For Standing Rock: 35–301. Standing Rock Tribal Department
of Education, Title 35 Education Code, approved November 13, 2012, Standing
Rock Sioux Tribal Code of Justice. Phone interviews with Remi Bald Eagle, January 22, 2020; Wayne Ducheneaux II, August 2021; Steve Vance, February 2021;
Doug White Bull, September 14, 2022.

AUTHOR'S NOTE

238 **Indigenous-led movements such as:** More about LandBack can be found at landback
.org. The Indian Land Tenure Foundation (iltf.org) has created school curricula that
can be found at: www.lessonsofourland.org. The Native Governance Center is an
excellent resource for considering how to make land acknowledgments meaningful: Beyond Land Acknowledgment Explainer Video, Native Governance
Center, www.nativegov.org/resources/beyond-land-acknowledgment-explainer-
video.

238 **Some descendants of settlers:** For examples of reconciliation efforts, read Mar-

garet D. Jacobs, *After One Hundred Winters: In Search of Reconciliation on America's Stolen Lands* (Princeton, NJ: Princeton University Press, 2021), and check out Reconciliation Rising, the website and podcast she codirects with Kevin Abourezk, a member of the Rosebud Sioux Tribe and an award-winning journalist: www .reconciliationrising.org.

238 **Jewish farmers, drawing for inspiration:** Author's phone interviews with Shani Mink (Jewish Farmer Network), January 26, 2022; Bruce Spierer (Hazon), February 1, 2022.

238 **created land taxes:** A couple of examples, though there are more: Real Rent Duwamish (Seattle): www.realrentduwamish.org; Shuumi Land Tax (Bay Area), https://sogoreate-landtrust.org/shuumi-land-tax.

239 **created "Sorry Books":** Jacobs, *After One Hundred Winters*, 197–98.

RESOURCES FOR FURTHER RESEARCH

Consider the place in America where you grew up or that you feel is your home. You can use the following resources to determine what Indigenous Nation or Nations once lived and hunted on that land: text the zip code of the location to 907-312-5085; or download the following app on your phone: www.native-land .ca/resources/mobile-app. To find out if your family received a free federal homestead, you can go to this site: www.glorecords.blm.gov/search/default.aspx.

Once you know the Nation or Nations connected to your home, determine if there was a treaty signed between that Nation and the United States. To find out about specific treaties, you can go to: www.arcgis.com/apps/webappviewer /index.html or www.narf.org/nill/triballaw/treaties.html. To find out more information about why treaties matter, you can visit: www.nativegov.org/resources /why-do-treaties-matter. The National Museum of the American Indian has an exhibit called *Nation to Nation* about treaties: www.americanindian.si.edu /explore/exhibitions/item?id=934. And, on a related note, learn more about Tribal sovereignty: www.nativegov.org/resources/what-is-tribal-sovereignty.

To learn more about specific Nations, you can visit this collection of geographically organized links to primary sources compiled by the University of Washington: https://guides.lib.uw.edu/research/history-nativeam/primary; or this treasure trove of information from the National Indian Law Library: www .narf.org/nill/resources/index.html.

Turtle Talk is the foremost website for information on legislation and current and ongoing court cases involving Indigenous Nations: www.turtletalk.blog.

The following are some resources to help you research by topic or learn more about federal policies that impacted and impact Indigenous peoples in the United States at great benefit to non-Native people. This is by no means a comprehensive list, but these resources were ones I found helpful in the course of my own research.

LAND-TAKINGS, POST-TREATY ERA

In 1871 the United States passed a law ending the signing of treaties with Indigenous Nations in America. In 1903, the *Lone Wolf* Supreme Court decision gave Congress the right to make all decisions on behalf of Indigenous Nations without their consent. Between 1887 and 1934, federal land policies stripped Native Nations and their citizens of ninety million acres.

Indian Land Tenure Foundation: www.iltf.org/get-involved/take-action.

A Matter of Honor: 125 Years of Living with the Legacy of the Dawes Allotment Act: www.youtube.com/watch?v=IhwSW2a_RPY.

FEDERAL BOARDING SCHOOLS

Either pick a boarding school near your home or consider learning about a boarding school where children from the Nation connected to your home were sent. Most children were sent far away from home to discourage visits with their families.

I'd suggest starting with this from the Heard Museum: www.heard.org /exhibits/boardingschool.

And also this from the Native American Rights Fund: www.narf.org/cases /boarding-school-healing.

Additional resources:

"Trigger Points: Current State of Research on U.S. Indian Boarding School Policy," National Native American Boarding School Healing Coalition: https:// boardingschoolhealing.org/resource_database/trigger-points-current-state -of-research-on-history-impacts-and-healing-related-to-the-united-states -indian-industrial-boarding-school-policy.

American Indian Boarding Schools by State: https://ee8.a33.myftpupload .com/wp-content/uploads/2020/07/2020-MAP-1500px.jpg.

The Genoa Indian School Digital Reconciliation Project: www.genoaindian school.org.

IMPACTS of HYDROPOWER

"Impact of Dams on Native People Case Study," National Museum of the American Indian: www.americanindian.si.edu/nk360/pnw-history-culture-barriers /dams.html.

Christina Rose, "Echoes of Oak Flat: 4 Pick Sloan Dams That Submerged Native Lands," *Indian Country Today*, August 14, 2017 (updated September 13, 2018): https://indiancountrytoday.com/archive/echoes-of-oak-flat-4-pick-sloan -dams-that-submerged-native-lands.

"Water," National Congress of American Indians (NCAI): https://ncai.org /policy-issues/land-natural-resources/water.

ATTACKS on the INDIAN CHILD WELFARE ACT

This Land (podcast): https://crooked.com/podcast-series/this-land.

LAND-GRANT UNIVERSITIES

Robert Lee and Tristan Ahtone, "Land-Grab Universities: Expropriated Indigenous Land Is the Foundation of the Land-Grant University System," *High Country News*, March 30, 2020: https://hcn.org/issues/52.4/indigenous-affairs -education-land-grab-universities.

REPRESENTATION and STEREOTYPES

"Fight Against Native Invisibility and Erasure," Illuminative: www.illuminatives .org/resources.

Before contacting an Indigenous Nation or organization to learn more about how to support their work, consider reading this guide to being culturally sensitive: www.store.samhsa.gov/product/American-Indian-and-Alaska-Native-Culture -Card/sma08-4354.

ILLUSTRATION CREDITS

INDEX

NOTE: *Italic page locators* indicate photographs.